THE
INTEREST GROUP CONNECTION
Electioneering, Lobbying, and Policymaking in Washington

EDITED BY

Paul S. Herrnson
University of Maryland

Ronald G. Shaiko
American University

Clyde Wilcox
Georgetown University

CHATHAM HOUSE PUBLISHERS, INC.
Chatham, New Jersey

THE INTEREST GROUP CONNECTION
Electioneering, Lobbying, and Policymaking in Washington

Chatham House Publishers, Inc.
Box One, Chatham, New Jersey 07928

Copyright © 1998 by Chatham House Publishers, Inc.

Publisher: Edward Artinian
Production supervisor: Katharine Miller
Cover design: Antler Designworks
Composition: Bang, Motley, Olufsen
Printing and binding: R.R. Donnelley & Sons, Co.

Library of Congress Cataloging-in-Publication Data

The interest group connection : electioneering, lobbying, and
    policymaking in Washington / edited by Paul S. Herrnson, Ronald G.
    Shaiko, and Clyde Wilcox.
        p.   cm.
    Includes bibliographical references and index.
    ISBN 1-56643-054-2 (pbk.)
        1. Pressure groups—United States.   2. Electioneering—United
States.   3. Lobbying—United States.   4. United States—Politics and
government—20th century.   I. Herrnson, Paul S., 1958–   .
II. Shaiko, Ronald G., 1959–   .   III. Wilcox, Clyde, 1953–   .
JK1118.I563   1998
324′.4′0973—dc21   97-21209
                                                                CIP

Manufactured in the United States of America
        10   9   8   7   6   5   4   3   2   1

Contents

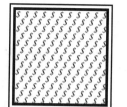

Preface

ORGANIZED interest groups—sometimes referred to as *special interests* or *factions*—have always played important roles in American politics. Factions weighed heavily on the minds of the Framers of the Constitution. They were a major focus of Populist and Progressive reformers at the turn of the twentieth century. At the dawning of the twenty-first century, individuals and reform groups claiming to be proponents of honest, clean government continue to label organized interest groups as the villains of American politics.

Nevertheless, interest groups play a positive role in the political arena. They organize constituencies affected by what government does—protecting their rights, defending their interests, and giving them a say in the political process. Without organized interests, many workers, business leaders, and issue advocates living across the United States and abroad would feel that they had no influence on the political process. Interest groups help connect Americans to their government.

Interest groups are pervasive in American political life. They spend money and mobilize voters in elections, lobby Congress and the White House, and attempt to influence the courts. The fortunes of interest groups rise and fall with political trends and events. Election outcomes; spending, regulatory, and redistributive initiatives introduced in Congress; executive orders; and judicial decisions can create or close down opportunities for interest group influence. Reforms specifically targeted at labor, business, and trade associations, and nonprofit group lobbyists who frequent Capitol Hill, can have a profound impact on the connection between American citizens and their government.

This book examines interest group activities in Washington, D.C., at a time of great change. The election of Bill Clinton as president in 1992 and the Republican takeover of Congress in 1994 were catalytic events for the interest group community. Clinton was the first Democrat to occupy the White House since Jimmy Carter departed in 1981; Newt Gingrich was the first Republican to be elected Speaker of the House since the GOP lost control of Congress as a result of the 1954 elections; and although Bob Dole had served as majority leader of the Senate from 1981 to 1986, he was the first Republican to hold this position while his party enjoyed control of both chambers of Congress since 1955. The elections of 1996 resulted in Clinton remaining in the White House and the Republicans retaining control of both the House and Senate, ensuring that a particular pattern of divided government that had not been present on the American scene for a very long time would persist at least a little longer. Lobbying regulations passed by the 104th Congress and recent Supreme Court rulings on issues pertaining to election campaign finance have also had a major impact on interest group activity in the nation's capital.

The chapters that follow demonstrate how groups have responded to these changes. The first two chapters give an overview of the role of interest groups in politics and provide an insider's view of how to lobby the federal government. The remainder of the book is divided into four sections, each covering one of the four areas in which interest groups interact with the federal government: the electoral connection, the congressional connection, the executive connection, and the judicial connection. Parts II, III, IV, and V have lead chapters that introduce the subject, several substantive chapters that use a variety of methodologies to explore interest group activity, and the commentaries of political practitioners who are experts in each area.

As with any collaborative enterprise, this book would not have been possible without the cooperation of many individuals. We must first thank our academic colleagues who participated in the project. We also wish to thank the political practitioners who offered their input, which appears in separate chapters in the book. The Consortium of Universities of the Washington Metropolitan Area; the School of Public Affairs, the Center for Congressional and Presidential Studies, and the Lobbying Institute at American University; the American League of Lobbyists Education Fund; and the Bryce Harlow Foundation deserve special thanks for cosponsoring a conference that facilitated the preparation of the book. Dale Weighill, Marc Wallace, and Desmonique Bonet helped organize the conference and prepare the manuscript for publication. To these individuals and groups, we express our deepest appreciation.

Finally, we dedicate this book to the memory of our publisher:
Edward Artinian: Friend and Publisher Extraordinaire.

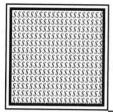

Part I

Introduction

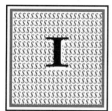

Ronald G. Shaiko

Lobbying in Washington: A Contemporary Perspective

ORGANIZED interests played a critical role in the birth and development of President Clinton's health-care-reform plan, and they were more responsible than any other factor for its death. Unions enthusiastically backed the plan, spending more than $10 million in cash and services to fight for its passage (Salwen 1994). The American Association of Retired Persons (AARP) spent an additional $2.5 million in support of health-care reform. Business interests, in contrast, were dead set against the Clinton health-care plan. The National Federation of Independent Business lobbied hard to kill it, and the Health Insurance Association of America spent millions to bring the skeptical dialogue of "Harry and Louise" to the television screens of America (West 1996). The American Medical Association also rallied in opposition.

Even religious organizations staked out positions on health-care reform. The National Council of Churches, the United Church of Christ, the American Jewish Congress, and numerous other religious groups embraced the idea of universal health care, but some bristled at the details of the Clinton package. The U.S. Catholic Conference and the Southern Baptists' Christian Life Commission, for example, opposed the health-care package because it included coverage for abortions (Anderson 1993; Mollison 1994).

Interest groups did not play unusual roles in the battle over health care. Organized groups have lobbied for and against a wide array of legislation, ranging from raising the speed limit on federal highways to subsidizing school lunches to raising price supports for beekeepers. The power of these groups has not gone unnoticed by politicians or ordinary Americans.

Elected officials of all political stripes, journalists, and scholars have assailed the undue influence of organized interests on the policymaking process in Washington (e.g., Greider 1992; Birnbaum 1992; Rauch 1994; Gais 1996). President Clinton echoed the sentiments of many of his predecessors when in his 1994 State of the Union address he stated: "Facing up to special interests will require courage. It will require critical questions about the way we finance our campaigns and how lobbyists peddle their influence." Ross Perot also targeted lobbyists for their corruption of the political system in his 1992 presidential campaign. Similarly, the vast majority of the Republican freshmen elected to the House of Representatives in 1994 ran on agendas that included lobby and campaign finance reform.

It should come as no surprise that the lawyers and lobbyists who represent organized interests in Washington are viewed as narrow, selfish, and even evil by most people. While serving as political scapegoats for a wide variety of governmental ills, the representatives of organized interests operate under the constitutional protection of the First Amendment. As long as citizens enjoy the "right to petition the government for a redress of grievances," lobbyists will continue to have an important role in making public policy.

This introductory chapter gives an overview of various connections between organized interests and policymakers in Washington. First, it addresses the forms of organized political representation in the nation's capital. Second, it analyzes the rules of the game for lobbyists and interest groups, including the federal laws governing the financing of congressional and presidential elections, the new lobby reform law that now regulates the lobbying profession, and the gift-ban provisions passed by the House of Representatives and the Senate. Third, it outlines the various electoral and lobbying resources available to organized interests in creating connections with members of Congress and their staffs, the president and the executive bureaucracy, and the federal judiciary.

Forms of Political Representation in Washington

In formulating our constitutional framework, the Founding Fathers wrestled with the dilemma of the political representation of individuals and groups in the American political process. On the one hand, if citizens are limited by government in their efforts to pursue their self-interest, then their political freedom is restricted. On the other hand, organized interests have the potential to dominate the policymaking process in favor of narrow segments of the population and at the expense of the general public, thereby undermining the democratic principle of majority rule. Contemporary "interest groups are no less a threat than they are an expression of freedom" (Berry 1984, 20).

James Madison, writing in *Federalist #10*, argued that organized interests or "factions" were an inevitable fact of life in American society, that the "causes of faction are . . . sown in the nature of man." Viewing factions as potential threats to democratic governance, Madison set forth a plan for "curing the mischiefs of faction." Erring on the side of protecting individual and collective rights to organize and voice support or opposition to government, he argued that any restrictions on individual freedom and liberty would be a remedy "worse than the disease." Madison believed that the republican form of government, outlined in the Constitution and the Bill of Rights, would be the safeguard against the worst impulses of factions and prevent a tyranny of the majority from developing (Madison 1961, 77–84). This structural safeguard was a democratic leap of faith that has not prevented powerful and sometimes small and narrow-based organized interests from exercising disproportionate influence. Madison's belief in protecting the rights of individuals and organized groups to participate in the policymaking process has endured for more than two centuries (Dahl 1956; Schattschneider 1960; Berry 1984).

Today, all citizens enjoy the First Amendment right to petition their government. As individuals, we may exercise this right by writing, calling, faxing, e-mailing, or meeting directly with members of Congress to discuss a particular policy issue or to ask for help in retrieving a lost Social Security check or expedite a passport request. Americans may also contact the president and officials in the federal bureaucracy. For example, federal agencies and departments must solicit public comments before implementing new rules and regulations. While fewer citizens tend to contact these executive branch entities, the right to petition extends to this branch of government as well (Verba, Schlozman, and Brady 1995, 56). Individuals who are not satisfied with the actions of these two branches have the right to take grievances to the judicial branch. As one of the most litigious nations in the world, we certainly do not shy away from "taking it to court" (Baum 1990, 245; Jacob 1995, 82–83).

While each of these methods of citizen contacting is widely used, the forcefulness of the message is often gauged by the size and importance of the messengers. Elected officials in Washington are responsive to the wishes of their constituents, often to a fault. Nonetheless, some constituents are more important than others in members' reelection efforts. Therefore, it has become increasingly important to make one's individual voice heard through the organization of common interests to provide more meaningful political representation. Throughout history, the United States has been viewed as a "nation of joiners," a "participatory democracy" (Tocqueville 1835; Almond and Verba 1963). Today such organized political representation is even more important, given the proliferation of organized interests in Washington during the past two decades (Rauch 1994, 36–44).

Apart from the representation of individual interests by citizens themselves, there are two basic forms of political representation in Washington: direct organizational representation and surrogate representation through lobbying firms. Three forms of direct political representation take place in the nation's capital: (1) direct corporate representation through Washington offices of American and international corporations; (2) direct representation through associations and unions; and (3) direct representation through special interest or "public interest" organizations. Three forms of surrogate representation are available for corporations, governmental entities, foreign interests, and other organized groups that are unable or unwilling to maintain a permanent physical presence in Washington or wish to call in the assistance of a hired gun: (1) multiple-client "boutique" lobbying operations; (2) major Washington law firms; and (3) megafirms that provide one-stop shopping for all public relations and governmental relations needs. Organized interests are not limited to any single form of representation in Washington; in fact, the more powerful interests in the federal policymaking process are represented in a variety of forms. Through these forms of representation, tens of thousands of organized interests are given a voice in the nation's capital.

Direct Representation: Interest Group Lobbying
Direct Corporate Representation

Before 1920, only one American corporation, U.S. Steel, had a permanent office in Washington, D.C. By 1940, the number of Washington offices of major corporations had climbed to five. Over the next two decades, particularly during the favorable business climate of the successive Eisenhower administrations, corporations flocked to the capital. By 1968, more than 175 corporations had established formal corporate offices in Washington (Epstein 1969, 90–91). According to Raymond Hoewing, president of the Public Affairs Council (an umbrella organization for corporate public affairs representatives), more than 600 corporations currently maintain full-time Washington offices and employ corporate representatives who hold titles such as vice-president for government relations or vice-president for federal affairs.

The vast majority of American corporations and American subsidiaries of foreign corporations do not maintain full-time offices in Washington. This does not mean that they are without political representation. These corporations are represented in the policymaking process through the next form of direct representation or through one of the surrogate forms discussed in the next section.

Association/Union Representation

Political representation through associations and labor unions predates the representation of corporations in Washington. Associations provide representation and other political services to their members, whether they are individual citizens, such as workers, or individual economic interests, such as business, professional, educational, industrial, or trade groups. The number of associations is growing rapidly. In 1955, there were about 5,000 national associations; two decades later, there were 13,000; today, more than 23,000 national associations (along with more than 64,000 regional, state, and local associations) provide representation for "seven out of ten adult Americans" (American Society of Association Executives [ASAE] 1996, 1).

The breadth and diversity of association representation in Washington is dramatic. Apart from the better-known associations such as the American Medical Association, American Bar Association, Chamber of Commerce, National Association of Manufacturers, American Association of Retired Persons, and American Automobile Association, thousands of lobbying organizations represent an immensely broad array of political interests, many of which operate under the title of National or American, Association, Society, Federation, Institute, or Academy. In the District of Columbia Telephone Directory, under Business-Professional-Organizational listings, there are fourteen pages of listings under the headings of American and National, with more than 2,500 entries. The organizational names listed in table 1.1 give one a sense of the narrow focus of some of the associations operating in Washington today. The lobbying profession it-

TABLE 1.1

"AMERICAN" AND "NATIONAL" ASSOCIATIONS
IN WASHINGTON, D.C.

American Association of Private Railroad Car Owners, Inc.	National Air Duct Cleaners Association
American Fishing Tackle Manufacturers Association	National Asphalt Paving Association
American Mushroom Institute	National Association of Miscellaneous Ornamental and Architectural Products Contractors
American Cotton Shippers Association	
American Society of Heating, Refrigerating, and Air Conditioning Engineers, Inc.	National Association of Pastoral Musicians
American Wire Producers Association	National Candle Association
American Butter Institute	National Cheese Institute
American Concrete Pipe Association	National Corrugated Steel Pipe Association
American Welding Society	National Electric Sign Association
	National Frozen Pizza Institute

self has a number of associations that provide political representation, including the American League of Lobbyists, National Association of Registered Lobbyists, Women in Government Relations, and the American Society of Association Executives. Associations provide political representation for a larger number of similarly situated interests at a more cost-effective level for individual members and corporations.

Union representation in Washington is similar to association representation in that these economic organizations are organized by craft, trade, profession, and industry. Moreover, there is a layering of representation from individual locals to national and international unions to umbrella organizations such as the AFL-CIO.[1] Today, labor unions represent approximately 12 percent of the American workforce. The AFL-CIO provides broad political representation for more than eighty national and international unions in Washington, many of which have their own lobbying teams. Recent leadership changes at the AFL-CIO have resulted in a reinvigoration of the labor movement in Washington and around the nation.

Special Interest/Public Interest/Governmental Representation

Beyond seeking direct representation through joining an association, union, or some other economic entity, individuals may also join membership organizations to advance their noneconomic goals in a collective fashion. Millions of people belong to groups that advocate a clean environment, consumer protection, animal rights, family values, gun control, abortion rights, immigration, and hundreds of other causes. Many ideological perspectives are often represented in the policy debate, although not always equally. More than 2,000 public interest organizations are active at the national level, according to the Foundation for Public Affairs. This sector also includes governmental entities such as state governments, city governments, and even small towns, public utilities, and regional authorities. Every state has a government relations office in Washington; in fact, many state offices are found in the same building, The Hall of the States, strategically located just off Capitol Hill. Public interest nonprofit organizations are granted special status by the federal government through tax exemption and subsidized mailing rates. During the past thirty years the political influence of public interest organizations has grown dramatically.

Surrogate Representation: Guns for Hire

Corporations and a wide variety of political organizations that are unwilling or unable to invest in direct representation through a permanent, physical presence in Washington often choose to "contract out" their lobbying services. These political interests may choose from a host of multiple-client lobbying firms, law firms, and large public affairs firms.

Multiple-Client Lobbying Firms

A growing number of multiple-client lobbying operations in Washington serve the needs of a broad array of interests. Some are organized around substantive policy expertise to serve a homogeneous client base, such as telecommunications companies, health-care providers, or oil/energy companies. Other firms serve the needs of a distinct client base, regardless of policy focus, such as state and local governments seeking appropriations funding on a variety of projects or colleges and universities that may have interests in the funding of basic research through the National Institutes of Health but also interests in competing for research funds through the Departments of Energy, Defense, and Interior. Still other firms provide lobbying services for special interests on a variety of issues; the clients in these firms tend to be attracted by a particular lobbyist in the firm. As few of these firms are able to cater to the entire spectrum of political interests, they have focused their lobbying efforts on specialized sets of policy or client interests; as such they have come to be known as "boutiques" or specialty shops. These "boutique" firms, such as O'Brien Calio, Timmons and Company, Cassidy and Associates, Capitol Associates, The Duberstein Group, and Podesta Associates, represent some of the most prominent corporations, associations, health-care providers, and universities in the nation, such as the American Medical Association, MCI, Northwestern and Tufts universities, Aetna-US Healthcare, General Motors, Capital Cities/ABC, and Time Warner.

The Lawyer-Lobbyists

Rather than seek surrogate political representation from a lobbying firm, some organized interests find greater comfort in the hands of Washington law firms. Top firms such as Patton, Boggs LLP, Wilmer, Cutler, and Pickering, and Akin, Gump, Strauss, Hauer & Feld also attract the top echelon of corporate America. Major corporations look to these law firms not only for their representation before Congress and relevant executive branch agencies but also for legal advice and expertise in managing their corporate affairs. In addition to the major law firms in Washington, representing a largely corporate client base, public interest law firms provide legal representation for traditionally underrepresented interests in the judicial arena.

Megafirms: Public Relations/Government Relations Services

A growing trend in Washington surrogate representation among multiple-client firms is the expansion beyond the traditional governmental relations (GR) services to include public relations (PR) services as well. Public relations work involves a broad range of services including advertising, media relations, marketing, and convention management. These services often have little to do with government relations. Nonetheless, a growing num-

ber of firms in New York, Washington, and around the country have attracted clients by offering to provide all the services relating to the external
affairs of corporations, associations, and other organized interest groups.
The traditional giants in merging public relations and government relations
services for clients are Hill and Knowlton Worldwide and Burson-
Marsteller. These international public affairs companies serve literally hundreds of corporations, associations, foreign governments, and organizations in Washington and around the world. Smaller firms, such as the
Dutko Group, have ventured into the PR/GR merger market, with significant successes.

Through one or more of these direct and surrogate forms, organized interests are provided with political representation in the federal policymaking process. Anheuser-Busch, for example, is quite representative of
the multilayered approach to lobbying in Washington. In addition to its
own Washington lobbying team, the beer giant contracts with several lobbying firms and belongs to a number of associations that serve their economic interests; it also operates a political committee that has contributed
more than $250,000 to federal candidates in each of the past three election
cycles (see table 1.2). Beyond these forms of representation, corporations,
associations, public interest groups, as well as citizens often expand their
political representation by joining forces with organizations with similar
interests in the policy debate by forming coalitions. Furthermore, they mobilize their memberships, employees, customers, and interested citizens at
the grassroots level. These two actions—coalition building and grassroots
lobbying—are necessary components in the interest group lobbying arsenal
in the late 1990s.

The Rules of the Game: Campaign Finance, Lobbying Disclosure, and Gift Bans

Interest groups, corporations, associations, unions, and the vast array of
organized interests in Washington, along with their attendant lobbyists,
operate under a variety of federal statutes and regulations. These rules of
the game encompass virtually all activities associated with influencing the
federal policymaking process, including electioneering and campaign financing, legislative branch lobbying, executive branch lobbying, and the
social interactions between lobbyists and government officials.

Federal Campaign Finance Provisions

The most hotly contested area of interest group regulation at the federal
level involves the financing of congressional and presidential election campaigns. In 1996 campaign finance reform bills were proposed in the House

TABLE 1.2

POLITICAL REPRESENTATION IN WASHINGTON:
ANHEUSER-BUSCH LOBBYING FORCE, 1996–97

Anheuser-Busch Companies, Inc. — Washington Office

Association memberships

Beer Institute[a]
National Beer Wholesalers Association
National Association of Wholesalers and Distributors
U.S. Chamber of Commerce
Grocery Manufacturers of America
Public Affairs Council

Lobbying firms representing Anheuser-Busch

Timmons and Company, Inc.	Bartley M. O'Hara, P.C.
O'Brien Calio	Public Strategies Washington, Inc.
Fleishman-Hillard, Inc.	Van Scoyoc Associates, Inc.
John Freshman Associates, Inc.	Washington Counsel, P.C.
Harmon & Wilmot, P.C.	Webster, Chamberlain and Bean
Howrey & Simon	The Wexler Group
Motley and Co., L.A.	Oldaker, Ryan, Phillips & Utrecht

Political Action Committee

AB-PAC, Anheuser-Busch Companies, Inc. Political Action Committee

SOURCES: *Government Affairs Yellow Book* (New York: Leadership Directories, Inc., 1997), p. 18; *1996 Washington Representatives* (Washington, D.C.: Columbia Books, Inc., 1996), p. 801.
a. Beer Institute membership includes Anheuser-Busch, Coors, Miller, and several smaller breweries.

of Representatives and the Senate that would have altered the relationships between organized interests active in the campaign financing of candidates for federal offices. Both efforts failed to garner sufficient support to change laws established more than twenty years ago. The 1996 elections for Congress and the presidency were conducted under the campaign finance laws passed by Congress and reinterpreted by the U.S. Supreme Court in 1976 and by a long series of rulings handed down by the Federal Election Commission (FEC), the regulatory entity created to disclose federal campaign finance transactions and enforce the law by the Federal Election Campaign Act of 1974 (FECA).[2]

Collectively, these laws prohibit corporations, unions, and other groups from contributing money from their treasuries to federal candidates or party accounts that are used to finance federal election campaigns, place ceilings on the amounts individuals can give to candidates and parties in federal election, and require the disclosure of money spent in congressional elections. The FECA also inspired the birth of the modern political action committee (PAC) because it allows corporations, trade associations, unions, and other groups to create campaign committees for the purposes of collecting contributions from their employees and members and redistributing them to federal candidates and party organizations. PACs allow interest groups to play an important role in federal elections. The provisions of the FECA that concern presidential elections created a voluntary system of federal matching funds for candidates for presidential nomination contests and federal block grants for general election candidates.

Current law allows PACs to contribute up to $5,000 per candidate per election and to give directly to party committees and other PACs as well. Members of groups can also contribute to candidates, parties, and other PACs, thereby magnifying the effects of the PAC contribution. PACs can also spend unlimited amounts, through independent expenditures, to advocate the election or defeat of a candidate, as long as they do not coordinate this spending with the campaign. Such expenditures by PACs must be disclosed to the FEC. In 1994 the National Rifle Association spent more than $100,000 on behalf of the Senate campaigns of Fred Thompson and Bill Frist of Tennessee.[3] Groups and their members can also make "soft money" contributions of unlimited size to state and national party committees to help in party building. Such contributions are often targeted by the party toward the presidential or selected congressional races. The June 1996 Supreme Court decision in *Colorado Republican Federal Campaign Committee et al.* v. *Federal Election Commission* (No. 95-489, 1996) secured the role of state political parties as recipients and spenders of unlimited soft money contributions as long as such expenditures are independent of the particular federal campaigns (see Marcus 1996). More recently, groups have mounted "issue advocacy" campaigns, in which they do not directly advocate the election or defeat of a candidate but instead spend unlimited amounts to inform the voters of the candidate's positions. In 1996 the AFL-CIO spent more than $35 million to inform voters of the perceived anti-union positions of many Republican incumbents.

Washington lobbyists and interest groups have readily adapted to the FECA's regulatory framework by making independent expenditures, carrying out issue advocacy campaigns, and making soft money contributions to political parties. During the year preceding the 1996 presidential and congressional elections, the Center for Responsive Politics tracked 300 Washington lawyer-lobbyists who had each given more than $1,500 to candidates, parties, and PACs. These top lobbyists (and their family members) gave more than $3.2 million in campaign contributions. While $2.2 million of their contributions went directly to congressional candidates, the top contributors also gave soft money contributions directly to party committees in order to skirt the law's aggregate $25,000-a-year contribution limit (see table 1.3).

Some of the nation's most powerful interests do not operate PACs, including the American Association of Retired Persons, the Christian Coalition, the U.S. Chamber of Commerce, and the National Association of Manufacturers; nonetheless they are heavily involved in federal elections. In fact, the latter three organizations joined forces with several other organizations allied with the Republican Party leadership in Congress in the spring of 1996 under the rubric of "The Coalition" to launch a multimillion-dollar issue advocacy campaign to counteract the AFL-CIO efforts. Neither the AFL-CIO issue advocacy campaign nor the efforts of The Coalition were disclosed to the FEC.

Federal Lobbying Disclosure Provisions[4]

The past four years have witnessed more changes in the relationships between organized interests and the federal government than in any other time during the last half century. In January 1993 President Clinton issued Executive Order 12834, increasing the restrictions on the postemployment lobbying activities of executive branch officials. The previous one-year cooling-off period banning contacts with former agencies or departments was extended to five years. A lifetime ban prohibiting former executive branch officials from working as agents on behalf of foreign governments or political parties was also created.[5] Later that year, the Clinton White

TABLE 1.3

TOP TEN POLITICAL DONORS
AMONG REGISTERED LOBBYISTS

Rank	Name	Firm	1995 amount
1	C. Boyden Gray	Wilmer, Cutler, and Pickering	$142,910
2	Lawrence F. O'Brien	O'Brien Calio	77,500
3	Steven M. Champlin	The Duberstein Group	49,500
4	Michael S. Berman	The Duberstein Group	46,822
5	J. D. Williams	Williams & Jensen	37,750
6	James H. Davidson	The Davidson Colling Group	32,250
7	Robert W. Barrie	O'Connor and Hannan	29,300
8	Charles T. Manatt	Manatt, Phelps et al.	28,681
9	Robert J. Thompson	R. Thompson & Co.	27,500
10-11	Vernon Clark	Vernon Clark & Assoc.	27,000
10-11	James V. Stanton	Stanton & Associates	27,000

SOURCE: Watzman and Youngclaus (1996).

House eliminated the tax deductibility of lobbying expenses by corporations and related business associations in its 1993 Omnibus Budget Reconciliation Act.[6]

The following two years proved to be a roller-coaster ride for those
championing broad lobby reform efforts. In 1994 a lobbying disclosure act
that would have provided comprehensive reporting requirements, established an independent registration and disclosure entity, regulated grassroots lobbying, and introduced gift-ban provisions was defeated (Shaiko
1995, 156–65). A year later, a similar but weaker bill—the Lobbying Disclosure Act of 1995—was passed. This law consolidates many of the provisions in existing law and makes many of them enforceable for the first
time, at least theoretically. Just as important, the new law acknowledges
additional realities of lobbying in the late 1990s.

As a result of the reform, communications from interest group representatives to congressional staff and executive branch officials on specific
policy issues is now considered lobbying. The new law defines a lobbyist as
any individual employed or retained by a client or organization for financial or other compensation, and whose lobbying activities constitute more
than 20 percent of his or her activities during a semiannual period. One is
exempted from filing if total income related to lobbying for a particular client is $5,000 or less during a semiannual period; similarly, an organization
that employs its own lobbyists and spends less than $20,000 on lobbying
activities need not register. Congressional testimony is exempted, as is information that lobbyists provide to members of Congress or senior executive branch officials at these officials' written request. Communications required by subpoena or similar action do not constitute lobbying, nor do
contacts made by a church or religious order. Communications by public
officials acting in their official capacities and by representatives of the media for the purpose of news gathering are also not considered lobbying.

Registration under the new law is a two-step process. Within forty-five
days of an initial lobbying contact, lobbyists are required to register with
the clerk of the House and the secretary of the Senate by providing pertinent information regarding the lobbyist, his or her clients, the issues, the
activities, and the governmental institutions associated with the lobbying
efforts. The second stage of lobby disclosure involves the filing of semiannual lobbying reports. The requirements for the semiannual reports consist
of responses to twelve items, including information about the lobbying
firm, the client, the firm's income or expenses, the firm's income from the
client, the lobbying issues (including bill numbers and specific executive
branch actions, the chambers of Congress and federal agencies contacted,
the name and title of each employee who acted as a lobbyist, and information on foreign entities).[7] Following the first deadline, an analysis of the
lobbying reports filed found that more than $400 million was spent on lob-

bying during the first six months of 1996 (Drinkard 1996, A1). Combined with the Year-End Reports filed for the last six months of the year, lobbying expenditures for 1996 totaled roughly $1 billion.

The Lobbying Disclosure Act of 1995 is a significant improvement over its predecessor, the Lobby Disclosure Act of 1946, and the various legislative remnants that constituted lobby regulation. Nonetheless, there are glaring weaknesses in the new law. First, there is no mention of grassroots lobbying, which emerged as a major interest group technique during the 1990s. Similarly, the language created to identify the activities of coalitions in Washington is too vague to capture the variety of ways in which coalitions operate. Many of the activities undertaken by coalitions are focused on grassroots mobilization and broad media campaigns. Neither of these activities constitutes lobbying under the new rules. Therefore, multimillion-dollar coalitions can avoid registering as lobbying entities as long as each of the coalition members provides less than $10,000 semiannually for lobbying purposes.

Various attempts by investigative journalists in Washington to uncover the hidden coalitions that are now forced to register under the new law have identified a grand total of six groups. In addition, the public will learn little about the specific targets of lobbying as Congress requires only that specific bills and the chamber that was lobbied be identified. It does not require lobbyists to report which members and congressional aides were contacted. Finally, although the number of individuals who have registered as lobbyists has increased, the new law does not provide an accurate count of the number of lobbyists who try to influence the federal government.[8]

The Gift-Ban Provisions

Perhaps more than the Lobbying Disclosure Act, the Senate and House resolutions relating to the acceptance of gifts and travel from lobbyists and organized interests have changed the political culture on the Hill. On 28 July 1995 the Senate passed S.Res. 158, which regulates the gifts, meals, and entertainment that senators can accept from lobbyists.[9] The gift resolution prohibits any senator or Senate aide from receiving a gift or meal valued at more than $50, or more than $100 per year in gifts from a single source. Meals over $10 count as part of the $100 annual gift limit. Senators and staff may receive commemorative materials such as plaques, trophies, or other awards of nominal value, but travel to events that are substantially leisure or recreational is banned.[10]

The rule "continues to allow Senators and their aides to accept: campaign contributions from lobbyists and others; contributions from those who are not lobbyists to a Senator's legal defense fund; gifts from other Senators and staff aides; anything of value resulting from outside business not connected with official duties; pensions and benefits; informational materials, such as books and videotapes; honorary degrees, including travel to ceremonies; items of little intrinsic value; inheritances; or any gift for which a waiver is approved by the Ethics Committee" (Salant and Scammon 1995, 234).

The House of Representatives went even further than the Senate by passing an outright gift ban on 16 November 1995. H.Res. 250 severely limits the ability of any member or staffer to accept meals or gifts from lobbyists or constituents. Only in widely attended events that include a range of participants, not simply lobbyists and members, may a member or staffer even accept a meal. Like the Senate gift-ban rule, the House reform has a "friends and family" limitation and an exception for awards, plaques, hats, and other items of nominal value. Members may also request from the House Ethics Committee waivers on the acceptance of certain gifts.

What is ironic about the gift-ban efforts in the House and Senate is that these attempts to limit the role of money in the political process through the acceptance of gifts and travel from lobbyists and other interested parties have made money more important in the political process. Now the only time that many lobbyists have access to a member of Congress outside the confines of the Capitol grounds is at a fund-raising event. Since the gift ban does not limit the abilities of members and senators to accept PAC contributions of up to $5,000 per election, some moneyed interests have continued to wine and dine elected officials under the guise of giving a campaign contribution. The House and Senate gift-ban provisions have changed the ways in which organized interests do business on the Hill. As time passes, more and more lobbyists will figure out new ways to operate under the new rules.

Creating the Interest Group Connection: Organized Interests in Elections, Congress, the Presidency, and the Courts

The chapters that follow examine the interest group connections in several distinct institutional settings: the electoral connection, the congressional connection, the executive connection, and the judicial connection. Each section includes a lead overview chapter that sets the institutional context for the chapters that follow and concludes with commentaries from relevant practitioners of lobbying, electioneering, or litigation. These lobbyists, lawyers, and PAC directors represent each of the six forms of political representation in Washington. The combination of scholars and practitioners offers an interesting mix of perspectives and insights into the interest group connections that link organized interests and government officials in the federal policymaking process. The next chapter offers a historical perspective on lobbying in Washington. Dr. Charls E. Walker, one of the deans of the Washington lobbying profession, gives a firsthand account of lobbying in Washington over the past four decades.

The substantive chapters, organized in parts II–V of the book, detail the rich tapestry of interest group connections. In the electoral arena they describe changes in the flow of PAC contributions after the 1994 election created a Republican majority in Congress and the role of groups in presidential elections. In the congressional arena they detail the ways in which groups engage in grassroots lobbying and coalition building and discuss the variety of resources that groups bring to bear when lobbying. Additional chapters address the way that budget deficit-reduction strategies have affected lobbying and the impact of PAC contributions in legislative outcomes in one specific issue area. In the executive arena the chapters focus on the administrative decision making in executive agencies, strategies for White House lobbying on Capitol Hill, and the role of interest groups in foreign policy formulation. The chapters on the judicial arena detail the rise of conservative Christian groups in church-state litigation and the impact of corporate litigation on free speech law. At the end of each part II–V, two political practitioners comment on some of the issues by drawing on their personal experiences.

Notes

1. Two additional pages of listings of interest groups in the District of Columbia Telephone Directory are found under "International." Many of these listings are unions.

2. On the FECA, see Magleby and Nelson (1990), esp. 13–20.

3. Bill Frist benefited from $187,127 in NRA independent expenditures and PAC contributions, while Fred Thompson benefited from $182,177 in similar NRA expenditures in the 1993–94 election cycle. See Anderson (1996, 167).

4. Much of the material in this section is drawn from Shaiko (1996).

5. The ban does not include a ban on lobbying for foreign corporations (Shaiko 1995, 160–61).

6. See Section 13222 of Title XIII of the Omnibus Budget Reconciliation Act of 1993 (OBRA); the elimination of the lobbying deduction will generate an estimated $500 million over five years. One may recall that the revenues generated by this action were to be used as the funding mechanism for a variety of proposed campaign finance reforms.

7. The Lobbying Disclosure Act of 1995 replaces the criminal penalties of the 1946 act with civil penalties for noncompliance, including fines up to $50,000. It is doubtful that the clerk of the House or the secretary of the Senate

will pursue unregistered lobbyists or sanction improper registrants because nothing in the act can be construed to grant audit or investigative authority to the clerk of the House or the secretary of the Senate.

8. For organizations with in-house lobbyists, reporting includes expenses incurred during each six-month period, in two broad categories: less than $10,000 and $10,000 or more, followed by a good-faith estimate to the nearest $20,000 if the income is more than $10,000. For additional details regarding the Lobby Registration and Reporting requirements, see Sachs (1996); see also Secretary of the Senate/Clerk of the House of Representatives, "Lobbying Disclosure Act Guidance," Legislative Resource Center, 1996. Since the passage of the Lobbying Disclosure Act of 1995, literally scores of lobbying firms and organizations have written legal briefs regarding its interpretation; two of the best are Roger S. Ballantine and Jeffrey L. Ross, "Patton Boggs, L.L.P. Memorandum—Re: The Lobbying Disclosure Act of 1995," 19 December 1995; and Robert A. Boisture, "What Universities Need to Know to Comply with the Lobbying Disclosure Act of 1995," American Council on Education, December 1995.

9. Gifts from family and friends also fall within the jurisdiction of the new rules, with personal gifts of more than $250 prohibited without the written approval from the Senate Ethics Committee.

10. Senators can accept travel in connection with their official duties.

2 Charls E. Walker

A Four-Decade Perspective on Lobbying in Washington

How DO YOU get a bill through Congress? How do you defeat a bill—get it changed, pigeonholed, or killed? My answer reflects my experience as a political appointee to the Treasury Department under Presidents Eisenhower and Nixon, a six-year stint as executive director of the American Bankers Association, and well over twenty years as the head of my own lobbying firm, Walker Associates. My answer is also somewhat oblique because I first insist on identifying the players in the lobbying game. A good place to begin a chapter on lobbying is with an examination of lobbyists themselves.

The Crowd on "K Street"

When the majority of Americans think of lobbyists, they think of a "hired gun"—the stereotypical Washington "K Street" insider wearing Gucci shoes and a $2,500 suit.[1] As we say in politics, perception is the name of the game. And although some political scientists have tried to set the record straight on members of the lobbying universe, the media are not cooperative, and perhaps the public does not really care anyway.

The fact is, of course, that Washington lobbyists are legion both in terms of number and the causes or institutions they represent. Organized labor lobbies—labor was "King of the Hill" from World War II until the early 1970s—and businesses, both large and small, lobby. Ralph Nader, Common Cause, and the Sierra Club lobby. The federal departments and agencies lobby. The University of Texas lobbies, as do the Ivy League schools and state universities and private colleges. Foreign governments and private interests lobby, but under stricter standards than domestic lobbyists. And churches lobby, from the Catholic church right on through the list.

A simple anecdote perhaps makes an important point about perception and reality. A likeable West Texan named Kent Hance was elected to Congress in 1978—incidentally, by beating George W. Bush, now governor of Texas. ABC asked to do a "day-in-the-life" documentary about what lobbying really is, and in the process interviewed Kent as to his views on lobbyists. Putting on his best West Texas accent and manners, he told a story about a stump speech he had made while campaigning for the Texas legislature some time back. When he had finished the speech, a nice little elderly lady came up to him and said, "Mr. Hance, I sure did like what you said, and I want to vote for you, but I cannot unless you promise me that you'll never talk to any of those lobbyists in Austin."

Kent responded: "Ma'am, I sure wish I could promise you that, but I simply can't."

"Why's that?" she asked.

Safely assuming that the nice lady was a Baptist, Kent went on: "Why, Ma'am, if a religious issue came up for a vote, I wouldn't think of taking a position until I had talked to the lobbyist for the Southern Baptist Convention."

"You mean," she said in great surprise, "that our church hires a lobbyist?"

"Yes, Ma'am, it does. And a fine Christian gentleman he is, too."

End of story.

"And Ike Said to Mr. Sam … "

Today's legislative process can be best understood by examining its evolution over a period of time. In answering the basic question about bill passage I go back to 1959–61, the last two years of the Eisenhower administration. In those days the federal government, on major domestic matters, was practically run by four people: Dwight D. Eisenhower, the avuncular national hero and highly popular president of the United States; Sam Rayburn, the legendary Speaker of the House of Representatives; Lyndon Baines Johnson, the equally legendary majority leader of the Senate; and Secretary of the Treasury Robert B. Anderson. This is, of course, an overstatement, but it says a great deal about these individuals' political skills and relationships.

Every week or so in those days the astute legislative operative Bryce Harlow would bring Rayburn and Johnson to a meeting at the White House with Eisenhower and Anderson over "bourbon and branch water."

President Eisenhower might say, "Fellows, I think we ought to do such-and-such." And Mr. Sam and LBJ might say: "That's a good idea, Mr. President. You propose it and Congress will approve it." And they'd be right, almost 100 percent of the time. Sometimes Mr. Sam and LBJ might state that the idea was basically good, but it needed a change here or there—a little different "spin." If that happened, then Congress would approve it. And they would be right again.

Mr. Sam and LBJ were no less partisan than Democrats of later years; perhaps more so. But instead of practicing the Democratic leadership approach in subsequent divided governments—that is, strongly adversarial to the administration—these two congressional leaders reasoned that they and the Democrats could only come out second in a spitting match with their fellow Texan who lived in the White House. Although they were deeply upset by Republican occupancy of the White House for two terms—in their view Democratic occupancy of the Oval Office was close to a divine right—and almost desperately wanted to recapture the presidency in 1960, they reasoned that the best course of action was to play the part of the "loyal opposition." They would go along with Eisenhower when they could and in the process get Democrats some of the credit. Thus on some occasions Mr. Sam and LBJ might say, in effect, "That's a good idea, Mr. President, but it won't sell to a Democratic Congress—[one that was also dominated by labor]. Let us propose it, you endorse it later, and Congress will approve it." And they'd be right again.

Which brings us to an important point about presidential leadership. There are things that a president of one party can do that the president of the other party cannot. Eisenhower and Anderson wanted to ask Congress for a comprehensive pro-growth tax-reform package—cuts in taxes on business and upper-income individuals (the top individual marginal rate was then 91 percent!), capital gains, and so on. But Rayburn and Johnson said forget it, arguing correctly that there was no way a Democratic Congress would respond positively to such a proposal from a Republican president. But, sure enough, that is exactly the type of tax proposal that President John Kennedy pressed in his brief presidency—and that LBJ pushed through Congress after Kennedy's death.

An example from the other side of the coin occurred when Richard Nixon was president. He had narrowly defeated Hubert Humphrey, LBJ's vice-president. Nixon deftly proceeded to open relations with Communist China, something Humphrey—a card-carrying member of the Americans for Democratic Action, which Republicans viewed as the epitome of "soft on Communism"—could never have done. And it was probusiness Ronald Reagan who engineered passage of a major "tax fairness" bill in 1986, something Democratic presidents and Congresses had failed to do over a long period of time.

Sometimes Rayburn and Johnson might act as a "front" for the Republican president and say, let us propose it, Mr. President, and then you support it. Or they might simply say, forget it; it's not doable and we might as well go on to other things.

The important point is not the substantive decisions but rather how Mr. Sam and LBJ could be so accurate in their forecasts of what Congress would or would not do. In recent years, congressional leadership has not only had a great deal of trouble keeping its troops in line, in a number of instances it has even failed to count votes accurately and has suffered embarrassing surprise defeats on the floor—something that seldom occurred in the earlier years. What has happened?

Some observers would have you believe that this nation no longer enjoys the caliber of leadership that these four men exemplified; that the explanation lies in the personalities and capabilities of the players. This is not so in my opinion. In fact, overall, we have more and better leadership material now than then. Most informed observers agree that the Congress of today is head and shoulders above the Congress of the earlier period in every way, including intelligence, education, dedication, sobriety.

The sobriety of Congress was highly questionable then, both figuratively and literally. The booze flowed mighty freely in those years, in members' offices, down the street at Hill bars, even in the cloakrooms. Its overuse sometimes affected the outcome of legislation. A major bill I was responsible for as deputy secretary of the treasury was the so-called Lockheed loan bailout in 1971. We went into the House floor debate on the legislation with a comfortable and accurately tallied margin of at least ten votes in favor the bill. But the debate went on so long and so many members got boozed up and upset with the unpopular floor manager of the legislation that on first count it was down the tube by seven votes. Working with the leadership, we scored a narrow three-vote victory on the final tally.

A similar occurrence took place on the same bill in the Senate: When the vote came, we thought that we had a margin of one vote or, if not, at least a tie; so we alerted the vice-president to be in the chair if his tie-breaking vote was needed. But during the roll call one of our "supporters" voted against us. The vice-president was rushed in to break the expected tie. Much to our surprise, however, a western senator known for his hatred of big business, but also for his devotion to John Barleycorn, surprised us by voting with us. I don't think he knew what bill he was voting on. Perhaps he didn't even know what day it was.

Still the voting was ending, the count was tied, and the vice-president was getting ready to do his thing. Whereupon a southern senator rushed in and voted aye, assuring passage. The vice-president wrote that senator a note: "You son-of-a-bitch; you just ruined my moment in the sun!" That vice-president was Spiro Agnew.

The Congress of those days contrasts sharply with the contemporary Congress. David Broder, the "dean" of political reporters, remarked on "the new sobriety" in the late 1970s, stating that he had sat through an all-night session in the House and it was amazing; there was not a single drunk on the floor!

Members of Congress are much better by any measure, but, paradoxically, Congress as a body stands in the lowest repute with the public since pollsters started asking voters to evaluate the institution. Thus the major difference between then and now must be institutional.

"Yes, Mr. Chairman, You Have My Vote!"

The institution that permitted Rayburn and Johnson to be so accurate was, of course, a relatively ironclad seniority system: positions of power were gained, not by ability, charm, or political prowess, but simply by longevity. For example, if you wanted to be chairman of the powerful House Ways and Means Committee back then, all you had to do was to get appointed to it (usually after several terms, with the approval of the party leadership and the support of members of your region), get reelected to the House of Representatives every two years, and outlive everyone else on the committee. It did not matter whether you were senile, a drunkard, or whatever; those were the requisites.

Two things should be noted. First, the situation did not differ much in the House and Senate. Second, the seniority system did not permit Sam Rayburn to run the House as he saw fit. Quite the contrary. Although the powerful committee chairmen owed him much, he was first among equals with what was power galore, but in the final analysis the committee chairmen ran their own shows. Thus the House in those days was "run," not by one man, or by 435 men, but by the Speaker, his top associates in the leadership, and some 10 to 15 top committee chairmen.

Those men—they were all men in those days—had prodigious power: the power to set committee agendas, ride herd on subcommittees, choose (or bar) members from junkets to beautiful foreign shores, and so on. Take, for example, Representative Howard "Judge" Smith and his Rules Committee. Judge Smith was definitely not a liberal. On social issues, particularly civil rights, he was a relic of the past, and he ruthlessly used the Rules Committee to block legislation he disagreed with. To be sure, he could do this only with the support of the southern Democrats and Republicans who together dominated the committee, but do it he did. For example, if a civil rights bill he disliked came to his committee, he might well repair to his farm in Virginia for a week or so. His committee could not meet without him: the legislation would languish and perhaps go away. Never mind that the Rules Committee was supposed only to be a "traffic cop" to assure an orderly flow of legislation from other committees to the House floor and to determine the terms of debate—a powerful prerogative. In those days, and from time to time since then, the committee in effect dealt with substance and not just procedure.

Small wonder, therefore, that early on newly elected President John Kennedy told Speaker Rayburn that he could not possibly get through his program with the Smith group controlling the Rules Committee. Would the Speaker take steps to "stack it" so as to release its hammerlock on legislation? Rayburn, an admirer of the presidency who had a special fondness for Jack Kennedy, said yes, but only reluctantly. To take such steps would be directly counter to the Rayburn system of running the House, in which the committee "barons" ruled their fiefs. But Rayburn took on the fight as his last big battle before his death in 1962 and eked out a narrow floor victory to "stack" the committee.

The most significant aspect of this seniority system for lobbying was that it made the job not necessarily easier but much less taxing and time-consuming. For example, if on a tax matter the "lobbyist" (the president, the secretary of the treasury, the AFL-CIO, Joe Smith, or whoever) had Speaker Rayburn, House Ways and Means chairman Wilbur Mills (D-Ark.), and highly respected ranking member John Byrnes (R-Wisc.) on his side, his work was in effect over. The bill would pass.

That is not to say the task was easier then than now—getting the sign-off from those three supermembers was a herculean task in itself. But it did mean that you did not have to fiddle around with other members of the committee. To be sure, Rayburn or Mills might ask you to lobby some other members in order to assure a good committee vote—the rule of thumb was that no bill should be taken to the floor without the support of a majority of the fifteen Democrats on the committee—or to help out when the bill reached the floor. But that was more like fun than work, and it put a lobbyist in a good light with these supermembers.

This system worked and worked well. Voters were more or less satisfied because the "leaders" got the job done. Moreover, most of the "followers" were happy; in fact, the leaders would protect the loyal and reward them in various ways. As Mr. Sam often said, if a member wanted to "get along," he (or she) had to "go along." Until December 1974, that is. Then the political earth moved, at least insofar as the U.S. House of Representatives was concerned.

The 1974 House Democratic Caucus: Blood on the Floor

The U.S. House of Representatives is not a "continuing body," at least insofar as assignments to committees, to committee chairmanships, and to other leadership positions are concerned. Consequently, in late November or early December of each election year, the two parties "caucus" separately in secret sessions to nominate their candidates for Speaker and committee chairmen, divvy up budget and staff, and take care of a variety of procedural and housekeeping matters. Then, after the caucuses, the majority party traditionally votes unanimously in the first "organizing" House session to implement its caucus decisions. Before 1974, election of committee chairmen had been pro forma—the senior member was automatically installed in each committee.

In 1975, however, rank-and-file Democrats rose up and kicked out the chairmen of three major committees—Agriculture, Armed Services, and Banking. To be sure, only in the first did the members get really bold by skipping several names on the seniority list; in the other two committees, the number-two member was elected in each case. The exception was in Agriculture, in which a talented young legislator named Tom Foley of Washington, later Speaker of the House, was moved up.

What happened? Restive Democrats of earlier classes, long wanting to move up the power ladder at a faster pace, had almost literally met the newly elected "Watergate Class"—all bright-eyed, bushy-tailed, and reform-minded—at the door and said, in effect, let's make a deal. And the deal was to loosen the seniority system and in effect put committee chairmen on notice that they were henceforth working not primarily for the people of a certain district in Virginia or Texas, the leadership, or the White House, but for members of the caucus. Committee chairmen were told if they forgot that fact, the members would have their scalp at the next caucus or perhaps through passing a petition even before then.

Why did this happen? And why did it happen at this particular time? Quite a few observers, especially in the press, considered Watergate the cause. This is wrong. Watergate was a catalytic factor and undoubtedly affected the timing, but it was the impatience that the increasingly qualified members of the House who were elected after World War II had with the seniority system that brought the system down. By 1974 they had had enough on the back benches and years of relative silence and impotence before real power was gained and found sufficient allies in the Watergate Class to initiate major reform.

The fallout was fast coming and far reaching. In essence, House committees had finally been democratized. Their chairmen became responsible to their party's caucus. With the younger members hungering for power and action, committee chairmen were forced to enlarge the number of subcommittees, even though such groups can be a pain in the rear of the chairman. More subcommittees meant more legislation and the possibility that more legislation that the chairman opposed would percolate up from the subcommittees. More subcommittees also upped the need for staff, thus contributing to the personnel explosion of recent decades.

From the standpoint of getting a bill through Congress, no longer could a lobbyist rely on a few powerful supermembers. On Ways and Means, for example (which had been "stacked" at the direction of organized labor and had grown from twenty-five to thirty-six members), a lobbyist would have to work both sides of the aisle, up and down, and would not feel at all comfortable unless upward of some twenty solid votes were in hand, including the chairman, who usually had firm control over his party's proxy votes.

The democratization of committees and indeed of the House itself, as chairmen's power declined, leads to some important questions: To what drummers do contemporary members of Congress march? What are they like? What appeals to them? How do they reach decisions? Such knowledge is the absolutely essential basic in the lobbyist's kit of tools.

Getting to Know You; Getting to Know All about You

Members of the "new" Congress—Congress after the great shoot-out of 1974—are, as noted, far superior in almost every way to the members who preceded them. That is good for the country and good for honorable lobbyists. The ethics of the "new" congressmen are higher, partly because of the exit of the stereotypical political hacks and machine-directed members of yesteryear (e.g., Richard Daley, mayor and "political boss" of Chicago, controlled all the votes of the delegation in those days); partly because the decline in the power of supermembers reduced the chances of chicanery; and partly because so many members of the "new" Congress came up through other than the traditional political routes, where cornercutting and even outright illegal practices were often accepted behavior.

Many if not most of the members of the "new" Congress are "quick studies." In 1959 Secretary Anderson asked me to explain to a very fine and intelligent southern senator how banks created money and where that power fit into monetary policy. It took a good half hour. Today most members already know the answer and, if not, can get a good fix on it from a short memo.

Second, it is stating the obvious to note that the "new" Congress is much more "independent minded" than the old—independent of the White House, independent of the leadership, independent of the "fat cat" contributors in their states or districts. The host of new political action committees (PACs), particularly the corporate and trade association variety, provided a major source of support for this increased independence.

With PACs making it much easier to raise even the larger amount of campaign funds needed in each election, members became "bosses" of their own operations, using the ample PAC funds to hire issue researchers, speechwriters, chauffeurs, hairdressers, pollsters, and others. Thus the victors came to Washington with the justifiable view that, in many if not most instances, they had won their seats largely by themselves and were not all that beholden to any powers-that-be in Washington or big shots at home.

This decline in the political power of "fat cats" emanating from the growth of PACs deserves special mention, since PACs are the institutions self-styled reformers constantly malign. An anecdote that illustrates this point comes from the 1978 ABC documentary on lobbying mentioned earlier. Then congressional correspondent Britt Hume interviewed a mid-American Republican congressman who was a very fine member. On network television, Britt hauled out a computer printout that unfurled around the room and confronted the representative: "What do you have to say about all of this PAC money you've received?" Taken by surprise, the congressman stammered a more or less incoherent—and to the television audience, incriminating—answer. What he should have said was, "Yes, that was indeed true, and isn't it a wonderful thing, Mr. Hume? For in the old days, there were a handful of major supporters in my district, any one of whom could call me before breakfast and tell me how to vote. If any PAC tries that, I can tell it to get lost—you're not that important to me." Then, as now, PAC limits were $5,000 per member, $10,000 if one includes the primary contest.

Third, there is much greater diversity of backgrounds in the "new" as contrasted to the "old" Congress. Before, there were too many lawyers and far too few other professional people, business men or women, educators, and so on. That increased diversity of backgrounds is also good for the country and good for the honorable lobbyist. When something like a shortage of oil and gas occurs, as in the 1970s, the lawyer unschooled in economics is likely to take out his legal pad and start drawing up a system of regulation as a cure. But the economist is likely to ask, why not let the price rise? That will increase the amount of oil and gas supplied and decrease the amount demanded—and after a while all will be right with the world. The lawyer-inspired regulatory approach to dealing with our 1970s energy shortage prevented us from dealing with this problem effectively for almost a decade.

"I Have a Ph.D. in Chemistry from Princeton"

In late winter of 1977, Jimmy Carter sent Congress his comprehensive legislative proposal to deal with the energy shortage that had started with the Arab trade boycott of Israel in the early 1970s. Unfortunately, neither he nor his top energy aide, Jim Schlesinger, had given any careful thought to the acronym for Carter's description of the program. He called it the "Moral Equivalent of War," or MEOW—an unfortunate acronym!

Carter and Schlesinger came up with what can only be described as a "Rube Goldberg" solution to the expected complete depletion of oil and gas, an event predicted by experts to occur in the 1990s. The basic assumption in MEOW wasn't all that bad, however; it was based on "two Cs": conservation and coal. The United States was using too much energy per unit of input of gross product and, with some regulatory and hortatory urging, industry could conserve more energy. And the role of coal in MEOW—there were several centuries' supply in the ground right here in the United States—would be as a substitute for the oil and gas that was being "wasted" in many applications, such as when used as a "boiler fuel" in manufacturing.

It was Carter's solution to the boiler-fuel problem that got Walker Associates into the act. The administration proposed an industrial use tax (IUT), a federal levy on the use of oil and gas in industry to reduce what it believed was a significant waste of oil and gas. The theory was that this increase in cost would cause companies to shift from oil and gas to coal and thus serve the Carter goals. The trouble with the theory was that because of heating characteristics, chemical qualities, and so on, this substitution could be very expensive, if not impossible. One affected company, the small but high-quality Lone Star Steel Company of Texas (LSS), hired Walker Associates to kill or at least ameliorate this provision, which would have had a very deleterious impact on its operations and profits.

Within a short time after Walker Associates was hired, something known as the "Lone Star Steel Amendment" to the energy bill was getting substantial attention in the press. How could a small steel company carry such clout? It didn't; a powerful coalition was behind it. Coalitions are the most important factors in getting a bill through Congress.

Within forty-eight hours after the firm began to work for LSS, representatives of four industries—automobiles, textiles, petrochemicals, and steel—each of which fully shared LSS's views on the IUT, were gathered in the lobbying firm's conference room. The IUT would cause serious and expensive production problems for each of these industries. The companies were willing to—and in fact did—establish tough and effective energy-conservation programs, but they wanted the IUT killed as soon as possible. This coalition had a great deal of political clout, as measured primarily in terms of jobs and payrolls in the states and districts where they had plants.

This leads to a second very important term in lobbying: *horse* (or *horses*). Unless an individual is lobbying from a position such as deputy secretary of the treasury, where you can join in the debate with congressional committee members as an equal (or almost an equal), you are left sitting in the audience. You may know more about the subject under discussion than anyone else in the room, but you cannot participate in the committee's proceedings. What if a proponent of IUT comes up with a compromise that looks good on the surface but is in fact a trap? You may (or may not) have time to send a note to your supporters in Congress through the cloakroom. You may be lucky enough for the committee to take a short recess so that its members can hike to the House floor to cast a vote, which affords you the opportunity to walk over with a key supporter and point out the problems with the compromise. But, then again, you may not.

What you need on the committee is one or more "horses." The "horse" will be on your side in wanting to kill or ameliorate the provision. He will be a quick study, articulate, and a good debater. He will know when to persist, when to compromise, when to sit there quietly, and when to walk away.

Why is the "horse" with you? It could be because of ideological reasons—the member shares your views. It also could be because of personal times—maybe you were both in the secret society known as "Skull and Bones" at Yale. Perhaps you helped the "horse" find one of his constituent's lost Social Security checks when you worked in the Treasury Department or did some other favor for him in the past. Maybe the member thinks the proposal is simply dumb. It is also possible that the member is convinced that what you are in favor of is good for his constituents.

The "horse" for the IUT in the Ways and Means Committee in 1977 was magnificent. The importance of the chemical properties of oil and gas as related to manufacturing can be a highly technical and complicated matter. But this "horse"—a very junior Republican member from North Carolina, where textiles are very strong—showed in the hearings that he knew more about the technical aspects of the matter than any administration witness. He tied its spokesmen in knots, and the result was a significant watering down of the IUT in the committee, which was later defeated in the Senate. As the bill moved out of the committee, the member was asked how he had come know so much about the technical aspects of the IUT. He responded that he had a Ph.D. in chemistry from Princeton University. That member was Jim Martin, who later became governor of North Carolina.

Having a handful of qualified scientists like Jim Martin as members of Congress, as well as a handful of economists, doctors, and others from diverse backgrounds, is for the good of the country. It is far too easy in Washington for policymakers to be led down the garden road by technical staff, many of whom may have hidden agendas, and none of whom was elected. The presence of a coterie of members who know the subjects themselves can help avoid foolish or even counterproductive legislation.

There is another lesson to be learned from MEOW. President Carter and his staff had made the mistake of sending up to a pluralistic Congress a massive proposal with too many interlocking parts. If not enacted in its entirety as a package, not only might the positive benefits be lost but damage could occur. Carter assumed—as Clinton and his White House staff perhaps did on health-care reform—that his proposal was so brilliant and indisputably effective that Congress would simply shout, "Eureka! Let's pass this bill today and get on to other things." That is *not* the way Congress works.

It's the People; Yes, the People

The trait held in spades by members of the "new" Congress, although emulated at least partially in the past by their predecessors, is a consummate, continuing, and copiously demonstrated concern for their constituents. It is relatively easy for the members to express this concern because of modern rapid transportation and instantaneous, real-time communications. Elected officials have always worked to stay in the good graces of their constituents, but hardly with the care, skill, and resources of the members of the "new" Congress.

The ways and means of constituent cuddling include newsletters, town meetings, and so-called casework to perform the ombudsman function. More important is the voting record that each member calculates will keep his supporters happy enough to reelect him. The drive to compile such a record is as strong as—or probably stronger than—at any time in the history of the Republic.

So the question of how you get a bill through Congress is easy to answer, although admittedly often difficult, and indeed impossible, to put into practice: all you have to do is to convince a majority of the members of Congress that what you are for is good for their constituents. If you are trying to stop a bill, you have to convince them of the opposite. And, if you are trying to change a bill, then the same rule applies. There is, however, one very important caveat: what counts is not what may be objectively good for constituents, but what they think is good for them. In some cases, voters may not know what is good for them; or they may even believe that some bill or program is good for them when in reality it would probably harm their interests.

The good politician will be keenly aware of this problem, as will the good lobbyist. A skilled lobbyist can make a strong case to a group of legislators and find them in agreement, but then learn they do not intend to vote against his or her position. When asked why, members are known to answer with something like, "The vast majority of my constituents do not understand the issue and in fact are against what you propose. Now if you go down there and change their minds, then I will be happy to vote with you." This explains a great deal about the modern surge in "grassroots" lobbying, which often relies on high-speed computers, telephone banks, and other modern technology.

A short anecdote demonstrates the importance of grassroots lobbying. In 1971 the railroad that provided economically vital freight transportation to seventeen northeastern states declared bankruptcy. The railroad—the Penn Central—limped along for a couple of years until January 1973, when a federal judge said, "No more; creditors' assets are being eaten away and this railroad will cease operating on November 1, 1973." Panic is probably too strong a word to describe eastern industrialists' reaction to this edict, but they knew that their operations would be severely cramped —in some instances, such as auto and steel production, even brought to a halt—by the demise of the railroad and the loss of essential freight transportation. Of course, Washington policymakers would never let this happen in the final instance, but their alternative would probably be federalization of the railroad—a dreaded event for the corporations. The trite but effective bogeyman for such federal intrusions into business is usually the U.S. Postal Service.

A coalition of major corporations, including four steel companies, two auto manufacturers, and three chemical producers, hired Walker Associates to help protect the railroad. It was a group with plenty of political clout, if mobilized properly. Not because of their PACs (they had none then), but because of the hundreds of thousands of jobs and hundreds of millions of dollars in payrolls they had in seventeen states.

The firm was hired to devise and enact a legislative solution to the problem very late in May 1973, less than six months before the railroad's scheduled demise. We quickly concluded that no free-market solution was possible. There was no investment banker who would or could raise the $8 billion to $10 billion necessary to resuscitate a railroad that was in awful shape both fiscally and physically. (Penn Central even suffered "standing derailments"—a freight car simply standing on the tracks would fall off because of the neglected, porous roadbed.) Only a public-private partnership could do the job.

We quickly found a plan that was drawn up by the executives of Union Pacific Railroad—a logical source given the need for dependable rail service from mid-America to the east. Union Pacific's plan called for creation of the "Consolidated Rail Corporation," or CONRAIL. Brock Adams (D-Wash.), a respected member of the relevant subcommittee of the House Commerce Committee (who later became a secretary of transportation and a senator) was the "horse" we relied on. Things came together in the House because the problem was pressing and the lobbying was good. By late July, with the month-long August recess just ahead, the firm confidently predicted House passage shortly after Labor Day.

Things did not go smoothly in the Senate. The chairman of the Transportation Subcommittee, Vance Hartke (D-Ind.), had pushed a bill through both his subcommittee and the parent Commerce Committee that directed the regulator of railroads, the Interstate Commerce Commission, to study the problem and report back in a year with recommendations for congressional action. My protests to Hartke that this would be far too late got nowhere; I suspect he shared many railroad workers' preferences for federalization of the railroads. Hartke stated flatly that his bill was scheduled for the Senate floor shortly after Labor Day and would be passed. What he did not say was that the conference between House and Senate on two such diverse bills could drag on and on until the deadline passed.

Walker Associates' task was to find a way to get a bill that had been passed by a strong majority of one of the Senate's most respected committees, which was chaired by Senator Warren Magnuson (D-Wash.), one of its most powerful elder members, pulled from the Senate calendar. We accomplished this "heavy lifting" by assembling representatives of our ten corporate clients in late July and recommending that, as a group, we will prepare a flip-chart presentation (today it would be a video) that will consist of two parts. The first part will be a "boilerplate" that explains how passage of the Senate bill would stop rail freight service in the Northeast and the passage of the House bill will keep it going. It will make the case that the Senate bill should not be taken up. The second part of the presentation will be prepared by and tailored to each of your companies and the states where you operate. For example, Bethlehem Steel of Pennsylvania will make a conservative calculation about what the stoppage of rail service will mean to jobs, payrolls, and output by Christmas—a good date for obvious reasons.

During the congressional recess Bethlehem's chief executive officer (CEO) will present its case to Pennsylvania's senators. Then, the CEOs of U.S. Steel, Alcoa, and some other companies will make their cases to the senators who represent the states in which they are headquartered. Because Bethlehem's Sparrows' Point plant in Baltimore provides a multitude of jobs in Maryland, Bethlehem will make presentations to Maryland senators. Other companies will follow suit: Ford's and General Motors' CEOs will meet with senators from Michigan, Indiana, and other auto-producing states; du Pont's CEO will meet with senators from Delaware and other states that host their production facilities; and General Electric's CEO will meet with the senators from Ohio, Pennsylvania, and other relevant states. They will tell their story in a low key but will make it clear to the senators that passage of the Hartke bill instead of the House bill will harm their state's gross domestic product and employment levels. The senators will recognize that a vote to shut down the Penn Central Railroad could be a vote for their retirement when they next run for reelection.

The CEOs did their jobs well. Immediately after Labor Day, Senator Magnuson stated that he was going to take the Hartke bill off the calendar and wait for the House bill to come over. Our plan succeeded because we convincingly documented our argument that passage of the Hartke bill would in all likelihood be very bad for the senators' constituents and that passage of the House bill could well be good for them. The battle was won by convincing most of the senators in seventeen states of the merits of this argument.

That was how the CONRAIL legislation got over the final hurdle. As we had hoped, and as the legislation provided, the public-private partnership brought forth a strong, well-run railroad that was returned to private ownership during Ronald Reagan's presidency. The Penn Central Railroad is now a premier, privately owned railroad with a very healthy bottom line.

Some Reflections

What lessons and conclusions can be drawn from the foregoing perspective on lobbying? First, the United States is a democracy. Members of Congress do what their constituents want. If my personal experience and the careful research of political scientists can be believed, members' votes are not for sale. At least no connection can be made between campaign contributions and the passage of truly important bills. And with the vigilance of today's press, even minor legislation that money used to help slip through unnoticed is now quickly brought to public attention and probable defeat. Much of the discontent voters are evidencing with respect to their Washington representatives is misdirected. Those constituents should perhaps direct their complaints to a mirror instead.

American democracy is fast becoming more "plebiscitary." Legislators can punch a few computer keys and find how their constituents stand on almost every issue, and adjust their positions accordingly. This is dangerous, especially with respect to economic policy, because people like high government spending, low taxes, and easy money—a sure recipe for inflation that could have disastrous economic and political consequences. Thus the increasingly strong efforts to help make voters better informed are all to the good and should be pushed even more strongly.

Second, Ann McBride of Common Cause, Ralph Nader of Public Citizen, and the lobbyist for the Southern Baptist Convention might be pained to hear this, but the techniques of lobbying are basically the same, regardless of whom your represent. But all these groups try to convince members of Congress that what they advocate is good for the members' constituents, and vice versa.

Third, the "Republican Revolution" of November 1994 did not change what constitutes effective lobbying. Effective lobbying is keyed to the democratic system. The Republican majority in Congress will do basically what their constituents want or that majority will again become a minority.

Fourth, ethics in the lobbying business have improved dramatically over the past four decades, not because of legislative edicts and regulation, but because of the quality of the members of Congress, the quality of the lobbyists, and the dispersion of power away from the Sam Rayburn proto-type to something close to a "one-person one-vote" regime in Congress. This last development carries with it some heavy baggage, however; legislative bodies need a structure that facilitates leadership. And that is difficult to manifest under the current system.

Note

1. Many corporate and association headquarters, as well as a number of the nation's most powerful lobbying firms, are located on or near K Street in Northwest Washington, D.C., between 13th and 22nd Streets—an area known as the "K Street corridor."

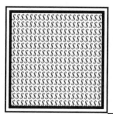

Part II

The Electoral Connection

3

Paul S. Herrnson

Interest Groups, PACs, and Campaigns

ELECTIONS are the most important connection between citizens and those who represent them in public office. Through elections citizens have the opportunity to express their approval or dissatisfaction with the job performance of individual officeholders or the government in general. Elections also provide the general public with the opportunity to have some input into the direction of public policy. Individual citizens, however, are not the only ones who use the electoral connection to express their views about politics. Businesses, labor unions, professional associations, and a variety of other groups—some of which are at best only loosely organized—also use elections to influence public policy. This chapter presents an overview of the activities of interest groups in federal elections.

From Pulpits to PACs

The potential for significant election-oriented interest group activity exists anywhere that a group can be found or organized. Churches, boardrooms, union halls, condominium association meeting rooms, and even the World Wide Web provide venues in which political organizing commonly occurs. The groups that assemble in these places often provide endorsements, volunteers, financial support, and other campaign assistance to candidates for the House, the Senate, the presidency, and state and local offices.

For most of the twentieth century, interest groups made three kinds of contributions to the election process. One had to do with the recruitment of candidates. Labor unions, civic clubs, and some other groups encouraged potential candidates to run for office and participated in their nomination campaigns. Interest group activity in this aspect of elections was important but was often secondary to that of political parties, which have traditionally played a more central role in candidate recruitment.

Another contribution that interest groups made to the election process was organizational. Labor unions, ethnic clubs, and business concerns provided campaign volunteers, sponsored rallies, endorsed candidates, and helped the candidates disseminate their messages. One of the groups' most important contributions to the campaign was to deliver the votes of their members on election day. Groups that had a large concentrated base strongly identified with and committed to the group's political causes were highly influential in elections. Some groups, particularly unions, had enough members and political clout to enable a candidate to secure a party nomination and win the general election.

The final contribution that interest groups made was financial. Corporations, trade associations, unions, and other groups historically have helped finance election campaigns. For much of U.S. political history, many groups have made contributions directly from their own treasuries or organized fund-raising committees and events (Alexander 1992, chap. 2).

Interest groups continue to participate in these aspects of federal elections, but they have adapted their activities to meet the opportunities and constraints that exist in the current legal, technological, and political environment. The modern political action committee (PAC), for example, emerged during the 1970s as a specialized form of organization that contributes money and other campaign support directly to federal candidates. A PAC can be most easily understood as the election arm of an interest group. In most cases, a business, union, trade association, or some other "parent" group is responsible for establishing a PAC. Yet, for most "ideological" or "nonconnected" PACs, the PAC is the organization itself.

The Federal Election Campaign Act of 1974 (FECA), its amendments, and Federal Election Commission (FEC) rulings are primarily responsible for the rise of PACs as a major force in federal elections. The law prohibits corporations, unions, trade associations, and most other groups from making campaign contributions to federal candidates, but it allows these organizations to set up PACs to collect donations from individuals and distribute them as campaign contributions to federal candidates. PACs are allowed to accept contributions of up to $5,000 per year from an individual or another PAC. In order to qualify as a PAC an organization must raise money from at least fifty donors and spend it on five or more federal candidates.

The FECA allows PACs to contribute a maximum of $5,000 per congressional candidate during each phase of the election cycle (primary, general election, and runoff). A PAC can also contribute up to $5,000 to a candidate for a presidential nomination and give another $5,000 to any presidential candidate in the general election who opts not to receive federal funds. Nevertheless, the rules governing presidential campaign finance deemphasize the roles of PACs in presidential elections. The public funding provisions for nomination contests provide matching funds for individual but not PAC contributions, thereby encouraging candidates to pursue individual rather than PAC contributions. The public funding provisions for the general election ban presidential candidates who accept federal funds from taking contributions from any sources, including PACs. The fact that every major-party candidate for the presidency between 1976 and 1996 has accepted public funding has encouraged most PACs to focus their efforts on congressional rather than presidential elections.[1]

There are other important aspects of federal elections in which some PACs, as well as corporations, unions, and other groups, participate. One is concerned with the financing of party committees and their campaign activities. PACs are allowed to contribute up to $15,000 per year to the federal accounts of national party committees. The parties can redistribute these funds as campaign contributions and expenditures made in direct coordination with federal campaigns or, as the result of a recent Supreme Court ruling, as independent expenditures made without the knowledge or consent of individual candidates.[2] PACs, individuals, and other organized groups can also make unlimited contributions to the soft money or nonfederal accounts that national parties use to help finance their internal operations, party-building activities, voter mobilization efforts, and generic campaign advertisements.[3]

A second activity is concerned with coordinating the campaign efforts of individuals. Many PAC directors, industry executives, and leaders of other groups work to coordinate the contributions of their colleagues and other big givers. They do this through sponsoring fund-raising events and serving on candidates' fund-raising committees. In some cases, these groups engage in a controversial practice called "bundling," in which a PAC or individual group leader collects contribution checks from individuals and delivers them under one cover to a candidate. Bundling is a highly effective form of contributing because it enables a group to steer more money to a candidate than it can otherwise legally contribute, and it allows both individual givers and groups to gain recognition for their contributions (Herrnson 1998, chap. 5).

Individuals, PACs, and parties can also make unlimited independent expenditures to advocate the election or defeat of a federal candidate as long as those expenditures are not coordinated with the candidate's campaign. Corporations, unions, and other groups are prohibited from spending money from their treasuries or operating accounts expressly to advocate voting for or against a particular candidate. Nevertheless a loophole in the law enables them to conduct "issue advocacy" campaigns in which they disseminate information designed to harm or help a candidate (or promote an issue) that does not directly tell people to vote for or against that candidate. Many groups, such as the AFL-CIO, have recently sought to take advantage of this loophole by carrying out issue advocacy campaigns designed to advance a candidate's standing with voters or detract from an opponent's level of support. Finally, these groups can also make unlimited expenditures to communicate with their members.

Pathways to Capitol Hill
Candidate Recruitment

Candidate recruitment and selection is an activity that has traditionally been carried out by local party organizations. During the late nineteenth and early twentieth centuries, local party bosses handpicked candidates for Congress and other offices. Organized interests did not have a formal role in candidate selection, but business owners, union leaders, and other local elites were sometimes part of the machine. They were often consulted because their support could be instrumental in winning elections (see, e.g., Hardesty 1976).

The introduction of modern primaries and caucuses opened the candidate selection process to a broader array of individuals and groups. By depriving the bosses of the ability to handpick their party's nominees, the new process created opportunities for a greater variety of individuals to compete for nominations. The process also increased the influence that ordinary citizens and organized groups could have on the nomination process. Individuals and groups began to play a larger role in shaping the pool of potential candidates and waging campaigns for the nomination.

Some contemporary interest groups work to encourage politicians who are sympathetic to their causes to run for Congress. Among them are EMILY's List, which recruits pro-choice Democratic women (Roberts 1993; Burrell 1994; Nelson 1994b), and the Clean Water Action Vote Environment PAC, which recruits environmentalist candidates of both parties (Hicks 1994, 177–78). These groups promise campaign contributions and other forms of support to those who ultimately decide to run for Congress. A few labor and professional association PACs, such as the AFL-CIO's Committee on Political Education (COPE) and the American Medical Association's AMPAC, take polls to encourage politicians who support their group's positions to run (Fowler and McClure 1989, 205–7). Before the 1996 election, the National Federation of Independent Business PAC went so far as to host a campaign training school for prospective candidates who supported the group's pro-business agenda. PAC activities can be important in helping an individual decide to run for Congress, but interest groups are less influential in candidate recruitment than are parties. Moreover, both groups and parties pale in influence when compared to a potential candidate's family and friends (Herrnson 1988, 85–88; 1998, chap. 2).

Campaign Activities

PACs play an important role in the financing of congressional elections. Over 4,500 PACs were registered with the FEC during the 1996 election cycle, and roughly 3,000 of these PACs actually contributed nearly $204 million to primary and general election candidates for the House and the Senate (FEC 1997). The biggest spenders were corporate PACs, which contributed roughly $78.2 million. These were followed by trade association PACs, which contributed $60.2 million; labor PACs, which contributed $48 million; and ideological PACs, which contributed another $24 million. PACs sponsored by corporations without stock and cooperatives contributed another $2.1 million and $4.4 million, respectively. The scales of PAC-giving are clearly tipped in favor of business over labor interests.

Moreover, PAC contributions are fairly concentrated among a relatively small number of groups. Fewer than 450 PACs, or approximately 10 percent of all registered committees, distributed roughly $165.6 million in contributions, or 76 percent of the total distributed in the 1996 elections. Just 180 PACs (4 percent of all PACs), accounted for nearly $124.6 million in contributions (57 percent of the total). Few elements of American society are represented in the top 4 percent of PACs, and most are not represented in the top 10 percent. Many groups, such as the poor and homeless, have no representation in the PAC community. Although PAC goals and strategies vary, and PAC contributions may offset each other under some circumstances, figures on PAC formation and PAC spending serve to dispel pluralist notions that all interests are equally represented in the PAC community and have a comparable impact on the financing of congressional elections.

The distribution of PAC contributions to congressional candidates further demonstrates that there are other systematic biases to interest group activity in elections. PACs contributed $140.4 million in major-party contested House elections in 1996.[4] The lion's share of this money—nearly 75 percent—went to incumbents. Contestants for open seats received 12 percent, and challengers received a mere 13 percent. The patterns for Senate elections were similar. Of the nearly $43.7 million that PACs spent in contested Senate elections, just 46 percent went to incumbents, slightly over 12 percent went to challengers, and 42 percent went to open-seat candidates.

The incumbent orientation of most PAC activity largely reflects the contributions of business-oriented committees, including most corporate and trade association PACs. Most of these committees focus on narrow issues that could affect their profits or those of their members. These PACs make contributions to ensure that their lobbyists have access to important policymakers (Sabato 1984, 78; Grenzke 1989; Langbein 1986; Wright 1990, 1996, chap. 5; Sorauf 1992, 64–65). Backing likely winners is one of their first decision rules. This results in most of their money going to incumbents, who enjoy reelection rates of over 90 percent in the House and roughly 75 percent in the Senate. A second rule is to back individuals who have the potential to influence legislation that is of importance to the PAC and its parent organizations. Access-oriented PACs give a great deal of their money to party leaders and the chairs, ranking members, and members of committees and subcommittees that legislate in areas of concern to their sponsors.

A second group of PACs is more concerned with influencing the composition of Congress than seeking economic gain or maintaining access to the legislature's current membership. Nonconnected PACs, often referred to as ideological committees, make contributions to candidates who share their views on one or more often highly charged issues. Ideological PACs contribute a greater portion of their funds to congressional challengers and open-seat contestants than do most other committees. Most ideological PACs seek to back candidates in competitive contests, but some give contributions to ideologically sympathetic candidates who are long-shots in order to encourage their political careers. Ideological PACs make more independent expenditures than any other group, accounting for nearly half of those made in 1994.

The last group of PACs consciously pursues both goals (Sorauf 1992, 74–75). PACs that follow "mixed" strategies, which include most labor union and some trade association committees, contribute to powerful incumbents to maintain access to important policymakers. They also contribute to challengers and open-seat candidates in hotly contested races in order to help elect candidates who share their views. As a group, PACs that use mixed strategies make substantially more independent expenditures than corporate PACs and substantially fewer than nonconnected committees.

Some PACs also provide candidates with assistance in a variety of aspects of campaigning, including fund-raising, strategic, and grassroots support. EMILY's List is credited with helping to steer millions of dollars worth of individual contributions to pro-choice Democratic women. The Wish List plays a similar role for pro-choice Republican women (Rimmerman 1994). The Business Industry–Political Action Committee (BI-PAC) and COPE are examples of "lead PACs" that seek to influence the contribution decisions of other pro-business and labor PACs (Nelson 1994a; Wilcox 1994).

The National Committee for an Effective Congress (NCEC) is unusual in that it gives candidates technical and strategic assistance in lieu of cash. It provides Democratic candidates with geodemographic targeting data that help them identify pockets of likely supporters and persuadable voters. It then helps the candidates formulate campaign strategies designed to maximize their numbers of votes. The PAC plays a role in elections that is similar to that of the parties' congressional campaign committees (Herrnson 1994).

Many ideological PACs, unions, religious organizations, and civic groups provide candidates with valuable endorsements and the volunteers needed to stamp envelopes, distribute campaign literature door-to-door, and mobilize voters on election day. Some also finance television, radio, and print advertisements criticizing congressional incumbents for their roll-call votes and failure to take action on issues that are of importance to their members. The AFL-CIO, which has traditionally been an important source of support for Democratic candidates, announced it would spend $35 million and target seventy-five vulnerable congressional districts, many occupied by GOP House freshmen, to help the Democrats in their unsuccessful attempt to regain control of Congress in 1996 (Edsall 1996). In addition to contributing money directly to the Democratic candidates through its PAC, the union aired television and radio commercials and organized its members at the grassroots (Marcus 1996a). "The Coalition," a group of thirty-one business organizations headed by the U.S. Chamber of Commerce, sought to counter the AFL-CIO's effort but fell short of matching the union's campaign expenditures and voter mobilization activities.

Churches have historically been the locus of much of the political activity of African Americans. The voter registration and mobilization efforts of black churches have usually helped Democratic candidates. In the early 1980s, church-based organizations, such as the Christian Coalition, began to play an important role in mobilizing grassroots support for conservative Republicans (Hertzke 1988, 65–68; Wilcox 1996). Before the 1996 election, the group announced plans to distribute 67 million voter guides (Marcus 1996b).

Some candidates find interest group assistance to be extremely helpful. A few who are involved in very close elections may even consider it to have been critical to their success. As a group, PACs are the second-largest source of campaign money in congressional elections, surpassed only by individuals. During the 1996 elections, PAC funds accounted for just 30 percent of the money collected by House and 15 percent of the money collected by Senate general election candidates. Congressional candidates and their campaign aides consider PACs and other interest groups to be a major source of assistance in fund raising (see, e.g., Herrnson 1998, chap. 5).

Congressional campaigners also consider interest groups helpful in other aspects of campaigning requiring technical expertise, in-depth research, political connections, and grassroots efforts. During the 1994 congressional elections, a number of interest groups, such as the National Association of Home Builders, Chamber of Commerce, National Federation of Independent Business, and the Christian Coalition, helped finance the research and advertising that went into the House Republicans' Contract with America and the nationalized election campaign that accompanied it. These groups and others representing various interests and causes across the political spectrum were even more active in the campaigns of Democrats and Republicans in 1996. Nevertheless, most candidates appraise the assistance they receive from interest groups to be somewhat less important than what they receive from party committees (Herrnson 1988, chap. 4; 1998, chap. 5).

The Road to the White House

Potential candidates for the presidency rarely need encouragement to run for office. The formal process by which one secures a major-party nomination lasts roughly a year, but aspirants for the White House spend years laying the groundwork for their campaigns. Interest groups often play important roles in this process by inviting candidates to address their members and donating funds to the PACs, tax-exempt organizations, and nonprofit foundations that the candidates use to finance these preliminary presidential forays (Corrado 1992).

As noted earlier, the FECA makes individual contributions more valuable than PAC contributions in presidential elections. PACs rarely account for more than 2 percent of the money raised by major-party candidates during the primary season. But the law does not inhibit other organized group activity in campaign funding and other aspects of presidential elections. Interest groups influence the financing of presidential nomination campaigns by organizing fund-raising events, sharing their mailing lists, and coordinating the contributions of their members (Brown, Powell, and Wilcox 1995, chaps. 4–7). Barred from contributing directly to candidates during the general election, groups assist candidates indirectly by contributing funds to their political party. A significant portion of these funds are contributed in soft money (Biersack 1994).

Corporations, trade associations, unions, ideological groups, and individuals representing these and other organizations contributed roughly $262 million in soft money to Democratic and Republican Party committees during the 1996 election cycle. The Democratic National Committee

(DNC) raised $101.9 million and other Democratic committees raised an additional $20.9 million, while their GOP counterparts raised $111 million and $27.2 million.[5] Corporations, such as Archer Daniels Midland (ADM), and labor unions, such as the United Steelworkers, are among the top soft money contributors. ADM and its chairman, Dwayne Andreas, contributed in excess of $1 million to Republican Party committees and Bush's prenomination campaign committee in 1992, $977,000 of which was contributed as soft money (Common Cause 1992). For safe measure, ADM and Andreas also contributed $90,000 to the DNC and an additional $50,000 to the Democratic Congressional Campaign Committee during the closing days of the general election campaign. Reflecting organized labor's staunch support for Democrats, the Steelworkers contributed $398,876 in soft money to the Democratic Party in 1992 and nothing to the GOP (Common Cause 1993). It is virtually impossible to pinpoint exactly where all these funds were spent, but significant portions went to voter registration and mobilization drives and party-building activities designed to influence the outcome of the presidential election (Alexander and Corrado 1995, 163–64).

Interest groups also campaign for presidential candidates using many of the same activities they use in congressional elections. They use independent expenditures on television, radio, newspaper, and direct-mail advertisements to advance the election of one candidate over another. In 1992 they spent $3.2 million to advocate the election or defeat of George Bush, Bill Clinton, and Ross Perot. The biggest beneficiary was Bush; PACs made over $2 million in independent expenditures on his behalf and less than $35,000 against him (Alexander and Corrado 1995, 247).

Interest groups carry out issue advocacy campaigns to support a candidate's efforts without expressly promoting the candidate's election or the opponent's defeat. Groups also use internal communications to influence their members' voting decisions and turnout, and to recruit campaign volunteers. Finally, interest group money plays an important role in financing the major parties' conventions. The host committees for the 1996 Democratic and Republican conventions raised $13.6 million and $12.4 million, respectively, from corporations, unions, trade associations, and individuals who represented these and other interests (Alexander and Corrado 1995, 98–104).

At the Crossroads

The 1992 presidential and 1994 congressional elections led to a significant reversal of the pattern of divided government. Most of the interest group activity in congressional elections that occurred prior to 1994 was conditioned by the Democrats' control over Congress. The Democrats had held a majority of House seats for an uninterrupted forty years between 1954 and 1994, and they controlled the Senate for most of this period. Not surprisingly congressional Democrats were the primary beneficiaries of most interest group activity before the Republican takeover.

The 1994 elections ushered in a new era on Capitol Hill. Republican control of both the House and the Senate created a new set of realities for interest groups, particularly PACs. How have PACs responded to these realities? Have most continued to support Democrats, or have they switched their primary loyalties to the GOP? The patterns for the House are particularly striking. The Republican takeover had a profound impact on the partisan distribution of early PAC money. The contributions that corporate and trade association PACs made during the 1996 election cycle are almost the opposite of those given during the 1994 election. In 1994 corporate and trade association PACs gave roughly 58 percent of their House contributions to Democrats; in 1996 they gave two-thirds to the Republicans (see table 3.1, pp. 48–49). These PACs' support for the GOP's pro-business agenda and desire to gain access to newly installed Republican committee and subcommittee chairs are principally responsible for the dramatic switch. Their concern with maintaining access to powerful members is an important factor in explaining both the PACs' switch to the Republicans and their continued contributions to incumbent Democrats. Democratic control of the White House also probably discouraged some PACs from abandoning the Democrats in favor of the GOP.

Ideological PACs were also influenced by the Republican takeover. They were able to galvanize their members, collecting and spending substantial sums. Their early contributions suggest that conservative PACs mobilized their members in order to help the GOP maintain control of the House. These PACs contributed over three times more money to House Republicans in 1996 than they did in 1994, while liberal PAC contributions to Democrats fell slightly.

Even some labor PACs, which have traditionally been among the staunchest supporters of Democratic candidates, changed their giving patterns in response to the Republicans' winning control of the House. Labor PAC contributions to Republican incumbents increased from 3 percent in 1994 to 7 percent in 1996 as these groups attempted to secure access to the newly empowered Republican majority. The Seafarer's Union, for example, gave only $51,100, or 10 percent of its House contributions, to fourteen House Republicans in the entire 1994 election, but gave $73,000, or 29 percent of its funds, to twenty-nine GOP House members during the first session of the 104th Congress—a full year before the 1996 election.

It is more difficult to assess the impact of the Republican takeover of the Senate on PAC activities because different Senate seats are up for election every two years and the idiosyncrasies of the states and candidates involved can have a major impact on campaign finance patterns. Nevertheless, the evidence suggests that many PACs, especially corporate committees, adjusted their early giving in Senate races in response to the GOP takeover of the upper chamber. Corporate PACs gave 59 percent of their Senate contributions to Republicans and 42 percent to Democrats in 1994 (see table 3.2, p. 50). In 1996 these numbers changed dramatically when corporate committees gave 81 percent of their money to Republicans and 19 percent to Democrats. Trade association PACs also responded to the GOP's 1994 success. These groups had distributed 44 percent of their Senate contributions to Democrats and 57 percent to Republicans in 1994, but gave nearly three-quarters of their Senate contributions to GOP candidates in 1996.

The partisan distribution of ideological and labor PAC money was also affected by the Republicans winning control of the Senate. Republicans collected 44 percent of the ideological PAC money distributed to Senate candidates in 1994. The mobilization of conservative PAC dollars enabled GOP candidates to gather two-thirds of the PAC money ideological PACs distributed in 1996. Republican Senate candidates made only small inroads into the labor community. In 1994 Republicans received only 3 percent of all labor contributions to Senate candidates. In 1996 GOP candidates collected 5 percent of these funds.

While the patterns of early PAC activity in congressional elections have changed, it would be wrong to state that PACs have deserted the Democratic Party. Instead, the giving patterns suggest that some PACs, including many representing corporations and trade associations, have responded cautiously to the new order on Capitol Hill. They are more supportive of Republican incumbents because the GOP has become the majority party in both chambers, but most PACs continue to give substantial amounts to powerful incumbents on both sides of the aisle. Candice Nelson's analysis (in chapter 4) of early PAC contributions to House committee leaders and House Commerce Committee members supports this thesis, demonstrating that PAC funds to the recently installed Republican committee chairmen have increased significantly, but Democratic committee leaders continue to hold their own in PAC fund raising.

The findings presented in chapter 4 and the figures presented in tables 3.1 and 3.2 suggest that the flow of early PAC dollars was informed by a sense of caution and a set of strategic considerations that emphasized supporting incumbents. PAC giving in 1995 and 1996 reflected the uncertainty surrounding the question of which party would control Congress following the 1996 elections and a strategic principle shared (then and now) by most corporate, trade association, and other business-oriented PACs that emphasizes maintaining access to powerful congressional leaders of both parties.

TABLE 3.1

THE DISTRIBUTION OF PAC CONTRIBUTIONS IN THE 1994 AND 1996 HOUSE ELECTIONS

	Corporate		Trade association		Labor		Nonconnected	
	1994	1996	1994	1996	1994	1996	1994	1996
Democrats								
Incumbents								
Competitive contests	35%	11%	33%	12%	44%	22%	36%	12%
Uncompetitive contests	19	16	18	16	26	27	13	11
Challengers								
Competitive contests	—	1	1	4	5	25	2	13
Uncompetitive contests	—	—	1	—	7	6	2	2
Open seats								
Competitive contests	2	1	5	3	11	10	8	4
Uncompetitive contests	1	1	1	2	4	3	3	1

Republicans

Incumbents							
Competitive contests	4	25	4	24	—	3	3	24
Uncompetitive contests	26	36	23	29	3	4	12	15
Challengers							
Competitive contests	6	2	6	3	—	—	10	7
Uncompetitive contests	—	—	—	1	—	—	1	1
Open seats							
Competitive contests	4	5	5	5	—	—	6	8
Uncompetitive contests	3	2	3	2	—	—	3	2
Total (in thousands)	$38,213	$46,118	$34,411	$40,054	$30,110	$35,781	$10,520	$13,718

SOURCE: Compiled from Federal Election Commission data.

NOTES: The figures include only PAC contributions to general election candidates in two-party contested races. Candidates involved in uncontested races, runoff elections, or contests won by independents are excluded.
"—" indicates that PACs spent less than 0.5 percent of their funds in these races. Some numbers do not add to 100 percent because of rounding.
N for 1994 = 776; N for 1996 = 812.

TABLE 3.2
THE DISTRIBUTION OF PAC CONTRIBUTIONS IN THE 1994 AND 1996 SENATE ELECTIONS

	Corporate		Trade association		Labor		Nonconnected	
	1994	1996	1994	1996	1994	1996	1994	1996
Democrats								
Incumbents								
Competitive contests	30%	6%	31%	8%	47%	19%	34%	11%
Uncompetitive contests	4	2	4	2	5	4	4	2
Challengers								
Competitive contests	—	1	1	3	13	15	2	5
Uncompetitive contests	2	—	1	—	8	2	2	—
Open seats	6	10	7	15	23	52	14	15
Republicans								
Incumbents								
Competitive contests	7	32	9	28	1	2	6	22
Uncompetitive contests	19	13	19	10	1	2	14	8
Challengers								
Competitive contests	9	9	7	7	—	—	10	8
Uncompetitive contests	—	—	—	—	—	—	—	—
Open seats	24	27	21	26	1	1	14	26
Total (in thousands)	$17,864	$16,547	$10,362	$10,982	$6,611	$6,316	$5,170	$6,292

SOURCE: Compiled from Federal Election Commission data.

NOTES: The figures include only PAC contributions to general election candidates in two-party contested races.

"—" indicates that PACs spent less than 0.5 percent of their funds in these races.

Some numbers do not add to 100 percent because of rounding.

N for 1994 = 68; N for 1996 = 68.

Unlike congressional elections, most of the interest group activity that took place in recent presidential contests occurred while a Republican was in the White House or was favored to capture it. In 1992, Democratic candidate Bill Clinton won the presidency, vanquishing incumbent Republican George Bush. Assessing the impact that a reversal of fortunes has on interest group activity in presidential elections is more difficult than it is for the House and the Senate because presidential candidates rely mainly on money collected from individual citizens and the federal government to finance their campaigns. PAC dollars do not play a big role in their campaigns.

Interest group money does, however, make its way into presidential election campaigns. As Stephen Wayne shows in chapter 5, both President Clinton and GOP nominee Bob Dole were able to help their respective parties raise substantial sums of soft money from corporations, unions, trade associations, and individuals who represent particular groups. These funds, and the independent expenditures, internal communications, and issue advocacy campaigns that these groups undertake, played an important role in the 1996 presidential election.

Notes

1. Candidate-sponsored PACs are the exception to the rule. These committees are frequently used to pay for some of the preliminary activities that politicians conduct before declaring their candidacies for the nomination (see Corrado 1992, chaps. 4–7).

2. See *Colorado Republican Federal Campaign Committee* v. *Federal Election Commission*, U.S. 64 U.S.L. 4663 (1996).

3. Soft money is raised and spent largely outside the federal law and is subject to limits imposed by state laws (Drew 1983; Sorauf 1992, 147–51; Biersack 1994; Alexander and Corrado 1995, chap. 6).

4. These figures are for general election candidates in typical races only. They exclude candidates involved in uncontested races, in runoff elections, or contests won by independents.

5. The figures have been adjusted to account for transfers among party committees (FEC 1997).

4

Candice J. Nelson

The Money Chase: Partisanship, Committee Leadership Change, and PAC Contributions in the House of Representatives

ON 15 March 1996 the *Washington Post* ran a story on its front page describing a phone call from Haley Barbour, chairman of the Republican National Committee, to the Republican speaker of the Arizona House of Representatives (Frankel 1996). The purpose of the phone call was to persuade the speaker to bring up for a vote a pro-tobacco bill. The more general point of the *Post*'s story was that the tobacco industry, after years of supporting both Democrats and Republicans with PAC contributions, increasingly was shifting its support to Republican candidates.

Labor unions have long overwhelmingly supported Democratic candidates, while corporations and trade associations have divided their PAC contributions between Democrats and Republicans (Magleby and Nelson 1990, 84). With the election of a Republican majority in both the House and Senate following the 1994 congressional elections, however, the incentives for business and trade association PACs to contribute to Democrats diminished. Democratic members of Congress had been the beneficiaries of corporate PAC contributions largely because Democrats were the majority party in Congress and thus chaired the committees and subcommittees where much of the initial legislative process takes place. With Republicans in control, corporate PACs had committee chairs who not only had power but also were more attuned to the ideological views of corporate America. In contrast, labor PACs, which had contributed little money to Republicans in past years, found that those in the majority were no longer the Democrats with whom labor shared a policy perspective, but Republicans with a policy view different from that of labor.

This chapter examines PAC contributions to Democratic and Republican committee chairs and ranking minority members during the 104th Congress and then compares those PAC contributions to PAC contributions to the same members of the House during the 103d Congress. The research seeks to determine if the new Republican chairs received more money from PACs in the 1996 elections than they did in 1994 contests, when they were in the minority, and if contributions to Democrats, in the minority in 1996, decreased from the same time period in 1994, when the Democrats were in the majority. The chapter looks at both the amount of money given to Republicans and Democrats and from whom the money came—business and labor.

PACs and the New Republican Majority

The 1994 congressional elections saw the Republicans gain control of the House of Representatives for the first time in forty years. With Republican control of the House came new party and committee leadership, as well as committee reorganization. Three standing committees were eliminated —Merchant Marine and Fisheries, Post Office and Civil Service, and the District of Columbia Committee—and other committee jurisdictions and names were changed. Republicans who had never chaired a standing committee suddenly found themselves as committee chairs; and Democrats, some of whom had been committee chairs for years, found themselves in the minority for the first time in their congressional lives.

Not only did the change in leadership in the House alter the positions of House members, but it also offered the potential for changing relationships for those who deal with House committee members. Interest groups with long-standing relationships with committee chairs suddenly found a new group of chairs to deal with. In most, but not all, cases the new chairs had been ranking minority members of the committees they now headed, so the players were not new, even if the change in leadership positions was.

Political scientists have long been interested in the relationship between money and policymaking. Some studies have found that PAC contributions do influence congressional voting (Kau and Rubin 1982; Silberman and Durden 1976), while others find that PAC contributions have little or no influence on congressional voting (Wright 1985; Grenzke 1989). Nevertheless, there is general agreement that PACs are not disinterested contributors to members of Congress; PACs make campaign contributions to, if not influence votes, at least gain access to members of Congress (Center for Responsive Politics 1988).

The election of Republican majorities in both the House and Senate in 1994 meant that political action committees and the interest groups they represent had new committee chairs to articulate their legislative interests before. This chapter examines how PACs faced the new situation. If PAC contributions are indeed made to gain access, we would expect PAC contributions to the new Republican committee chairs to increase. Similarly, we would expect PAC contributions to Democrats, former chairs but now ranking minority members, to decrease, as their influence over legislation at the committee stage diminished somewhat.

In the 104th Congress, there were nineteen standing committees in the House of Representatives. In the analysis that follows, the PAC contributions to committee chairmen and ranking minority members of fourteen of these committees will be analyzed for 1993–94, when the Democrats controlled the committee chairmanships, and for 1995–96, when the new Republican committee chairmen first took their positions (see table 4.1).[1]

Table 4.2 compares PAC contributions to fourteen Republican committee chairs during the 1994 and 1996 election cycles. As expected, PAC contributions to those Republicans who sought reelection in 1996 increased substantially after they became committee chairmen. The contributions to Kasich, Bliley, Young, and Shuster, chairs of the Budget, Commerce, Resources, and Transportation committees, increased more than $200,000, and the contributions to Robert Livingston, chair of the Appropriations Committee, increased more than $400,000. The Commerce, Resources, and Transportation committees all have large substantive jurisdictions, while the Appropriations Committee has responsibility for all congressional appropriations.

Contributions to the other committee chairs, while more modest, still exceeded $100,000 in the cases of Henry Hyde, chair of the Judiciary Committee, and Floyd Spence, chair of the National Security Committee. Only Ben Gilman, chair of the International Relations Committee, and Robert Stump, chair of the Veterans Affairs Committee, received PAC contributions in amounts only slightly larger than in 1994.

While PAC contributions to Republicans increased when they became committee chairmen, the reaction of the PAC community to the Democrats demotion to the minority was more mixed (see table 4.3). Five Democrats—Obey, Dingell, Hamilton, Brown, and LaFalce—received more money from PACs in 1996 than they did in 1994, even though four of the five (Dingell, Hamilton, Brown, and LaFalce) had moved from committee chairs to ranking minority members. The other four ranking minority members who ran for reelection in 1996 received less money from PACs in 1996 than they did in 1994.[2]

Although the decline in the amount of money given to Democrats is not as large as the increase in the amount of money given to Republicans, it

TABLE 4.1

COMMITTEE LEADERSHIP, 103D AND 104TH CONGRESSES

	Committee	1995–96	1993–94
Republicans			
Pat Roberts	Agriculture	Chair	RMM[a]
Bob Livingston	Appropriations	Chair	5th[b]
John Kasich	Budget	Chair	RMM
Tom Bliley	Commerce	Chair	2d
William Clinger	Government Reform	Chair	RMM
Ben Gilman	International Relations	Chair	RMM
Henry Hyde	Judiciary	Chair	3d
Floyd Spence	National Security	Chair	RMM
Don Young	Resources	Chair	RMM
Robert Walker	Science	Chair	RMM
Jan Meyers	Small Business	Chair	RMM
Bud Shuster	Transportation	Chair	RMM
Bob Stump	Veterans Affairs	Chair	RMM
William Archer	Ways and Means	Chair	RMM
Democrats			
Kika de la Garza	Agriculture	RMM	Chair
David Obey	Appropriations	RMM	5th
Martin Sabo	Budget	RMM	Chair
John Dingell	Commerce	RMM	Chair
Cardiss Collins	Government Reform	RMM	2d
Lee Hamilton	International Relations	RMM	Chair
John Conyers	Judiciary	RMM	3d
Ron Dellums	National Security	RMM	Chair
George Miller	Resources	RMM	Chair
George Brown	Science	RMM	Chair
John LaFalce	Small Business	RMM	Chair
Norman Mineta	Transportation	RMM	Chair
Sonny Montgomery	Veterans Affairs	RMM	Chair
Sam Gibbons	Ways and Means	RMM	Chair

a. Ranking minority member.
b. Rank within party on committee.

does appear that PACs changed their contribution patterns as a result of the change in party control of the House of Representatives. Republican chairs received more money from PACs than they had when they were in the minority, and four of the nine Democrats seeking reelection received less money than they had when the Democrats were in the majority, and when three of the four were committee chairs. If PAC contributions are made to gain access, PACs clearly wanted more access to the new Republi-

TABLE 4.2

PAC CONTRIBUTIONS TO REPUBLICAN COMMITTEE CHAIRS,
1993–94 AND 1995–96 (IN DOLLARS)

	1993–94	1995–96	Change
Roberts	222,137	—[a]	—
Livingston	182,044	642,295	460,251
Kasich	193,490	487,513	294,023
Bliley	451,033	699,082	248,049
Gilman	214,370	231,105	16,735
Hyde	171,445	322,583	151,138
Young	394,842	595,043	200,201
Walker[b]	119,720	98,000	−21,720
Meyers[b]	181,416	42,263	−139,153
Shuster	331,985	544,431	212,446
Archer[c]	—	—	—
Clinger[b]	171,810	106,200	−65,610
Spence	145,670	259,650	113,980
Stump	107,478	122,616	15,138

SOURCE: Federal Election Commission data.
a. Ran for the Senate in 1996.
b. Did not seek re-election in 1996.
c. Did not accept PAC contributions.

TABLE 4.3

PAC CONTRIBUTIONS TO DEMOCRATIC RANKING MEMBERS,
1993–94 AND 1995–96 (IN DOLLARS)

	1993–94	1995–96	Change
De la Garza[a]	398,213	38,300	−359,913
Obey	319,552	441,998	122,446
Sabo	309,210	242,688	−66,522
Dingell	756,110	881,560	125,450
Hamilton	193,616	431,853	238,237
Conyers	337,537	163,143	−174,394
Miller	223,875	151,250	−72,625
Brown	342,512	346,864	4,352
LaFalce	255,005	287,074	32,069
Mineta[c]	571,612	133,726	−437,886
Gibbons[a]	829,667	144,822	−684,845
Collins	294,750	—[b]	—
Dellums	175,591	118,325	−57,239
Montgomery[a]	244,950	16,625	−228,325

a. Did not seek re-election in 1996.
b. Did not accept PAC contributions in 1996.
c. Resigned from Congress, October 1995.

can chairs and were willing to risk losing some access to Democrats in the minority.

Not only is the amount of money given to Democratic and Republican leaders of interest, but so are the sources of PAC contributions. Past research has shown that business and trade association PACs divide their campaign contributions roughly evenly between Democrats and Republicans (see, e.g., Magleby and Nelson 1990), while labor PACs give overwhelmingly to Democrats. But the change in party leadership in the House following the 1994 election changed the incentives for corporate and labor PACs to contribute to Democrats and Republicans. Corporate PACs no longer needed to contribute to Democrats because of their majority status, while labor unions no longer had Democrats, who shared their policy perspectives, in the majority.

Table 4.4 examines the total contributions each Republican committee chair received from business and labor PACs in the 1994 and 1996 election cycles. In both years, Republicans received an overwhelming amount of support from the business community. Only Ben Gilman, chair of the International Relations Committee, received less than 80 percent of his PAC contributions from business PACs in both 1994 and 1996, and eight of the

TABLE 4.4

PAC CONTRIBUTIONS FROM BUSINESS AND LABOR PACS
TO HOUSE REPUBLICAN CHAIRS,
1993–94 AND 1995–96 (IN DOLLARS)

	Business		*Labor*	
	1993–94	*1995–96*	*1993–94*	*1995–96*
Roberts	217,482	—[a]	500	—[a]
Livingston	177,709	599,678	3,610	31,651
Kasich	189,720	483,497	0	4,000
Bliley	449,293	698,566	700	0
Gilman	116,220	156,305	89,180	65,700
Hyde	161,125	316,351	6,000	3,000
Young	305,842	487,806	69,200	90,249
Walker	117,300	94,962	1,500	2,000
Meyers	166,090	41,757	1,500	0
Shuster	295,545	504,281	26,000	29,000
Archer	—[b]	—	—	—
Clinger	159,690	91,825	7,150	12,300
Spence	140,650	237,650	3,000	19,000
Stump	106,358	114,850	1,000	3,500

a. Ran for the Senate in 1996.
b. Did not accept PAC contributions.

committee chairs received more than 90 percent of their PAC contributions from the business community in both years.

There is some indication that organized labor did alter its contributions as a result of the Republican takeover of the House. Six of the thirteen chairs received larger PAC contributions from labor PACs in 1996 than in 1994, though for three of the six the increases were a very modest 1 or 2 percent. Yet William Clinger, chair of the Government Reform Committee, received almost twice as much money from labor PACs in 1996 as he did in 1994. Only five Republican chairs received less money from labor PACs in 1996, and for three of the five the differences in the two cycles were quite small. Republicans, while still largely dependent on business PACs for contributions, did seem to make modest inroads into the labor community in 1996.

As discussed earlier, the affiliation between business PACs and Democrats in the House was based more on the Democrats' majority status than their ideological and issue positions. Table 4.5 compares the contributions that Democratic ranking minority members received from business and labor PACs in the the 103d and 104th Congresses. Nine of the thirteen Democrats received less money from business PACs in 1996 than in 1994.

TABLE 4.5

PAC CONTRIBUTIONS FROM BUSINESS AND LABOR PACS
TO HOUSE DEMOCRATIC RANKING MEMBERS,
1993–94 AND 1995–96 (IN DOLLARS)

	Business		Labor	
	1993–94	*1995–96*	*1993–94*	*1995–96*
De la Garza	374,363	37,300	12,450	0
Obey	203,952	221,498	109,100	209,500
Sabo	203,260	143,288	97,950	92,900
Dingell	617,910	763,650	126,250	110,660
Hamilton	164,416	288,528	18,200	126,375
Conyers	171,237	88,646	154,800	70,600
Miller	133,825	64,300	82,300	81,450
Brown	214,162	125,075	103,600	144,750
LaFalce	209,505	223,199	45,000	60,875
Mineta	460,035	124,546	109,077	8,180
Gibbons	773,667	116,122	48,500	21,500
Collins	223,250	—[a]	67,250	—[a]
Dellums	100,141	43,075	72,950	72,750
Montgomery	232,950	15,625	2,000	0

a. Did not accept PAC contributions in 1996.

The largest decline was in George Brown's case. In 1994 Brown relied on business PACs for almost two-thirds of his PAC contributions; in 1996 only one-third of his PAC contributions came from business PACs. Nonetheless, nine of the thirteen Democrats received over half of all their PAC money from business PACs. While business PACs seem to be somewhat less supportive of Democrats when they are in the minority, they still provide a substantial portion of the PAC contributions Democrats receive.

Beyond the Committee Leadership

PACs have changed their contribution patterns based on the changes in the committee leadership in the House in the 104th Congress. Republican chairs received more money from PACs and, in many cases, a larger percentage of their money from labor PACs than they did when they were ranking minority members. A number of Democrats received less money from PACs, and a smaller percentage of their money from business PACs, than they did when they were committee chairs. How did PACs react to the change in party control beyond the committee leadership? Given that the Republicans had been in control of the House for only two years and that the Democrats needed a net gain of only nineteen seats in the 1996 elections to regain control of the House, it would make sense for PACs to increase their support of Republicans but not to abandon Democratic members who could had the opportunity to regain their majority status in the 105th Congress.

To investigate PAC contributions to Republicans and Democrats, I examined PAC contributions to members of the House Commerce Committee, a committee with one of the largest substantive jurisdictions in the House. Tom Bliley, the chair of the committee, received more money from PACs in 1996 than did any other committee chair; and John Dingell, the ranking minority member and former chair, received more money from PACs than any other ranking minority member in 1996. Excluding the committee chair, the ranking minority member, and committee members who did not accept PAC money, Republican members of the Commerce Committee averaged $461,157 from PACs in 1996, while their Democratic counterparts averaged $381,094 from PACs in 1996. Republicans received on average $80,000 more from PACs than did rank-and-file Democrats, suggesting that, at least on this committee, PACs were supporting Republicans substantially more than they were supporting Democrats.

While PACs have an incentive to support both Republicans and Democrats with whom they have an ongoing relationship, the incentives for supporting newly elected freshmen are different. Most PACs give the majority of their campaign contributions to incumbents (Magleby and Nelson 1990, 82), so freshmen House members generally were not dependent on PAC contributions for funding their 1994 campaigns. PACs interested in gaining access to majority-party members would be expected to be more supportive of Republican freshmen than Democratic freshmen. When we compare PAC contributions to Republican and Democratic freshmen during the first six months of 1995, a time when freshmen were both retiring debts from the 1994 campaign and developing resources to run in 1996, we find that PACs were, indeed, more supportive of Republican freshmen than of Democratic freshmen. The average PAC contribution to Republican freshmen during the first six months of 1995 was $67,329; the average PAC contribution to Democratic freshmen was only two-thirds of that, $46,122, during the same time period.

The disparities in PAC contributions to Republican and Democratic freshmen are smaller when contributions for the entire year are compared. During 1995 PACs gave, on average, $99,470 to Republican freshmen and $81,424 to Democratic freshmen, or 82 percent of what their Republican colleagues received. What is also interesting is that all but three of the Republican freshmen received over half their PAC contributions in the first six months of 1995, while 25 percent of the Democratic freshmen received over half their PAC contributions in the second half of the year. While PAC contributions in the first half of 1995 seemed to favor Republican freshmen, by the end of the year PACs were contributing more equally to both Democratic and Republican freshmen.

Moreover, when PAC contributions to Democratic and Republican freshmen members for the entire 1995–96 cycle are compared, there is almost no difference between Democrats and Republicans. Republican freshmen received, on average, $368,954 from PACs.[2] Although PACs seem to have been more receptive to Republican freshmen's pleas for help with debt retirement early in 1995, PACs were no more supportive of Republican freshmen than they were of Democratic freshmen for the entire cycle.

Discussion

These data suggest that a change in party control of the House of Representatives has meant a change in the patterns of PAC contributions to Democratic and Republican committee chairs and ranking minority members. By becoming committee chairs Republicans received more money from PACs than they did when they were in the minority, even though twelve of the fourteen had been ranking minority members on the committees they now chaired. Four of the nine Democratic ranking minority members who accepted PAC contributions in 1996 and who sought reelection received less money from PACs than they did when they were chairs in 1994. The patterns of PAC support also showed subtle changes in 1996. Business PAC support of Democratic ranking minority members weakened somewhat, while labor support of Republican committee chairs increased in 1996 over labor support of the same members in 1994.

Although PACs do seem to have responded to changes in the control of the House as we hypothesized they would, seeking to use campaign contributions to attain access to the new Republican majority, PACs have not abandoned Democrats. In comparing PAC contributions to two groups of Democratic and Republican House members outside the committee leadership, we found that the differences in PAC contributions to Democrats and Republicans were varied. Republicans on the Commerce Committee averaged more money from PACs than did Democrats on the committee, yet when we compared average PAC contributions to Republican and Democratic freshmen, we found Republicans averaged only slightly more money from PACs than did Democrats.

If Republicans were getting more money from PACs in the 104th Congress than they were in the 103d and Democrats were not getting substantially less, then these results suggest that there was more special interest money being contributed to members of Congress in the 104th Congress than in the previous Congress. Aggregate figures compiled by the Federal Election Commission support such a claim. The commission found that Republicans received more money from PACs than did Democrats in the 1996 election cycle. Republicans received $118.2 million from PACs, a 60 percent increase over the 1994 cycle, while Democrats received $98.9 million from PACs, a 16 percent decrease from the 1994 election cycle.[3]

This analysis suggests that there was more special interest money being given to committee leaders in the 104th Congress than there was in the 103d. PACs have increased their support of new Republican committee chairs without substantially decreasing their support of Democratic ranking minority members. Faced with uncertainty over which party would control the House of Representatives in the next Congress, PACs seemed to be supporting House incumbents on both sides of the aisle.

Implications for Campaign Finance Reform

At the end of the 103d Congress, compromise on campaign finance reform legislation was finally reached between the House and the Senate leadership, but too late for a majority of senators and House members to agree to the compromise and send a bill to the president. The final point of negotiation in the 103d Congress was a reduction in the amount of money a House member could receive from PACs. House Democrats resisted, until the last minute, any lowering of PAC contributions, and it was only at the very end of the negotiations that a phased-in reduction of PAC contributions from $5,000 per election to $3,000 per election was accepted. Republicans, in contrast, supported eliminating PACs altogether, or, at the least, reducing the amount of money PACs could contribute to candidates to $1,000.

Campaign finance reform was not part of the Contract with America, and during the first half of 1995 campaign finance reform was far from the forefront of the 104th Congress's legislative agenda. Bipartisan campaign finance reform bills were introduced in both the House and Senate during the summer and fall of 1995 but were defeated in the summer of 1996. Both the House and Senate bills would have eliminated PAC contributions entirely or, if the courts had found such a ban unconstitutional, would have limited PAC contributions to candidates to $1,000 per election.

Some analysts think that the PAC contribution limit was the final sticking point in the negotiations over campaign finance reform in the 103d Congress because House Democratic incumbents, who receive, on average, more than half their campaign contributions from PACs (Magleby and Nelson 1990, 82), were unwilling to vote for a reduction in such a ready source of campaign funds. If that conjecture is true, this study suggests that neither House Democrats nor House Republicans will be very supportive of any campaign finance reform that eliminates or sharply reduces PAC contributions to candidates for the House of Representatives. At least among committee leaders, Democrats continue to receive substantial support from PACs, and Republicans receive even more money from PACs than do Democrats. Democratic incumbents who were reluctant to support reductions in PAC contribution limits may well now be joined by Republicans, the new beneficiaries of PAC contributions.

Democratic House members may find, at some point in the future, that they are not the beneficiaries of the PAC contribution limits they fought so hard to keep. If there is no campaign finance reform, or if reform does not include a reduction in PAC contributions, and if the Republicans retain control of the House of Representatives for some time to come, Democrats may see their contributions declining much more than they have in the 104th Congress. Corporate and trade association PACs have historically divided their contributions between Democrats, because they were the majority party, and Republicans, because they were closer to corporate and trade association PACs on the issues. But with Republicans in control of the House, corporate and trade association PACs have much less reason to contribute to Democrats. The research in this chapter suggests PACs have not moved away from Democrats in large numbers, but it has shown that Republicans received a slightly larger proportion of their PAC contributions from labor in 1996 than they did in 1994, and Democrats received a somewhat smaller proportion of their contributions from business PACs in 1996 than they did in 1994. If Republicans appear to be headed for longer-term control of the House, corporate and trade association PACs may continue to alter their contributions to favor Republicans much more than

Democrats, as the *Washington Post* story cited at the beginning of this chapter suggested. Labor unions, in turn, may find themselves forced to split their contributions between Republicans, because of their majority status, and Democrats, because of their ideological affiliation with labor's interests, just as corporate PACs have done in the past. Because there are many more corporate and trade association PACs than there are labor PACs, Democrats, particularly those in the House, may find themselves on the short end of PAC contributions.

Conclusion

This chapter has examined PAC contributions to House Republican committee chairs during the 1996 election cycle and has compared those contributions both to what the same Republicans received from PACs during the 1994 election cycle and to PAC contributions to Democratic ranking minority members on the same committees during the same two time periods. The analysis shows that, as expected, the amount of PAC money contributed to Republicans increased when Republicans took control of the House of Representatives and became committee chairs.

While PACs increased their support of Republican committee leaders, there was only a modest decline in the amount of money PACs contributed to Democratic committee leaders. Perhaps not surprisingly, PACs that supported Democrats during their long reign as the majority party in the House continued to support Democratic committee leaders in the 104th Congress, albeit at more modest levels than before. Consequently, with more PAC money flowing to Republicans, and not a great deal less flowing to Democrats, PAC contributions from special interests to congressional candidates reached an all-time high in the 1995–96 election cycle. PACs contributed $429.9 million to congressional candidates, an 11 percent increase over 1994.[4] For campaign finance reform advocates who support eliminating or reducing PAC contributions, support may be hard to find on either side of the aisle in the 105th Congress.

Acknowledgments

I would like to thank my research assistants, Dennis Bailey, Jordana Schmier, and Todd Young, for their assistance with this chapter.

Notes

1. Of the nineteen standing committees, three were excluded from the analysis because their jurisdictions deal with internal House procedures (House Oversight, Rules, and Standards of Official Conduct); two additional committees,

Banking and Economic and Educational Opportunities, were excluded as the committee chairmen do not accept PAC contributions.

2. These figures exclude freshmen who ran for the Senate and who did not seek reelection to the House.

3. Federal Election Commission, "PAC Activity Increases in 1995–96 Election Cycle," 22 April 1997.

4. Ibid.

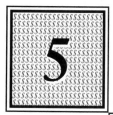

Stephen J. Wayne

Interest Groups on the Road to the White House: Traveling the Hard and Soft Routes

THE ROAD to Congress may be paved with PAC contributions, but the road to the White House is not. The latter is an expensive road to travel, and political action committees contribute to the costs, but the bulk of their funds does not go directly to presidential candidates. Nonetheless, substantial amounts do find their way into party coffers or are spent independently for or against presidential candidates. These monies, which provide indirect help to the presidential nominees and supplement the parties' get-out-the-vote activities, raise the same serious questions that have been debated about PAC contributions and activities at the congressional level as well as more generally. How do interest groups try to influence presidential politics and government? Who contributes how much, and what do they get for their money? Do PACs, individually or collectively, make the playing field unlevel? Should they be constrained, and can they be, without impinging on First Amendment rights?

This chapter attempts to answer these questions by describing patterns of PAC contributions and expenditures in recent presidential campaigns and by pointing to some of the tangible and intangible benefits that seem to accrue from these monies.

Precandidacy

PACs, notably leadership PACs, play a large role at the precandidacy stage of presidential campaigns. The law permits candidates to form their own

PACs, and many do so in anticipation of their official presidential quest. These PACs are used primarily by prospective candidates to fund and promote their activities before they declare their candidacy and create their campaign committees.

One of the earliest and most successful of these leadership PACs was Citizens for the Republic. Started in 1977 with $1.6 million left over from Ronald Reagan's 1976 presidential campaign, this organization had within a year raised $2.5 million and spent $1.9 million on operations. Total expenditures were over $6 million (Alexander and Corrado 1995). Most of this money was used for fund raising, travel, and other expenses of the PAC's principal speaker, Ronald Reagan. In the process of raising money, the organization developed a list of more than 300,000 contributors. This list was purchased for a nominal fee by the Reagan campaign committee.

The Reagan PAC became the prototype for other presidential candidates. By the end of 1985, PACs established by aspirants for the 1988 Republican nomination had raised over $10 million. Much of this money was used to support a sizable national staff, field coordinators for the early primary and caucus states, and a range of prenomination activities.

The Democrats used PACs during this period as well. In 1981 Walter Mondale and Edward Kennedy each formed a PAC to his expected candidacy in 1984. When Kennedy withdrew by 1982, his PAC had already raised $2.5 million. Mondale had raised a similar amount and amassed a donor list of 25,000 names, which he used to launch his presidential campaign in 1984.

Mondale's use of PACs in that election also got him into trouble. His campaign organization had encouraged the formation of delegate PACs, that is, organizations that raised money and provided support to slates of individuals who were seeking direct election as Mondale delegates to the Democratic nominating convention. A letter from a Mondale official indicated how such PACs could be established and suggested that any legal question concerning them should be referred to the campaign's legal counsel. PACs for Mondale delegates were organized and raised money in nineteen states. In several of them funds raised were used to pay the salaries of individuals who had been previously paid by the national campaign organization. There were even transfers of money among PACs of different states. Gary Hart, Mondale's principal opponent in that nomination contest, charged that this PAC activity violated the law, which prohibited collusion between the official campaign organization and the PACs. After trying to sidestep the issue, the Mondale campaign was finally pressured into repaying the sums his delegate PACs had spent, approximately $400,000.

The Democratic PAC controversy in 1984 led some Democrat aspirants for their party's 1988 nomination to denounce leadership PACs and seek other ways to fund their precandidacy activities. One device used by Hart,

Governor Bruce Babbitt, and others, including Republicans Jack Kemp and Pat Robertson, was the creation of a tax-exempt foundation. Although foundations cannot provide direct support for candidates for office, they can provide support for the development and articulation of their ideas—for research, speechwriting, and travel. They can also produce valuable donor lists.

The indirect use of these foundations for political activities has also generated controversy, not only because it circumvents the election law but because it conflicts with an Internal Revenue Service regulation that tax-exempt organizations cannot engage in political campaigns on behalf of any candidate. This issue resurfaced in 1995 when it was revealed that GOPAC had partially funded an education foundation that supported a college-level course, "Renewing American Civilization," which House Speaker Newt Gingrich taught while he was a member of Congress. One issue was whether GOPAC's money and organizational support violated the foundation's nonpartisan status. A subsidiary issue involved Gingrich himself and his use of GOPAC money to supplement his own partisan, electoral activities during the early 1990s. A special counsel engaged by the House Ethics Committee found that Gingrich had not properly maintained the separation between partisan and nonpartisan electoral activities. Moreover, the counsel determined that the Speaker provided the committee investigating the charges with incomplete, unreliable, and misleading information about his campaign finances. Gingrich was subsequently reprimanded by the House of Representatives in January 1997 and fined $300,000.

With competitive campaigns for the nominations in both parties in 1988, leadership PACs played an even larger role in the precandidacy period. Four Democrats (not including Michael Dukakis) and five Republicans established their own PACs, raising and spending over $25 million. George Bush's Fund for America's Future was the fund-raising winner. His organization received and spent over $10 million (Alexander and Bauer 1991). The PAC languished after Bush's victory, however, and was disbanded prior to the president's reelection campaign.

In 1992 leadership PACs did not play as prominent a role as they had in 1988. Bush's large lead discouraged challengers in both parties. Democrats Jesse Jackson, Dick Gephardt, and Al Gore, who had created leadership PACs prior to their 1988 presidential campaigns, decided not to run for the Democratic nomination in 1992. With the campaigns starting late, both for the Democratic nomination and Buchanan's challenge to Bush, there was a very short precandidacy period, not sufficient time to create and fund a leadership PAC and perhaps also less need to do so.

Leadership PACs have proven valuable in several respects. In addition to the organizational functions they serve and the financial support they provide, they establish a foundation on which a donor base for the pre-nomination campaign can be built. Potential contributors can be tapped several times, first by the leadership PAC and then by the campaign committee. Moreover, money raised during the precandidacy period can be given to other candidates for federal office in the midterm elections, thereby creating the potential for reciprocal endorsements and financial support later.

Senator Robert Dole is a good example of a presidential candidate who benefited from the prepresidential activities of his PAC, Campaign America. Not only did Dole receive endorsements from many of the Republican officials to whom his PAC had contributed, but his presidential organization began its own fund-raising efforts with a list of 500,000 donors to Campaign America.

Dole also created an educational foundation, entitled Better America Foundation, to develop and promulgate policy on a broad range of national issues. The foundation, which raised millions of dollars from individual and corporate donors, was not subject to contribution limits and reporting requirements. Nor did its tax-exempt status permit it to promote a particular candidate. Critics, however, alleged that the Dole presidential campaign used funds from the foundation to raise money and broadcast advertisements that featured Senator Dole. The criticism, voiced by Dole's opponents, prompted the senator to close the foundation in June 1995 and return $4.6 million of remaining funds to contributors.

Lamar Alexander created still another mechanism for extending his visibility and developing a contributor base for his presidential ambitions in 1996. He established a nonprofit corporation, the Republican Exchange Satellite Network, that produced and distributed monthly television shows about public policy, starring none other than Lamar Alexander. Funding for the network, raised from private donors, was not subject to reporting requirements or contribution limits of the Federal Election Campaign Act. Thus Alexander was able to obtain relatively large sums of money from a few wealthy individuals. He received 13 gifts of $100,000 and 200 of $10,000 or more. He was able to go back to these same donors for an additional $1,000 contribution for his campaign and, more important, to get them to raise similar amounts from their wealthy friends (DeParle 1995).

Prenomination

Once individuals declare their candidacy, all campaign expenditures must be paid by their official campaign committee. In most instances, candidates will transfer the personnel and sell the assets of their leadership PACs, such as its donor mailing lists, to their campaign committee. The PACs that then play a role in the presidential nomination campaign are the traditional nonparty groups: PACs connected to existing organizational structures such as corporations, labor unions, and trade associations, and nonconnected PACs that create their own organization. Nonconnected PACs that were active in the 1996 Republican nomination included the Republican Majority Fund, Republicans for Choice, and the Log Cabin Republicans, all of which contributed to Dole's campaign.

Although the election law prohibits corporations and labor unions from making direct contributions to political campaigns, it does allow their employees, stockholders, or members to form political action committees and fund them through voluntary contributions. These groups can directly affect the presidential selection process in four ways: by endorsing a candidate, by giving up to $5,000 to a single candidate, by spending an unlimited amount of money independently for or against a candidate, and by communicating to their members and then using their organization to turn out voters.

Direct contributions are probably the least important of these activities because of the limit placed on the size of the contribution, a limit that is not subject to adjustment for inflation. Thus direct PAC contributions to candidates in presidential nominations rarely exceed a small percentage of the total amount raised by the candidates. In 1992 they constituted only $920,976, less than 1 percent of the total revenues; this was the least amount contributed directly by PACs since 1976.

One of the reasons that PAC contributions were low in 1992 is that several Democratic candidates chose not to accept them. These included Bill Clinton, Paul Tsongas, and Jerry Brown. The principal PAC men for the Democrats in that election were Senators Tom Harkin and Bob Kerrey. Harkin received $492,069, mostly from labor PACs—8.7 percent of his total revenues (including matching funds); Kerrey got less, $349,757, or 5.4 percent of his total. On the Republican side, George Bush received only $44,250 in PAC contributions compared to over $27 million in individual donations, and Pat Buchanan received $24,750 from PACs, compared to $7.15 million from individuals.

In 1996 PAC contributions were small, less than 1 percent of total revenues. Through 30 June, candidates received $231 million, only $2.5 million from PACs. The benefactors were the principal Republican candidates. They ranged from Robert Dole, who received $1.2 million in PAC contributions, to Steve Forbes, who financed his own campaign and did not solicit contributions, but still netted contributions of $2,000, and Robert Dornan, who received $1,000. Although Dole received the most money, it represented only 2.7 percent of his total.

One of Dole's gifts proved controversial and ultimately embarrassing to his candidacy. Log Cabin Republicans, a gay group that focused on raising money for AIDS research but supported other causes such as the admission of homosexuals to the military, sent Dole a check for $1,000. When the orientation of the group and its contribution became public knowledge, the Dole campaign returned the money on the grounds that it could not accept money from a group whose political agenda was fundamentally different from Dole's. Nonetheless, Dole had accepted and kept money from individuals and groups in the entertainment media, which he had criticized in a well-publicized speech for its emphasis on sex and violence. The senator, who prides himself on his sensitivity to the plight of various minority groups, particularly the disabled, later called the return of the funds a mistake by his staff. He claimed he had no personal knowledge of the contribution or its return until the episode became public (Fritsch 1995). Subsequently the Log Cabin Republicans endorsed his candidacy against President Clinton.

Dole received the bulk of his contributions from national corporations and trade associations such as Aetna Life and Casualty Company Political Action Committee, RJR Political Action Committee, RJR Nabisco, Inc., Pepsi-Cola Bottlers Association PAC, as well as the BAKE PAC (the PAC of the Independent Bakers Association), the BUILD PAC (the PAC of the National Association of Home Builders), and the CIGAR PAC (Political Action Committee of the Cigar Association of America, Inc.). But he also received contributions from such groups as Citizens Concerned for the National Interest, English Language Political Action Committee, and the Free Cuba PAC.

PAC contributions followed traditional patterns for the other Republican candidates. Alexander, Phil Gramm, and Richard Lugar disproportionately benefited from PACs located in their states. Although Buchanan received only a very small amount of PAC support, it was from nonconnected ideological groups. PAC help during the nomination phase is not limited to money. The ability of PACs to organize their supporters and turn them out to vote may be even more important. Table 5.1 lists total adjusted revenues and the contributions of nonparty groups for the 1996 nomination process as of 31 August of that year.

Convention Activities

The support of nonparty groups does not end with the winning of the nomination. Goodwill, expressed in dollars and in-kind contributions, continues to flow to the parties and indirectly to their nominees at the national conventions. Despite the fact that these conventions are party affairs and are funded in part with a grant from the federal election campaign funds —in 1996 that grant was $12.4 million—and from the states and cities that host them, corporations, labor unions, and trade associations continue to "help out."

TABLE 5.1

PAC CONTRIBUTIONS DURING THE 1996 PRECONVENTION
PROCESS, THROUGH 31 AUGUST 1996 (IN DOLLARS)

	Total revenues (adjusted)	PAC contributions	Percentage of total
Republicans			
Alexander	17,614,978	286,766	1.6
Buchanan	24,501,176	18,280	<1
Dole	44,604,092	1,208,655	2.7
Dorman	346,885	1,000	<1
Forbes	41,693,481	2,000	<1
Gramm	28,791,502	400,879	1.4
Keyes	4,348,165	3,500	<1
Lugar	7,769,383	129,015	1.7
Specter	3,490,295	158,791	<1
Taylor	6,516,850	0	0
Wilson	7,363,215	242,349	3.2
Democrats			
Clinton	42,489,548	40,580	<1
LaRouche	3,684,253	1,000	<1

SOURCE: Federal Election Commission.

At the 1992 and 1996 Democratic and Republican conventions, corporate giants such as Anheuser-Busch, AT&T, Bank America, and Philip Morris/Kraft were major sponsors, giving at least $100,000 to each party in addition to their PAC contributions to party candidates and their soft money contributions to each party. They and other corporations also hosted elaborate receptions to which the delegates were invited and at which they were wined and dined (Salant 1996).

In addition to funding events, groups have also been active trying to influence the party in its policy positions, especially the platform, and its rules and procedures. The Christian Coalition exercised considerable influence at the 1992 and 1996 Republican conventions, particularly with respect to the platform position on social issues. Organized labor regularly exerts its muscle at Democratic conventions, as does the National Education Association and several gender, racial, and ethnic groups.

The General Election

Although PAC contributions are not permitted to the major-party candidates in the general election, they are permitted for third-party and independent candidates. In 1992, however, Ross Perot did not solicit such money, and only a small amount of PAC contributions filtered to the minor-party candidates. Soft money contributions and independent activities of nonparty groups are a more important influence on the presidential election, primarily for the major-party nominees.

Soft Money

Although PAC contributions to the presidential candidates are not allowed, soft money contributions to the parties are not only permitted but encouraged. In fact, despite persistent calls for campaign finance reform and limiting these large contributions, the presidential and vice-presidential candidates spend a considerable amount of time helping their parties to raise these funds, which indirectly help their presidential campaign.

Ostensibly soft money is used in nonpartisan voluntary efforts to get-out-the-vote by party organizations at the national, state, and local levels. In actuality, it is used to maximize the party's vote for all its candidates, especially those at the top of the ticket. The national party solicits the bulk of soft money contributions and distributes it to its state party affiliates. The money distributed depends on the party's opportunities in the states, however, based on previous elections and current polling data. It also takes into account the states its presidential nominees have targeted.

Soft money tends to come from large donors. There are no ceilings on these contributions, as there are on contributions to individual candidates for federal office. In 1988 George Bush raised $100,000 or more from 267 individuals and Michael Dukakis from 130. In 1992 it was more of the same. More than 198 people contributed $100,000 or more to the Republicans, while 375 gave $100,000, the maximum that Clinton and the Democrats would allow. Even after he had the nomination, Clinton continued to raise soft money for his party, approximately $40.5 million from July 1992 to the end of 1993. This figure was almost double the amount George Bush raised during a similar period (Alexander and Corrado 1995).

And the soft money has continued to flow. In the 1995–96 election cycle the Republicans raised $141.2 million (through 31 December 1996) and the Democrats $122.3 million, almost tripling the amount raised during the previous election cycle. Corporations have been the source of most of the soft money, particularly to Republicans. Labor unions have been big Democratic benefactors. The five largest donors to each party during the 1995–96 election cycle and their contributions are listed in table 5.2.

Most business, labor, and individual donors view their contributions as sound political investments. Doors open to large contributors. They have the access to make their cases and the resources to support their positions. They can hire the best lobbyists and public relations firms, who also have access, to represent them.

There are also personal benefits, such as invitations to meet with top-

TABLE 5.2

THE LARGEST SOFT MONEY CONTRIBUTIONS IN 1995–96
(IN DOLLARS)

Company or union	Total
Republicans	
Philip Morris	2,520,518
RJR Nabisco	1,188,175
Atlantic Richfield	764,471
News Corp. (Murdoch)	654,700
Brown & Williamson Tobacco	635,000
Democrats	
Seagram & Sons	1,261,700
American Federation of State, County, and Municipal Employees	1,134,962
Communications Workers of America	1,130,300
Walt Disney Co.	1,063,050
Food & Commercial Workers Union	727,500

SOURCE: Center for Responsive Politics from Federal Election Commission data, 1 January 1995 through 31 December 1996.

ranking officials. During the 1995–96 election cycle, Republicans offered their big donors, those in the $100,000-plus category, meals with the Senate and House GOP leadership as well as briefings by congressional committee chairs. The Democrats, with the active encouragement of President Clinton, used their control of the White House to entice large donations. Big contributors were invited to coffee hours and small dinners with the president and vice-president, briefings by cabinet officials, and trade missions with the Commerce secretary. Some even received invitations to sleep in the Lincoln Bedroom of the White House. Clinton entertained 938 people overnight during his first term in office. Many of these "friends of Bill" were also large Democratic contributors. The president hosted 103 coffee klatsches in which donors or potential donors were invited to chat informally with the president. Vice-President Gore made over fifty telephone calls from his White House office to raise money for the 1996 Democratic war chest, in seeming violation of federal law that prohibits solicitation from federal buildings.

Even noncitizens were considered targets of opportunity as were American affiliates of foreign companies. Since the Federal Election Campaign Act prohibits noncitizens who are not permanent residents of the United States from contributing and precludes foreign companies from making donations unless the money donated came from U.S.-made profits, the Democrats were forced to return millions of dollars when the party was unable to verify the legal status of its donors. The extent of these campaign finance activities became the subject of press scrutiny and congressional investigation, leaving the Democrats in considerable debt following the 1996 election.

The appointment of ambassadors, particularly to Western Europe, has served as the traditional means of rewarding big party donors. Although Bill Clinton promised to appoint 70 percent of his ambassadors from the foreign service, political appointees constituted 40 percent during the first year and a half of the administration (Greenhouse 1994). These included the following Democratic "fat cats," along with their ambassadorial appointment and their contributions to the Democratic Party effort: Swanee Grace Hunt, ambassador to Austria ($328,700); K. Terry Dornbush, ambassador to The Netherlands ($253,750); M. Larry Lawrence, ambassador to Switzerland ($196,304); Edward Elson, ambassador to Denmark ($182,714); and Pamela Harriman, ambassador to France ($130,902).

Soft money always finds its way into presidential campaigns. Until 1988, the Republicans enjoyed a large advantage in this respect. Since 1988, they have not. In 1992 the parties raised close to the same amount. According to Herbert E. Alexander and Anthony Corrado, Republican committees raised more than their Democratic counterparts in 1992, but the Democrats spent more on the presidential contest than did the Republicans (Alexander and Corrado 1995). In 1996, it was the same story. Table 5.3 lists soft money expenditures that have been spent on presidential campaigns from 1980–96.

Soft money is used by the parties in a variety of ways. It is spent operating telephone banks, printing and distributing campaign literature, and recruiting field organizers and other political operatives. In 1992 and again in 1996, both parties' presidential candidates depended on the state parties

TABLE 5.3
SOFT MONEY EXPENDITURES IN PRESIDENTIAL CAMPAIGNS,
1980–1996 (IN MILLIONS OF DOLLARS)

Year	Republican	Democrat
1980	15.1	4.0
1984	15.6	6.0
1988	22.0	23.0
1992	15.6	22.1
1996	24.0	45.0

SOURCE: Citizens' Research Foundation as reported in Herbert E. Alexander and Anthony Corrado, *Financing the 1992 Election*, 110; Ira Chinoy, "In Presidential Race, TV Ads Were Biggest '96 Cost By Far," *Washington Post*, 31 March 1997, A19.

for these activities and to pay for staff based in the states. This arrangement enabled them to operate with relatively small national offices, thereby reducing their administrative overhead, their need to fund large grassroots organizations, and fund generic advertising campaigns. Much of the advertising was paid for by state party affiliates using soft money raised and disbursed by the national party committees in order to avoid spending "hard dollars," which were limited to $12 million in coordinated expenditures in the 1996 presidential election.

The soft money raised by committees of the national parties for the 1992 and 1996 presidential elections was considerably greater than the public financing grants given to their candidates by the FEC—$55 million in 1992 and more than $60 million in 1996. According to the FEC, "if all of the soft money spent by the national party committees in 1992 had been spent to support Bush and Clinton, it would have represented 23 percent of the total funding available to the two candidates during the entire election cycle or 32 percent of the funding available in the general election period" (Federal Election Commission 1993). Four years later the proportion of expenditures from soft money was even greater. During the 1995–96 election cycle, the campaigns of Clinton and Dole spent a combined total of $232 million. Democratic and Republican soft-money expenditures totaled $263.5 million.

Independent Expenditures and Issue Advocacy
Since the Federal Election Campaign Act was repassed after the Supreme Court's *Buckley* v. *Valeo* decision in 1976, which overturned two provisions of the legislation, the law has permitted independent expenditures by individuals and groups.[1] PACs engage in most of the independent spending (Alexander and Corrado 1995).[2] The Republicans have been the principal benefactors. In 1980, $2.7 million was spent in the prenomination campaign, with most of it going to Ronald Reagan. With Reagan assured of the nomination in 1984, independent spending declined substantially in the preconvention period and has remained small since then.

Independent spending in the general election is another story. Again the Republican candidates have gained the most. Even when enthusiasm waned for George Bush in 1992, he still received 75 percent of the independent expenditures on behalf of a candidate, and Clinton was the target of 70 percent of expenditures against a candidate (Alexander and Corrado 1995).

Citizens for Bush, a PAC established by Floyd G. Brown, executive director of Citizens United, a conservative interest group with approximately 100,000 members, spent the most on the 1992 presidential race—over $2 million. In 1988 Brown, as political director of National Security PAC (NSPAC), raised more than $9 million for the PAC's "Americans for Bush" campaign. It was NSPAC that sponsored the infamous Willie Horton ad, which many believed had strong racial overtones (Shaiko 1994, 181–85). In 1992 Brown continued to maintain his reputation as a no-holds-barred Republican advocate by releasing tapes of alleged conversations between Clinton and Gennifer Flowers. These tapes could be accessed by calling a 900 number at a charge of $4.99 with the money going to Brown's PAC. The Bush campaign committee sought to distance itself from Brown's PAC activities, even filing a complaint against it with the FEC.[3] The second-largest expenditure of funds for Bush in 1992 was the National Right to Life Committee, which spent almost $800,000 on his behalf. The Freedom Leadership PAC spent over $190,000 against Clinton in that election. Of the $4.25 million spent in 1992 in support of presidential candidates through independent expenditures, $2.7 million was spent for Clinton, almost all by labor unions and the National Education Association (Alexander and Corrado 1995).

Labor unions have traditionally been the principal independent spenders on behalf of Democratic presidential candidates. They do so primarily by communicating with their members and the general public about "their" issues. These communications can take the form of letters and memorandums, telephone calls, and radio and television advertisements. Communications can be partisan or nonpartisan. The distinction is important. Partisan communications are more restricted than nonpartisan communications. Organizations such as corporations may communicate partisan information to their stockholders, executives, and administrative staff, and labor unions can do so to their members. Nonpartisan communications can be made to a much wider audience, including the general public.

The federal courts have broadly interpreted what constitutes nonpartisan communications. Since *Buckley* v. *Valeo*, they have given nonparty groups considerable leeway in issue advocacy as long as they do not support specific candidates for office. A good example is the 28 February 1996 federal district court decision in *FEC* v. *GOPAC*, which found that GOPAC did not engage in partisan electoral politics as a political committee when it advocated removing the Democrats from power and building a new Republican majority in 1990. A partisan group, the court contended, was one whose major purpose was the election of a particular federal candidate or candidates (Federal Election Commission 1996).

The partisan versus nonpartisan issue was raised again in 1996 by organized labor's $35 million "nonpartisan" voter education campaign, aimed at turning out a sizable prolabor vote. A special assessment of $1.80 for each of the 13 million union members was used to raise money to be spent on radio and television commercials and training and organizing a rank-and-file grassroots movement. The campaign was concentrated in seventy-five congressional districts that had a large union membership. The majority of these districts were represented by Republican members of Congress.

Naturally, the Republicans saw the campaign as blatantly partisan and instituted legal action to prevent it. From the GOP's perspective, labor was violating the law by engaging in partisan political activity and by colluding with the Democrats in their independent expenditures. Labor officials saw it differently, contending that its issue advocacy, like GOPAC's, was protected by the First Amendment to the Constitution.

Americans for a Balanced Budget, a conservative advocacy group, responded with a campaign of its own in some of the same districts labor had targeted. Additionally, with the encouragement of several key Republicans in Congress, the Chamber of Commerce, the National Association of Manufacturers, together with several other business organizations, as well as the Christian Coalition, formed "The Coalition" in order to merge their resources in a multimillion-dollar campaign to try to blunt labor's efforts across the country in this hotly contested election year (Kuntz and Burkins 1996, A12). Another PAC that was extremely active in 1996 was EMILY's List, an organization that contributes to women candidates, primarily Democrats.[4] This group sponsored a $3 million get-out-the-vote project aimed at women voters in several of the most competitive states. Table 5.4 indicates the communication expenses in presidential elections from 1980 to 1992.

TABLE 5.4

COMMUNICATION COSTS IN PRESIDENTIAL ELECTIONS,
1980–92 (IN MILLIONS OF DOLLARS)

	1980	*1984*	*1988*	*1992*
For presidential candidates	2.0	4.7	2.0	4.2
Against presidential candidates	0.6	0.05	0.1	0.05

SOURCE: Citizens' Research Foundation, based on Federal Election Commission data as they appear in Alexander and Corrado, *Financing the 1992 Election* (1995), 249.

The Inauguration

Political contributions do not cease after the election is over and the winner is decided. Business and labor unions are important sources for "loans" for the festivities that surround the presidential inauguration. Charles Lewis notes in his book *The Buying of the President* that of the $32 million spent on inauguration events in 1992, $14 million was lent by 192 corporations, labor unions, and prominent wealthy contributors (Lewis 1996).

Even though all of the 1992 inaugural money was paid back in 1993, and the Inauguration Committee ended up with a profit of over $9 million, many of the companies and law firms loaning the money had interests in the legislative and regulatory arenas of the federal government (Lewis 1996). In the words of Neal McCoy, managing partner of a law firm that made a sizable loan, "We think that in order to be a participant in public life, it was desirable to make the loan" (Chaplain 1993).

Similarly in 1996, labor unions, corporations, and wealthy individuals helped finance the festivities. Although the Inaugural Committee refused to accept contributions of more than $100, it did permit, even encourage, large-scale purchase of tickets to inaugural events. The American Federation of State, County, and Municipal Employees bought $322,000 worth of tickets while the American Federation of Teachers spent $116,000 on the inauguration. Companies such as Beacon Management made purchases totaling $148,600 while IBM spent over $100,000. There were also individual "buys" of over $25,000 by several wealthy Democrats, all of whom coincidentally had slept in the Lincoln Bedroom during the previous four years. In all the Inaugural Committee reported receipts of almost $24 million with expenditures of approximately $20 million.

Conclusion

PACs supplement the presidential selection process. They provide an organizational entity that candidates can use to lay the foundation for their campaigns in the period prior to their official candidacy. They provide some direct funding during this time and during the prenomination stage of the presidential campaign, although the amount they provide is only a small percentage of the total revenues that candidates receive and much less than the sum that individuals donate. The independent expenditures of PACs, particularly communications to their members, sympathizers, and the general electorate, represent a larger but more indirect form of electoral help. These expenditures have also generated the most controversy when they are expended under the guise of voter education efforts. Issue advocacy is permitted for nonpartisan educational campaigns, but the advocacy of particular candidates for federal office is not.

The solicitation of funds for voter education efforts has had the effect of circumventing several intents of the Federal Election Campaign Act: to limit the influence of wealthy donors, to reduce the dependency of party and candidates on indirect funding, and to eliminate the time and effort that presidential nominees spend raising money, and presumably the debts they incur as a result, so that they can spend more time campaigning for office and communicating with the electorate.

The connection between big bucks, open doors, personal benefits, and prestigious appointments is one that remains a bone of contention and a source of persistent criticism by those who wish to reform campaign finance to level the playing field. Although the presidential campaign is not the principal conduit through which PAC money travels and on which it is spent, that campaign still benefits from these contributions and expenditures. In this sense it is part of the problem by those who see PAC contributions, soft money, and/or independent spending as having harmful consequences for a democratic selection process.

Let us be clear about that impact. PACs do not buy presidential elections. Their resources, however, tend to be attracted to those who have the "right" ideas or positions, especially those who are perceived to have the best chances of winning. To paraphrase Damon Runyon, the race is not always won by the swiftest or the fight by the strongest, but most of the smart money bets that way.

Notes

1. The original limitation on expenditures by individuals and groups was seen by the Court as violating the free speech protection of the First Amendment. The original appointment process in which Congress designated some of the six commissioners impinged on executive authority, thereby violating the separation of powers, according to the Supreme Court.

2. Alexander and Corrado (1995, 115) note that PACs accounted for 98 percent of the independent spending in 1992.

3. The complaint alleged that Brown's PAC violated the law by not clearly indicating that it was sponsoring the recorded tapes, and it was soliciting money for its Citizens for Bush PAC, not the official Bush campaign. See Marcus (1992, A9).

4. The name EMILY's List is an acronym that stands for "Early Money Is Like Yeast"; it makes the dough rise.

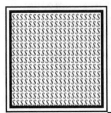

Ellen S. Miller and Donald L. Goff

Comments on the Electoral Connection

Ellen S. Miller, Public Campaign*

After the dramatic changes in Congress that resulted from the 1994 elections, it is appropriate to explore an old adage about the role of money in American politics: "where flows the power, there flows the money." The primary mission of the Center for Responsive Politics is to analyze the relationship of money to politics. We look at two sides of this issue: the impact of money on elections and the effect of money on the making of public policy. Our analytic starting point is the creation of databases of campaign contribution information. These databases show us in great detail where the money comes from for federal campaigns. We use these databases for our own analyses, and we make them available to others; journalists, activists, and educators are the most frequent users. We have developed a system of more than 400 interest group codes through which we filter all PAC and large individual contributions (over $200). What we find tells us the money and politics story of who gets elected and how policy gets made on Capitol Hill. The Center regularly publishes reports that explore the highways and byways of campaign cash. The Center's books and newsletter, *Capital Eye*, illuminate various aspects of the campaign finance issue.

In an article for the November 1995 issue of *Capital Eye* Larry Makinson, the Center's deputy director, pointed out that two-thirds of the PAC money in the first six months of the 1995 election cycle went to Republicans—a flip-flop from the prior election cycle. And most surprisingly, he

* Ellen S. Miller served as executive director of the Center for Responsive Politics from 1984 to 1996.

found that some twenty labor PACs, historically the most reliable of Democratic funders, shifted the majority of their dollars to the newly dominant Republicans. Apart from some of these abrupt shifts to the Republicans, other PAC trends remain the same as in previous cycles. For example, the finance, insurance, and real estate sector continues its dominance as the biggest funding source in congressional elections, with $6.9 million in contributions in the first half of 1995, 76 percent of it to Republicans. The Center has also found that business PACs gave the lion's share of money in the first half of 1995, providing 79 percent of total PAC giving. Contributions from labor PACs represented only 14 percent; ideological PACs trailed, with only 5 percent. In the last 1995–96 election cycle, business PACs dominated labor PACs by a factor of three to one. Three-quarters of the business money in early 1995 went to Republican candidates. A similar proportion of labor money went to Democrats. The ideological money split nearly evenly between candidates of both parties.

Because 95 percent of labor's money normally ends up in the campaign war chests of Democrats, it is surprising to find that in the first half of 1995, only 76 percent went to Democrats. Some of the transportation unions went even further, giving a majority of their funds to Republicans. The most GOP-oriented labor PAC was the Maritime Engineers PAC, which gave 57 percent of its money to Republicans. Two other sea transport unions—The Seafarers International and Masters, Mates & Pilots Union—tilted heavily toward Republicans, 52 and 66 percent, respectively, to GOP candidates.

Of the roughly 100 industries and interest groups in our system of categorization, insurance groups were the biggest overall givers in the first half of 1995, contributing nearly $2.4 million. Transportation unions were next, with just under $2 million. These interests were followed by commercial banks and health professionals, both of which gave $1.5 million. All of the leading business contributors gave a majority of their money to Republicans.

Reflecting the fact that PAC dollars are strongly linked to lobbying efforts, many of the contributions were targeted at specific congressional committees. Members of the House Commerce Committee, which has jurisdiction over telecommunications, health care, finance, and energy industries, among other important policy areas, were the biggest beneficiaries of the PAC spending spree. Committee members collected $4.2 million in PAC contributions from January through June in 1995. The Center has also undertaken a series of studies to determine whether campaign contributions affect policymaking. We have found interesting correlations with regard to the sugar industry, farm subsidies, the defense industry, and environmental issues. Even when competing interests are involved, those with the most money usually win.

I would like to close with one final comment on the implications of proposed campaign financing plans for reforming the campaign finance system. Let me be clear: the Democrats have never wanted to change the system substantially, and I think the Republicans, the current beneficiaries of the system, will be even less likely to want to make significant changes, if and when that time comes.

Donald L. Goff, Conventional Wisdom

Having spent some twenty years as lobbyist, staffer, and PAC manager, and having completed academic training with some focus on political economy, I feel very strongly that there is a need to bridge the gap between theory and practice and to take every opportunity to refine our methods of research and practice. So what follows will be, basically, a suggestive essay, with observations from both the perspective of a practicing politician and that of an academic.

Political action committees evolved from the model developed as the Committee on Political Education (COPE) of the AFL-CIO back in the 1940s. They proliferated in the 1970s as a product of reforms and a series of favorable court rulings. The Federal Election Campaign Act (FECA) and its amendments established the rules of the current campaign financing system. FECA created the reporting mechanisms, participation rules, and contribution limits; it also required timely reporting from both the PACs and the campaign organizations. Limits on contributions and the audit trail are the two distinguishing characteristics of the PAC system of campaign contribution management.

These two characteristics have led also to a high degree of cynicism about the leverage that PAC contributions presumably provide to special interests seeking, if not to buy a vote, at least to rent one for a while. The relative ease of identifying contributions through the FEC databases has given many critics an opportunity to attack the system by using the public disclosure rules that it generated. And PACs organized to contribute based on commonly held beliefs are almost tautologically a definition of "special interest."

It is important to note this negative context in any scholarly PAC analysis because it may tend to suggest relationships that may or may not really exist. The PAC bashing in journalistic or popular treatment has suggested that PACs are somehow inherently evil, repugnant, or otherwise negative. This observation is not meant to excuse or otherwise be an apology for abuses perpetrated by some PACs. But the continued criticism of legal campaign contributions based on a differing value about the propriety of the law has obscured far more than it has clarified. It is important, too, because many scholarly treatments of PACs have fallen into the polemics of the debate, rather than focused on an objective evaluation of their role and function.

Second, it is important to note that there are significant resource limitations on all PACs. No single political action committee has ever offered a maximum legal contribution to every candidate for Congress. Each PAC must pick and choose among the various candidates to support. Even a $1,000 contribution, only 20 percent of the maximum allowable, to one candidate in each House and Senate race would require a PAC to raise close to $500,000 for each election cycle. Yet most PACs have far less than that, usually less than $100,000 to spend.

This resource limitation has some implications. It reinforces, intuitively, the notion that PACs will spend the money where it will do the most good for their issues, that is, for the reasons they banded together in the first place. Implicitly, the members of Congress most likely to receive the greatest contributions would be those who can most affect the legislative outcome. PACs should tend to give to members on the committees and subcommittees having direct jurisdictional sway over their issues. Members solicit membership on committees in the same way. They forfeit a stronger voice on certain issues in order to have a significant influence on a narrower set of issues.

It is important to remember that organized interests, having no vote or position at the legislative table, must work through surrogates. They must invest considerable time and effort into educating members and preparing them to deal with the vicissitudes of negotiation in the early stages of the legislative process. Members will support the positions that facilitate their own political positions and allow them to grant public policy benefits simultaneously to as many interests as possible. PACs, presumably, will focus their support primarily on the legislators who can help them most in achieving the public policy benefits they seek; note the bias toward incumbents.

The important factor in practical politics, yet to get full academic treatment, is competition among these groups seeking to obtain favorable public policy treatment. Most of the journalistic treatments, in my opinion, lump these competing interests together when they describe the effect of campaign contributions on member votes. They write of the "telecommunications industry"as if the viewpoints of local companies were not dramatically different from long-distance companies, for example. Yet clearly, competing forces within that industry (e.g., the Regional Bell Operating Companies and the long-distance companies) have fought an expensive, long-term legislative battle since 1984, when the old Bell System was disbanded.

This competition within industries or among interests has several implications. It tends to drive up the contributions to members on key committees, as competing interests seek to get ahead of their competitors. This fact advantages the large givers over the small. And it tends to dilute the effect of one contributor at a given level if there are many at that level. That is, if one competitor gives a maximum contribution of $5,000 and no one else does, the contribution stands out as a major gift by the benefactor. But if many competing interests give at that same level, the value is diminished. There are many benefactors, none of whom the incumbent or challenger will wish to offend, seeking to maximize political benefit from the broadest possible array of contributors.

Perhaps the greatest factor diluting the impact of any single contribution is the overall cost of campaigning. The average expenditure by a congressional candidate was above $400,000 in 1994. The average Senate candidate spent nearly $4 million. Even a large PAC contribution represents a very small percentage of the total cost of a House or Senate campaign. Taken together with the fact that PAC contributions come from a wide array of competing interests, the effect of any one PAC contribution on the financing of the campaign is meager.

Apart from direct PAC contributions to candidates, soft money played a major role in the 1994 election cycle. The Republicans worked hard to solicit contributions to the national and state parties that could be used for all their candidates running for office. Such funds, outside the direct contribution rules of the FECA for congressional candidates, allow voter registration drives, media buys, polling, or telephone banks in support of all the candidates of the party within each state. Congressional candidates get a push from such efforts, but the PAC and individual contribution limits do not apply. After the election, the Republicans organized to solicit more soft money. Members of the House were essentially tasked and taxed to produce contributions to the National Republican Congressional Committee (NRCC), the party organization in the House that supports Republican incumbents and Republican candidates running for Congress. The drive culminated in a major event in early February 1995 in Washington. It was a stellar success. Many newly elected committee chairs served as active fund raisers for the NRCC at this event.

In contrast, the Democratic Congressional Campaign Committee (DCCC) seems largely to have been shell-shocked. Unprepared for the loss of majority control, the DCCC seem to have been less prepared institutionally to raise significant contributions during the first six months of 1995. The Republicans, in contrast, jubilant in victory and spurred by their party fund raisers to capitalize on it, may have been prompted by these general party actions to be more aggressive in fund raising for their personal campaigns. Republicans may also have anticipated that election finance reform might come about in 1995, and that failure to raise large dollar amounts early would be a mistake. The passage of reform legislation could have precluded their raising large amounts to be used to consolidate their gains and, for the individual chairs, their positions.

In closing, I would like to caution once again about becoming embroiled in the contemporary debate about the inherent goodness or evil of PACs and of trying to generalize about their behavior too broadly. Taking several thousand organizations whose only commonality is their legal form of organization and attempting to adduce motive or effectiveness will require more precision in hypothesis testing than has been evident so far. Scholarship will need a precision in methodology that builds on the raw data provided through the Federal Election Commission by taking into account related political context, competition among PACs for member support, coalitions, the power of the chair, and the degree of party organization, among other important variables. But well-constructed studies should be fruitful.

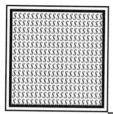

Part III

The Congressional Connection

6 Clyde Wilcox

The Dynamics of Lobbying the Hill

IF POLITICAL scientists were charged to design a national legislature to maximize interest group influence, they would be hard pressed to improve on the American Congress. Because any member can introduce legislation, groups can often find someone to write their pet policy into a bill and drop it in the hopper. Because any member can vote the way he or she chooses, groups can bargain with and persuade individual members of both parties instead of dealing with the central party leadership of a parliamentary system. Because policy gets rewritten in subcommittees and committees of both the House and Senate and in conference, and is sometimes amended during floor debates, there are many opportunities to insert special provisions that benefit the group. The multiple steps at which majorities must be assembled give groups who favor the status quo many chances to convince enough legislators to kill a bill. Clearly groups have many points of access to the U.S. Congress.

Members of Congress also have incentives to listen to interest groups. First, members must frequently make decisions on several very large, highly technical pieces of legislation in a single day, especially at the end of the legislative session. Because any single vote can become an issue in the next campaign, members are often quite interested in obtaining information from groups about the policy and political implications of legislation. Second, members must assemble their own electoral coalitions, sometimes without a great deal of help from their party. Groups have important resources to help candidates reach voters, including infrastructure, communication channels, and volunteers. Moreover, candidates must raise their own money for the campaign, and the ever-increasing costs of modern campaigns make the financial contributions of interest groups very attractive.

For all these reasons, Congress is quite open to interest group influence. The institution has been permeable to groups throughout its history, but changes in institutional arrangements, in the interest group universe, and in technology have affected the extent and the manner of group influence, as well as the kinds of groups that are influential. For as long as political scientists have been studying congressional lobbying by interest groups, however, two main strategies have been used by interest groups in lobbying Congress: an "inside" and an "outside" strategy.

Inside Strategies

Inside strategies generally focus on quietly persuading a member of Congress in a meeting with interest group lobbyists. Lobbyists generally present information in these meetings—usually some combination of technical information about the likely impact of legislation and political information about the constellation of actors who might support and oppose a bill. The arguments and information that the lobbyists present do not always carry the day, but they do so often enough to lead many groups to use in-house and hired lobbyists to try to influence the content of legislation and its odds of passage.

Inside strategies work only for groups that are able to gain access to members and key congressional staffers. There are a variety of strategies to gain access. One of the most common is to contribute to the campaign of the member, most commonly through a PAC, but occasionally through coordinated member giving. There is considerable evidence that campaign contributions do help groups gain access to the member (see, e.g., Langbein and Lotwis 1990).

Giving money is not the only way to gain access to a member of Congress. Interest groups with sizable numbers of members in a given state or district can often gain the ear of their senator or representative simply because they represent many voters. Grassroots organizations may have access because of their ability to mount voter mobilization campaigns, or because of their ability to communicate with their members. Organizations that possess important technical information can often find a member or key staff aide to attend to their data. Groups with large budgets may hire professional lobbyists who have access to certain key legislators or committees. In chapter 9, Christine DeGregorio describes the various resources that a variety of groups have used to gain access to members of Congress.

She notes that lobbyists find ingenious ways to use whatever resources their group possesses to open doors on Capitol Hill.

Sometimes groups seek only to connect with congressional staffers. Committee staff often play a major role in drafting technical legislation, and they frequently meet with lobbyists who have information to convey. Lobbyists also seek to meet with members' personal staff, who are often involved in meetings to decide key votes or to discuss possible legislative initiatives. Before the passage of the congressional gift bans, free tickets to hockey games were a frequent entree to staff discussions. Today, staffers may join lobbyists at hockey games or other sporting or entertainment events, but must pay for their own tickets.

Of course, most groups do not get direct access to every member. Republicans with strong ties to polluting industries may not take the time to meet with lobbyists from the Sierra Club, for example, and Democrats from socially liberal constituencies may not meet directly with lobbyists from the Christian Coalition. Generally, groups that contain a sizable membership can at least meet with office staff, but in some cases even these meetings cannot be arranged.

Many groups not only gain access to some members but also enlist them to champion their cause. Charls Walker refers to these champions as "horses." When a group succeeds in forming a close relationship with some legislators, it may provide them with useful political information, with short speeches to deliver on the floor and longer speeches to deliver elsewhere. In some cases, the staff of the interest group takes on some of the functions of congressional staff. The member in turn may introduce legislation, offer amendments, or try to change legislation during committee markup.

In the House, interest groups especially try to gain access to members of substantive committees, appropriation committees, and the Rules Committee because legislation that comes out of committee usually passes on the floor, often under restrictive rules that limit amendments. In the Senate, however, any member can "hold" a bill until his or her substantive issues are addressed, allowing interest groups to cultivate any member for any issue. In that body, policy negotiations are often more informal, including senators from the substantive committee and others with an interest in the legislation (see, e.g., Cohen 1992).

Once a group has gained access to a member of Congress, its lobbyists must persuade the member to support its position. Here information is generally critical, both technical information on the merits of the case and political intelligence about the constellation of actors supporting or opposing a bill.

It is often argued that campaign contributions not only buy access but also political support for legislation, but political science research has to date uncovered only a weak link between PAC contributions and roll-call voting—far less than the impact of constituency opinion or strong persuasion by the president or party leaders (Chappell 1981; Grenzke 1989; Wright 1985). The conclusion of this research is that you can buy some of the votes some of the time, but you can't buy all of the votes all of the time.

Yet many political actors charge that money has a very strong influence on congressional policymaking. Retiring members frequently complain that their colleagues (but not themselves) have been bought by special interests, and one survey by the Center for Responsive Politics found that a substantial number of members who answered an anonymous survey admitted to having changed a vote because of a PAC contribution. Many journalists who cover campaign finance believe that contributions have a profound influence on legislation and can supply numerous anecdotes to support their claims (see, e.g., Drew 1983; Jackson 1988). Some PAC directors will even admit to having influenced votes by contributions, though never on the record.

How can we reconcile the political science finding that contributions have only a modest impact on roll-call voting with the widespread view that Congress is for sale? There are several possibilities. First, it may be that the widespread cynicism about Congress that generates the conventional wisdom is simply wrong and that sound scientific research has dispelled a common myth. As Walker notes in his chapter, when PACs can give only a maximum gift of $10,000, their influence is limited, for this represents only a tiny fraction of total receipts for any credible incumbent candidate. Second, it may be that political scientists and insiders are focused on different questions, and that both claims are true. On any given roll-call vote, most votes may be determined by ideology, partisanship, and elite cues, but those votes that are swayed by contributions may be sufficiently numerous to affect the outcome. This would lead political scientists to conclude that contributions influenced few votes and journalists to see that the bill passed or was defeated because of political money.

Third, it may be that roll-call votes are not the main way that money influences the legislative process. Major legislation frequently contains many paragraphs, sentences, or even clauses that can greatly affect groups, and it may well be in the formal and informal negotiations and bargaining that decide the final wording of legislation that the impact of money is most important. Finally, the linkage of roll-call voting to campaign contributions also ignores the fact that much of the relationship between interest groups and their lobbyists and members of Congress, as it relates to money and politics, revolves around making sure a roll-call vote never happens. Therefore, the absence of legislative activity is a much more perplexing measure of interest group influence. Political scientists are only starting to wrestle with this aspect of the interest group connection in Congress.

Whatever the impact of campaign contributions on voting or nonvoting, it is clear that the information provided by interest groups does influence legislation. Groups seek access using whatever resources they can muster and then try to use that access to persuade members to back their policy proposals. Inside lobbying is most successful when it is not noticed—when a group quietly succeeds in getting its proposals through Congress or in blocking legislation that it finds objectionable. In chapter 11, John Wright assesses the impact of PAC contributions from the tobacco lobby on legislative outcomes in the U.S. Senate.

Changing Inside Strategies

Although inside strategies have been a part of Congress throughout most of our history, the problems and opportunities that confront groups that use this strategy have changed over time. Three factors stand out: (1) changes in the levels of decentralization in decision making affect a group's ability to target lawmakers; (2) changes in the control of Congress have an impact; (3) changes in congressional budgetary policies and norms have affected the way that groups seek to practice insider lobbying.

After the revolt against Speaker Cannon early in the twentieth century, Congress was ruled by a few powerful men who chaired influential committees. Interest groups could influence legislation by cutting deals with a few committee chairs and party leaders, confident that these men could control the committees and the floor debate. In his chapter, Charls Walker recounts how party leaders and committee chairs once dominated policy-making (see also Davidson 1981). The corporate and labor interests that dominated the interest group environment of the time formed stable and cozy relationships with committee chairs and other leaders.

The 1974 election, however, brought to Congress many new liberal Democratic members, who immediately sought to change the institutional norms and power arrangements. The norm of deference of younger members to committee chairs and party leaders was seriously eroded by this eager class of reformers, who helped to increase the power of subcommittees and create mechanisms to remove committee chairs who abused their power. They were aided in this task by a series of scandals that beset powerful committee chairs. For example, the House Ways and Means Committee chairman Wilbur Mills was caught dancing in the Tidal Basin with stripper Fannie Foxe, and this ended his reign as one of the most powerful men in Washington.

Decentralization presented interest groups with new opportunities and new problems. As subcommittees proliferated, important legislation was often referred to several committees and subcommittees. Where once a powerful interest could block a bill by approaching a single committee chair, now there were many committee and subcommittee chairs involved, and none of them could guarantee the votes of other committee members. The opportunities to insert special provisions into legislation multiplied, but so did the opportunities for other groups to insert provisions that would be harmful to the group's interests.

Because of the difficulty of gaining access to so many members, a surprising number of whom were relatively new to Congress, groups began to rely much more frequently on coalitions. Some of these coalitions are formal and enduring, others ephemeral and informal. Some are predictable, as when environmental groups worked together on Clean Air legislation in 1990; others are surprising, as when the Christian Coalition and the ACLU joined forces to oppose elements of lobby reform legislation. Coalitions are vital in the modern Congress, as groups combine their various resources and lists of friendly members to lobby more effectively. By working together in coalitions, groups expand the number of key members with whom they have some degree of contact.

Professional lobbying firms began to offer a brokering service whereby they could assemble a coalition of actors who would support or oppose specific legislation on an ad hoc basis. For example, in the debate surrounding the North American Free Trade Agreement (NAFTA), the Wexler Group, a Washington-based lobbying firm that specializes in coalition building, managed the pro-NAFTA forces. Some of these coalitions adopt names and couch their appeals in terms of the public interest, but in fact they are financed by one or a few economic interests. For example, the National Wetlands Coalition is a group of oil drillers, land developers, and major gas companies; the Consumer Foundation is dominated by Sears, Woolworth, and Walgreens; and the Coalition for Health Care Choices is primarily financed by Health Insurance Association of America (HIAA), the organization that did the "Harry and Louise" commercials during the national debate on health care in 1994 (Shaiko 1995, 168). Yet some coalitions are genuine cooperative efforts. During considerations of the Clean Air bill in 1990, the major environmental groups met regularly and coordinated their efforts under the name of the Clean Air Coalition, while industry groups worked together under the name of the Clean Air Working Group.

The new Republican majority in the House in 1994 restructured power relationships by significantly concentrating power in the hands of the Speaker. As Colton Campbell and Roger Davidson point out in chapter 8, Speaker Newt Gingrich had great influence over the choice of committee chairs and presided over a reduction in the number of committees as well as committee staff and a sorting of jurisdictional boundaries. More significantly, the early agenda of the House was set by the Contract with America, a set of policy promises signed by most House Republican candidates during the 1994 campaign. Thus interest groups were forced to bargain more centrally with the party leadership than had been the case in the past few decades.

This does not mean that groups were in an especially weak bargaining position. Many organizations such as the National Rifle Association (NRA) and the Christian Coalition claimed credit for electing the new Republican majority, and many Republicans were willing to give them a share of the credit. The NRA-organized hearings on the Ruby Ridge shootings are an example of the close ties between interest groups and the Republican leadership, which approved of the hearings.

More important, the actual implementing legislation for the Contract with America was written, in part, by a set of lobbyists who contributed significant amounts to the Republican Party and who agreed to support the entire package of proposals that came out of the process. Thus the American Petroleum Institute helped draft legislation that would reduce liabilities from toxic wastes. Lobbyists for corporations wrote the legislation on regulatory relief that limited the ability of the bureaucracy to enforce existing environmental and worker safety rules (Greider 1992; Judis 1995).

That interest groups draft legislation is not new: Democrats often allowed their allies to help craft bills. But Democrats balanced a constituency of labor, environmentalists, women, and minorities with business interests, while the new Republican House majority essentially froze out liberal groups from the formulation process. The consequence has been legislation that has often included lobbyists' wildest dreams but has failed to pass the more moderate Senate, resulting in very unfavorable public evaluations of Gingrich and the Congress.

Finally, the changed budgetary rules and norms that developed during the late 1980s and early 1990s have altered the nature of interest group lobbying. Whereas agricultural groups once lobbied together for price supports for all crops and defense contractors for additional military spending, spending decisions in an era of a fixed or shrinking pie have become a zero-sum game. If one group wins an additional allocation of public funds, it must come at the expense of a different group. This has forced many former allies to lobby at least on occasion against programs of their closest competitors. In chapter 10, James Thurber analyzes the impact of years of mounting budget deficits on lobbying activities in the congressional budget process.

Overall, the use of inside strategies has increased somewhat over time. The number of PACs peaked in the late 1980s at more than 4,000, but many groups have expanded their campaign finance activity in an effort to gain greater access to members. Schlozman and Tierney (1986) found that substantial majorities of interest groups they surveyed reported engaging more often in a variety of inside strategies: direct contact with policy-makers, testifying at hearings, presenting research results or technical information, engaging with informal contacts with policymakers, helping to draft legislation, and making financial contributions to campaigns. Such trends continued in the following decade.

Outside Strategies

If the inside strategy is the carrot, the outside strategy is the stick. Grass-roots lobbying involves using group members (or the general public) to pressure policymakers to support the group's agenda. Generally there is an implicit or explicit threat that these members will work to defeat the member if she or he refuses to support the group's policies, sometimes coupled with the promise of electoral support if the member agrees to promote the group's goals. In chapter 7, James Gimpel examines the changing grassroots tactics of interest groups in the new Republican Congress.

Outside strategies involve contact between the group's members and the offices of legislators. The oldest and still most common means of grass-roots pressure is the letter-writing campaign. Until the late 1960s only a few groups, such as the NRA with its network of gun clubs and frequent newsletters, could mount coordinated mail campaigns. With the advent of powerful desktop computers and word processing programs, however, nearly any group can now contact its membership, provide them with information, and urge them to sign a postcard or form letter, or to draft a letter in their own words. Improvements in computer technology have allowed groups to mobilize only special segments of their constituency through mail messages, for example, members from particular districts or states, or members who have shown a special interest in a key issue (Fowler and Shaiko 1987).

Congressional offices are routinely barraged by postcards and form letters, and most of them by now merely count these mass-produced communications but do not reply to them. More effective are handwritten, individual letters. The NRA often instructs their members to write a letter in their own hand and in their own words, expressing their view on a bill. Although the letters may miss some of the details of the legislation under consideration, they nonetheless reflect constituent intensity in a way that mass-produced mail does not.

Because legislative offices receive an enormous volume of mail daily, some groups have adopted novel tactics to get the member's attention. One group representing the elderly instructed its members to include two pennies with each letter to "get in your two cents worth." The National Association of Home Builders, together with timber interests, once coordinated a campaign of notes written on short pieces of 2-by-4 lumber. Such campaigns are more likely to be noticed by the legislator, although there is little evidence that this results in more effective lobbying.

Grassroots pressure also comes in the form of coordinated calls, which can tie up the phones on Capitol Hill for days. In one such effort by the Christian Right in response to a bill that would have reversed some recent Supreme Court decisions on civil rights, conservative pastors called to complain that the bill would "force churches to hire known, practicing homosexuals as youth pastors," although no such language was contained in the bill.

Perhaps the most effective form of grassroots lobbying involves having group members meet directly with the legislator or her staff. After major pro-choice and pro-life demonstrations, delegations from each House district seek to meet with their representatives and then band together to meet with the senators from their state. Some groups, such as the Sierra Club, have a membership lobbying corps, which come to Washington when key bills are under consideration to lobby members and their staffs. A number of professional and trade associations hold their national conventions in Washington and then schedule a "lobby day," when their members contact their representatives and senators.

Groups need not have ready access to a member to pursue an outside strategy; indeed many organizations use the tactic only when dealing with members who are "on the fence" on an issue. Pressuring legislative allies is not usually good politics, and the Moral Majority was the subject of much ridicule when it was disclosed that it had flooded the offices of Senator Orrin Hatch with mail and phone calls in the early 1980s, a process that succeeded primarily in irritating one of their strongest supporters in the Senate.

Many groups do not use grassroots strategies in dealing with members who strongly oppose their policy preferences because at best it would be a waste of effort and at worst might actually motivate the member to work harder against them. But many highly ideological groups do urge their members to bury their opponents in letters and postcards, and the rationale for this behavior has more to do with the dynamics of fund raising than with lobbying strategies. Members of conservative groups may find it satisfying to send a strongly worded postcard or letter to Senator Ted Kennedy and therefore be more likely to contribute to the group.

Groups with large and ideologically cohesive memberships are best able √ to use grassroots strategies. Organizations such as the National Rifle Association, the Christian Coalition, the National Abortion Rights Action League, and Common Cause are able to mobilize their large and geographically diverse memberships into political action. But organizations with fewer members but members who possess significant resources can also use grassroots strategies. The Business Roundtable has on occasion mobilized its members, who are primarily CEOs of major corporations, to make direct contact with key members of Congress.

Changing Grassroots Tactics

Where once only a few highly organized groups such as the NRA could generate grassroots pressure, technological change has made it much easier for groups to use the tactic. As a consequence, as offices become buried in piles of mail and burdened by the demands of coordinated phone campaigns, legislators increasingly distinguish between genuine grassroots passion and coordinated efforts that require little initiative from group members. Most congressional offices have boxes of postcards that the staff will not answer and complicated computer routines to handle the growing avalanche of mail.

A number of companies now specialize in generating grassroots campaigns even when there is little interest among group members for an issue. These firms can print many versions of letters to create the appearance that the letters are drafted by constituents, and a few have gone so far as to print signatures of group members on the letters. The Competitive Long Distance Coalition, later organized as the Unity Coalition, representing MCI, Sprint, and AT&T, reportedly called individuals who used their long-distance services, asked them a question, and then sent multiple letters on behalf of those whose answers conformed to the coalition's positions. These campaigns, often called "astroturf" campaigns, are designed to create the appearance of strong opinion in the district or state. As Congress slowly modernizes its technology, the possibilities for grassroots contact increase. A growing number of members of Congress now have Web pages and e-mail addresses. Today, hundreds of political organizations have Web sites that attract millions of contacts every day. And, for the first time, several significant grassroots campaigns were successfully conducted in cyberspace during the 104th Congress (Browning 1996).

Interest Groups, Lobbying, and Congress: An Evaluation

Interest groups serve several vital functions in the American Congress. By aggregating individual preferences and relaying them to the legislature, they are a conduit for public opinion to influence public policy. By presenting technical information to key committee members and their staff, they help inform the legislative process. By providing aid to members during their reelections, they help to organize the electoral process, and provide resources to help candidates communicate their policy positions to voters.

Yet these benefits come with real costs. Although the flourishing of public interest and citizens' groups in the 1960s and 1970s served to increase diversity in the interest group community, it is nonetheless the case that not all groups are represented. Bob Dole has often noted that there is no "Foodstamps PAC," and it is clear that lobbyists for corporate interests have a dominant position on Capitol Hill. Moreover, often differences in interest group resources may produce public policy that is clearly opposed by the public. When the House Republicans voted to repeal the ban on assault rifles in 1996, the power of the NRA and other gun groups relative to handgun control and various police organizations was obvious. Yet surveys showed that a substantial majority of Americans opposed the repeal.

The balance between the positive and negative aspects of interest group lobbying in Congress is influenced by lobby and campaign finance regulations, which provide the rules of the game and limit the excesses of resource-rich, interested groups. In the concluding chapter, we consider some proposed reforms that would affect the way that groups press their case to government.

James G. Gimpel

Grassroots Organizations and Equilibrium Cycles in Group Mobilization and Access

INTEREST groups in America can be categorized by their dominant strategies of influence—the principal activity the group engages in to ensure that the doors of policymakers are opened to its ideas and goals. A group's dominant strategy is its path to power, its means for obtaining access. For some groups, the dominant strategy is the campaign contribution; for others, it is litigation and legal expertise; for some, it is information and technical expertise; and for still others, it is the capacity to mobilize thousands of donors and other members at the grassroots.

This chapter examines interest groups whose dominant strategy of influence is the activation of a mass base to bring pressure to bear on Congress. Drawn from interviews conducted in 1995, the chapter further focuses on activities by a variety of conservative and liberal groups in response to the Republican takeover of Congress. The 1994 elections changed entrenched patterns of access and influence. Groups that were closely aligned with the Democrats were fenced out, while groups allied with the out-party found that they had unprecedented access. This dramatic reversal of fortune suggests that interest group mobilization and influence are subject to the same kind of equilibrium fluctuations that are observable in the American two-party system.

Why Do Grassroots Matter?

The standard model of constituency control posits that representatives act in accordance with the preferences of their constituents because (1) representatives want to be reelected, and (2) constituents are likely to reward or punish their representative at the polls on the basis of the representative's behavior in office (Arnold 1990; Mayhew 1974; Key 1964). Elections provide voters with a sanction, a means by which behavior on the part of the accountable individual can be induced into being responsive or punished for failing to respond. It is fear of the use of the electoral sanction that prompts our representatives to act in accordance with the preferences of the represented (Kingdon 1989; Kuklinski 1978; Mayhew 1974). Grassroots organizations are especially influential because they draw principally on large member-donor bases made up of informed voters positioned to hold their elected officials accountable (Goldstein 1995).

The most politically influential groups have a very large and widely distributed member-donor base, usually in the hundreds of thousands. The National Education Association (NEA), with its 2.2 million members, is one of the larger membership-based grassroots organizations, although only a fraction of this membership is active and much of its membership is coerced through closed-shop work rules in local public school systems. The Christian Coalition currently has one of the strongest volunteer bases, claiming an estimated 1.9 million members.[1] It is clearly an exception, however, even among conservative groups. Concerned Women for America (CWA), a conservative Christian women's group, boasts a membership of 600,000. The Family Research Council (FRC) has approximately 250,000 regular donors. On the left, grassroots social issues groups such as the National Organization for Women (NOW) and the National Abortion and Reproductive Rights Action League (NARAL) also have extensive member-donor bases. Sources in each of these organizations reported NOW's membership to be 250,000 and NARAL's to be 500,000. The Sierra Club, the well-known national environmental group, has an extensive nationwide membership of more than 500,000.

Groups active in congressional and budget reform, such as U.S. Term Limits, the National Taxpayers Union, and Americans for Tax Reform, also have extensive grassroots bases ranging from 100,000 to 600,000 members. Business groups such as the National Federation of Independent Business (NFIB) can also claim a grassroots base of 600,000 small business owners, most of whom operate firms employing fewer than ten workers. What all these groups have in common is the ability to use the size of their membership to open doors on Capitol Hill. Non-grassroots organizations cannot get the bulk of their membership to do much more than write a check. By contrast, the grassroots groups ensure that thousands of members can be depended on to do more than make financial contributions. Contributing to the organization is broadly defined to include letter-writing campaigns, calling Hill offices, appearing at town meetings, engaging in political demonstrations, and volunteering in local political campaigns.

A second important characteristic of grassroots groups is the extensive distribution of the mass base across electoral districts. Since reelection is their overriding concern, members of Congress are far more likely to open their doors if the grassroots organization has a chapter in their district (Kingdon 1989, 150; Mayhew 1974). If members do not see a constituency connection, they know the group has no negative sanction to impose on those who resist its petitions (Kingdon 1989, 151). While all the organizations discussed here have Washington offices run by between 5 and 100 full-time staff, group representatives were quick to point out that their strength is not based on their concentration of policy wonks "inside the Beltway." There is a high premium placed on the geographic distribution of their membership as the key to their influence in Congress. "Clearly we open doors because members go home to a town hall meeting and run into our people," said Ralph Reed, head of the Christian Coalition (Reed 1995). "They [members of Congress] see that we turn people out to vote." "Activism matters," said NOW's Mia Arnold. "The more active the members are, the more likely we are to get in" (Arnold 1995).

Along with the characteristic of a widely distributed membership, many of these groups have avoided locating their headquarters in the nation's capital. In an era of strong anti-Washington sentiment, this helps them maintain the image of being close to their citizen constituents—distant from the loathsome and corrupt Beltway elites. The Christian Coalition is based in Chesapeake, Virginia. The NFIB is based in Nashville, Tennessee. Ross Perot's United We Stand is based in Texas. Having a headquarters away from Washington also may keep the organization focused on its constituents and away from being taken over by Capitol Hill politics.

Activating or Following the Grassroots

A third defining feature is that the organization take a significant degree of direction from regular assemblies of members from the state and local chapters. In a wide variety of grassroots organizations, active members are influential in defining the policies and goals of their groups. While generalizations about policy direction and governance are difficult, grassroots groups ordinarily have a governing structure that heavily involves representatives of local or state affiliate chapters, or both. The National Education Association holds a representative assembly every year. Delegates to the assembly are elected from the local chapters and set policy and budget priorities for the organization. Involvement by the grassroots in governing and policy direction obviously raises a question about the extent to which these organizations are leaders or followers of their membership. The answer is that most of them both lead and follow but that leadership and followership often depend on the issue. At times, the local organizations will call attention to a particular issue and encourage the national leadership to take a stand. "Lesbian and gay rights was an issue where the grassroots prepared the Washington leadership to speak out," explained NOW's Mia Arnold (1995). "We followed the grassroots on airborne toxic chemicals," said the Sierra Club's Dan Weiss. "The idea bubbled up because we had activists out there who saw what was happening" (Weiss 1995).

Grassroots groups are formed from a complex mixture of widespread popular discontent and the political entrepreneurship of leaders who translate this discontent into the kind of pressure that will generate policy change. On the issue of balance between leading and following, Ralph Reed pointed out that most of the members of the Christian Coalition are not newcomers to politics and are not so easily led. "They carry the battle scars of many political skirmishes in state, local and national politics. But we do try to teach them a language to use. We try to provide leadership on style and vernacular" (Reed 1995).

Dan Danner, the chief lobbyist at the NFIB, was more insistent that his organization was a follower of the grassroots: "This is a member driven organization. We don't take positions that our members don't tell us to take. We go to great lengths to be open and fair and allow the members to decide. We regularly poll them and do market research on their problems and priorities. We have lots of data on what our members think" (Danner 1995).

At U.S. Term Limits, the national director, Paul Jacob, described the relationship between Washington and the grassroots as symbiotic:

> Everyone in this world is both a leader and a follower. We're following the lead of the people—that itself is a sign of leadership. What we're really doing is facilitating. We're not shy about saying what we think works. We provide many services. In that sense we're following. But in another way, we are pointing the movement in a certain direction. Leaders of term limits have to facilitate what is happening. We don't have to produce it. It is such a popular issue that it will happen if we just set up the machinery. (Jacob 1995)

Other organizations saw themselves more explicitly in an entrepreneurial role with an accent on leading the grassroots. "I consider myself a leader," said Beverly LaHaye (1995) of Concerned Women for America. "I believe very strongly that traditionalist women are looking for someone to give them a voice." Joan Blum, NARAL's chief lobbyist, assessed her organization's role in the same terms: "We are here to shape the decisions of policymakers. We see ourselves as an opinion leader" (Blum 1995). From these comments, it is clear that in spite of having a mass membership, there is considerable variation in whether these groups consider themselves leaders or followers of their base. Most would agree that they spend considerable resources "educating" their members about what is going on in Washington. Even the NFIB's Danner admitted that regular communications with the grassroots were designed to educate and mobilize the membership behind certain goals broadly consistent with what the leadership considers to be the members' interests. The NFIB's operation is an excellent example of a successful grassroots organization. Its membership database includes information on the phone and fax numbers of its members, their legislative districts, type of business, issue positions, and political backgrounds (Faucheux 1995). This level of detail greatly facilitates the targeting of NFIB's grassroots pressure toward individual members.

Several of these organizations have regular radio programs. Grover Norquist, head of Americans for Tax Reform, regularly hosts conservative talk shows: "I spend an hour per day doing talk radio shows and I am in constant phone contact with local taxpayer groups" (Norquist 1995). Beverly LaHaye also has a daily radio show on Christian radio stations across the country. All the groups spend large portions of their budget on direct mail, fax, and e-mail communications. Some organizations, such as the Christian Coalition, operate phone banks to keep members and chapters aware of developments in the nation's capital. These efforts are productive of the kind of discussion and activism that maintains the interest of the locals in the causes for which the organization is fighting.

Activating Support versus Manufacturing Support

The distinction between groups that occasionally use a grassroots strategy to build local support for their interests and groups chartered on the basis of their grassroots support is important, but increasingly hard to draw. Traditionally, one of the distinctions between groups whose genesis was at the grassroots and those who use grassroots as a strategy was that members of "true" grassroots organizations were motivated by the fulfillment of purposive and expressive goals, instead of securing economic benefits (Olson 1971; Salisbury 1969). Grassroots groups are able to rely on local activists, not because the member-donors have some economic interest at stake, but because they are ideological and issue oriented. The proliferation of groups that are turning to grassroots mobilization efforts indicates that such efforts no longer rely on the animation of purposive or expressive sentiment. Some of the latest grassroots campaigns are waged to activate citizens around a short-term, immediate concern; the older, more permanent organizations are looking to have a long-term impact for social and political justice (Woliver 1993, 1995). Many of the business- and labor-oriented organizations have turned to episodic grassroots mobilization efforts to minimize economic costs for key constituent groups. While these organizations may occasionally take a position on social issues, their primary focus has always been on improving the economic position of their members. Whether the organization seeks to secure economic or political benefits, however, is increasingly irrelevant to whether it can mobilize a grassroots base.

Realizing that members will open their doors to grassroots organizations, interest groups that have heretofore been active only with corporate representation in Washington have increasingly turned to the manufacture of grassroots opinion in areas where opinion on an issue may lack salience. Enterprising consultants in Washington and elsewhere are making huge profits by building mailing lists and developing activation strategies that they then sell to organizations with no ready-made grassroots base of their own (Goldstein 1995). In a 1995 article, *Campaigns and Elections* magazine listed some sixty-two firms competing to locate and activate a grassroots base behind virtually any issue (Faucheux 1995). One grassroots-for-sale strategy involves the generation of mass support for a viewpoint based on misinformed and deceived respondents to organizational propaganda. Derisively labeled "astroturf" to denote its artificiality, this ad hoc creation of fake opinion is losing favor as politicians have become more skeptical of mass mailings.

Most manufactured grassroots activity is not quite as cynical and unsophisticated as astroturf. The efforts of the Health Insurance Association of America (HIAA) to defeat President Clinton's health-care-reform proposal in 1994 indicate how effective a mix of grassroots strategies can be. HIAA hired Washington consultants to do direct mailings, set up phone banks, and mobilize the "grasstops"—small numbers of influential citizens and opinion makers to contact public officials through personal correspondence, phone calls and visits. Somewhere there is a line to be drawn separating groups that manufacture grassroots pressure and more conventional grassroots groups that rely on the stable ideological and purposive activism of their members, but so many organizations are now involved in grassroots mobilizing that such distinctions are beginning to lose their meaning. Like everything else in politics, grassroots activation is for sale, and, as the HIAA effort shows, it appears to succeed whether it is manufactured on an ad hoc basis or permanently in place.

Equilibrium Cycles: In-Groups and Out-Groups

While the proliferation of the use of grassroots strategies has blurred the distinction between grassroots organizations and Washington-based groups, it is worth wondering how the more permanent grassroots groups, such as CWA, NOW, NARAL, NEA, the AFL-CIO, the Christian Coalition, and the Sierra Club, have fared with the redirection of the congressional agenda in the mid-1990s. The fortunes of more ideologically oriented grassroots groups appear to wax and wane with the ebb and flow of national political tides. The fate of grassroots groups appears to be closely linked to political party fortunes.

Political scientists and historians in a previous generation often spoke of "equilibrium cycles in two-party politics" (Sellers 1965; Stokes and Iverson 1962). When the fortunes of one party are on the rise, the fortunes of the other are on the decline. If one were to graph electoral margins for each party over time, one would see a familiar pattern of peaks and troughs. Party competition in a two-party system functions according to these regular oscillations. These predictable in-party, out-party cycles are generated by the fact that politicians of both parties are deadlocked in a fierce competition to maximize their support (Sellers 1965, 29–31). One party may gain the ascendancy for a time, but its fortunes will inevitably wane as the other party makes competitive adjustments. When the out-party fails to make appropriate adjustments, it is generally replaced.

It is no long stretch of the imagination to understand how grassroots groups would be subject to such cycles. John Mark Hansen (1985) has shown that group mobilization is greatly enhanced by the perception of threat. Threats can include the kinds of economic crises that have periodically mobilized farm groups (Key 1964, 25), or the threat posed by an administration that is pushing a hostile health-care-reform proposal.

But few things are more threatening to one of these ideologically oriented groups than losing its access as a result of the poor fortune of the party with which it is aligned. Because these organizations have interests that are well defined, interests on which the parties have often taken clear positions, the mass membership is sympathetic to one party or the other. Members of the Christian Coalition, Concerned Women of America, and many of the anti-tax and congressional reform groups are overwhelmingly Republican (Guth, Green, Kellstedt, and Smidt 1995). Members of the strong environmental and abortion rights groups work mainly with the Democrats. In spite of its purported nonpartisan doctrine, as early as 1960, the AFL-CIO gave its financial support to 194 Democratic House candidates, but only 6 Republicans (Key 1964, 63).

If a group does not have an explicit partisan orientation, such as the National Taxpayers Union, it has often developed strong working relationships with one group of partisans or another. In this respect, grassroots groups come to resemble auxiliary party organizations, something their Washington-based counterparts in the interest group community cannot boast. Given their close association with political parties, it is not surprising that group access and the perception of threat varies with the fortunes of the party to which they are most closely tied. Their relationship to party success and failure makes it reasonable to suggest that there are equilibrium cycles in interest group influence and access.

In-Groups and Out-Groups, 1992–94

Ironically, as grassroots organizations succeed in reaching their goals and obtaining the benefits they seek, it becomes more difficult for group leaders to maintain the activism that brought that success. There is a tendency for members or donors to think that once they have won, everything will be taken care of. The idea is that success ultimately leads to complacency and a decline in the level of activism. Hence, the pro-choice movement dissolved for a time in the wake of the *Roe* v. *Wade* decision (Staggenborg 1991; Graber 1996). Through the one-party dominance of Congress by the Democrats, liberal groups maintained access to the corridors of power on Capitol Hill for years. In the comfort of their Washington domain, they had deemphasized the grassroots underpinnings they had once drawn on to build their legitimacy and reputation.

On the other side, with the loss of the executive branch following the 1992 elections, conservative, pro-Republican groups—anti-tax, pro-family, pro-business, anti-abortion, and congressional reform organizations— faced the frightening prospect of having nowhere to turn but to the grassroots. These groups now had every incentive to mobilize. At the same time, many of the liberal leaning groups had lost whatever measure of threat they had used to retain and build their membership through the Reagan and Bush years. Congress and the presidency were firmly in Democratic hands, or so it appeared. Many of these groups believed the Democrats would surely take care of everything now.

Just as donations to liberal activist groups fell off after 1992, activism and money began to pour into conservative religious groups in reaction to the lead President Clinton took on gays in the military. These impressions are bolstered by at least one recent study that strongly suggests that grassroots communications to Congress helped frame the fall campaign attacks of Republican challengers in 1994 (Goldstein 1995, 23). The Republican grassroots efforts were especially influential because it is often easier to mobilize voters against something, such as the in-party's agenda, than it is to mobilize them in favor of something. Growing negativity against the party in power naturally benefits members of the out-party. Political psychologists have been studying the strong impact of negativity in political perception and have come up with several explanations for its influence (Kernell 1977; Lau 1982, 1985; Fiorina and Shepsle 1989b; Fiorina and Shepsle 1990). Negative information may have higher salience against a background of generally prevalent positive information. Alternatively, people may be more motivated to avoid costs than to approach gains (Lau 1985). Those who are against certain proposals will put in far more effort to defeat them than supporters of those proposals will put in to see that they are passed. The Christian Coalition's opposition to the Clinton administration's policy agenda helped inspire the group's increased activities. They spent all of 1993 and 1994 reacting to the president's initiatives, beginning with the fight to prevent the integration of gays into military service and ending with the fight over health care and the crime bill.

Interest Groups and the Formation of the Contract with America

Grassroots organizations that seek political and purposive gains often work hand-in-hand with the parties to which their fortunes are tied. Out-parties and out-groups face a shared goal that readily unifies them: gaining control and access by becoming the in-parties and in-groups. How an out-party gains in-party status has been a topic of study for some time. One explanation is that the out-party can make more extravagant promises of future benefits and stronger attacks on political institutions than the in-party, which is limited by its actual performance in office (Stokes and Iverson 1962). This makes it easier to run as an outsider. Certainly the Republicans in the House took this approach in the 1994 elections with some success, drawing attention to many social and economic problems that persisted in the face of unified Democratic government. The ambitious reforms promised in the Contract with America were far more likely to come from an out-party seeking to be an in-party than an in-party trying to maintain its position (Gimpel 1996).

Another explanation for equilibrium cycles relevant to the formation of the Contract is that the out-party has a stronger incentive to innovate. In his recent book, *The Losing Parties*, Philip Klinkner argues that out-parties in American politics have a tradition of risk taking and invention (Klinkner 1994). In the flush of victory, an in-party is less likely to reflect critically on its strategy and tactics. After all, the in-party can claim that it speaks for the majority. Out-parties, in contrast, are forced to figure out what's wrong and fix it. Grassroots influence on the Contract with America during the time of its formation in mid-1994 helps illustrate the extent to which out-groups are willing to cooperate in supporting innovative strategies for obtaining in-party status. The Christian Coalition, the National Federation of Independent Business, Americans for Tax Reform, the National Taxpayers Union, Concerned Women for America, and U.S. Term Limits were are all part of the interest group coalition allied with the Republican leadership through 1994. As the Contract was framed, Republican leadership staff and members would invite the regular input of these grassroots groups in Capitol Hill meetings. By gathering the groups together, Republicans ensured that each member of the alliance would contribute the highest level of effort. Research has shown that when alliance allies interact on a regular basis, their contributions increase (Hojnacki 1995). It is not clear how much influence these groups had on the content of the legislation. Their invitation to the meetings was probably designed more to co-opt their political and financial support than invite their input. For instance, House Republicans avoided social legislation that the conservative Christian groups badly wanted to include. The Christian Coalition asked for school choice and school prayer to be included, but then–Minority Leader Newt Gingrich (R-Ga.) and then–Conference Chair Dick Armey (R-Tex.) refused to capitulate. Ralph Reed explained the position in which the Christian groups found themselves: "One thing that really restricted what went into the Contract was their [Republican leadership's] insistence that every single member had to sign. This automatically took many issues off the table. I didn't have any problem with this. I understood what Gingrich was trying to do, but it meant that many of our issues wouldn't be included" (Reed 1995).

As Reed's comments indicate, conservative grassroots groups may not have controlled the Contract agenda, but the involvement of these groups was critical to building mass support for the legislation and maintaining the loyalties of activists (West and Francis 1995). Business and anti-tax groups attended meetings and later lobbied on welfare reform and family tax relief—issues that were not strictly related to their interests. Conservative Christian groups lobbied for term limits, business deregulation, and tort liability reform even though these are not issues that motivate their membership. When asked about this strong cooperation among grassroots groups with differing bases, Ralph Reed explained that there is some overlap in the membership. "Some 40 percent of small business owners say they are born again evangelical Christians," he explained. "But in reality, I think it is realpolitik that keeps us together. We hang together or we hang separately. We don't control Congress by huge majorities. If we work at cross-purposes that could lead to a Democratic majority again. We don't want that" (Reed 1995). Reed's remarks illustrate a simple point: groups choose to work with other groups when their collective effort is more likely to bring them success than if they were to go it alone (Hojnacki 1995, 4–5). Grover Norquist (1995) echoed an even simpler calculus behind the cooperative effort: "You have to work on everyone's issues or they won't be helpful to you on your issues."

As part of these larger coalitions, grassroots groups trying to secure in-party status will often invent sophisticated and elaborate justifications for lobbying on issues not clearly related to their central mission. Grassroots leaders are constrained by their core activists from going too far astray on unrelated issues. There is considerable freedom within those boundaries. On term limits, Bob Morrison of the Family Research Council explained that at first glance there is nothing pro-family about the issue. "Our argument to the grassroots was that the Washington establishment is indifferent to family concerns. Washington spending priorities are clearly hostile to family interests. Look at how the personal tax exemption has been watered down" (Morrison 1995). Morrison also indicated that government spending cuts and the balanced budget amendment are sold to the grassroots on the basis that fiscal austerity will help squeeze out controversial programs such as the National Endowment for the Arts and the Legal Services Corporation. "You can stretch the pro-family theme to some degree," said LaHaye (1995). "We worked on SDI [Strategic Defense Initiative] under the guise that we wanted to protect American families." Although these groups have some room to stray from their bailiwick, some issues are too controversial among member-donors. LaHaye's organization opposed NAFTA and remained silent on the capital gains tax reduction. Similarly, the Family Research Council went along with a capital gains tax reduction because the Republican proposal included some tax relief for families.

It is noteworthy that the input of certain groups on the Contract's formation was not invited. The excluded groups possessed the status of the in-party Democrats. The Sierra Club and other strong environmental groups, such as Defenders of Wildlife and the National Resources Defense Council, had no place at the Republican table. And the abortion rights and feminist groups were not invited. These groups had a history of strong working relationships with the Democratic leadership as well as loyal Democratic constituencies at the grassroots. In the end, these organizations were effectively fenced off from the Republican leadership in the House following the November elections.

Consistent with the notion that in-parties suffer from ambivalence and a false sense of security, it is clear that the liberal grassroots groups failed to take the innovative Republican campaign strategy seriously. While their ambivalence may not quite have reached the level of complacency, several group leaders clearly pointed to inactivity and nonvoting at the grassroots as the cause of defeat. In some cases, not even the leaders were aware of the potential threat that the Republicans posed to their interests. "I didn't take the Contract seriously last year. Honestly, it didn't seem like a viable legislative program," NOW's Mia Arnold (1995) recalled. Few predicted that the Republicans would capture the House after their forty years of minority status, so the liberal groups predictably played the role of the non-threatened in-partisans. Although some groups did attack the Contract on their own, there was no teamwork among the liberal groups to campaign against the Republican proposals. Their leadership bought the conventional wisdom coming out of the White House that the Republican effort was simply a public relations gimmick.

Role Reversal: The Aftermath of the 1994 Elections

Group leaders and followers on both sides were surprised by the results on 8 November 1994. Even though conservative organizations had enthusiastically participated in the deliberations on the Contract, and most figured that the Republicans would win the U.S. Senate, few expected such a stunning reversal. Insiders had counted on remaining insiders. Outsiders had hoped that this would be the year, but they had hoped that in many previous elections. While they willingly participated in the Contract formation process, probably few thought they would actually have to lobby for its passage in the 104th Congress.

Liberal Groups: The New Outsiders

Liberal groups with political action committees could see that there were many vulnerable seats, but no one thought they would lose all those seats. Waking up to the reality on 9 November was quite sobering, "We found after the election that Congress had shifted decidedly against reproductive rights. We no longer hope to use this Congress to advance our agenda" (Blum 1995). But being on the defensive gave these new outsiders a chance to go back to their neglected grassroots and stoke their membership base:

> On defense, you try to help articulate what is happening in this Congress. The grassroots doesn't really know about the true agenda of the members. People assumed that choice was secure at some level. So now our goal is to help people realize who they have put into office. The majority supports choice. They don't want Congress dictating that. We need to rebuild the grassroots. We have a major public education program ahead. To do that, we've gone to press conferences, opened booths at state fairs, held house meetings and made media appearances. On social issues, *when people feel threatened, it's easier to mobilize.* (Blum 1995; emphasis added)

It is not accidental, given the existence of equilibrium cycles, that contributions to liberal activist groups have been rising: "The silver lining in the Republican election is that our membership and contributions have gone up. We're banking on people getting pissed. There will be no proactive legislation for women in this Congress" (Arnold 1995). The Sierra Club's Dan Weiss echoed the new imperative to rebuild and energize the grassroots: "For us it's back to basics. During the first 100 days, 61 of the freshmen voted anti-environment on every vote. This was unbelievable party unity! We have to go to the grassroots and to the media. We are going to spend $100,000 on radio ads in the next two years" (Weiss 1995). He admitted that with the comfortable relationships that had been developed with the Democrats in power, the Sierra Club had not been well organized to fight at the level they are now having to fight. The imperative is now to organize, and this imperative has been helped immeasurably by having something to organize against: "But being on the defensive is a motivating tool. The media loves conflict. That the Republicans are rolling back twenty-five years of environmental law is a good story. The incremental changes we gained under Democratic rule weren't a good story. Our press coverage dropped drastically after Clinton was elected, now it is going back up" (Weiss 1995).

For groups such as the National Education Association, this was the single most threatening time in recent memory, far more threatening than the early 1980s because Ronald Reagan never had control over the appropriations process. As their chief lobbyist explained:

> We are launching a four-month crisis campaign of free and paid media. Our goal is to turn around the appropriations process. The basics are at stake. The Republicans have made draconian cuts. Many of our rank-and-file don't know the relevance of the federal government to their classroom. Now that relevance should be very clear. . . . We have to energize the grassroots more than ever. We need them more than ever. (Teasley 1995)

The liberal groups would have to turn back to their grassroots because they were going nowhere with the new Congress, as the NEA discovered soon after the 104th Congress convened:

> Our lobbyists don't have access. When we do see Republicans we go from one office to the next and they tell you the same thing, "These programs need to be cut because they don't work." The moderate Republicans like [John] Porter [Ill.] and [Bill] Goodling [Pa.] have been pushed way to the right by their leadership. The leadership in this Congress has a radical agenda. They admit that. The moderates have to do it the Armey, Archer, DeLay way. In every office there is a standard line of the day. So people who might otherwise be persuadable don't listen. (Pons 1995)

Consistent with in-group, out-group oscillations, the forces of outsider liberalism were showing the same signs of cooperation and innovation that marked their Republican opponents following the 1992 elections. Groups as diverse as labor unions, environmental groups, and feminist and civil rights groups convened to brainstorm about how to win back a Congress that would be more favorable to their agenda. In the 1995 fall appropriations process, several liberal groups joined forces to try to defeat the Labor/Health and Human Services spending bill. There are obviously obstacles to this kind of cooperation insofar as agendas are not identical, but as the threat to their interests continues to grow, one can count on considerable cooperation and innovation in the liberal effort to regain the keys to the corridors of power.

Conservative Groups: The New Insiders

Republican-aligned groups also woke up to a sober reality on 9 November 1994. The Contract would constitute their lobbying agenda in the early days of the new Congress. While Gingrich and Armey succeeded in delivering most of the Republican votes during the first 100 days without interest group involvement, groups did play a role in three important areas: taxes, welfare, and term limits.

On taxes, the lobbying of the conservative coalition of interest groups helped ensure party unity behind the $500 per child tax credit. On welfare, the absence of pressure-group activity may have jeopardized the leadership's more conservative provisions in the welfare reform bill. On term limits, the activism of the grassroots groups ensured that there was a floor vote on a substitute term limits measure offered by Van Hilleary (R-Tenn.) that would have allowed states to maintain lower limits than those enacted by Congress (Gimpel 1996). The reversal of fortune experienced by the Republican takeover has left the lobbyists at the NFIB scarcely enough time to breathe:

> During the first 100 days, we were up on the Hill all the time. We were called to testify, to review language. Through the end of July, we testified 45 times, 30–35 of those were during the first 100 days. We could hardly keep up. Those appearances involved writing testimony and we tried to bring in outside business owners. It was a hectic, crazy time.... In this Congress we've been asked for more opinions, more times than in any three previous Congresses. This is a very small business interested and oriented Congress. (Danner 1995)

LaHaye (1995) of CWA echoed Danner's sentiments: "We're invited to more meetings than we ever were before. Last year, they didn't want to see us in Congress."

Although the Republican-aligned organizations now had unprecedented access and influence, at the same time they faced some ominous but predictable challenges. "Donations have really dropped off," said David Keating of the National Taxpayers Union, an anti-tax group with a dues-paying membership of some 300,000 members. "The feeling is that now that the

Republicans are here, they'll take care of it" (Keating 1995). The potential side effects of this new insider status are twofold: (1) the grassroots will wither as a result of the complacency of their membership, and (2) the leadership of these grassroots groups may become too Washington focused and spend less time grooming and building their base. Group leaders admitted that it was always easier to mobilize people against something. Perhaps this reflects the power of negativity in political perception or some other force; the conservative groups lacked the motivating tool they had held firmly for two years. "The effort to enact these [Contract] proposals is not the same task as defeating Clinton's health plan," admitted the Christian Coalition's Marshall Wittman (1995), now with the Heritage Foundation. "It's difficult to maintain the fervor that generated the revolution."

Conclusion

With the dawning of the new Republican Congress, the liberal out-group leaders fiercely criticized the new majority for being more special interest oriented than the Democrats had ever been. "Do people really believe that handing the keys of government over to corporate America is the way to go to ensure their economic security?" asked the NEA's Micheal Pons. "Armey and DeLay believe that putting business in charge is the best course. But what will business do? Keep wages low, not clean up their messes, cut education so their workers can't command as much in the work force, lower taxes so they don't have to pay for the nation's infrastructure" (Pons 1995). Conservative leaders retorted that the liberal groups no longer spoke for the majority of Americans and that the new in-groups did: "The left likes to whine. Environmental groups wrote all of the environmental laws when the Democrats were in power," Grover Norquist pointed out. "Now they're shocked and horrified that the American people have suggested writing legislation" (Norquist 1995).

This highly partisan exchange underscores a couple of points I have tried to make in this chapter. First, many grassroots groups and their constituents are firmly if not explicitly aligned with one party or the other. Second, because of these alignments with the parties, interest groups face the same equilibrium cycles in their support that political parties face. The grassroots groups described in this chapter are poorly equipped to work with the other side. So when out-groups become in-groups, naturally they seek to maximize the impact of their newfound access. It is totally predictable that environmental groups would seek to craft legislation for the Democrats and that the NFIB and the U.S. Chamber of Commerce would be invited to the Republican table. One could hardly expect business groups to be warmly welcomed by the Democrats, nor environmental groups by the Republicans.

That grassroots groups are subject to these partisan shifts provides evidence that there is considerable strength and vitality in the American two-party system. Far from being independent of partisan and other institutional forces, grassroots groups are subject to them. When Republicans are threatened by out-party status, Republicans and Republican-aligned groups build, innovate, and cooperate. When Democrats find themselves threatened, they rise to the occasion. Far from presenting a danger to our democratic system, these cycles of grassroots access and influence are a sign that there is opportunity for citizens to take part in governing through means other than the ballot box.

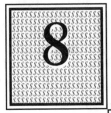

Colton C. Campbell and Roger H. Davidson

Coalition Building in Congress: The Consequences of Partisan Change

THE 1994 congressional elections were a turning point in American politics. The midterm earthquake shifted party control in both the House and the Senate. The new Republican majority in the House quickly implemented significant procedural reforms, which disadvantaged or marginalized some special interests and advantaged others. What effect did this have on the base of interest group participation? This chapter explores new patterns of coalition building in policymaking within the 104th Congress.

The Role of Interest Groups in Legislation

Students of politics have long realized the importance of interest groups in the governmental process. In his celebrated *Federalist #10*, James Madison held that people, having an innate propensity for pursuing their self-interest, will organize in some fashion to further their common interests. Inevitably, different groups and interests emerge and compete against one another based on their differing occupations. Most analysts of U.S. society have noticed the propensity of Americans to form groups and act collectively to achieve common goals, nonpolitical or political. In his book *The Governmental Process* David B. Truman makes the potent assertion that politics can be understood only by looking at the interaction of groups. Public policy is seen to be the outcome of a highly pluralistic process that engages a multitude of actors in many decision-making systems. According to a subsequent, specialized theory of interest group behavior, these groups have increasingly tended to organize around discrete programs and issues (Loomis and Cigler 1991). Lowi (1979) labels this proliferation of groups and their linkage to government as "interest-group liberalism." Politically active interest groups interested in influencing public policymaking direct their attention and effort toward key congressional leaders and committees whose decisions affect them either positively or negatively.

From Iron Triangles to Issue Networks

Contemporary discussions of group theory formation often rely on two predominant metaphoric images for explaining how groups have influenced the policymaking process: "iron triangles" and "issue networks." Both images seek to characterize the connection between groups and legislators and suggest how coalitions manifest and sustain themselves. They further address the issue of "subgovernments" and their respective methods of decision making in the policy process (McCool 1989).

The iron-triangle metaphor postulates a triad formed by executive bureaus or agencies, congressional committees or subcommittees, and interest group clienteles having a stake in particular programs. It implies a relatively closed and autonomous policymaking system marked by more or less stable relations among a limited number of participants. Control is often said to be vested in the leaders of each segment of interest who collectively operate in symbiotic interdependence; that is, the arrangement is an interlocking of elite actors who engage in reciprocal behavior to control the decision-making process of policy (Heclo 1978; Adams 1981; Thurber 1991b). Participants, whatever their motives, work to defend and protect the whole triangle, as well as their own share, by trading off support for each others' projects. In this context, every legislative step forward in Congress is by agreement between a number of semiautonomous bodies.

During the 1970s and 1980s, however, observers recorded a dramatic expansion in the size and complexity of government activities and of the interests that sought influence over them. The iron triangle seemed an increasingly inaccurate metaphor for describing or explaining domestic policymaking. Critics contended that the notion of closed systems of policymaking was oversimplified and outdated. Many of the old symbioses were destabilized when new groups sprang up to challenge previously dominant interests. Previously unorganized or underorganized interests surged into the political arena, for example, groups representing consumers, minority and women's issues, and the environment. New legislation, new agencies, and new programs were fashioned in response to these and many other group demands.

On Capitol Hill, congressional reform efforts redistributed and decentralized the power structure of Congress. This wider range of access points to congressional affairs permitted greater participation and influence on policy, which in turn led many external groups to take a more active interest in the operations of Congress, further destablizing the policymaking process. This called into question the legitimacy of otherwise stable cozy relationships among self-interested groups (Salisbury 1990). Change in the general nature of interest groups as a result of the breakup of interest group hegemony and an invasion of external groups transformed the distribution of influence. This growth and professionalization in government and the unabated growth of self-interest groups is not factored in by proponents of the iron triangle (Berry 1989). Interest group politics is thus conceived in terms of more open and fluid issue networks (Heclo 1978; Thurber 1991b). As groups seek access on Capitol Hill and elsewhere, their degree of access depends on many factors, not the least of which is an affinity with the party in power.

Interest Group Coalition Patterns

After decades of entrenched partisan division, there has been a propensity for Democrats and Republicans in Congress to align themselves with their own interest group supporters, to form distinct issue networks, to protect and advance their interests (Ginsberg, Mebane, and Shefter 1995). Democrats have fixed themselves primarily in the social service and regulatory agencies of the domestic state; Republicans and their allies have sought to create a similar base in the military and national security apparatus, as well as with groups that actively promote business and family values. Such alliances are not new to our political system. During the New Deal and postwar decades administrations expanded their social base and constructed new mechanisms of governance to connect significant political interests to their party (Ginsberg and Shefter 1995). Nevertheless, this trend in coalition formation raises important questions concerning the interaction of party and interest group politics on the contemporary scene in Washington.

The congressional electoral earthquake of 1994 brought a surprising shift in power and significant structural change to Capitol Hill, dramatically altering which policy issues are pushed to the top and how such policies are processed (Thurber 1995b). Issues that had been hidden or subordinated suddenly came tumbling from the closet (Davidson 1995). The party fortunes of nearly two generations were upended. For the first time in forty years, the Republican Party controlled both the House and the Senate. The Democratic Party lost fifty-two House and eight Senate seats, and two Democratic senators and five House members switched their allegiance after the election. After a brief interregnum—which hardly brought interbranch harmony—divided government again reflected the deep partisan political fault line.

This chapter explores the special character of coalition building in policymaking within the 104th Congress. The changing of the guard on Capitol Hill resulted in attempts to dislodge the "welfare-industrial complex" —the policy networks linking federal departments and agencies, liberal advocacy groups, and their allies in Congress. It brought to the fore new issue networks affecting participation and influence on policy and altering the distribution of influence. New House rules, crafted in the Republican Conference and adopted on the floor with dizzying speed, affected the base of interest group participation. Like the Democrats who preceded them, the new GOP majority put into place rules and practices that enhanced the fortunes of certain special interests and weakened the influence of others.

Our examination begins with a brief review of the recent changes in rules and procedures, which have centralized power and closed points of access. Following this section is a brief analysis of the Contract with America. Interest group involvement was present at every stage, from inception to drafting, to advertising and lobbying, and finally to its passage during the first 100 days. Third, we examine patterns of group involvement in the legislative process, from traditional lobbying activities to more active participation in lawmaking, for example, testifying before hearings, writing legislation, and sitting in on markups. Our case study involves controversial legislative initiatives to roll back environmental regulations, especially a proposed revision of the Endangered Species Act.

Finally, we consider the new congressional majority's efforts to limit activities of opposition lobbyists, both in the public and private sectors. A particularly clear case that illustrates the shifting coalition patterns is tax exemption for nonprofit and charitable organizations. Efforts by the conservative wing of the Republican Party to limit the amount of private money that nonprofit organizations can spend on political advocacy have exacerbated cleavages among interest groups and have especially threatened groups traditionally aligned with the Democrats.

Partisan Earthquake on Capitol Hill

Since 1994, life on Capitol Hill has become commonly acrimonious because of escalating warfare between increasingly cohesive parties that have built coalitions with distinctive clienteles. In the 104th Congress, new tactics and relationships emerged. Democrats for forty years formed alliances with kindred interest groups to advance their liberal agenda. Like the Democrats, the Republican leadership embraces organizations consistent with and committed to common objectives. These special interests, some of which were previously excluded from the policymaking process or relegated to working politically with Democratic leaders whose policy interests they did not share, were among the prime political beneficiaries of the

GOP revolution of 1994. They have been privy to the deliberations of the Republican leadership; they have worked with member and staff task forces drafting and developing legislation; they have been invited to testify and participate in the markup of legislation; and the new majority has encouraged them to campaign actively for public support and passage of the Contract with America and subsequent GOP-sponsored initiatives. Reciprocally, these interest groups acknowledge that their work for the Republicans has been prompted by their commitment to the party's conservative agenda.

Changes in the relations of key interest groups and Republican leadership reveal an altered pattern in the nature of coalition structures. Political marriages between interest groups and lawmakers have always existed: groups join coalitions for a variety of reasons, some of them only tangentially related to strategic public policy goals (Hula 1995). But the conservative interest group connection is unusual in its ideological coherence and its open affinity with the legislative goals of congressional leaders (West and Francis 1995). The union between Republican leaders and a coterie of new (and some old) conservative groups is built around common convictions and not just single issues. This relationship naturally has excluded many of the groups and causes that enjoyed preferred access when the Democrats were in control. In addition, a number of Republican lawmakers have set out to restrict the activities of some segments of the political world that have traditionally aligned themselves with Democrats (Barnes 1995). "They are caught up in this Orwellian net of political regulation," charged Representative David E. Skaggs (D-Colo.), ringing the fire alarm for groups to the left that were systematically losing in the policy process (CR, 21 August 1995, 9406).[1] As one indication of this effort Republicans removed the word "labor" from the House Education and Labor Committee, with jurisdiction over employment issues, changing its name to Economic and Educational Opportunities, and later to Education and the Workforce.

Centralizing Reforms: A Return to "Cannonism"?

Forty years of minority frustration swiftly materialized in 1994 into a GOP reform package that significantly altered the way the House does business. The initial order of business of the first session of the 104th Congress was to reshape the procedural environment in which the institution operates. This is apparent from the number of changes in rules, structure, and procedure that embody the GOP pledge to rewrite or wipe out the vestiges of forty years of Democratic rule. House Republicans passed a package of reforms that extended to the committee system, administrative offices, staffing practices, and floor procedures. By recasting the committee system, the Republican leadership was able to impose its agenda on committees and subcommittees long accustomed to charting their own course. Further, under these new rules predominantly Democratic coalitions of the past were disadvantaged or marginalized.

The most prominent of these reform efforts was the establishment of a strong party hierarchy, embodied by augmenting the House Speakership, in both its formal and its informal powers. The revitalized Speakership has its antecedents in the 1970s, when Democratic Party reformers attacked the power of committee barons not only with caucus restrictions but also with enhanced powers for elective leaders (Sinclair 1983). Democratic Speakers took some advantage of their new powers, though in varying degrees and with mixed success (Davidson 1995). Under the Republicans, further consolidation of formal powers sent a clear message to all parties involved who wish to shape and organize the legislative agenda: the epicenter of power would be the Speaker's office—the "Dinosaur Room"—in the Capitol building. In addition to the standard parliamentary functions performed by his predecessors, Speaker Newt Gingrich has used the office as a pulpit that embraces his ideas about leadership and his Whiggish vision for Congress: a dominant first branch of government as the prime mover in national politics, able to set and implement policy.

Bypassing the Committee Alliances

Even before his formal election as Speaker, Gingrich was quick to enlarge his influence over committee personnel and procedures by exercising leadership control of committee assignments and housekeeping matters. Using the leverage of his singular support among the rank and file, he named the new chairmen of all standing committees, departing in four instances from seniority to lend his support to more activist and committed conservatives. Rotation of chairs was assured by a conference provision that they can serve no more than six years of leadership (compared to an eight-year limit for the Speaker).

In an unprecedented move Gingrich stocked several of the most important committees with freshmen. The Appropriations Committee, traditionally one of the most bipartisan committees in Congress, emerged as a major facilitator of the Republican agenda. In a tactical move reminiscent of Speaker Joseph G. ("Uncle Joe") Cannon (D-Ill.), Gingrich preemptively safeguarded himself and the Republican leadership's agenda by asking that all the subcommittee chairmen sign a statement that they could be removed if they did not adhere to the Republican Conference's agenda (Bruck 1995, 72). Attached to its bills have been a large number of limitation amendments ("riders"), many used to advance the GOP leadership's policy or ideological agenda, or to reward interests allied with the party. In the past, riders had been employed frequently for a variety of purposes, such as to protect a friendly industry from deregulation; but the number of riders fastened to spending bills in the Republican-controlled 104th Congress had not been reached in decades (Bruck 1995, 72).

The three committees and twenty-eight legislative service organizations (LSOs) that were eliminated were predominantly linked to Democrats' allies. The three standing committees were the District of Columbia Committee, whose clientele is mostly Democratic voters; the Post Office and Civil Service Committee, with strong ties to postal and public employee unions; and the Merchant Marine and Fisheries Committee, closely associated with environmentalists, maritime unions, and seaport cities (Davidson 1995). The Small Business Committee, targeted for extinction by many reformers, was preserved in large part because the small business community provided one of the cornerstones of the Republicans' interest group base.

The twenty-eight LSOs—noncommittee member groups granted House office space and financed from their members' clerk-hire allowances—were defunded primarily to remove them as independent power centers with a knowledge base predominantly in the service of liberal or interest-based members. Of these groups, eleven were associated primarily with liberal causes, eleven were regional or industry based, two were Democratic Party groups, two were GOP groups, and two were bipartisan state delegations. The most notable examples were the Democratic Study Group (DSG) and several liberal-oriented entities such as the Congressional Arts Caucus, the Congressional Black Caucus, the Congressional Caucus for Women's Issues, the Congressional Hispanic Caucus, and the Federal Service Task Force.[2]

A frequent tactic of the Republican leadership in the 104th Congress was to bypass the committee system altogether: by using leadership-dominated committees, especially Budget and Rules, to shape legislation, or by shifting from a committee-based system to an informal task force system. To improve a bill's chances of passage the GOP leadership attached a large number of substantive measures to appropriations bills. With variations to fit the circumstances, task forces dealt with issues as disparate as gun control and political advocacy. These temporary entities not only bypassed committees and their established issues networks, but they allowed friendly groups more points of access to the members. For example, special interests could come before them to plead their case, out of public view. Further, because these task forces had no staff, their members were more inclined to rely on those interest groups for information and advice.

The Republicans' procedural innovations significantly reduced congressional staffing. Section 101 of H.Res. 6 required House committee staff to be reduced by at least one-third.[3] Furthermore, committee chairs were granted control over the hiring of subcommittee staff with subcommittee chairmen and ranking minority members losing the authority to hire one staffer each. Although committee staffs had come to be regarded as overblown and overactive, they provide indispensable services to members and have become intricately involved in shaping legislative outcomes. As legislation became more complex, congressional staff became more professionalized. Growing committee staffs also helped Congress oversee the huge and intimidating bureaucracy over the past several decades (Aberbach 1990).

Enlarged committee staffs have also allowed members to participate more effectively in a broader range of issue areas (Malbin 1981). Staffers tend to share members' ideologies and often serve as extensions of members' activities. Kingdon (1989) suggests that staff aides and members work as one decision-making unit. The relationship allows members to pursue other objectives while staffers pursue the detail work of the legislative process. Faced with losing staff aides, members (especially those in the minority) must function with a substantially reduced support system. The loss of these professionals may have repercussions on the legislative output of Congress. For example, Democratic members and staffers in the 104th Congress complained that legislation was being drafted by lobbyists and interest groups instead of policy professionals (Love 1995b). This extreme centralization of power, an artifact of the 104th Congress, was a high-water mark but in no way inconsistent with long-term trends. By the time the 104th Congress adjourned, it was apparent that House leaders, having overreached their powers, needed to accommodate committee leaders and internal factions, not to mention the Senate and the White House. As the 105th Congress convened, House leaders had to beg for support among various factions, promising to give committees and their chairs more leeway in developing legislation. The new Senate leadership, especially Majority Leader Trent Lott, pursued the classic course of seeking consensus among the Republican Conference members. The larger trends—mainly strengthened party leaders with the capacity to influence or bypass committees—seems likely to survive. As Sinclair (1997, 31) points out, the trend toward leadership management of legislation predated the Republican takeover and is likely to survive temporary leadership setbacks. "The new practices and procedures," she explains, "... make it easier for the majority party leadership to advance its members' legislative goals. The leadership now has more flexibility to shape the legislative process to suit the particular legislation at issue."

Interest Groups and the Contract with America

Policymaking is a process driven by the transactional politics needed to sustain coalitions. While it is often a straightforward process to attract a coalition in favor of general statements of principle in a coalition, forming actual language and detailed policies can divide solidified interests and splinter coalitions. To overcome this pitfall the House Republican Party constructed a national platform for the 1994 congressional elections, the Contract with America, which was primarily the brainchild of Representative Gingrich. The national manifesto was officially unveiled on 27 September 1994, as more than 300 Republican congressional candidates met on the steps of the U.S. Capitol's West Front to pledge that, if elected, they would support changes in congressional procedures and bring the Contract's ten proposals to a vote on the House floor.

From the beginning, the GOP leadership understood the importance of interest groups in determining the shape of legislative conflict (West and Francis 1995). Groups sympathetic with the party's conservative agenda were invited to a series of Republican Conference retreats in Maryland to help formulate, and later to promote, the Contract with America. To be certain that key organizations were on board, Republicans established several working symposiums composed of legislators, staff members, and outside groups to craft specific language for each of the Contract's ten points. Based on their particular interests and areas of expertise, different groups participated in the various working groups.

Interests not in tune with the Republican leadership's objectives were denied access to this process. Big business, for instance, tended to be passed over in favor of small business groups because, as Representative Richard Armey (R-Tex.) noted, "small businesses tend to be more ideological and principled in what they expect from the government" (Berke 1995). Among the more active organizations were the Christian Coalition, the Free Congress Foundation, Citizens for a Sound Economy, Americans for Tax Reform, Family Research Council, the National Federation of Independent Businesses, the National Taxpayers Union, and U.S. Term Limits. A staff aide to Representative John Boehner (R-Ohio), who helped coordinate the meetings with outside groups, reported that "we had meetings with outside groups every week where we let them know what was going on and let them know what we were doing. Our natural allies were Citizens for a Sound Economy, Americans for Tax Reform, the Heritage Foundation, the National Federation of Independent Businesses, and the Chamber of Commerce" (West and Francis 1995, 11). Table 8.1 lists some of the more prominent groups involved in fashioning the Contract with America.

Groups that participated in formulating the Contract were subsequently active in drafting specific legislative proposals (Engelberg 1995; Miller 1995a). Key lobbyists were seated with Republicans during certain formal hearings on issues of interest to their clients. For instance, a lobbyist for a trade association used office space on Capitol Hill to work on strategy for the product liability bill (Engelberg 1995). In another well-publicized instance, the staff of the Senate Judiciary Committee allowed a lob-

TABLE 8.1
GROUP PARTICIPATION IN THE CONTRACT WITH AMERICA

Balanced budget and line-item veto — The Fiscal Responsibility Act
    Citizens Against Government Waste

Crime — The Taking Back Our Streets Act

Welfare — The Personal Responsibility Act

Children — The Family Reinforcement Act
    American Family Association, Christian Action Network, Christian
    Coalition, Family Research Council, Traditional Values Coalition

Middle-class tax cut — The American Dream Restoration Act
    Americans for Tax Reform, National Taxpayers Union, Citizens for a Sound
    Economy

Congressional term limits — The Citizen Legislature Act
    U.S. Term Limits

National security — The National Security Restoration Act

Senior citizens — The Senior Citizens Fairness Act
    Senior's Coalition, Sixty-Plus Association

Capital gains — The Job Creation and Wage Enhancement Act
    National Federation of Independent Business, U.S. Chamber of Commerce,
    National Association of Home Builders, National Association of
    Manufacturers

Tort reform / product liability — The Common Sense Legal Reform Act
    Trial Lawyer's Association, Civil Justice Reform, Citizens for a Sound
    Economy, U.S. Chamber of Commerce, National Federation of Independent
    Business, American Tort Reform Association[a]

SOURCES: Darrell M. West and Richard Francis (1995); and a compilation of materials from *Congressional Record, Congressional Quarterly Weekly Report, National Journal, Washington Post, Washington Times, New York Times,* and witness lists from McIntosh hearings.
NOTE: Key think tanks were instrumental in helping write the Contract with America, most notably the Heritage Foundation and Cato Institute.
a. The American Tort Reform Association is a national umbrella group of 400 different organizations representing small businesses, medical people, and nonprofit associations.

bying firm representing electric utilities and other corporate interests before federal regulators to brief it before markup sessions on the Comprehensive Regulatory Reform Act (Shear 1995). This prompted bitter complaints from Democrats, who charged that such an intimate relationship threatened the public interest. "Whatever boundaries existed between lobbyists and legislators have been pretty well erased," Representative George Miller (D-Calif.) said. "These people are sort of becoming adjunct staff to the Republican leadership (Stone 1995, 1641).

Interest Group Access to the New Regime: The Case of Environmental Protection

Speaker Gingrich had followed pollsters' advice in keeping environmental policy out of the Contract with America. Once in office, however, the new Republican majority set about altering a string of environmental policies involving, for example, funding for the Environmental Protection Agency, reauthorization of clean air and water laws, wetlands protection, and further acquisition of federal lands.

For years, environmental activists had been able to count on a Democratic Congress. But in the 104th Congress, they were forced to deal with a trio of Alaskan lawmakers who controlled the committees that oversee most natural resources legislation, and who shared an antipathy for what the House Republican Conference called "the environmental lobby and their extremist friends in the eco-terrorist underworld" (Mathews 1995). As one indication of this effort, Representative Don Young (R-Alas.), the former trapper and riverboat captain who now chaired the House Committee on Resources, changed the name of the Arctic National Wildlife Refuge to the Alaska Oil Reserve. To tighten his control of the committee, he adopted what is known as the "Young Rule": Republicans who wanted a seat had to promise to vote with him on Alaska and other issues; in return, he would trade his support for their projects. Young filled the ranks with such self-proclaimed champions of the West as Representative Helen Chenoweth (R-Idaho), who had campaigned at an "endangered salmon bake" (Brant 1995). Environmental advocates depicted the new committee arrangement as a morality play, pitting the environment against "corporate welfare." House GOP leaders countered that human and economic prosperity outweigh traditional preservation apprehension.

One attempt to roll back federal environmental regulations came with reauthorizing the Endangered Species Act (ESA) of 1973. The law was intended to identify species of plants and animals threatened with extinction and to require steps to ensure their survival. It had been used to restrict land and water development encroaching on the habitats of threatened species.

The twenty-two-year-old statute had become a source of contention between environmentalists, who support species protection, and property rights advocates, who resist governmental incursions into the use of private lands. According to the latter, the statute was being abused. "For decades the liberals in Congress have distorted the original intent of the Endangered Species Act to further their extreme agendas," charged Representative Ron Packard (R-Calif.). "It is time to give human needs at least as much consideration as those of birds, fish, insects, and rodents" (CR, 18

July 1995, E1456). Reforming the ESA was an effort that encapsulated the goals of conservative lawmakers, especially from western states, to curb excessive federal regulatory actions and allow state and local governments to fashion their own ways of accomplishing environmental goals.

The vehicle for this effort was an endangered species task force, coordinated from Young's office. In this instance, Young effectively circumvented the subcommittee on Fisheries, Wildlife and Ocean and its chair, Representative James H. Saxton (R-N.J.), a moderate who favored the existing law. Young turned the task force over to Representative Richard W. Pombo (R-Calif.), a fourth-generation rancher who claimed that his own ranch had been devalued when it was declared a critical habitat for the kit fox (Rauber 1996b). At Young's direction, Pombo scheduled twelve field hearings in rural western counties to showcase property owners' hardships.

What Pombo and the task force heard were stories of local landowners who questioned why they should lose the right to develop their property because an endangered species made itself at home (Lacayou 1995). Environmentalists complained that speakers sympathetic to the law were squeezed out. During the question-and-answer session of one task force hearing, Representative Wally Herger (R-Calif.) rebuked an environmental group spokesperson who had criticized another witness, a builder who had to relocate a housing project because of a protected wetlands habitat. "These are hard-working, salt-of-the-earth families that are being denied the American dream, that are being denied any semblance of fairness. And I can say this, there was an election last November 8 and we have had enough of what is going on and, by golly, we are going to change it" (quoted in Rosin 1995, 13). "It is critical that people are put in this equation of the endangered species," declared Representative Chenoweth. "Because truly, the American producer, if the trend continues, will be the endangered species" (CR, 12 September 1995, H8789). Sensible reform, declared Representative Jim Kolbe (R-Ariz.), must remove regulatory mandates that "prevent any sensible or rational interpretation/implementation of our environmental laws" (CR, 8 February 1995, E304).

The measure drafted by the Endangered Species Act task force would have required the federal government to compensate private property owners for lost use of their lands as a result of restrictions caused by protecting endangered species and mandated additional scientific review before the government could list a species as endangered. The bill also would establish incentive programs to encourage property owners to conserve critical habitat and shift more responsibility to states and landowners to work out recovery plans for threatened species and their ecosystems. Lastly, the bill would emphasize protecting species on lands already set aside for conservation—protected wilderness and national parks—but on federally owned lands that are not set aside—national forests managed for logging and

other commercial purposes—the bill would curb conservation requirements (see table 8.2).

Critics—a broad spectrum of conservation groups and pro-environment
members—complained of a "frontier atmosphere," exhibited by a coalition
of industry lobbyists, advocates of property rights, and conservatives, in
which members of industries were invited to draft bills affecting their companies' interest.[4] "The task of rewriting our nation's most important environmental laws is being done by the major corporate interests whose
practices created much of the problem in the first place," said one environmental lobbyist (Egan 1995b). Vice-President Al Gore agreed, accusing
GOP lawmakers of allowing industry lobbyists to reshape environmental
policy to their advantage. "They have invited the lobbyists to walk right
into the halls of Congress, they've held their chairs, given them a pen and

TABLE 8.2

GROUPS SUPPORTING AND OPPOSING
THE YOUNG/POMBO BILL

Supporting the bill	Opposing the bill
American Forest and Paper Association	California Biodiversity Alliance
Coalition for Property Rights	Citizens for Sensible Safeguards
Competitive Enterprise Institute	Defenders of Wildlife
Endangered Species Act Reform Coalition	Endangered Species Coalition
Endangered Species Coordinating Council	Environmental Information
Grassroots Endangered Species Act Coalition[a]	Center
National Association of Home Builders	Environmental Information
National Endangered Species Coalition[a]	Services
National Wetlands Coalition	Environmental Media Services
National Wilderness Institute	Environmental Working Group
Nationwide Public Projects Coalition	Greenpeace
Northwest Sportfishing Association	National Wildlife Federation
Pacific Coast Federation of Fishermen Assn.	Natural Resources Defense
Reynolds Metal Company	Council
Society of American Foresters	O.M.B. Watch
The Hudson Institute	Sierra Club
The Peregrine Fund	The Izaak Walton League
United Paperworks Union	

SOURCES: A compilation of materials from *Congressional Record, Congressional Quarterly Weekly Report, National Journal, Washington Post, Washington Times, New York Times, Los Angeles Times*, and witness lists from Endangered Species Act Task Force hearings.
a. The Grassroots Endangered Species Act Coalition is an umbrella group of some 200 organizations representing a range of groups from the Alaska Loggers Association to the Sugar Cane Growers Co-op of Florida. The National Endangered Species Coalition represents 185 different groups and companies such as Chemical Corporation, Chevron U.S.A., Inc., and Kaiser Aluminum.

invited them to rewrite all of our environmental laws," he charged (*Washington Post,* 6 October 1995, A21). Republicans disputed this point, noting that the help they received in drafting laws was no different than the services environmental groups had offered other politicians in the past. "In the last Congress, rats, bugs, and even weeds were more important than people," claimed Representative Ken Calvert (R-Calif.) (*CR,* 24 February 1995, H2182).

Opponents saw the effort to reform the Endangered Species Act as an attempt by House Republican leaders to allow widespread destruction of habitat and give strong priority to economics over species survival. At issue in the Young/Pombo bill was the goal of habitat protection as the key to species recovery. Since 1975, the Fish and Wildlife Service had included habitat modification as "harmful" to endangered species, which the Supreme Court reaffirmed. The GOP version would define "harm" as direct action against a species that causes physical injury—not habitat modification—and would allow permits for activities that have less minimal environmental effects. Representative George Miller (D-Calif.) called the bill "an out-and-out effort by extremist antienvironmentalists to destroy a crucial law" (quoted in Bornemeier 1995). "The Republican majority is turning back the clock," noted Representative Rosa DeLauro (D-Conn.). "They are wiping out decades of improvement to the environment ... they are taking a wrecking ball to environmental protections in this country" (*CR,* 6 December 1995, H13942).

The outcome of the new regime's war on environmental regulations remains in doubt. On the one hand, Congress effectively banned new listings of endangered species for fiscal 1995 as part of a supplemental spending bill. And a House-passed regulatory overhaul bill (HR. 9) would compensate landowners whose property had declined by 20 percent because of federal actions to protect endangered species. On the other hand, it became clear that extreme reversals of environmental laws would be difficult to enact. Public support for environmental protection was stronger than the Republican leaders and their allies had foreseen, and on more than one occasion a coalition of environmentally minded Republicans and Democrats overpowered the GOP leadership and their allies in House floor votes.

Changing Rules of the Game

Under pressure from junior members, mostly from its conservative wing, the new Republican majority initiated a project coordinated by the office of House Majority Leader Richard Armey (R-Tex.), which some described as a campaign to "defund the left." The effort consisted of a series of proposals to restrict "political advocacy" by federal agencies and nonprofit groups paid to run government-sponsored programs. Although these groups cannot use federal money to influence the government, conservatives contend that they commingle public and private funds to subsidize lobbying and political activity. Seeing such groups as part of a liberal infrastructure, opponents vowed to "hunt [them] down one by one and extinguish their funding sources," according to Grover Norquist, head of Americans for Tax Reform and a Gingrich ally (Norquist 1995).

One set of proposals was aimed at curtailing lobbying by agencies of the federal government itself. Republicans complained that federal employees, prompted by the White House and political appointees, had used taxpayer dollars to lobby against Republican-sponsored legislation. As examples they cited the Department of Veterans Affairs, which distributed paychecks to its employees with messages from Secretary Jesse Brown urging opposition to the GOP budget plan, and the Department of Commerce, which briefed lobbyists on why a GOP bill to restructure the cabinet-level office was a "bad idea" (Jacoby 1996).

Spurred by such stories, House Governmental Reform and Oversight Chair Bill Clinger (R-Pa.) and Senate Governmental Affairs Chair Ted Stevens (R-Alas.) introduced a bill in March 1996 that would curtail executive lobbying. According to Clinger and Stevens, their bill would not curb political appointees in Senate-confirmed posts from advocating the administration's views. Nor would it forbid career employees from helping political appointees draft speeches or testimony, or providing factual information to outside groups. But career federal employees would be barred from: taking part in public events designed to promote public support for the administration, engaging in grassroots distribution of literature, soliciting outside groups to contact Congress, or providing outside groups with lists of lawmakers to be lobbied.

Clinger vowed to "move this bill as rapidly as I can through my committee," and Stevens promised to act following House approval. Two months later, Clinger held a singular hearing involving a secret witness called "Mr. X," a small business association lobbyist who claimed to fear retribution from the government if his name were known. "Mr. X" told of a series of unsolicited faxes from the Environmental Protection Agency outlining the agency's view of the Contract with America and related bills. "When an association receives lobbying materials from an agency that directly regulates the business of its members," the lobbyist contended, "there is an implicit suggestion that supporting the administration and agency position will result in more favorable treatment." Representative Henry A. Waxman (D-Calif.) called the hearing "very bizarre." Other Democrats ridiculed the hearing as a "publicity stunt" and were skeptical about the witness's fear of retribution (Barr 1996).

The Clinger-Stevens bill was but one of numerous Republican moves to check opposition from the executive branch. House committees launched investigations into alleged abuses of travel rules by cabinet members, and other panels requested voluminous records on agency officials' travels and public statements.

Other proposals were aimed at private organizations that receive federal funds. One of these, authored by Senator Alan Simpson (R-Wyo.), became law as part of the Lobbying Disclosure Act of 1995. It bars federal grants to large groups with a 501(c)(4) tax status, which covers such "lobbying machines" as the American Association of Retired Persons (AARP) and the Environmental Defense Fund.

A more extreme measure, pushed with leadership support by freshman Representatives Ernest J. Istook (R-Okla.) and David M. McIntosh (R-Ind.), would cover an even larger category of charitable 501(c)(3) and 501(h) groups. The Istook proposal would curb "political advocacy" by nonprofit groups that receive federal grants, preventing such groups from spending more than 5 percent of privately raised funds, up to $20 million, on "political advocacy," broadly defined. Such groups would be subject to audits by the General Accounting Office and would have to prove their compliance with the law, under penalty of fines or perhaps loss of grants. They would also have to disclose basic information about their operations, their grants, and their advocacy activities. Federal agencies, in turn, would be directed to send a list of grant recipients and their annual reports to the Census Bureau, which would make the data available through the Internet. To counter some objections to his measure, Istook later presented a revised version that would have limited any organization that received more than one-third of its revenue in federal funds to spending no more than $100,000 on advocacy activities. Nonprofit groups with annual revenues of $3 million or more that engaged in political activities would be prohibited from receiving federal grants. The new measure would exempt any group that spent less than $25,000 on political activities.

For years, conservatives argued, Democrats had been rewarding non-profit organizations associated with liberal causes. "This is an amendment that exposes what has been going on in this town for many, many years, where organizations from the left like Act-Up all the way to the U.S. Chamber of Commerce have taken Federal funds and have lobbied for more Federal funds," Representative Tom DeLay (R-Tex.) stated during an angry House floor debate (*CR*, 3 August 1995, H8389). Shrouded in tax-code language and other legal technicalities, the issue at hand was whether tax-exempt groups or other organizations that receive federal grants may lobby the federal government on their own behalf. The initial vehicle for this campaign was an amendment to the Labor, Health and Human Services (HHS) and Education Departments spending bill sponsored by Representatives Istook and McIntosh, along with Representative Robert L. Ehrlich Jr. (R-Md.).[5]

Limiting nonprofits was an effort that encapsulated the conservative goal to put an end to taxpayer-subsidized lobbying or "welfare for lobbyists." Table 8.3 lists groups supporting the Istook proposal, along with some of the advocacy groups identified as opponents. Federal grant dollars, it was contended, were being transferred to organizations that engaged in political activity, thus freeing up private funds to increase that organiza-

TABLE 8.3
GROUPS SUPPORTING AND OPPOSING
THE ISTOOK AMENDMENT

Supporting the amendment	*Opposing the amendment*
American Family Association	American Association of Retired
American Walnut Manufacturers	Persons
Association	AFL-CIO
Association of Concerned Taxpayers	American Bar Association
Christian Action Network	AFSCME
Christian Coalition	American Heart Association
Citizens Against Government Waste	Alliance for Justice[a]
Citizens for a Sound Economy	Association of Head Start Grantees
Committee for a Constructive To-	Association of Retarded Citizens
morrow	Boy Scouts of America
Concerned Women for America	Children's Defense Fund
Eagle Forum	Child Welfare League
Fine Hardwood Veneer Association	Families USA
National Association of Manufacturers	Girl Scouts of America
National Association of Wholesale	National Council of La Raza
Distributors	National Council of Senior Citizens
National Beer Wholesalers Association	National Fish and Wildlife
National Federation of Independent	Foundation
Business	NAACP Legal Defense & Educa-
National Restaurant Association	tion Fund
National Rifle Association	National Society of Fundraising
National Taxpayers Union	Executives
Right to Work	OMB Watch
Senior's Coalition	Planned Parenthood Federation of
Sixty-Plus Association	America
Tobacco Institute	Sierra Club
Traditional Values Coalition	United Way
U.S. Chamber of Commerce	YMCA of the USA

SOURCES: For supporters: Office of Rep. Ernest J. Istook, Jr. (R-Okla.); Peter Stone, "Follow the Leaders," *National Journal* (24 June 1995), 1640. For opponents: a compilation of materials from *Congressional Record, Congressional Quarterly Weekly Report, National Journal, Washington Post, Washington Times, New York Times,* and witness lists from McIntosh hearings.
a. The Alliance for Justice is an umbrella organization whose members include such groups as the Children's Defense Fund, OMB Watch, the Advocacy Institute, and Congress Watch.

tion's activity, or used directly to engage in prohibited political activity. "When this Congress sheds light on one of Washington's dirty little secrets, the Washington lobbyists are going to scream," said Representative Istook. "Unfortunately for them, the truth will point out how the taxpayer is subsidizing Washington lobbying" (Kellman 1995). Systematic reform, he declared on another occasion, "must not be targeted at any particular group nor any particular philosophy but must allow the U.S. Congress to perform its fiduciary responsibility to the American taxpayer." "That responsibility requires the Congress to track Federal budget dollars to their usage point" (*CR*, 30 June 1995, H1388).

Critics—a broad spectrum of public charities and nonprofit groups —charged that the version singled them out while not imposing the same restriction on for-profit groups, such as federal contractors and veterans service organizations that receive free office space from federal hospitals and state and local governments. "This amendment stifles nonprofit service groups while continuing to allow defense contractors, agribusiness, professional paid lobbyists and a host of others who also receive billions of dollars of tax dollars in Federal money not be gagged," said Representative Jerrold Nadler (D-N.Y.). "Why do we not gag these lobbyists, too? Because it is not in your ideological purpose to do so" (*CR*, 3 August 1995, H8391). Republicans disputed this point: "This language is content neutral," said Representative Armey. "It applies equally to the left and to the right.... We are not favoring any special interest, we are imposing openness and honesty on all special interests in order to benefit the public interest" (*CR*, 3 August 1995, H8396). To throw light on what he considered a deliberate attempt by an "Imperial Congress" to target liberal advocacy groups, Representative Martin Olav Sabo (D-Minn.) noted:

> In order to uncover the true intent of this provision, I offered an amendment to the Istook amendment when the Appropriations Committee considered the Labor, Health and Human Services bill. My amendment would have extended the same prohibitions to the beneficiaries of Federal contracts and loans. If the intent of the original amendment was to safeguard taxpayer dollars, then proponents should have viewed my amendment as an improvement. If, however, the intent of the original amendment was to curb a certain type of political advocacy, then my amendment would have been regarded as an unacceptable obstruction to that goal. My amendment failed in an 18-29 vote, and the Istook amendment was adopted. (*CR*, 3 August 1995, H8393)

Liberal advocacy groups and their allies in Congress saw the Istook amendment as an attempt by House Republican leaders to regulate and silence nonprofit organizations that opposed Republican goals. "The intent of this language is obvious," noted Representative Alcee L. Hastings (D-

Fla.). "It is to send the message to labor-oriented persons, nonprofits, and grassroots organizations not to disagree with the conservatives. It tells those groups that they may participate in the democratic process only if they agree with the Republicans. . . . Senator McCarthy is dead, but his legacy clearly lives on" (*CR*, 3 August 1995, H8391). For instance, the measure would directly affect groups such as Planned Parenthood Federation of America Inc., a powerful pro-choice advocate; the American Bar Association (ABA), which sparred with the new GOP majority over a constitutional amendment to ban flagburning; and the American Association of Retired Persons, which opposed Republican efforts to overhaul Medicare. Other nonprofit organizations that would be limited by this measure include: the YMCA, whose local branches received federal funds yearly for child care services, youth sports programs, and educational campaigns promoting childhood immunization and AIDS prevention; and the National Council of Senior Citizens (NCSC), which used federal grant monies to subsidize minimum-wage jobs for seniors.

Although Congress may clearly limit, regulate, or condition the use of the funds it appropriates, critics further charged that the Istook bill would restrict the rights of federal grantees to use their own money to engage in core activities protected by the First Amendment, including public debate on issues of public concern, communication with elected representatives, and litigation against the government (*CR*, 3 August 1995, H8390). The activities of "lobbying"—that is, persons individually or in association with one another engaging in advocacy communications to public officials on political, social, and economic issues of interest to the individuals and groups—are intertwined with implicit fundamental rights protected in the Constitution[6] (Maskell 1995, p. 11). At issue in the Istook proposal were compliance provisions that would require nonprofit organizations to disclose basic information about their operations, their grants, and their advocacy activities, as well as questions by witnesses concerning the political activity of federal grantees.[7] During acrimonious committee debate, Representative Steny H. Hoyer (D-Md.) called the proposal unconstitutional and "a device to intimidate those with whom you disagree" (Barr 1995a). "The goal is not and never should be to restrict free speech," Representative Istook answered. "Instead, the goal is to avoid the use of tax dollars to subsidize the private speech of those who have political connections or who rely on taxpayers' money to advocate their political views" (*CR*, 30 June 1995, H1388).

Istook's efforts were supported by many of the groups associated with the Contract with America. "I have heard about and have been indirectly a part of these efforts to identify the various channels in which traditionally liberal institutions are funded and to cut those pipelines," the budget director of the Heritage Foundation reported (Shear 1995).

As with many of the new GOP majority's more ambitious plans, the Istook amendment faced concerted opposition. It was dropped from pending bills during 1995, though not without conflict: having been supported by majorities on the House floor, it was a bone of contention in more than one House-Senate conference that year. But the initiative's spirit surfaced in the 105th Congress with a new House rule requiring committee witnesses to disclose the amount and source of federal grants or contracts that they or their organizations had received over the previous three years (House Rule XI, clause 2(g)). Though aimed at nonprofit organizations, this requirement particularly embarrassed corporations whose witnesses the Republicans might presumably receive more favorably. Whether more extreme measures will resurface is uncertain. But the provisions of the Istook amendment demonstrated the lengths the new regime was prepared to consider in limiting the effectiveness of groups associated with post–New Deal liberal causes and further pursuing the new regime's policy goals.

Conclusion

Today's political parties are organizations located at the center of extensive and distinctive networks of interest groups. The ties between parties and groups are complex and symbiotic: the party's elected officials (and their nonelected aides) are in a position to confer policy benefits, in exchange for which interest groups can supply funds, volunteers, and mobilization efforts necessary for underwriting campaigns. Some of these relationships are marriages of convenience. For example, political action committees (PACs) of whatever type tend to support majority-party candidates and incumbents because they can best confer access and policy benefits. Other interests tilt toward one party or another on the basis of deeply shared ideological or policy goals. When voters choose one party over another, therefore, they in effect cast two ballots: one for the party's candidates, the other for those interests most closely allied with that party. Thus, shifts in party control have the effect of rearranging the relative influence of individual interests and coalitions. Partisan turnovers in the executive branch are visible and not infrequent: since the New Deal era there have been no less than six such turnovers. On Capitol Hill, however, these transitions are less familiar: only three bicameral shifts occurred over the same period of more than sixty years.

The Republicans' sweep of the House and Senate in 1994 constitutes the most dramatic recent example of how partisan change can affect group coalition structure and influence. Indeed, a coalition of conservative and business groups collaborated in shaping and selling the Contract with America. Once in power, the new majority changed congressional rules, structures, and operating modes in ways that had the effect (often intended, sometimes unintended) of promoting certain interests and disadvantaging others. These arrangements themselves further encourage the formation of supportive coalitions and in turn force excluded groups to form defensive alliances. Finally, we have seen how several of these coalitions were involved in drafting, developing, and passing specific legislation. This same legislation was opposed by coalitions traditionally aligned with the former Democratic majority. A close examination of the new majority's coalition structure, in contrast with that of the previous majority, validates once more the "group basis of [congressional] politics."

Notes

1. *Congressional Record* references are presented throughout the chapter in the following manner: *CR,* date, page.

2. The DSG is not officially part of the Democratic Caucus. Its two staffers are now part of the Democratic Steering Committee and operate as shared employees with several offices. Many of the banned LSOs have reappeared as Congressional Member Organizations (CMOs), some of which have affiliated nonprofit, tax-exempt organizations located off the Hill.

3. Originally, GOP plans included a reduction in personal staff from eighteen to sixteen positions, but members successfully thwarted efforts to reduce personal staff.

4. These included representatives from oil and gas companies, mining and logging interests, and developers and growers.

5. The three sponsors later sought to attach the measure to the appropriations bill that finances the Treasury Department and the Postal Service to improve the measure's chances of passage. The appropriations process has the traditional advantage of complicating matters for the White House. The president cannot put back into appropriations bills money that Congress has zeroed out. To kill the nonprofit language in the appropriations bill, the president might have to cancel a program he especially favored.

6. The term, according to the measure, includes "carrying on propaganda, or otherwise attempting to influence legislation or agency action, including, but not limited to, monetary or in-kind contributions, preparation and planning activities, research and other background work, endorsements, publicity, coordination with such activities of others, and similar activities." *CR,* 3 August 1995, 8385.

7. It has been a principle of federal constitutional law that the government may not condition the receipt of a public benefit upon the requirement of relinquishing one's protected First Amendment rights. See, generally, Jack Maskell, "Restrictions on Lobbying Congress with Federal Funds," *CRS Report,* 95-382A (March 3, 1995). See also *U.S.* v. *Harriss,* 347 U.S. 612 (1954); *U.S.* v. *Rumeley,* 345 U.S. 41 (1953); and *Eastern Railroads President Conference* v. *Noerr Motor Freight, Inc.,* 365 U.S. 127 (1961).

9 Christine DeGregorio

Assets and Access: Linking Lobbyists and Lawmakers in Congress

THE SEEDS of the welfare reform legislation passed in the 104th Congress were sown in the 100th Congress with the passage of the Family Support Act of 1988. For the first time in over a decade, lawmakers agreed on a way to attack the crippling cycle of poverty that ensnared 20 percent of American children (Rich 1988). The bill represented a marked departure from old welfare policies in that it was openly intended to get recipients of Aid to Families with Dependent Children off welfare and back to work.

This would be accomplished, it was hoped, through a mixture of mandatory work requirements (exempting only mothers of children under three years of age), subsidized child care, job training, and financial aid (Rich 1987). The legislation would also provide transitory health and welfare benefits to ease the transition from welfare dependency. It would help single mothers track down delinquent fathers who had reneged on paying child support, which would lessen the costs to taxpayers.

One group of winners in the new legislation were poor, intact, and functioning families—the so-called deserving poor—who could for the first time count on some temporary government aid. The losers in this skirmish included single mothers who preferred to stay at home with their children than to work, absent fathers who had up until now escaped their financial responsibilities, and conservative American taxpayers who objected to any expansion of the welfare rolls as a wrong-headed solution to the problem of poverty.

The case of welfare reform clearly demonstrates that there are winners

and losers whenever government steps in to redistribute rights and resources. The preferences of the many often win out over the preferences of
the few, but vocal minorities can and do win the day. The cumbersome
structure of Congress, with its two chambers and numerous committees,
slows down the policymaking process, giving ample opportunity for evaluation, promotion, and compromise along the way. Yet, although interested
parties organize to advance their goals and, in so doing, establish close
working relationships with the sponsors and champions of legislative initiatives, some participants get better access than others. Most popular accounts of Washington politics hold that the disparities in access are often
related to disparities in money.

Clear advantages accompany the value officeholders place on money, in
particular campaign contributions that assist with their reelections, yet the
conventional wisdom in this case is too simplistic. In this chapter, I offer
and empirically test a more subtle story about the exchanges entailed when
lobbyists seek for their own ends the time and talents of busy legislators.
The theory rests on a familiar assumption. Power seekers of every sort, be
they lawmakers, congressional aides, or issue advocates inside and outside
government, have preferences about what Congress enacts into law, and
they enter the fray to achieve what they can for themselves and their organizational sponsors. For House members especially, who face electoral
challenges every two years, the twin goals of running for office and making
good public policy and the activities they engender are inextricably en-
tangled. And while students of campaign politics have it right when they
say the electoral imperative creates an ever-present chase for money, the
money does not wholly satisfy either goal (see Jacobson 1987; Magleby
and Nelson 1990).

Notwithstanding numerous references to the evils and omnipresence of
money and politics, financial wealth is neither the best nor the only asset
that piques legislators' interest in working with lobbyists. The nature of
Congress and the electoral process dictate that other assets, especially information, are more important. Although lawmakers have substantial resources including a large staff, considerable uncertainty remains. The
agenda is too large and the issues are too complex for any one lawmaker
to assess the ramifications of every choice that presents itself. To overcome
the confusion and to stay out of trouble with constituents, legislators rely
on one another for voting cues (Sullivan et al. 1993; Kingdon 1989). Spe-
cialists from the Agriculture Committee give advice on farm policy to colleagues from other committees. The tables then turn, and the members of
Ways and Means and Commerce, respectively, give cues on the issues they
know best to their colleagues on Agriculture.

If the promoters of controversial issues are to succeed in winning over
the support of reluctant rank-and-file lawmakers they must have informa-

tion and contacts that rival contrary information from other quarters, including the decision makers' usual sources. It is this highly individualistic side of decision making and coalition building that gives rise to the leaders' insatiable need for what only lobbyists have to offer: myriad, tailor-made explanations of events and district-level grassroots support that make allies out of adversaries.

Both lawmakers and lobbyists gain by entering into these policymaking partnerships. The advocates need accommodating leaders to interject their points into the formal decision-making process. Legislators need information, brokers, and confidants to help them build congressional support for passage. Because both parties to the exchange get something for their trouble, I call this explanation of events an *exchange theory of access*. It is fully delineated below.

The empirical evidence I use to test this interpretation of promotional politics comes from personal interviews with ninety-seven advocates who represent the diverse community of interests that engage in advocacy. The groups include private for-profit, nonprofit, and intergovernmental organizations. The participants describe the way they secured access to key House leaders—officeholders and aides—who championed to passage six major initiatives of the 100th Congress (1987–88). The policies, disparate in subject matter and scope but uniformly serious in their consequences to the country, include *Contra* aid (HJ Res. 523), farm credit reform (HR 3030), omnibus drug (HR 5210), nuclear testing limitations (Sec. 924 of HR 4264), omnibus trade (HR 4848), and welfare reform (HR 1720).

An Exchange Theory of Access

On matters of great national significance, lawmakers rarely agree on what constitutes the best governmental response. Almost always, the serious conflicts over policy stem from lawmakers' views of how their votes will be interpreted in their districts, where their reelection fortunes hinge on making the correct choices in Washington. While it is true that most citizens are inattentive to the actions of their representatives, legislators conduct polls, tally incoming calls, and devote plenty of time, staff, and money to avoid trouble at home. And while the odds are very good that citizens will return incumbents to their congressional offices, legislators experience close races often enough to warrant fear of reprisals (Jacobson 1987), and most can point to a friend who was an apparently safe incumbent who lost in a recent election. Incumbents, knowing the volatility of citizens' support, are always on the lookout for information about how this or that action in Washington will be perceived by potential voters.

As a consequence, officeholders who take the lead in assembling coalitions either for or against passage do so slowly and with great finesse. The issue leaders often, but not always, hold positions of prominence in congressional party and committee hierarchies (DeGregorio 1997). Here they receive the procedural legitimacy to structure choices (agendas in committee rooms and vote schedules on the floor) and the substantive expertise to craft provisions (markups in committee and amendments on the floor) that unite rather than divide would-be followers (Fiorina and Shepsle 1989a; Bach and Smith 1988).

The shepherds of major legislation also woo supporters through material means that may or may not be related to the issue at hand (Sinclair 1983; Little and Patterson 1993). This may come in the form of substantive or political information and analysis, a vote on an unrelated issue, an endorsement, a campaign contribution, a hearing in a colleague's district, a photo opportunity, a favor for a constituent, or a speech on behalf of the targeted coalition member.

Congressional leaders bring to these political relationships a variety of resources derived from personal attributes and the perks that come with formal positions within the committee and party hierarchies (DeGregorio 1997; Hall 1993; Mayhew 1974). Others come from outside the institution, from professional lobbyists and the myriad organizations they represent.

I expect several organizational attributes to be instrumental in opening doors for lobbyists on Capitol Hill. While money can buy some of these, it cannot furnish all of them. They include the organization's (1) budget and staff, (2) PAC affiliations, (3) number and location of members, and (4) credibility. The advocates also possess skills and talents that may gain them access apart from what their institutional affiliations afford, including (1) personal credibility, (2) prior experience, (3) professional in-kind service, and (4) position.

Budget and Staff
Of all the resources that an organization can muster to win access, money and staff are surely the most versatile. Staff may be deployed on myriad projects. If available, money and staff can be used to conduct targeted public opinion polls, acquire and analyze economic data pertinent to affected districts, and sponsor retreats in which officeholders and community leaders consult with one another in a relaxed setting (prior to the passage of more restrictive gift/travel rules). When an organization has money and a talented staff, it has enormous potential for access and influence. Money and staff can provide nearly everything a political leader needs, except perhaps politically useful information and the added legitimacy that comes with a mass volunteer, citizen-based effort.

PAC Affiliations
While informed observers, scholars, and practitioners disagree over the

power of campaign money to buy legislators' votes, there is little disagreement that contributions buy legislators' time (Smith 1995; Conway 1991). Organizations that sponsor PACs are sure to be granted an initial audience with their now-elected beneficiaries. Nevertheless, the extent to which this preliminary contact translates into long-term access or supportive votes has more to do with such factors as the quality of the consultation and the persuasiveness of the presentation than it has to do with the size of the donation. This is why it is important to consider nonmonetary resources along with the monetary ones.

Membership Size and Diffusion

When interest groups publicly endorse a bill, legislators take notice. Size alone matters because it offers a degree of institutional legitimacy. In 1987 legislators' appeals for an end to our government's financial support of the *contras*' fighting in Nicaragua received notice when several large church groups organized with the same goal in mind. The advocates for the United Church of Christ, the American Baptist Church, and the National Council of the Churches of Christ could boast of several million members.

The more geographically dispersed one's members are, moreover, the greater the likelihood that there will be a constituent-legislator connection. Also, a group's capacity for high-volume, constituent-oriented networking is an asset that can be parlayed into access with the House leaders, who are themselves on the lookout for well-placed political allies (see Wright 1996). Groups without large complements of civic-minded volunteers (for-profit organizations and some research institutions) will likely build access on different grounds (e.g., sound and timely analysis and a persistent presence).

Institutional Credibility

Like money, institutional credibility is crucial on Capitol Hill. Unlike money, it is difficult to identify and measure. According to the study participants, however, it is not just a matter of size. "Even though our organization is quite small in comparison to some of the church groups, its credibility is high and that opens doors for us." Institutional credibility is inextricably linked to trust, follow-through, and being perceived to be on the "right side of the issue." Success also breeds credibility and more success. Savvy lobbyists know this and make strategic choices about when and when not to pressure Congress. In the words of one lobbyist, "You have to demonstrate that you can win, even if it means carving up what you want to achieve into tiny pieces. You have to demonstrate that you can be successful. That's how you gain credibility with members of Congress and with your grassroots." In part, an organization's credibility is associated with the commitment and talent of its administrators and staff.

Personal Credibility

Although it is difficult to measure the impact of advocates' contributions in terms of policy successes, it is reasonable to think that their congressional partners formulate impressions of the advocates' value to their leadership enterprise. In study after study, advocates speak of the importance of their own credibility (Walker 1991; Berry 1989; Schlozman and Tierney 1986).

Prior Experience

Call it experience, the old boys' network, or the revolving door, it adds up to the same thing. Congressional leaders work with people they trust. Where the trust is initially established may be immaterial, but we can consider a few options besides the service provision discussed above. Many leader-lobbyist relationships start on Capitol Hill with the lobbyist serving first as an officeholder or aide (congressional alumnus). In other instances, leaders learn to trust an advocate after a series of successful ventures with that advocate.

Professional Service

Sometimes advocates offer professional services—speechwriting, preparation of issue briefs, and policy analyses—to congressional insiders in the hope that they will be remembered favorably and be granted the access they desire with influential legislators and aides. They do this even on matters unrelated to their lobbying efforts. Their sole aim is access. Over time, this strategy may result in a healthy ongoing relationship in which the advocates and the House leaders continually rely on each other for valuable assistance, in part alleviating the advocates' worries about gaining future access.

Position

An important determinant of executive-legislative liaisons not present anywhere else is the structural link that derives from Congress's formal budgetary and oversight roles vis-à-vis the executive branch of government. The link should be particularly strong for civil servants who develop long-term relationships with the officeholders and staff of the congressional committees that have jurisdictions over their policy domains.

In sum, what advocates have and issue leaders need are the resources required to build coalitions. To the extent that the organizations with the biggest budgets and the largest staffs are also best able to satisfy the resource needs of the issue leaders that rank-and-file House members turn to for cues and coalition work, they have advantages over other groups seeking access. But if valuable assets such as substantive expertise, personal credibility, and well-placed constituent contacts are uncorrelated with the organizations' financial wealth, access may be more equal than critics would have us believe. Money, while a highly valuable asset, may not be the best or the only predictor of congressional access.

The following sections present the empirical test of this exchange theory of access. First, we want to know who participates because to have influence in anything, one must be a player. We also want to know if the characteristics of pending policies and their political environments encourage some organizations to participate more than others. Next, to test the proposition that different organizational resources account for much of the variation in who works with whom and with what degree of success, we focus on three additional aspects of interest group access: (1) the organizational assets relied on by various groups, (2) the variations in access achieved by groups, and (3) the rewards of access achieved by different classes of organizations.

Shifting Involvements

Most studies of interest group politics ignore the promotional activities of government officials. Common practice notwithstanding, the evidence in this chapter includes public-sector lobbyists at all levels because, just like participants from the private sector, they must talk their way into Capitol Hill offices. On the issues in question, federal, state, and local advocates constituted 37 percent of the entire pressure community. And twenty-six of the thirty-five public-sector participants lobbied for the administration. The composition of private-sector groups conforms well to other studies of interest group behavior. Occupational groups such as the National Association of Manufacturers (NAM) numerically dominate almost three to one the nonoccupational (citizen) groups such as Mothers Against Drunk Driving (MADD) and Greenpeace. The nonprofits such as NAM and the International Ladies Garment Workers' Union hold the same relative advantage over the for-profits such as American Express and AT&T. Compared with other group classifications, the for-profit occupational groups possess a decidedly small share (17 percent) of the entire distribution. The baseline composition of the interest group community provides a point of departure for understanding the link between organizational participation and the nature of the issues and their political environments.

The technical complexity of a policy and the scope of its intended application have a bearing on decision making and leadership inside Congress (DeGregorio 1997; Sinclair 1995; Rohde 1991). And while it stands to reason that these conditions might affect the play for influence from outside Congress, there are no tests of the extent to which these factors affect the participation levels of different organizations. Nor do we know if some types of organizations excel in bringing out the troops when issues kick up a lot of controversy and capture plenty of media attention.

Table 9.1 shows the proportionate involvement of disparate organizations (e.g., citizen based v. occupation based and public v. private) as they participated in selected policy domains and political contexts. The six issues are clustered according to their technical complexity, scope of application, and public salience. The table demonstrates that involvement of advocacy groups varies with the characteristics of the issues under consideration. The information on scope shows that two types of organizations experience dramatic increases in their rates of participation when issues are broadly construed. Nonprofit occupational groups and those from the public sector eclipse almost two to one other promotional groups on the scene at the time. Citizen groups are vastly outnumbered by their occupational complement. Only when the issues capture extraordinary media attention (salience) does the rate of citizen-group participation exceed that of other groups. Also, when issues are salient, public-sector entities appear to suffer the consequences.

The connections demonstrated here between organized promotional activity and the nature of the issues reflect the membership base of various

TABLE 9.1

ORGANIZATIONS CATAGORIZED BY TYPE, ISSUE
COMPLEXITY, SCOPE, AND PUBLIC SALIENCE

Organization type	N	Complexity	Broad scope	Public salience
Private	61	37.7	37.7	41.0
Public	35	31.4	65.7[a]	17.1[b]
Not for-profit	81	32.1	49.4	32.1
For-profit	15	53.3	40.0	33.3
Not nonprofit	69	37.7	40.6	36.2
Nonprofit	27	29.6	66.7[a]	22.2
Occupational	68	39.7	55.9	25.0
Citizen	28	25.0	28.6[a]	50.0[a]
Not administration	70	32.9	45.7	35.7
Administration	26	42.3	53.9	23.0

NOTE: The proportions reveal activity levels when the condition (complexity, scope, and salience) holds. *Complexity* includes farm credit, testban, and omnibus trade. The texts of these bills and the controversies they engendered include highly technical language. *Broad scope* includes welfare reform, omnibus drug, and omnibus trade. The potential that these issues hold for affecting sizable audiences within society is reflected in the above-average number of indexing terms they attract in the Library of Congress's on-line system for locating legislative initiatives. *Public salience* refers to the action that surrounded the two initiatives—*Contra* aid and omnibus trade—that received above-average numbers of articles in the media.
a. $p < .05$.
b. $p < .01$.

advocacy operations. Broad-based national legislation inevitably affects diverse occupational groupings throughout the country. President Clinton's plan for health-care reform triggered a broad array of reactions from countless sources because the proposal threatened an industry that comprises one-seventh of the U.S. economy. The two omnibus bills and welfare reform bill included in this study illustrate the point. Advocates with occupational interests intervened in large numbers because in each case they correctly perceived both opportunities and challenges to the distribution of rights and resources with which they were accustomed.

Citizen groups and the saliency of issues are particularly susceptible to the influence that policies have on the populace. First, when it comes to attracting new members, the group's mission may be decisive in persuading an individual to join one group and not another. This scenario is extremely likely when groups have comparable stores of selective benefits to bestow on their prospective members, differing only in the policies the groups promote. Second, issue saliency comes into play again when group organizers prod their grassroots members to lobby Congress or write letters to the editors of their local papers. Only when their interest is piqued will group members take the time to respond as directed. Third, lobbyists like to boast of a large citizen base. Whether active or not, it grants them a degree of credibility in the eyes of the officeholders.

By contrast, the advocates from occupational groups need none of these properties that saliency spawns. They need not wait for mass opinion to solidify; it is sufficient that the administrators (and perhaps the members) of the labor union, trade, or professional association are watchful and interested. It is often enough to analyze the economic ramifications of the policy change and produce arguments that resonate with what lawmakers interpret to be in their own or their constituents' interests, whether or not the issue engenders widespread attention and concern.

The disparities that appear in the column headed *complexity* are also enlightening, although their instability warrants caution. It is plausible that citizen-based organizations may be less equipped to intervene over technically complex matters than are their for-profit and executive branch counterparts. Only the citizen-based, cause-oriented groups with specialized knowledge will be equipped to speak with authority on the matter. Other interested citizen groups, because they lack expertise, will be forced to play secondary roles.

This is not to imply that nonoccupational groups cannot educate themselves on the arcana of a complicated issue. They can and do. The Council for a Livable World and Women's Action for Nuclear Disarmament (WAND) are examples of citizen-based groups that have acquired enormous credibility on their subject. The point is that the knowledge they acquired in a dozen years of promotional work is readily available to the scientists who make a living doing research in the area. A mystery that is not so easily explained is the dip in the participation rate of nonprofit groups when issues are complex. Affected occupational groups such as these should have an ample supply of experts on whom to draw in the event that highly technical disputes break out.

An issue-by-issue analysis shows that the administration constituted 100 percent of public-sector activity when the president's autonomy was in question (omnibus trade). By contrast, when states had the most to lose, as was the case in reforming state-run poverty programs, their lobbyists outnumbered administration officials three to one.

Taken together, the evidence on participation affirms the conventional wisdom that occupational groups have the upper hand in their visibility on the political playing field. There are some important caveats, however. Participants from citizen cause-oriented groups and government agencies at all levels are abundant when the media bring issues to the attention of the public. Second, the public sector is not a monolith. Lobbyists for the administration dominate state and local participants when presidential autonomy is at stake. Just the opposite asymmetry occurs when states' interests are at issue.

Variations in Assets

Organizational resources, such as money, staff, and members, for private-sector organizations, are the raw materials that can be transformed into assets of greater consequence, including credibility. For-profit occupational organizations are the most advantaged; a larger share of these organizations have average or above-average budgets, staff, and membership numbers.[1] Nonprofit occupational associations come next. They outflank the citizen groups in all dimensions except membership levels. The findings presented in table 9.2 show that 20 to 25 percent of all private-sector organization lobbyists believe that having a PAC helps considerably in gaining access to decision makers. Of greater merit, however, are two nonmonetary assets: issue expertise and professional service. Between 36 and 61 percent of lobbyists interviewed agreed that both were useful.

There are two dissimilarities of interest as well. First, the lobbyists from nonprofit organizations possess the widest array of useful assets. Second, there is a remarkable lack of correspondence among what lobbyists value across organizational types. The lobbyists stress the assets that they have in ample supply. Nonprofit lobbyists stress membership and organizational credibility, while for-profit lobbyists emphasize their personal credibility and knowledge of the issues. Lobbyists for the administration rate their institutional positions as the best resource for accessing House leaders. To a lesser degree, they see the desirability of three assets that their nonadminis-

TABLE 9.2
ASSETS THAT DIFFERENT TYPES OF ORGANIZATIONS
REPORTED AS VALUABLE IN SECURING ACCESS
(IN PERCENTAGES)[a]

	For-profit	Nonprofit	Citizen	Administration
Organizational assets				
Credibility	6.7	51.9	21.4	3.8
Membership	.0	77.8	22.2	.0
PAC affiliate	20.0	22.2	25.0	.0
Personal Resources				
Credibility	40.0	18.5	25.0	23.1
Issue expertise	40.0	55.6	60.7	23.1
Congressional alumnus	26.7	37.0	17.9	26.9
Professional service	40.0	44.4	35.7	15.4
Position	20.0	18.5	7.1	53.8
Percentage in sample	15.6	28.1	29.2	27.1

SOURCE: Interview responses to the question: "In reflecting on these and other assets (list provided), what ones do you consider to be important in explaining your access to the leaders you just identified?" (N = 96)
a. Because only positive responses from each organization type are included in the table, the cells do not sum to 100 percent.

trative counterparts also value: personal credibility, issue expertise, and former career ties to Congress.

Lobbyists from corporations, which lack a volunteer base, such as American Express and BankBoston, explain their access in terms of their own personal resources. This frees them to boast of something within their control—their trustworthiness and reputation for hard work. A twelve-year veteran from a large public relations firm that represented Mexico in the omnibus trade bill put her experience in these terms. "We don't have any campaign connections. We don't have a PAC. The members have to trust you. You have to be a straight shooter."

Lobbyists from the AFL-CIO, the National Association of Manufacturers, and the National Association of Governors give primary credit for their access to the size and credibility of the organizations they represent. An advocate from the farm lobby affirms the sentiment. "It's our size and scope. Ninety percent of farm co-ops in the country are part of this organization, and when you figure that every farmer is a member of about three cooperatives, we've got every farmer represented." Legislators cannot afford to be inhospitable to these organizations.

Large grassroots citizen organizations benefit from their constituency connections as well. A spokesperson from a church group explains, "Our group represents 44 million constituents. The nature of the group and the number of members made it next to impossible for any member to shut the door in my face." More than citing the value of membership, however, citizen-group representatives emphasized their PAC affiliations and their knowledge of the issues. "I've met with members for over twenty-seven years. It's experience. They know me well. They enjoy my expertise, and this is the primary reason for access." These advocates, like no other, remarked on their long-term devotion to their issues and their organizations.

The high percentage of "position" in the column headed "Administration" is attributable to agency bureaucrats who describe being completely nonstrategic in gaining Hill access. One civil servant explained his circumstance. "A member of the Department of Energy once got into trouble because of the appearance of lobbying. I would never think to call a member of Congress. The requests come from them to us. They ask us for a briefing." In sharp contrast to this characterization, the presidential appointees are strategic and discerning about whose time they seek in Congress. In the words of one appointee, "I advocated that we do an omnibus trade bill, and ultimately, after a lot of work it happened. As White House liaison I was coordinating the effort, but you've got to remember that the cabinet secretaries would contact the members themselves."

These findings demonstrate that, first, lobbyists perceive that an exchange is occurring when they receive access, and money is only part of the equation. Second, the organizations with the most money and staff (for-profits) are not the most advantaged in the intangible assets such as experience, professional service, and credibility. Here, the nonprofits excelled with the most eclectic range of personal and organizational assets. Third, and perhaps most important, lobbyists play to their strengths. When you have mass support and members who can be relied on to overwhelm legislators with mail and phone messages, you use them. When this is lacking, as is the case with think tanks, some corporations, and law firms, you use your expertise and record of trustworthiness.

Resources and Linkages

When the organizations in this study took promotional stands on high-stakes issues, their lobbyists linked up with an average of twelve issue leaders, mostly officeholders and their staff. Roughly 80 percent of the identified elected leaders were from the Democratic Party, the majority party in the 100th Congress. The basic profile of contacts is similar for groups with above- and below-average stores of money and staffs.

As the analysis in table 9.3 shows, interest groups and their lobbyists rely mainly on four assets—two organizational and two personal—to secure access. Advocates who cite their organizations' credibility as a key to

TABLE 9.3

THE IMPORTANCE OF ORGANIZATIONAL AND PERSONAL
RESOURCES IN DETERMINING WHICH ISSUE LEADERS
ARE CONTACTED

Valued resources	Mean leaders cited (N)	Mean office-holders (%)[a]	Mean Democrats (%)[b]	Mean party leaders (%)
Organizational resources				
Credibility				
No (72)	10.7	68	72	13
Yes (22)	13.8[c]	72	74	9
Membership				
No (67)	12.2	63	81	12
Yes (23)	11.8	84[c]	73	8
PAC affiliate				
No (78)	10.9	69	73	13
Yes (16)	13.4	68	75	09
Personal resources				
Credibility				
No (70)	11.7	72	72	14
Yes (24)	10.8	61[c]	77	09
Issue expertise				
No (50)	10.2	68	71	14
Yes (44)	13.0[c]	70	76	11
Congressional alumnus				
No (69)	11.1	69	73	14
Yes (25)	12.4	70	73	9
Professional service to leaders				
No (62)	10.9	69	70	14
Yes (32)	12.9	70	80[d]	10

SOURCE: Interview responses to the question: "In reflecting on these and other assets (list provided), what ones do you consider to be important in explaining your access to the leaders you just identified?"
a. References to staff issue leaders plus officeholders sum to 100.
b. References to Democrats plus Republicans sum to 100.
c. $p < .05$ in one-tailed test.
d. $p < .05$ in two-tailed test.

access are more likely to contact party leaders, committee and subcommittee chairs, and members of the Rules Committee, while those who place importance on their membership base include more rank-and-file officeholders in their networks.

The connection between the personal resources and access is best explained by the major role congressional aides play as gatekeepers in Con-

gress. Staff members who screen calls and information have witnessed firsthand the in-kind professional services that lobbyists can provide. A lobbyist from a citizen-based group explains the way he uses professional service
to ensure that his phone calls are answered: "I circulate our publications
and research on issues of interest to various congressional committees. The
staffers, in particular, get to know me. It boosts my credibility. And when
an issue comes up that we organize around, the staff recognize me and return my calls."

Lobbyists who rely on personal credibility recognized the key role of
staff in the decision-making process, and 11 percent more of them reached
out to staffers than did others when assembling a Hill network. The connection between professional service and greater reliance on Democrats
when that party controlled the Congress may result from the fact that Democrats had one-third more committee staff than their Republican counterparts. Thus advocates who use professional service as an inroad to the
House leadership rely more heavily on the party in formal possession of the
perks of office, including a disproportionate share of staff.

It is noteworthy that lobbyists, almost without exception and regardless
of their organizational wealth, secure access with leaders from standing
committees (74 percent) more than from subcommittees (40 percent), subcommittees more than party leadership posts (14 percent), and party leadership posts more than the House Rules Committee (9 percent). The lobbyists give two explanations for eschewing the help of party leaders and
members from the Rules Committee. For practical reasons they do not
want to use up precious access over minor conflicts or over serious and un-
winnable ones. For strategic reasons, they often defer the task of meeting
with these officials and those on the Rules Committee to their elected allies, who can speak with them as fellow members of the institution.

The sequential nature of the lawmaking process dictates where you
look for leaders. According to a lawyer-lobbyist, "You start with a small
nucleus and just build and build." Similarly, a labor union representative
concludes, "What you do is build as you go. You try not to drop anybody
off the coalition but basically build throughout. And you try to get ready
for a floor fight. I mean you'd like to avoid the floor fight, but you're always getting ready for it." Most lobbyists do not abandon their leaders
along the way. Instead, they build their networks as the issue wends it way
from one venue to the next.

Organizational Rewards

The issue of impact was addressed by asking, "On a 100-point scale (with
100 being high), how close does the actual policy outcome resemble the
one you were attempting to achieve?" Eleven interest group representatives

reported obtaining everything they wanted in the legislation. And a full 50 percent reported receiving 70 percent or more of what they were attempting to achieve. Only six participants reported getting nothing for their efforts. The two groups that reported the lowest level of success, oddly enough, were the for-profits and the administration. The perceptions of the lobbyists from these settings are that they receive no advantage from their enviable stores of organizational wealth (for-profits) and formal position (administration). The nonprofit occupational groups report the greatest success, followed by citizen groups. Overall, the findings suggest that Congress has earned its reputation as a responsive institution.

A comparison of the levels of satisfaction between two groups shows that neither baseline resources (budgets, staff, and members) nor exploited assets (personal credibility and organizational credibility) account for the difference. The organizations that get involved in legislators' political campaigns, however, whether through grassroots volunteer efforts or through financial support, report higher achievement scores than do others. The lobbyists who work with an above-average number of leaders report higher levels of satisfaction (72 percent) than do their counterparts (62 percent).

Conclusion

There is ample evidence, through anecdotal experience and systematic inquiry, that money is an important ingredient in gaining access to policy movers on Capitol Hill. The evidence assembled here enlarges and refines that picture by revealing the nonmonetary assets that link lobbyists to issue leaders in the U.S. House. Occupational groups numerically dominate the scene, and they are visible regardless of an issue's complexity or its obscurity. Citizen groups excel, however, when issues capture extraordinary attention in the media. Administration officials are out in force when the president's autonomy is in question. State and local governmental associations emerge in large numbers when initiatives threaten their turf. The interest group community is not a monolith, unwaveringly dominated by big business and trade associations. Organizations' participation rates ebb and flow with what is at stake, the nature of the issues, and their political environments.

For-profit occupational groups excel in gaining access; they have more money and staffs than other promotional groups. Nonprofits place next, outperforming citizen groups in their stores of money and personnel. Citizen groups, however, possess high numbers of member-volunteers. This pattern of advantage is undermined to some degree when we examine lobbyists' own accounts of what opens doors for them in Congress. From this perspective, for-profit organizations are somewhat constrained. Their representatives cannot evoke organizational credibility the way membership-based groups can. On this dimension, in particular, occupational non-profits and citizen cause-oriented groups have the upper hand. And while all lobbyists, regardless of organization type, tap into both personal and organizational assets, the occupational nonprofits show unparalleled advantage in the diversity of these assets.

Perhaps it is the lobbyists' ingenuity and their diverse resources that explain the remarkable similarity we see when we compare the size and the composition of the leadership networks across group types. With few exceptions, lobbyists, regardless of sponsor and auspice, reach out to incredibly similar combinations of leaders: officeholders more than aides, majority party legislators more than minority party legislators, full committee members more than subcommittee members, and so on.

Congress is indeed a permeable place, and lobbyists find kindred spirits to herald their causes in remarkably similar corners of the institution. The disparities that exist in baseline resources either do not matter in their quest for access or are compensated for by other means. The participants from the most well-endowed organizations are not demonstrably happier than everyone else. Indeed, those in the for-profit category, which includes corporate and business interests, are less satisfied than other types of organizations. Highlighting this difference in perceptions, however, distracts from a more important point. By and large, the advocates are pleased with the policy outcomes the institution produces. Congress upholds its reputation for responsiveness.

Appendix: Sampling Procedures

This analysis is based on personal interviews with advocates chosen randomly from 400 promotional organizations that took a stand on one of six major policies. The initial sample of 180—30 individuals per issue —shrank to 97 because 26 percent of the original group could not be located and roughly 7 percent of those contacted refused to participate.

The focus is exclusively on the U.S. House of Representatives and six "key" bills considered during the 100th Congress. Key bills are defined by *Congressional Quarterly Weekly Reports* as those in which the president's position was known and controversy swirled. The issues differ markedly along two dimensions that affect the policymaking process: the substance of the issue and the political atmosphere in which it is debated.

Through personal interviews, the respondents identified by name anywhere from two to forty-four issue leaders in the House. Because the participants were asked to name "the insiders, who by some mix of position or personal talent attract the attention and compliance of others in the chamber," the lists omit minor players who commanded no following.

Among other things, the advocates assessed whether or not each of the following attributes contributed to their success in gaining Hill access: personal credibility, prior experience with the issue, professional in-kind services, PAC affiliation, and organizational membership.

Note

1. Because some of the participants did not want to disclose this information, the analysis supplements personal interviews with secondary data from such sources as the *Encyclopedia of Associations* (1988). In every category there are extreme outliers, so the group in the middle of each distribution (the median) is used as the cutpoint for comparing the percentage of groups having average and above-average levels of these resources. The medians include a $2 million budget, a staff of 35, and a membership of 7,000. In this sample, farmer cooperatives are counted among the for-profit organizations. And these membership-based groups no doubt account for the for-profits' outstanding showing on this dimension.

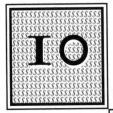

James A. Thurber

Interest Groups and the Congressional Budget Process: Lobbying in the Era of Deficit Politics

DECISIONS about the federal budget are battles over where federal money for public programs will be spent and who will pay for them. They are battles among organized interests in society. It is at the heart of American politics and the essence of interest group politics. Successful budgetary lobbying strategies and techniques are dynamic and adjust to the policy and program under consideration, as has been shown in the congressional budget process from 1974 to present. All kinds of tactics and lobbying techniques are used in the congressional budget process: direct contact with members of Congress and staff, coalition building among groups with common goals, grassroots organization (also "grasstops" and "astroturf"), media campaigns, interest group involvement in election campaigns with finances and volunteers, and high-tech lobbying such as the use of the Internet are all commonly used in trying to influence the formulation and passage of the annual budget in Congress.

If the budget policies being lobbied are macropolitical issues that involve major confrontations between the White House and Congress, such as the proposed cuts in Medicare and Medicaid in the fiscal years 1996 and 1998 budgets, then all strategies are brought to bear on the issue. If the issue is an appropriation of funds for a single project in a congressional district or state, a micropolitical issue, then it is likely that only direct lobbying with a narrow focus and scope of conflict is used. But the most common form of budget decision making is structured around policy systems (congressional committees, executive branch agencies, the specialized media, interest groups, state and local governments, the White House, and other interested stakeholders) that are competitive, dynamic, and require constant adjustment of lobbying techniques, often using the entire range of lobbying tools available to lobbyists. Successful interest groups and lobbyists adapt to the constantly changing realities of the congressional budget process and are part of the policy subsystems that have a direct impact on the federal government issues and programs they follow. The politics of the congressional budget process has been in constant change since 1974 as have the lobbying techniques that have been used to attempt to influence budget making (Thurber 1996). Budget summitry, reform, and most recently the deadlock, government shutdown, and failure of the budget process in 1995 and 1996 are directly linked to the power of special interests and the lobbying techniques they used in American politics. This chapter describes and analyzes these congressional budget reforms and lobbying from 1974 to the present.

The 1994 election of Republican majorities in the House and Senate for the first time in forty years had a direct impact on lobbying the federal budget of the United States (Thurber 1995). The first Republican congressional budget agreement in early 1995 was historic in that it ignored President Clinton's budget preferences and directly confronted hundreds of special interests by proposing to balance the budget by 2002; cut Medicare, Medicaid; reform welfare; eliminate the Department of Commerce (and hundreds of other federal programs); and provide for $245 billion in tax cuts. Upon agreement between the House and Senate over the budget, House Speaker Newt Gingrich (R-Ga.) announced that "throughout the conference, Republicans have been unified in fashioning a budget which keeps our promise to the American people." Senate Majority Leader Robert J. Dole (R-Kans.) stated that the budget agreement would "put more money in the pockets of American families and provide incentives for savings, economic growth and job creation" (Pianin 1995, A1). Congressional Republicans dismissed President Clinton's budget plan, and Clinton dismissed the Republican plan, which actions led to a historic deadlock and weeklong shutdown of the federal government. The congressional Republican Party plan was a major shift from Clinton's first two budgets when he enjoyed unified party government in 1993 and 1994. The confrontation over the fiscal year 1996 budget changed the strategy of most lobbyists on Capitol Hill.

The struggles over the federal budget in the 1990s, whether with unified or divided government, have continued toward a zero-sum game, pitting budgetary commitments and interest groups against one another. Until the 1994 election, the battles tended to favor existing programs and strong interests over new programs and weak interests. Congressional budgeting became more centralized and independent of the president under the Republican leadership of the 104th Congress, thus causing interest groups to focus their attentions at a much higher level in the budget process. Republican budgeting in the 104th Congress was in direct conflict with President Clinton and the desires of many specialized interests. It is centralized, disciplined, and top-down, designed to limit deliberations, the power of agencies and their supportive interest groups, and discourage individualism by members of Congress. Concern about the deficit and cutback management of federal programs, first by President Clinton in his 1992 election campaign and continued with greater earnestness by the Republican Congress in 1995, guaranteed partisan and institutional battles between the president and Congress over the budget and a more complex and difficult environment for organized interests.

To combat rising deficits and improve accountability over the budget process, the congressional budget process has undergone five major reforms in the last two decades: the Congressional Budget and Impoundment Control Act of 1974, the Balanced Budget and Emergency Deficit Control Act of 1985 and 1987 (known as Gramm-Rudman-Hollings or GRH I and II), the Budget Enforcement Act of 1990 (BEA), and the Contract with America agenda of balancing the budget within seven years (see Thurber 1995, 1991; Thelwell 1990; LeLoup, Graham, and Barwick 1987; Havens 1986; Fisher 1985). Supporters of these reforms suggested that they would promote more discipline in congressional budgeting, reduce deficits, control runaway spending, and make the process more timely and effective. In the years since the adoption of the first four reforms, however, concerns about spending, taxing, deficits, debt, and the budget process itself have not abated. The GOP takeover in 1995 brought a new round of budget reform efforts and a major shift in spending and taxing priorities, thus causing major changes in lobbying strategies in Washington, D.C.

Lobbying and the 1974 Congressional Budget Process

The most important change in the way Congress collects and spends money in the past fifty years was the Congressional Budget and Impoundment Control Act of 1974 (also referred to as the Congressional Budget Act).[1] The act forced interest groups and lobbyists to focus on a more centralized and often more open decision-making system in Congress. It created standing Budget committees in the House and in the Senate that are responsible for setting overall tax and spending levels. It also required Congress annually to establish levels of expenditures and revenues with prescribed procedures for arriving at those spending and income totals.

The procedures include three important elements having a direct impact on lobbying in Congress. First, a timetable was established that set deadlines for action on budget-related legislation. This timetable was intended to ensure completion of the budget plan before the start of each fiscal year. Second, the Congressional Budget Act required the annual adoption of concurrent budget resolutions (which do not require presidential approval). Initial concurrent budget resolutions establish targets for total budget authority, budget outlays, and revenues for the upcoming fiscal year. Then, a final "binding" resolution with ceilings on budget authority and outlays and a floor on revenues is adopted. Finally, the act instituted a reconciliation process to conform revenues, spending, and debt legislation to the levels specified in the final budget resolution (Thurber 1987).

These elements required interest groups to follow the budget process at a higher level of aggregation than the traditional decentralized authorization and appropriations processes. It was more difficult to build cozy relationships between the Budget committees and special interests than between those interests and the Authorization committees and Appropriations subcommittees that had jurisdiction over relevant programs. It required lobbyists and groups to build broad-based coalitions, use grassroots lobbying techniques, and use traditional direct lobbying interventions, as was the case before implementation of the new congressional budget process. In addition, term limits were created for House Budget Committee members and chairs to prevent long-term cozy relationships from developing.

The reconciliation process is the procedure under which the Budget committees may direct other committees to determine and recommend revenue and spending actions deemed necessary to conform authorizations and appropriations to the determinations made in the budget resolutions. The Budget committees have the option of mandating that House and Senate committees "report" legislation that will meet budget authority, outlays, and revenue targets (see Schick 1981; Tate 1981). Reconciliation centralizes the budget process by giving the Budget committees the authority to direct one or more of the legislative committees to make changes in existing laws to achieve the desired budget reductions. It adds another complex stage of lobbying for groups that are trying to create, expand, or save government programs.

Reconciliation permits actions to be taken in tandem that would never survive alone, thus making it more difficult for specialized interests to influence the budget process. Combining spending reductions and revenue increases in the same legislation communicates "shared sacrifice" to the American public and allows members of Congress to build a coalition to reduce the deficit, as was the case in 1995. The use of reconciliation made basic changes in the budget much more open and competitive, thus making lobbying for specific programs over others much more difficult.

Lobbying the Budget Process
under Budgetary Constraints

By the early 1980s projected budget deficits were about $200 billion, far more than ever before experienced.[2] The Office of Management and Budget (OMB) estimated the FY 1990 deficit at $218.5 billion in July 1990 (the final figure was $195 billion) and the FY 1991 deficit at $269.4 billion—$205 billion over the GRH target (see table 10.1). Changing economic conditions and adjustments in the estimates for expenditures for the savings and loan bailout continued the FY 1991 deficit estimate to rise to nearly $331 billion by October (Kee and Nystrom 1991).

Congress, concerned with its continuing inability to control large deficits, turned to more drastic measures: the Balanced Budget and Emergency

TABLE 10.1

DEFICIT REDUCTION TARGETS AND ACTUAL DEFICITS,
FY 1986–96[a] (IN BILLIONS OF DOLLARS)

Year	1985 GRH limits	1987 GRH limits	1990 BEA limits	CBO deficit projections[b]	Actual deficits
1986	172	—	—		221
1987	144	—	—		150
1988	108	144	—		155
1989	72	136	—		152
1990	36	100	—		195
1991	0	64	327	331	269
1992	—	28	317	425	290
1993	—	0	236	348	255
1994	—	—	102	318	203[d]
1995	—	—	83	162[c]	193[d]
1996	—	—	—	176[d]	174[e]

a. CBO estimates of the deficit taken from *An Analysis of the President's Budgetary Proposals for Fiscal Year 1991* (Washington, D.C.: Congressional Budget Office, March 1990), 8; and *The Economic and Budget Outlook: An Update* (Washington, D.C.: Congressional Budget Office, July 1990), x.

b. Deficit projections excluding social security and postal service from CBO, *Economic and Budget Outlook: An Update,* August 1991, xiii. Note: The budget figures include social security, which is off-budget but is counted for the purposes of the Balanced Budget Act targets. For comparability with the targets, the projections exclude the Postal Service, which is also off-budget.

c. These deficit figures are from CBO, *The Economic and Budget Outlook: Update,* August 1994, 31.

d. These deficit figures are from the Office of Management and Budget as reported in the *Washington Post,* 7 February 1995, A13.

e. *Historical Tables, Budget of the United States Government, Fiscal Year 1998* (Washington, D.C.: Government Printing Office, July 1997), 20.

Deficit Control Acts of 1985 and 1987. The GRH legislation revised established budgetary deadlines for each of the major aspects of the congressional budget process in order to bring more discipline to congressional budgeting, to make the process more efficient, and to focus attention on reducing the deficit. These deadlines significantly altered prior budget process deadlines. Notably, the new deadlines have been delayed or modified each year since GRH I and GRH II were passed.

The central enforcement mechanism of GRH is a series of automatic spending cuts that occur if the federal budget does not meet or fall within $10 billion of the deficit targets; these automatic spending cuts are referred to as *sequestration* (Penner and Abramson 1988). Sequestration requires federal spending be cut automatically if Congress and the president do not enact laws to reduce the deficit to the maximum deficit amount allowed for that year. If the proposed federal budget did not meet the annual deficit targets established by GRH (listed in table 10.1), then the president had to make across-the-board spending cuts evenly divided between domestic and defense programs until those targets were met. Most entitlement programs (then approximately 43 percent of the budget) and interest payments (then approximately 14 percent of the budget) were "off-budget," partially or totally exempt from the potential cuts.

The 1985 GRH legislation gave the General Accounting Office (GAO) the responsibility for triggering the across-the-board cuts. In 1986, the Supreme Court, in *Bowsher* v. *Sinar* (106 S.Ct. 3181), declared that part of the legislation to be unconstitutional because it gave the GAO, a legislative support agency, executive functions. The Supreme Court's decision would have prevented the implementation of GRH, but Congress responded by passing a revised version of the act in 1987 (GRH II). GRH II altered the original GRH deficit-reduction plan by directing the Office of Management and Budget (OMB), an executive agency, to issue the report that would trigger sequestration if deficit-reduction targets were not met. GRH II also revised the original deficit-reduction targets in accordance with more realistic economic assumptions.

The Failure of GRH and the Success of Specialized Interests

The Gramm-Rudman-Hollings deficit-reduction plan promised long-term progress toward lower deficits and a balanced budget, but these goals proved to be elusive and overly optimistic. But since the Gramm-Rudman-Hollings balanced budget legislation was enacted in 1985 and revised in 1987, the deficit was never as low as the law requires. The failure of GRH reflects the power and success of strong specialized interests maintaining full funding and tax expenditures for the programs they monitor. Some of the largest parts of the budget that have well-organized interests in society, such as Social Security, Medicare, and veterans benefits, could not be touched by sequestration.

GRH sequestration was supposed to threaten the interests of all participants (including organized interests outside of Congress) in the congressional budget process enough to make them want to avoid it. But the threat of sequestration did not have the intended effect. Comparing the projected impacts of sequestration on their favored programs with the potential impact of cuts from regular legislation, lobbyists and policymakers simply decided that their interests were better served by delaying the passage of bills until after sequestration occurred.

Two other factors contributed to the failure of GRH. The most important was that sequestration could be avoided by using overly optimistic economic and technical assumptions as substitutes for actual policy changes, a common practice in recent years. Also the enforcement of the deficit targets was not effective after the final budget "snapshot." Before 1990, Congress evaluated the budget only once a year to ascertain whether it was meeting the GRH deficit-reduction targets. The result was a "snapshot" of the budgetary situation. After that evaluation, Congress was free to add new expenditures to the budget, which often increased the budget deficit. After the snapshot was taken, indicating that the deficit target had been met, legislation could be adopted that raised the deficit in the current year and following years as well (see Schick 1988, 52).

The Budget and Impoundment Control Act and Gramm-Rudman-Hollings I and II, despite their expressed goals, did not curb the growth of federal spending, bring an end to the growth in uncontrollable spending, reduce the deficit, force Congress to complete budgeting processes on time, reorder national spending priorities, allow Congress to control fiscal policy, eliminate the need for continuing resolutions, or reduce the power of specialized interests. Clearly something more needed to be done to counteract these problems; that turned out to be the 1990 Budget Enforcement Act.

Lobbying in a Zero-Sum Game

By early 1990, it was obvious to congressional budgeteers and those lobbying the process that the balanced budget target was not going to be reached. The deficit in 1993, the year in which the revised targets were to require a balanced budget, turned out to be $255 billion; thus the budgetary rules were changed again with passage of the Omnibus Budget Reconciliation Act of 1990 (OBRA 1990). The significant programmatic and procedural restrictions made in spending and taxing resulted in reducing the deficit by almost $500 billion over a five-year period (1991 through 1995). The bipartisan agreement was intended to bring more control over spending while easing potential conflicts over the budget, allowing more efficient negotiated compromises to difficult economic and political questions, solving the problems of increasing deficits, and providing political cover over unpopular election-year decisions (Yang and Mufson 1991).

The 1990 BEA reforms further centralized power within Congress by forcing Congress and coalitions of interest groups to make "zero-sum" choices: that is, trading visible reductions in one program for visible increases in another, or tax cuts for some in exchange for tax increases for others. The BEA included changes in substantive law and budgetary procedures designed to bring more top-down party leadership control over the budget process and to reduce the deficit, thus increasing the centralization of budgetary decision making and the power of interest groups. In December 1990 the Congressional Budget Office (CBO) estimated that the tax hikes, spending cuts, and procedural changes of the BEA summit agreement promised to reduce the cumulative deficit by about $496 billion for the 1991–95 period (CBO 1990a). The most visible change was the elimination of fixed deficit targets as established in GRH I and II, but other innovations—such as categorical sequesters, pay-as-you-go (PAYGO) provisions on taxes and spending, and a new enhanced role for the OMB—had a major impact on the budgetary powers within Congress and for the president and further forced changes in the strategies of lobbyists (see Doyle and McCaffrey 1991).

The 1990 budget reform changed the process of sequestration, or automatic cuts in programs if deficit limits were not met, that had been the hallmark of the GRH legislation. The 1990 BEA requires a specified amount of savings for each of five years covered by a multiyear budget plan. Through FY 1993, sequestration was not linked to the total federal budget but to discretionary spending (spending for programs that must be appropriated each year) "ceilings" in three categories of government programs: defense, domestic, and international (Kee and Nystrom 1991, 8). The BEA eliminated the $10 billion cushion between the actual deficit and deficit targets for FY 1991 and 1993 that was the norm under GRH.

Perhaps the most significant aspect of the BEA reforms are the spending ceilings it establishes, a serious limit for those lobbying for expanded program funding. The ceiling of each discretionary spending category (defense, domestic, and international) is enforced by an end-of-session sequestration applied across the board to all the programs *within* the category or categories that exceed their spending limits (e.g., if the ceiling for discretionary spending in the international category is exceeded, the end-of-session sequester applies to all programs within the international category). This process is referred to as "categorical sequestration." It is triggered only if the spending limits of any or all the categories are exceeded due to changes in legislation (e.g., an extension of the benefits of a program or of the number of people eligible to receive benefits or tax cuts). If the spending limits are exceeded because of changes in economic conditions (or, as is the case with many domestic programs, the number of eligible recipients increases), sequestration would not be triggered. If more is appropriated for discretionary spending than is allowed under the discretionary limits, automatic sequestrations will be imposed but only on the accounts in the category in which the breach has occurred.

In FY 1994 and 1995, the system was supposed to return to fixed deficit targets enforced by the same sequestration rules used prior to the 1990 act, but President Clinton wanted to reduce the deficit further so he proposed another five-year deficit-reduction package. The goal of this plan was to reduce cumulative budget deficits by a total of $500 billion between fiscal years 1994 and 1998. With few changes, the Congress passed the 1993 OBRA with a codified new five-year deficit-reduction plan that embraced tax increases, discretionary spending cuts, and more stringent limitations on discretionary spending. The BEA's enforcement procedures, including the discretionary caps and the PAYGO process, were extended through 1998. There continued to be spending ceilings for defense, international, and domestic discretionary programs in FY 1994 and 1995. All these changes created a zero-sum game for lobbyists. To have expanded funding for a federal program, those lobbying for the program had to show where the money was going to come from; because it would not come from taxes, it had to come from cuts in other programs. Powerful groups thus found themselves competing against one another.

The 1990 BEA and President Clinton's 1993 Omnibus Budget Reconciliation Act called for all tax and direct spending legislation to be "deficit neutral" in each year through FY 1998. This major reform was called a pay-as-you-go procedure. PAYGO cuts nonexempt entitlement spending automatically to make up for any increase in the deficit due to the passage of legislation that increases entitlement benefits or extends benefits to more people or legislation that would lead to revenue reductions. This makes the budget process a zero-sum game, the most important consequence of the budget reforms of the 1990s for interest groups and lobbyists. It forced organized interests to fight each other or join broad coalitions to lobby for tax expenditures or increases in spending.

PAYGO reforms were not necessarily intended to reduce the deficit but to limit growth in spending and deficits by requiring that new expenditures be linked to cuts in expenditures for existing programs or to tax increases (CBO 1990b). According to former CBO Director Robert D. Reischauer, "To date, this pay-as-you-go requirement has proved to be an effective poison pill that has killed a number of legislative efforts to cut taxes and expand entitlement" (Reischauer 1991). The primary impact of PAYGO has been to dampen lobbying for new spending. The difficulty of either raising taxes or cutting popular existing mandatory programs (like Social Security) has resulted in PAYGO effectively closing out new mandatory programs (like Clinton's 1993 health-care reforms). In the FY 1996 budget deadlock, the PAYGO provision made it much more difficult for all parties to negotiate an agreement to balance the budget in seven years.

Lobbying a Centralized Budget Process

Before the budget reforms of 1974, 1985, 1987, and 1990 were passed, the stable roles, relationships, and routines of the president, OMB, executive branch agencies, congressional party leaders, congressional committees, and interest groups led to few surprises in the federal budget process. Predictable "preferential" pluralistic incrementalism with a narrow scope and low level of political conflict predominated over distributive budgetary processes (Jones 1994). Since 1974, two oil crises, stagflation, high interest rates, Reaganomics, large deficits, and debt have changed the economy and destabilized the budget process. Reagan-era tax cuts forced Congress to make redistributive budget decisions that widened the number of organized interests in the conflict over the budget and increased the conflict's visibility. A consequence of the budget reforms since 1974 has been increased budgetary conflict, confusion, visibility of decisions, stalemate between Congress and the president, and deadlock among the interest groups.

The budget reforms centralized budget decisions and caused some jockeying for jurisdictional turf between the Budget committees and the other standing committees, especially the Appropriations and Taxing committees, thus shifting the focus of lobbying the process. The Authorization committees have lost power because of the Appropriations committees' right to cap new back-door spending.[3] The 1974 budget reforms restricted the Authorization committees' use of contract authority and borrowing authority. But pre-1974 entitlement programs and net interest payments continue to reduce the ability of both Congress and the president to control the budget.

The 1974 budget act requires all standing committees to estimate the cost of programs within their jurisdiction early in the budget cycle. These estimates of authorization tend to limit the committees' freedom and that of executive agencies and interest groups, which have a natural tendency to push for new programs and higher authorizations. The committees are forced to state priorities and to make difficult choices among programs very early in the process; they are much less vulnerable to twelfth-hour lobbying by agencies and strong, well-organized interest groups. Before the 1974 reform program, authorization levels were commonly double and even triple the final appropriations. The Authorization committees would often approve programs at very high levels to placate strong pressures from outside Congress, knowing full well that the Appropriations committees would decrease the funding to more reasonable levels. After 1974 and GRH, the Authorization committees could no longer play this game. The requirement to estimate program costs reduces the gap between authorizations and appropriations and puts a cap on the political pressures from agencies and interest groups.

Interest groups and lobbyists now find it necessary to work Congress constantly in order to win spending battles. They cannot simply rely on direct contacts with a few powerful members on key committees of jurisdiction over the issues they are following. In the 1990s the process is relatively open and thus more difficult for lobbyists and specialized interests, forcing them to bargain more openly with members of Congress and to monitor the budget process carefully and continually. Lobbyists attend Budget Committee hearings and markups, but they also try to sit at the bargaining table with Budget Committee leaders when they mark up the final budget resolutions, as was the case in the 104th Congress.

The Impact of Budget Reforms in the 1990s on Organized Interests

The budget reforms of the 1990s have affected the budget process, the internal workings of Congress, congressional-presidential budgetary powers, and lobbying by external organized interests (Thurber 1989; Thurber and Durst 1991). Collectively, the budget reforms of the 1990s establish more budget control, expand the power of the Appropriations committees, and narrow the scope of influence other committees had enjoyed because the changes establish a zero-sum budget game. At the same time, the congressional budget process is made more accessible and accountable to the public, interest groups, and the administration by publicly revealing the tradeoffs that must been made in discretionary and entitlement program spending. A zero-sum game with controls on the number of behind-the-scenes budget tricks that can be played makes the budget process more visible to everyone. Although the combination of an open and more accountable zero-sum budget game may have the potential for more conflict over the budget, the 1990 reforms were *intended* to create a more congenial budget process. The 1990 and 1993 budget agreements assured that the president and the Congress would not fight over the size of the deficit, but they would battle over domestic discretionary spending in a controlled zero-sum budget game. However, the battle to balance the budget was center stage again in the 104th and 105th Congresses.

Notably, the 1990 and 1993 reforms have had mixed consequences for the distribution of power within Congress and for the power of lobbyists outside Congress. The pay-as-you-go, zero-sum reforms had a centralizing impact: the reforms discouraged individual members from initiating their own "budget proposals" (with the help of outside interests) because cuts and revenue enhancements had to be instituted in other programs in order to save their proposals. On the other hand, stricter enforcement of categorical sequestration, PAYGO provisions, and taking the Social Security Trust Fund surplus "off-budget" raised the public's understanding of spending priorities and the specter of heavy lobbying; intensifying pressure on members and committees to protect their favorite programs and to make cuts in other programs. Such controls also centralized budget decision making with the party leadership and the Budget committees, institutions with the power to negotiate tradeoffs in the zero-sum game, as shown clearly with the Republican leadership in the 104th Congress. Reconciliation, Congressional Budget Act (CBA) 302(b) constraints, and the 1990 BEA categorical sequestration centralized power by calling for more top-down budgeting.

Although the more rigid constraints set by the 1990 BEA have further reduced the autonomy of the Appropriations committees, most budget participants argue that the Appropriations committees were the big winners in the 1990 pact. The new budget process rules diminish the role of the House and Senate Budget committees, by giving more degrees of freedom to the Appropriations panels. One budget expert summarized this shift: "Since the pot of money the Appropriations Committees will have to work with has already been decided, they needn't wait for a spending outline from the Budget committees before divvying it up" (Yang 1991, A12).

Appropriators are more able to determine the legislative details within the BEA constraints than through the old reconciliation process and sequestration under GRH. The appropriators have more control over "backdoor spending," which has been done regularly by the authorizers in reconciliation bills. The budget process reforms of the 1990s also encouraged appropriators to favor "pain-deferral budgeting" or slow-spending programs over fast-spending programs in order to reduce the projected spending for the next year. An example of pain-deferral budgeting was the failure of Congress (and the administration) to terminate major programs whose budgetary requirements are likely to escalate sharply in future years, such as the space station, although they did cut the Superconducting Supercollider (SSC). "The camel's nose is being allowed under the tent; next year the camel's shoulders will want in, and then his hump," according to CBO's Reischauer (CBO 1990a). All of this changed with the drive to balance the budget in seven years by the Republican 104th Congress.

The budget reforms of the 1990s have made the congressional budget process more open to the public and interest groups. The discretionary spending limits and PAYGO controls over entitlement spending for five years were visible and well known to all the players. The 1990 BEA new rules reduced degrees of freedom for the actors while revealing the budget decisions to interest groups and the administration.

According to Irene Rubin, "closing the budget process is often considered one way to help control increases in expenditures; opening it is usually a way of increasing expenditures" (Rubin 1993, 66). The BEA attempted to do the opposite; it opens up the process and places more controls on expenditures. The reforms opened the process and revealed the tradeoffs within mandatory spending and the three discretionary spending categories, thus putting tough spending and taxing decisions in full public view.

The 1990 and 1993 budget agreements simplified the process only if members abide by the agreement. The innovations tend to work at cross-purposes when it comes to timeliness. A five-year budget agreement theoretically should make it easier to pass budget resolutions on time. If the budget resolutions are not passed on time, the appropriators may still pass money bills, which was not the case in 1995.

But several other reforms of the 1990s increased the complexity and thus the potential delay in Capitol Hill budget making. Steps in the process have multiplied, as have the decision-making rules. Typically, the more complex the process, the more time it consumes. Categorical sequestration and PAYGO provisions have slowed the process by increasing the number of confrontations within Congress and between Congress and the president. Alternatively, confrontations increase complexity and delay in the process as more cuts (or tax increases) are required to meet the caps. Already vexing budget decisions were made more difficult for lobbyists because of the budget process changes of the 1990s.

The Contract with America and Budgetary Lobbying

The 1994 congressional election transformed the budget reform agenda significantly. The major impact of the 1994 election and the Republican Contract with America was to bring the balanced budget amendment, the line-item veto, and the unfunded mandate reform to the top of the congressional budget reform agenda.

The foundation of the Contract budget reforms were proposals developed in the 1990s. The 1990s brought numerous recommendations for budget process reforms that promised to reduce the deficit and balance the budget. More than forty budget reform proposals were introduced in the 103d Congress, such as the drive to require a balanced budget, to limit the size or growth of the federal budget or of the public debt, or some combination of these ideas. The basic thrust of these reforms was that "total outlays shall not exceed total receipts for a fiscal year." Another popular reform was the line-item veto/enhanced or expedited rescissions (fifty of these proposals were introduced in the 103d Congress). A CBO listing of budget process reform legislation in the 103d Congress included 186 major budget process reform proposals, most being the balanced budget amendment and the line-item veto/enhanced rescission (Joyce 1994). The Joint Committee on the Organization of Congress (JCOC) considered dozens of budget proposals, but none was adopted in the 103d Congress.

The first promise in the Contract with America in the 104th Congress was the Balanced Budget Amendment (HJ Res. 1), a constitutional amendment requiring the president to propose and Congress to adopt a balanced budget each fiscal year starting in FY 2002 (or for the second fiscal year following its ratification) (see table 10.2). Congress may not adopt a budget resolution in which total outlays exceed total receipts unless three-fifths of the membership of each house approves. Congress may waive these provisions for any fiscal year in which a declaration of war is in effect or the country faces "an imminent and serious military threat to national security." A majority of each chamber must pass and the president must sign a joint resolution identifying the threat. This was a popular proposal with the public. A Gallup poll conducted 28 November 1994 revealed that 77 percent of those questioned ranked the amendment either a top or high-priority item for the 104th Congress. Congress had previously rejected several balanced budget amendments since the first one was introduced in 1936. The closest Congress had come to passing one was in 1986 when the Senate defeated the proposal by a single vote.

The second major budget reform in the Contract with America was the Line-Item Veto Act (HR 2), which gives the president a permanent legisla-

TABLE 10.2
MAJOR BUDGET PROCESS REFORM PROPOSALS
OF THE 104TH CONGRESS

The line-item veto (House vote: 430–1)
Unfunded mandate reform (House vote: 418–0)
Budget reform (House vote: 421–6)
Prohibit authorizations of less than two years
Abolish baseline budgeting
Restore "firewalls" between defense and nondefense discretionary spending
Three-fifths super majority for tax increases (House vote: 279–152)
Balanced budget amendment (HJ Res. 1) (House vote: 300–132)

SOURCE: *Congressional Quarterly Weekly Report*, January 1995–April 1996.

tive line-item veto. Under this procedure, the president may strike or reduce any discretionary budget authority or eliminate any targeted tax provision in any bill. The president must prepare a separate rescissions package for each piece of legislation and must submit his proposal to Congress within five working days after the original legislation arrives on his desk. The president's proposed rescissions take effect unless Congress passes a disapproval bill within thirty legislative days after receiving them. The disapproval bill must pass by a simple majority vote in both houses. The president can veto the disapproval bill, and Congress will then need a two-thirds majority in both houses to override. This confers substantial new budgetary powers on the president. Proponents of the line-item veto maintained that given large deficits, the president should have the authority to single out "unnecessary and wasteful" spending provisions in bills passed by Congress. Critics of the line-item veto argue that the line-item veto cedes too much power to the executive branch to control federal spending, a responsibility clearly given to the legislative branch in the U.S. Constitution.

The Unfunded Mandate Reform Act (HR 5) amended the 1974 Budget Act (PL 93-344) to restrict the imposition of unfunded requirements (mandates) by the federal government on state and local government entities. Unfunded mandates are provisions in federal legislation that impose enforceable duties on state and local governments without appropriating funds to pay for them. Examples of unfunded mandates include provisions in most environmental legislation (e.g., the Clear Air Act Amendments of 1990, the Clean Water Act, and the Safe Drinking Water Act), the Motor Voter Act, and the Americans for Disabilities Act. The bill established a Commission on Unfunded Federal Mandates to investigate and review the impact of current unfunded state, local, and private entities. According to the reform, the commission must report to Congress and the president (within nine months after enactment) recommendations for suspending, consolidating, simplifying, or terminating mandates, as well as suggesting flexible means and common standards for complying with mandates. The bill requires federal agencies to assess the effects of federal regulations on state, local, tribal, and private-sector entities. CBO is required to prepare an impact statement assessing the cost of the proposed mandates for any legislation. The CBO statement must detail estimates of the total direct costs of compliance exceeding $100 million in the first five years. The bill repeals mandates at the beginning of any fiscal year in which no funds are provided to cover their costs and assigns responsibility to determine the appropriate mandate funding levels to the Budget committees.

The balanced budget amendment, line-item veto, and unfunded mandate reform all (1) favor a more conservative agenda for federal spending, (2) increase complexity, (3) shift power between the president and Congress, and (4) have a major impact of the nature of lobbying the budget process. Further cutbacks in federal spending and federal legislation would occur as a result of these three Contract with America reforms. Adoption of the presidential line-item veto substantially decreases congressional power to control budget outcomes. Not only the president gained a power-ful tool for preventing funds from being distributed in accordance with the wishes of Congress, but he is able to use the threat of the line-item veto to negotiate and build support for his budget and other policies. The drive to balance the budget by 2002 by the Republican leadership (primarily in the House) in the 104th and 105th Congresses helped centralize budget deci-sions around the leadership and the Budget committees, increasing the level of conflict and forcing lobbyists to make appeals to the leadership, rather than to specific Authorization and Appropriations subcommittees of juris-diction.

Lobbying the Budget after the 1994 Election

The major impact of the 1994 election and the Contract with America was on the House of Representatives (not the Senate) in the budget process. Speaker Newt Gingrich attempted to centralize power in the House and wanted to become the strongest Speaker since Thomas Bracket Reed and Joseph G. Cannon around the turn of the twentieth century. Because of a strong, unified party that ran on a common ideology, the Contract, Ging-rich effectively consolidated power in the Speakership and dominated the budget process until December 1995. This forced lobbyists to work with the leadership, build broad coalitions, or go to the public through grass-roots strategies to save or dramatically change programs they support. Af-ter December 1995 when the negotiations over the FY 1996 budget became mired in deadlock with President Clinton, Republican members of the House became more difficult to control. The more traditional individual-ism of the members began to undermine the discipline and centralization of the leadership's control of the budget process. Speaker Gingrich enjoyed high levels of loyalty from the GOP in the House until the spring 1996 budget negotiations and the impending 1996 election changed the behavior of House Republicans. The loyalty of Republicans, and especially Republi-can freshmen, to their party was exceedingly high in the first session of the 104th Congress. The party unity scores were 92 for veteran House Repub-licans and 94 for freshman Republicans, compared to 82 for veteran Dem-ocrats and 87 for freshman Democrats. The loyalty of the Republican Budget Committee members was especially impressive compared to Demo-crat Budget members and the 102d Congress with President Bush. The House and Senate GOP members of the Budget committees in the 104th Congress had party unity scores of 93 and 91, respectively, compared to the House and Senate Democrats with party unity scores of 80 and 85. The party unity scores of House GOP Budget Committee members increased dramatically from the 102d Congress when they had a score of 79. The highest party unity score (96) of Budget Committee members was the House freshmen GOP in the 104th Congress (Thurber 1995b).

The symbiotic relationship between House GOP freshmen and Speaker Gingrich paid off in their strong support for his early negotiations over the FY 1996 budget but fell apart during the final confrontation with President Clinton in the spring of 1996 and the decentralized construction of the FY 1997 budget. Gingrich helped build this unity through several dramatic actions. He effectively appointed all the chairs of House committees, ignoring seniority by passing over the most senior members in several cases, including the Appropriations Committee. Chairmen feel they owe their positions to him (and the Republican Conference), rather than to seniority. He restricted the power of the chairs by placing term limits of six years on their positions. He also pushed through a ban on proxy voting by the chairs, which undermines their ability to act independently of the Speaker in the budget process. He made all freshman committee assignments, putting freshmen on the Rules, Ways and Means, Appropriations (six out of eleven open Republican appointments), and Commerce committees. Putting freshmen on the four most important committees in the House is unprecedented and has helped build exceedingly high party unity scores from House GOP freshmen both on and off the Budget Committee. Three-fifths of the Republicans have been elected to the House in the past two elections; many feel they owe their seats to Gingrich and are naturally his backers generally and in the budget process specifically. The consequences of the 1994 elections and the subsequent reforms in the House have been to centralize budget power in the House leadership until the spring of 1996 and the decentralization of the process into the House Appropriations subcommittees, Ways and Means, and several Authorization committees. There were fewer roadblocks within the House to putting together a balanced budget until popular opinion reacted to the proposed cuts in Medicare, Medicaid, education, and environmental regulations.

Conclusion

Specific policy outcomes did not change dramatically as a result of the budget process reforms during the past twenty years. Change came as a result of the transformational 1994 election and the will of Congress and the president to balance the budget within a specific number of years. The real growth in government spending happened almost automatically through pluralistic incrementalism and the strength of specialized interests over the past fifty years. Interest groups, agencies, and committees were as successful under the 1974 budget process and GRH in protecting their base funding and securing their "fair share" of increase as they were before Congress centralized budgetary decision making. No major groups were significantly disadvantaged by budget reform until the new budgetary priorities of the Republican 104th Congress were established. No major programs were cut until the partisan change came in both the House and Senate after the 1994 election. No congressional committees tried to abolish major programs under their jurisdiction until the 104th Congress. Spending priorities were not greatly changed as a direct result of the 1974 budget process reforms, GRH, and the 1990 BEA. Change came with a new will of the Republican members of the House and the strong desire to balance the budget in seven years.

The BEA further diffused the target of responsibility for spending and the deficit (although the latter is dropping rapidly). In a complex budget process, who will be blamed (or get credit) for the deficit? Not the Budget committees, the Tax committees, the Appropriations committees, the party leadership, or the president. President Clinton understood this with his FY 1996 budget proposal that abandoned serious deficit reduction. Clinton's FY 1996 budget invited the Republicans to show how they could balance the budget while cutting taxes and increasing defense spending. Realizing that he was not getting credit for deficit reduction, Clinton "punted the ball" to the Republicans to pursue the politically thankless task of deficit reduction. They proposed major cuts in Medicare, Medicaid, education, the income tax credit, and other social welfare programs in their drive to balance the budget. This led to a major confrontation over the scope and role of the federal government and pushed special interests to the side of the battle. Members of Congress learned that Americans did not like the government shutdown and cuts in popular programs, so the FY 1997 budget was passed quickly with the lead from the Appropriations committees, the traditional focus on lobbying in the allocation of federal dollars.

Budgets are political documents, and budgetary battles will continue to hold center stage for both Congress and lobbyists. Budget and party leaders will continue to build coalitions in the formulation of the budget and to negotiate with the president about spending priorities, as was the case in divided party government under President Bush and unified party government under President Clinton and again under divided party government after the 1994 election. The major impact of the 1990 pact and the 1994 Republican win on lobbying the congressional budget process is a tighter zero-sum budget game with more control, top-down, centralized budgeting by the congressional party leadership. The tradeoffs between program reductions and increases are more visible at the aggregate level, as are tax reductions and increases, but the responsibility for them is more diffuse. The emphasis of the 1990 BEA reforms was on spending, not deficits, and the budget battles of the 104th Congress was on deficits and program cuts.

The lobbying strategies have been over spending priorities and cuts in programs within zero-sum limits defined by the reforms of the 1990s and the realities of a more conservative and centralized leadership in the House. These reforms make spending tradeoffs more visible and impose more control over the process. The reforms have added more complexity to budget making and thus lobbying (e.g., categorical caps on discretionary spending and PAYGO) and enlarged the roles of budget and party leaders, thus reducing individualism and the power of organized groups external to Congress. Ultimately, conflict over further centralization of budget power is inevitable; however, the impact of the budget process in the 104th Congress was to reduce the power of special interests.

The features that make the Budget Enforcement Act, the Balanced Budget Act, and other reforms in the 1990s insulated Congress from accountability also make it difficult to assign responsibility for the growth of the federal budget or the size of the deficit. The reality of the congressional budget process in the 104th Congress is the opposite. It is open and transparent. The policy differences between the president and Congress are clear. The centralized drive in Congress to balance the budget has hurt many specific organized interests. Accountability is clear in the era of the Contract with America.

Congressional budgeting has become more democratic yet more conflicted. Frequently, the result is policymaking gridlock as was the case over the FY 1996 budget. Congress is fundamentally a representative institution with access for interest groups and lobbyists. Because it responds to political pressures from organized groups and public preferences generally, any effort to make the budget process more efficient is in direct conflict with its constitutional design and natural state. The struggle inside Congress vacilates between centralization and decentralization of authority as shown clearly in 1995 (centralized budgeting) and 1996 and 1997 (decentralized budgeting), and it will continue to cause delay, deadlock, and even a breakdown in congressional-presidential budgeting until the American people wish something different.

The centralization of power over the budget process in the House in 1995 and the increased discipline of the congressional Republican Party reduced the power of many organized interests outside Congress, which in turn led to increased campaign contributions, grassroots activity, and coalition building among special interests. Further change in lobbying strategies and techniques regarding the federal budget came in 1996 as a result of the impending 1996 elections and turnover in membership, as it did in 1994. If voters want a balanced budget, Congress will respond, and successful interest groups and lobbyists will adjust to an even tighter zero-sum budgetary game, just as they did in the battles over the FY 1995 and 1996 budgets.

Acknowledgments

I would like to thank the School of Public Affairs and the Center for Congressional and Presidential Studies at American University for supporting the research for this analysis. This chapter is partially based on interviews with White House staff, House and Senate members, staff, and informed observers. I am grateful for the time they gave and for their observations about the congressional budget process. I would especially like to thank Dr. Patrick J. Griffin, assistant to the president for legislative affairs, for his insights about the relationship between President Clinton's White House, Congress, and interest groups in the congressional budget process.

Notes

1. One of the important reforms instituted by the 1974 Budget Act was the creation of the Congressional Budget Office (CBO). This agency serves as Congress's principal source of information and analysis on the budget, and on spending and revenue legislation. The CBO has a specific mandate to assist the House and Senate Budget Committees and the Spending and Revenue committees. Secondarily, it responds to requests for information from other committees and individual members of Congress. Prior to the creation of CBO, Congress was forced to rely on the president's budget estimates and economic forecasts and the annual analysis of the economy and fiscal policy done by the Joint Economic Committee.

2. Another measure of budget deficit problems is the imbalance of outlays and receipts as a percentage of the gross national product (GNP). The deficit is declining as a percentage of GNP. For example, outlays were 24.3 percent of the GNP and receipts were 18.1 percent of the GNP in 1983; 23.7 percent outlays to 18.4 percent revenues in 1986; and 22.2 percent outlays to 19.2 percent revenues in 1989. See U.S. Congress, Congressional Budget Office, *The Economic and Budget Outlook: Fiscal Years 1991–1995* (January 1990), appendix E, table E-2, at 123.

3. There are three kinds of back-door spending techniques: *Contract authority* permits agencies to enter into contracts that subsequently must be liquidated by appropriations. *Borrowing authority* allows agencies to spend money they have borrowed from the public or the Treasury. *Mandatory entitlements* grant eligible individuals and governments the right to receive payments from the national government.

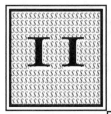

11   John R. Wright

Tobacco Industry PACs and the Nation's Health: A Second Opinion

IT HAS been more than two decades since data on campaign contributions from special interests to members of Congress first became publicly available. These data have spawned countless studies by academic scholars, journalists, and other analysts into the relationship between special interest money and congressional voting. Within this considerable body of research, there still is no consensus about whether and to what extent campaign money determines legislative outcomes (Grenzke 1990; Smith 1995). There is, however, a noticeable difference in the analytical methods used by academic scholars and those used by journalists and other analysts, and there is also a noticeable difference in research conclusions. In general, academic scholars tend to be much more careful about controlling for possible influences other than PAC money and, as a result, have generally discovered *weaker* relationships between PAC contributions and legislative voting than journalists and those interested in reform or other policy agendas (see Sorauf 1988, 307–17; Sorauf 1992, 20–28, 163–74).

A recent study of the impact of campaign contributions from the tobacco industry on congressional voting provides a vivid illustration of the differences in methods and conclusions between academic scholars and analysts advocating specific policy agendas (Moore, Wolfe, Lindes, and Douglas 1994). As reported in a *Journal of the American Medical Association (JAMA)* study, the strongest explanation for congressional opposition to tobacco-control legislation during the 102d Congress was the money that representatives received from tobacco industry political action committees. The authors of the study alleged that tobacco contributions "strongly influence the federal tobacco policy process," and that the ability of the tobacco industry to thwart tobacco-control legislation through campaign money contributed to the loss of "hundreds of thousands of lives a year" (Moore, Wolfe, Lindes, and Douglas 1994, 1171).

This chapter offers a second opinion on the diagnosis reported in the *JAMA* study. On further analysis, it turns out that PAC contributions from the tobacco industry only *weakly* affected congressional voting decisions on important tobacco-related issues. In fact, the evidence indicates that had the tobacco industry made no campaign contributions whatsoever from 1987 to 1992, congressional policy in 1992 would have been no different than it was given the full participation of the tobacco PACs. The critical flaw of the *JAMA* study is its failure to take into account the ideological divisions in congressional voting on tobacco issues. The scope of political conflict over tobacco-related issues in recent years has expanded to include concerns of public health in addition to the traditional economic issues of tobacco production and marketing. As a result, tobacco-related issues now involve broad ideological conflict between those who advocate or oppose stronger governmental regulation of tobacco as a means of providing for the public's health. This conflict is fundamental to representatives' basic liberal-conservative philosophies and bears directly on their voting decisions.

In the remainder of this chapter, I reexamine the relationship between tobacco industry contributions and congressional voting and present what I believe to be a more realistic assessment of the impact of the tobacco industry's PACs on national tobacco policy. I begin by first providing an overview of the methodological issues involved in specifying and estimating congressional voting models. Next, I discuss the specific theoretical and methodological issues that gave rise to the incorrect diagnosis in the *JAMA* study; and, finally, I present new estimates of the impact of tobacco PAC money on roll-call voting in the U.S. Senate.

An Overview of Congressional Voting Models

One of the principal ways political scientists study legislative behavior is by constructing and testing statistical models of roll-call voting. In the context of legislative voting, a voting model is simply a precise description of the factors believed to determine a representative's announcement of yea or nay. Roll-call voting models are constructed from specific hypotheses about how legislators make decisions, and these specific hypotheses are typically derived from one or more general theories about legislative behavior.

A common, shorthand method of describing voting models is to specify the possible connections between the vote choice and the explanatory variables as a functional relationship. For example, if one hypothesized that representatives' votes are related to the policy preferences of constituents, one might employ the following notation:

$$\text{votes} = f(\text{constituency preferences}),$$

to be read "votes are a function of constituency preferences." The concept of a function here connotes various ways that representatives might translate constituency preferences into a voting choice. Listed in figure 11.1, for example, are three possible translations. Under f_1, representatives vote exactly as their constituents prefer; under f_2, representatives vote just the opposite of what their constituents prefer; and under f_3, representatives vote yea no matter what their constituents prefer.

Typically, researchers will specify exactly which functional relationship—f_1, f_2, or f_3—they believe to be correct and then proceed to test

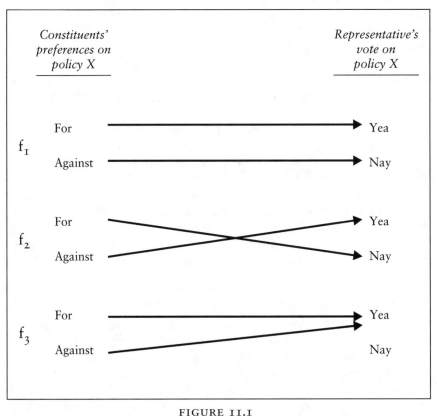

FIGURE 11.1

FUNCTIONAL RELATIONSHIPS BETWEEN CONSTITUTENTS'
PREFERENCES AND REPRESENTATIVE'S VOTE

their expectation using available data. Suppose, for example, that a researcher has valid and reliable measures of representatives' voting preferences and of their constituents' policy preferences on some policy X. Suppose also that these measures assign numbers to votes and preferences that range from zero to one, where a value of one indicates complete support for X and a value of zero indicates complete opposition. The functional relationships f_1, f_2, and f_3 then correspond to the graphical representations in figure 11.2. The line connecting the points (0,0) and (1,1) has a positive slope for f_1—as the value of constituents' preferences increases from zero to one, so also does the value of the representative's vote. The line in the graph corresponding to f_2, however, has a negative slope. If the value of constituency preference changed from zero to one, the value of the legislator's vote would change from one to zero. Finally, the line associated with f_3 has zero slope, indicating that the value of the representative's vote does not depend on the value of constituents' preferences—the representative votes yea no matter what the constituents prefer.

If one had data for votes and constituents' preferences across many legislators, one could determine statistically the relationship between votes and constituents' preferences more generally. One widely used statistical technique to estimate the direction and magnitude of these relationships is regression analysis. Application of this technique yields a *regression coefficient,* which, roughly speaking, is the numerical value of the slope that best characterizes the relationship between any two variables such as those in figure 11.2. Typically, of particular interest is whether a given slope is positive or negative, and how confident one can be that it is different from zero. In figure 11.2, the numerical value of the slope for the function f_1 is +1; for f_2, −1; and for f_3, 0.

A convenient way of representing diagrammatically the various relationships proposed by any given voting model is to construct a *channel map* of the connections among the variables in the model. Displayed in figure 11.3 is a channel map for the simple model involving the roll-call vote (V), constituents' preferences (C), and pressures from party leader (P). The arrows leading from C and P to V indicate that V is a function of both C and P; that is, $V = f(C, P)$. To isolate the effect of any one factor in the model, the effects of all other factors must be held constant. Each arrow in the model represents the independent, or isolated, effect of that variable, and numerical estimates of the strength and direction of the effect are provided by the regression coefficient associated with that variable.

Voting models generally contain both *systematic* and *random* factors. Systematic factors, like constituents' preferences, are large factors that affect roll-call voting in a regular and predictable manner. Random factors are small factors that, even though they affect voting, do not do so in any

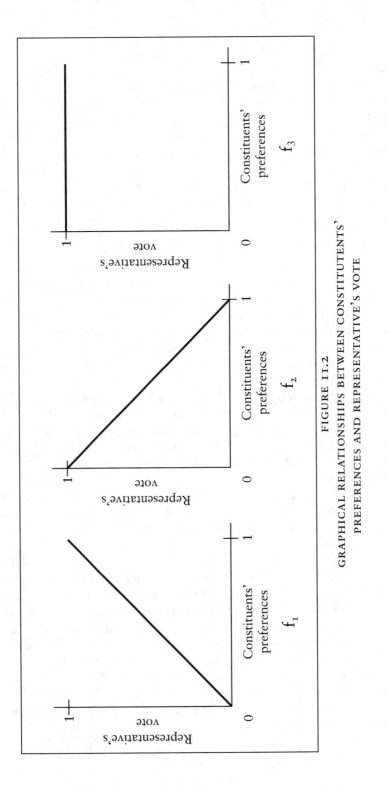

FIGURE 11.2

GRAPHICAL RELATIONSHIPS BETWEEN CONSTITUTENTS'
PREFERENCES AND REPRESENTATIVE'S VOTE

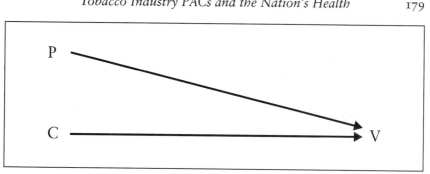

FIGURE 11.3
VOTING MODEL WITH CONSTITUENCY AND PARTY

regular or predictable fashion. A traffic jam that prevents the representative from receiving important information before voting is one example of a random effect that could have a small impact on the legislator's decision. Since one cannot be sure when or where these nonsystematic factors might be operating, they must be treated as unobserved or unmeasured.

Ideally, the random component of a model will contain only random effects. Sometimes, however, nonrandom effects that are not perfectly measured and captured by other variables in the model will be reflected in what is presumably the random component. Interest groups' lobbying efforts, for example, which are not a matter of public record, are difficult to observe and often can be measured only imperfectly. In practice, systematic factors like lobbying that are difficult or impossible to measure are often reflected in the random term of the model, in which case it obviously is not truly random. The critical objective in constructing a model is to identify and isolate as many systematic factors as possible. The exclusion of important systematic effects can lead to distorted estimates of the included systematic factors.

To see what can go wrong when the random term varies systematically, consider the model in figure 11.4. This model is identical to that in figure 11.3, except that the model now includes an explicit disturbance term, U, which presumably reflects all of the nonsystematic effects on V. In the model of figure 11.4, however, U reflects not only random factors but also the systematic effect of lobbying, L, which is not explicitly measured and specified as a direct effect on V. (The incorporation of L in U is represented in figure 11.4 by the arrow leading from L to U.) This situation could arise if the researcher has no quantitative indicator of lobbying activity or is simply unaware that lobbying efforts can systematically affect roll-call voting.

Suppose that an interest group lobbies representatives to vote yea, and that this group lobbies only representatives from districts where the group

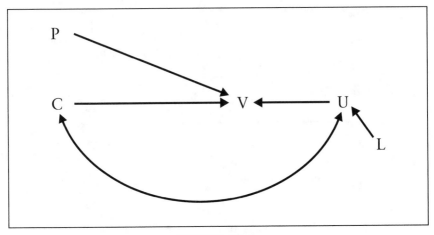

FIGURE 11.4

VOTING MODEL WITH CONSTITUENCY, PARTY, AND
SYSTEMATIC DISTURBANCE

has a large number of members or supporters who can write letters and make telephone calls. In other words, the group targets its lobbying efforts to representatives from districts where constituents are supportive of the group's objective. This coordination between lobbying and constituency support means that constituency preferences, C, will be positively correlated with lobbying activity, L. In fact, not only will L be correlated with C, but if L is left unmeasured and therefore included in U, then U will also be correlated with C. Thus the general problem with letting U contain systematic factors is that U may then be correlated with one or more explanatory variables in the model. This situation is depicted in the channel map of figure 11.4 by the double-headed arrow between U and C.

The statistical problem with estimating the strength of the relationship between C and V in figure 11.4 is that it is impossible to hold constant the effect of lobbying, L. Lobbying surely affects V, in which case V changes when L changes (e.g., representatives who are more heavily lobbied are more likely to vote yea). The problem is that L and C are also related: greater lobbying effort occurs in constituencies with a stronger interest in a yea vote. Thus, to get a true estimate of the effect of C on V, lobbying must be held constant; otherwise, the effect of L on V will be indistinguishable from the effect of C on V, as both C and L vary together. Unfortunately, when L is unmeasured and reflected only in the U-term, as in figure 11.4, it is impossible to control for its effects. In this situation, the regression coefficient for C, the estimated effect of constituency preferences on voting, will be *biased*. The regression coefficient will not reflect the true effect of C

on V, but the effect of C on V and the effect of L on V. In general, the direction and strength of this bias will depend on two things: (1) the strength of the correlation between the omitted factor and the included explanatory variable in question, and (2) the effect of the omitted factor on the dependent variable.

The problem with the model in figure 11.4 is essentially the same problem that plagues the *JAMA* study. In the *JAMA* study, however, the bias is in the estimated coefficient for campaign contributions. The main cause of the bias is the omission of an important systematic factor from the model —representatives' ideological preferences—which is correlated with contributions and relegated to the error term. Before reestimating the model to correct for this bias, I first replicate the analysis of the original *JAMA* study in order to establish a baseline for evaluating the extent of the bias.

The *JAMA* Model

The voting model presented in *JAMA* proposes that senators' roll-call votes on tobacco-related issues are positively related to campaign contributions from tobacco industry political action committees. The study analyzed voting in the U.S. Senate on two amendments, the so-called Bingaman and Harkin amendments, considered during the 102d (1991–92) Congress. In addition, the *JAMA* study analyzed voting on one bill in the U.S. House of Representatives, 102d Congress, as well as decisions by House members and senators to sponsor or cosponsor legislation. I confine my attention here to the two roll-call votes in the Senate. Only the Senate roll calls were relatively close—the House vote was a lopsided 331–82—and thus it is plausible a priori that only the outcomes in the Senate were actually determined by tobacco money.[1] I choose not to analyze sponsorship or cosponsorship for two reasons: these activities are often poor indicators of representatives' final positions on bills or their commitment to legislation, and the theoretical reasons behind sponsorship or cosponsorship activities are not always clear (Kessler and Krehbiel 1995; Krehbiel 1995; Schiller 1995).

The Bingaman amendment in the Senate was formally Amendment No. 1046 to the National Defense Authorization Act for Fiscal Years 1992 and 1993. Offered principally by Senator Bingaman of New Mexico, the amendment sought to raise the prices of tobacco products sold in military commissaries, exchanges, and ships' stores. The key provision of the amendment read as follows: "In the case of a commissary store, military exchange, or ship's store located in the United States, the price charged for any tobacco product shall be the prevailing price charged by private commercial businesses for the retail sale of such tobacco product in the retail market area in which the commissary store, military exchange, or ship's store is located" (*Congressional Record* 1992, S-12321). After the amendment was introduced and debated, Senator Ford of Kentucky moved to table and asked for the yeas and nays. The motion to table passed by a 56–43 margin—a yea vote was a vote in favor of the motion to table—on 2 August 1991, and thus the amendment itself was effectively defeated and never directly voted on.

The Harkin amendment was Amendment No. 3170 to HR 11, an urban aid and miscellaneous tax bill. The purpose of the amendment, offered by Senator Tom Harkin (D-Iowa), was to limit tobacco industry tax deductions for advertising and promotional expenses for tobacco products from 100 percent to 80 percent, and to apply the resulting revenues to antismoking campaigns. The Senate passed a motion to table this amendment by a 56–38 margin on 24 September 1992. As with the Bingaman amendment, the position favored by the tobacco industry was a (yea) vote in favor of tabling the amendment.

The basic voting model employed in the *JAMA* study posited that senators' roll-call votes (V) are a function of their partisan affiliation (P), the preferences of their constituents (C), and campaign contributions from tobacco industry political action committees (T). More succinctly, $V = f(P, C, T, U)$, where U stands for all other omitted factors, both random and systematic. I have estimated the effects of these factors on voting with data comparable to that used in the original *JAMA* analysis. I coded senators' votes, V, as either yea (value of 1) or nay (value of 0), and party, P, as either Democrat (value of 0) or Republican (value of 1). As an indicator of constituency preferences, I use the actual amount of tobacco produced in the state (in millions of pounds) as reported in the 1987 U.S. Census of Agriculture—State Data. Similar to the *JAMA* analysis, I have measured tobacco contributions, T, as the total contributions from ten tobacco PACs to members of the U.S. Senate during three election cycles: 1987–88, 1989–90, and 1991–92. The PACs were affiliated with the Brown & Williamson Tobacco Company, the Cigar Association of America, the National Association of Tobacco Distributors, Philip Morris, the Pinkerton Tobacco Company, RJ Reynolds, the Smokeless Tobacco Council, the Tobacco Institute, the Universal Leaf Tobacco Company, and U.S. Tobacco Executives.

My sample of senators includes those members of the U.S. Senate who served in the 102d Congress. Not all of these individuals, of course, were members of the Senate in 1986 or even in 1988. Thus, tobacco PAC contributions from 1987–88, for example, include only those contributions to members of the 102d Senate who were either in the Senate at that time or else who first ran for election to the Senate in 1988. Similarly, data on contributions for the 1989–90 cycle include contributions only to members of the 102d Senate who were in the Senate in 1989–90 or who first ran for election during that cycle.

Presented in table 11.1 are the estimated direct effects of P, C, and T on senators' votes on the Bingaman and Harkin amendments.[2] The estimated effects of campaign contributions on voting easily exceed traditional levels of statistical significance—the probability of finding effects this much larger than zero by chance is extremely small—for both the Bingaman and Harkin amendments. These effects of money are not only large statistically, they are also large substantively in terms of what they imply for senators' actual voting decisions. For example, the coefficient for campaign contributions on the Bingaman amendment yields the following interpretation: If all Democrats from nonproducing tobacco states had received zero tobacco contributions instead of those they actually received, their average probability of voting to table the Bingaman amendment would have decreased from .36 to .21. This change is substantial enough that seven of these Democrats would theoretically have voted *against* the tobacco industry had they not received PAC contributions. Thus, my replication yields conclusions consistent with those reported in the *JAMA*: the tobacco industry determined the Senate's policy on tobacco through their campaign contributions.

This voting model is flawed in two significant respects, however. First, a

TABLE 11.1
JAMA VOTING MODEL
FOR BINGAMAN AND HARKIN AMENDMENTS

Explanatory variable	Bingaman probit coefficient	Harkin probit coefficient
Party[a]	0.60 [1.98][b]	0.093 [0.31]
Tobacco production, 1987[c]	0.006 [0.76]	0.016 [1.29]
Tobacco PAC contributions, 1987–92[d]	0.072 [3.55]	0.04 [2.70]
Constant	−0.82 [−3.54]	−0.31 [−1.48]
N	98	94
Pseudo R^2	.26	.15

NOTE: Dependent variable: 1 = vote to table the amendment; 0 = vote against tabling.
a. Party codes: 0 = Democrat; 1 = Republican.
b. Values in brackets are *t*-ratios.
c. In millions of pounds.
d. In thousands of dollars.

variety of factors that systematically influence voting have been relegated
to the error term because of imprecise measurement and misspecification of
the theoretical model. The critical omission from the model is any general
consideration of senators' personal ideological preferences for or against
tobacco. The omission of a proxy for ideology inflates the estimated impact of campaign contributions on voting. Second, since the vote on the
Bingaman amendment occurred nearly a year before the 1992 election,
some of the contributions that senators received during the 1991–92 election cycle came *after* the vote, and thus these contributions may be a consequence of, not a cause for, opposing Bingaman. In short, there is potentially a problem of reciprocal causation. I elaborate on each of these in
turn, beginning with the issue of ideology.

Ideology

The theoretical and empirical significance of ideology in representatives'
voting decisions is well established in the social science literature. In his
seminal *Theory of Committees and Elections,* Duncan Black (1958) demonstrated that when voters' preferences over alternatives are arrayed along a
single ideological dimension, the median alternative will prevail under majority voting. This powerful result has served as the foundation for virtually all subsequent theoretical research on legislatures and legislative voting
(see Krehbiel 1995 for a review). A key assumption in this research is that
legislators' preferences and the alternatives over which they vote can be arrayed along ideological continua, ranging, for example, from liberal to
conservative.

Considerable empirical evidence buttresses the notion that legislative
voting reflects one or more ideological dimensions. Although there is some
debate over exactly how many ideological dimensions are relevant (see,
e.g., Clausen 1973; Poole and Daniels 1985; Koford 1989), the evidence
uniformly indicates that legislators have little difficulty arraying themselves
and various alternatives on ideological continua. John Kingdon (1989, 268)
has noted, for example, that "congressmen are quite comfortable with
thinking in terms of general valuative dimensions and placing political objects (amendments, groups, congressmen) along those dimensions at points
they perceive to be appropriate."

The standard practice for measuring the ideological positions of representatives' is to use interest group ratings, such as the Americans for Democratic Action (ADA) support score, as approximations of liberal-conservative positions. The ADA's rating, for example, is a simple percentage of
roll calls—usually a sample of fifteen or twenty taken from each legislative
session—on which a representative votes in favor of the ADA's position.
The voting scores of various interest groups are typically highly correlated,
suggesting that all reflect a common ideological continuum (Poole 1981).

A persistent question concerning the use of ADA and similar voting scores is, "What, exactly, do they stand for?" Quite often, researchers interpret them as standing for the representative's *personal ideology*—that is, the representative's independent beliefs and judgments about whether public policy in general should follow liberal or conservative principles. This is surely part of what they stand for, but obviously not all of what they represent. Since voting scores are summary measures of representatives' voting behavior, they necessarily reflect all those forces that bear on their roll-call decisions. In addition to personal ideology, these forces include pressures from party leaders to follow the party line, constituency preferences, and the balance of interest groups' lobbying efforts. As Jackson and Kingdon (1992) argue, voting scores meld a variety of factors into a single variable.

Despite the "catchall" nature of voting scores, their use in roll-call voting models is firmly established, especially in models attempting to isolate the effects of campaign contributions on legislative voting (see, e.g., Chappell 1982; Kau and Rubin 1982; Welch 1982; Frendreis and Waterman 1985; Wright 1985; Schroedel 1986; Grenzke 1989; Langbein and Lotwis 1990; and Langbein 1993). Unfortunately, however, the inclusion of voting scores in statistical models of voting can produce distortions in the estimated effects of other factors in the model. Jackson and Kingdon (1992) demonstrate that the use of voting scores leads to estimates that *overstate* the relationship between personal ideology and voting and *understate* the relationship between other factors such as constituency preferences on voting. Both types of bias occur because voting scores reflect factors other than just the personal ideology of legislators. Voting scores are themselves functions of party, constituency, and related factors, and thus the impact of voting scores on specific roll-call decisions includes the effects of these factors, which typically are falsely attributed to personal ideology. That the influence of factors such as party and constituency are incorrectly attributed to personal ideology also means that the true effects of party and constituency are understated. Voting scores capture some of the effects of those variables that should be directly attributable to them.

The potential problems associated with the use of voting scores are of obvious concern in models of campaign contributions and legislative voting. Since the estimated effects of contributions on voting have important practical implications for the perceived relationship between representatives and special interest contributors, it is important that these effects not be systematically over- or understated. Most problematic, however, is the situation where voting scores are excluded from models of contributions and voting. Then it becomes highly likely that the estimated effects of contributions will be overstated, because personal ideology can affect both the vote itself and the type and amount of campaign contributions representatives receive. Consequently, the omission of voting scores from the model can lead to statistical estimates that incorrectly attribute the effects of personal ideology to campaign contributions.

The seriousness of the bias in the estimated contribution coefficients resulting from the omission of ideology will depend on the strength of the relationships between contributions and ideology and between ideology and voting. The nature of these relationships for tobacco contributions, ideology, and voting on the Bingaman and Harkin amendments are illustrated in table 11.2. There, the roll-call votes, together with average tobacco contributions from 1987 to 1992, are arrayed for various types of senators. The ideological positions of senators are established in table 11.2 by the voting scores assigned to senators by the Americans for Democratic Action in 1991. Of all roll-call votes cast in the U.S. Senate in 1991, the ADA chose twenty to rate senators. Each senator's ADA score was computed as the percentage of the twenty votes on which the senator supported the ADA's position. Scores of 100 reflect perfect alignment with the ADA, a group with an avowedly liberal agenda.

Table 11.2 clearly reveals that the senators receiving the largest average contributions from the tobacco industry were Republicans, conservatives, and senators from major tobacco-producing states. These senators also voted overwhelmingly against both the Bingaman and Harkin proposals. Senators receiving the smallest average contributions were Democrats, lib-

TABLE 11.2

CAMPAIGN CONTRIBUTIONS FROM TOBACCO PACS
TO SENATORS AND VOTING ON BINGAMAN AND
HARKIN AMENDMENTS

	Mean tobaccco contributions, 1987–92	Senate votes			
		Bingaman amendment		Harkin amendment	
Characteristics of senator		For	Against	For	Against
Senators from					
Major tobacco-producing states[a]	$32,287	1	11	0	10
Minor and nonproducing states	$9,311	42	44	38	46
Conservatives[b]	$18,206	7	26	9	24
Moderates[c]	$12,294	13	21	11	22
Liberals[d]	$5,081	23	8	18	10
Republicans	$15,361	11	31	14	28
Democrats	$9,584	32	24	24	28

a. Georgia, Kentucky, North Carolina, South Carolina, Tennessee, and Virginia.
b. N = 34; ADA scores < 25.
c. N = 35; 25 ≤ ADA scores ≤ 75.
d. N = 31; ADA scores > 75.

erals, and senators from minor or nonproducing tobacco states. These senators were much more supportive of the Bingaman and Harkin amendments. On the surface, therefore, the association among ideology, contributions, and voting appears quite strong, and thus it is quite conceivable that ideology could rival party, constituency, and contributions as an explanation for voting.

While there is preliminary evidence favoring the inclusion of voting scores in statistical models, their use can also lead to an understatement of the effects of campaign contributions. Voting scores will lead to an underestimate of the effect of contributions, however, only if the votes that make up the voting score are *directly* influenced by campaign contributions. If the votes that make up the voting score are *not* affected by PAC money, then the voting score cannot "steal" some of the effect of contributions. Thus, when constructing a voting model, it is extremely important to choose a voting score that does not contain votes that one would expect theoretically to be directly affected by the PAC contributions under study. Fortunately, the twenty issues that constitute the ADA's 1991 voting score are not issues in which it would appear that the tobacco industry had great interest. The 1991 ADA index includes votes pertaining to sanctions on Iraq, racial discrimination, gun control, abortion, the Strategic Defense Initiative, the Head Start program, appeals of death row prisoners, the Clarence Thomas nomination, the National Endowment for the Arts, and so forth.

Given the potential problems with using voting scores, their inclusion requires a strong theoretical justification for the expected influence of personal ideological considerations on voting. There is such justification present for voting on tobacco legislation. The controversy over public health and smokers' rights transcends the narrow considerations of subsidies and other benefits that defined tobacco policy for years. In terms of the issue types introduced by Lowi (1964), tobacco policy has evolved from a pork-barrel or *distributive* issue to a *regulatory* issue. As with most regulatory issues, those favoring regulation typically frame the debate in terms of the public interest versus private interests, and a call is made to bring the state's coercive powers to bear on private interests. Such issues generally entail broad ideological conflict between those who advocate a stronger governmental role in regulating private economic activity and those who oppose it. Tobacco usage is clearly one such issue.

Reciprocal Causation

As mentioned earlier, because the vote on the Bingaman amendment took place so early in the 1991–92 election cycle, contributions in 1991–92 may have been a function of voting rather than vice versa. In other words, contributions in 1991–92 may have been a reward for, not a cause of, senators' decisions to oppose the Bingaman amendment. Unless some correction is made for this possibility, contributions given as rewards may incorrectly be interpreted as causing votes.

To gain some insight into the substantive problem of reciprocal causation, consider two hypothetical legislators. The first type, which I shall call the *appreciative legislator,* receives money from an interest group for reasons unrelated to any particular roll-call vote. These legislators may receive money because they are members of the majority party, because the group has a strong economic interest in their geographic districts, because they sit on committees with jurisdiction over issues of concern to the group, or because of their general ideological outlook (Grier and Munger 1986, 1991; Romer and Snyder 1994). Having received money, or else *expecting to receive money,* these legislators then vote as the group prefers as a way of expressing their appreciation for the money. Importantly, appreciative behavior can apply even to legislators who actually receive contributions *after* a particular vote has taken place, as long as their votes are based on appreciation for money promised, or understood, to be delivered in the future.[3]

The second hypothetical legislator, whom I shall call the *compensated legislator,* receives money only because he or she has voted as a group prefers on a particular roll call. Unlike the appreciative legislator, this legislator would not ordinarily receive a contribution. Being a member of the minority party, or else not having appropriate committee assignments or constituency interests to motivate a campaign contribution, this legislator nevertheless supports the group on an important roll call. Compensated legislators may be either sincere or strategic, although in practice it is very difficult to distinguish between the two. Sincere legislators are those who vote in accordance with their personal judgments or the preferences of unorganized voters in their constituencies, not as a ploy to raise campaign money. Strategic legislators, however, vote in a deliberate and calculated manner to raise campaign money.

One problem with the *JAMA* study is that no distinction is made between compensated-sincere legislators and other types. All legislators are assumed to be appreciative or else compensated strategists, and this assumption overestimates the extent of appreciative or strategic behavior, as some legislators are surely compensated for sincere behavior. Since the votes of the compensated-sincere types are not determined by contributions, the greater the share of sincere legislators, the greater will be the estimated bias.

Statistically, there are a couple of ways to handle the problem of compensation versus appreciation. One is simply to exclude all 1991–92 contributions from the analysis under the assumption that all of these are motivated by compensation. This approach, however, has the drawback of underestimating the effect of money on voting by eliminating the possibility of appreciative behavior for the anticipation of contributions received *after* the Bingaman vote. A second approach is to attempt to purge the 1991–92 contributions of contributions that are the result of compensated behavior. This approach, which does not distinguish between sincere and strategic compensation, may also underestimate the true impact of contributions on voting if most compensated legislators are strategic types. As reported in the next section, however, my best estimate is that compensated-sincere legislators outnumber compensated-strategic legislators by two to one. Thus it would appear that the second approach is better than ignoring the problem entirely.

The campaign contributions senators received in 1991–92 depend not only on factors such as constituency interests, reelection, and so forth, but may also depend on their voting decisions on the Bingaman amendment. One statistical method for purging the compensated contributions from the total of 1991–92 contributions is to obtain an estimate of 1991–92 contributions that does not depend on senators' votes on the Bingaman amendment, and then use this estimate of contributions to predict voting on Bingaman. Voting on the Harkin amendment is much less problematic because that vote occurred very late in the 1991–92 election cycle—not until late September 1992. For the Bingaman amendment, however, the statistical task is to obtain a measure of campaign contributions that varies independently of voting.

Presented in table 11.3 is a statistical estimation of 1991–92 contributions that does not depend on voting. Contributions are estimated in table 11.3 as a function of party, ADA scores in 1991, tobacco production in senators' states, membership on the Senate Commerce and Agriculture committees, campaign contributions from 1989 to 1990, whether the senator was running for election or reelection in 1988 and 1992, and whether the senator was expected to retire in 1992. Some of the predictor variables in table 11.3—the election year and retirement variables—are not expected to affect roll-call voting directly and presumably are independent of any nonsystematic factors affecting voting on Bingaman. Importantly, these variables are two of the most potent predictors of 1991–92 contributions, and this provides some assurance that contributions estimated from this model will vary independently of senators' votes on Bingaman. The expected contributions for 1991–92 for each senator are derived by simply multiplying the coefficient for each variable in table 11.3 by each senator's value on that variable and then summing over all of the variables.

The Full Voting Model

The full voting model includes a measure of ideology in addition to the factors of party, constituency, and money. Notationally, $V = f(P, C, I, T)$,

TABLE 11.3
PREDICTION OF TOBACCO PAC CONTRIBUTIONS, 1992

Explanatory variable	OLS coefficient	t-ratios
Party[a]	−1208.05	−0.49
ADA voting score, 1991	−69.75	−1.80
Tobacco production[b]	40.47	4.06
Member of Commerce committee[c]	1452.73	0.86
Member of Agriculture committee[c]	189.21	0.105
Tobacco PAC contributions, 1987–88	−0.04	−0.23
Tobacco PAC contributions, 1989–90	−0.17	−1.39
Candidate for election or reelection, 1988[c]	521.36	0.27
Candidate for reelection, 1992[c]	13684.97	7.82
Retiring in 1992[c]	−12417.43	−4.33
Constant	4352.19	1.173
N	100	
Pseudo R^2	.62	

NOTE: Dependent variable: Total tobacco PAC contributions to U.S. senators, 1991–92 election cycle.
a. Party codes: 0 = Democrat; 1 = Republican.
b. In millions of pounds.
c. 0 = no; 1 = yes.

where I stands for ideology, measured by the ADA voting index for 1991; P and C stand for party and constituency interests, respectively, with constituency interests approximated by the number of pounds (in millions) of tobacco produced in each state; and T stands for the money given by tobacco PACs .

Three alternatives for the money variable permit alternative estimations. The first alternative, denoted by $T(3)$, is the total actual contributions from the ten tobacco PACs over the *three* election cycles from 1987 to 1992. This is the measure used in the *JAMA* study. The second alternative, denoted by $T(2)$, is the sum of actual contributions from the 1987–88 and 1989–90 election cycles only. The third alternative, denoted by T^*, includes *expected* money and is the sum of actual contributions from the 1987–88 and 1989–90 election cycles and the expected contributions for 1991–92. (The expected contributions are derived from the procedure described above and the coefficients reported in table 11.3.)

The computed effects of P, C, I, and the alternative money variables on senators' roll-call votes for the Bingaman and Harkin amendments are reported in table 11.4. For the Bingaman amendment, estimates from three different models—one for each of the three money variables—are reported; for the Harkin amendment, however, only effects based on model $T(3)$ using total actual contributions are reported. The noteworthy result in the estimation of voting on the Harkin amendment is that PAC contributions from the tobacco industry do *not* have a statistically significant effect. The coefficient for $T(3)$ in the full model, 0.016, is less than half the estimated effect of .04 in the *JAMA* model, and given its level of statistical significance, one can have little confidence that the true impact of money is greater than zero. In contrast, the ideology variable is statistically significant in the full model, indicating that its omission from the *JAMA* model causes a significant upward bias in the estimated impact of money on voting.

For the Bingaman amendment, the estimated effects of the three money variables are as anticipated. The largest estimated effect is for $T(3)$, the actual total contributions for all three election cycles. At a value of .042, however, this coefficient is considerably less than the corresponding value of .072 in the *JAMA* model. That the ADA voting index is statistically significant in the full model indicates that, just as in the case of voting on the Harkin amendment, the omission of any measure of ideology in the *JAMA* analysis causes a significant upward bias in the estimated impact of money on voting. The coefficient for $T(3)$, however, is still inflated in the full model because it does not take account of the possibility that tobacco contributions were given as rewards to senators voting to table the Bingaman amendment.

The full voting model based on T^* corrects for the reciprocal effect of voting on contributions, and as one would expect, this correction results in an even smaller estimated effect of money. The effect of the correction, while not dramatic, does lead to a decrease of .004, from .042 to .039. Finally, the full estimation using $T(2)$, actual contributions from just the first two election cycles, results in the smallest estimate of the effect of money on voting. At a value of .014, however, this coefficient surely underestimates the true impact of money on voting, as this correction presumes that all contributions given in 1991–92 were compensation for opposing Bingaman, and that none of the senators opposed Bingaman out of appreciation for anticipated contributions.

Of the three money variables, the best estimate of the effect of tobacco PAC contributions on senators' votes on the Bingaman amendment is that associated with T^*. As discussed earlier, however, because the measure of T^* is designed to eliminate the reciprocal effects of voting on contributions, it may understate the impact of contributions if a large number of senators opposed Bingaman simply in order to raise campaign money. The correction essentially adjusts for all effects of voting on contributions, whether they were strategically induced or not.

I have devised a rough estimate of the number of sincere versus strategic legislators who were compensated for their votes by examining the votes and contributions of senators who were running for election in 1992.

TABLE 11.4

FULL VOTING MODEL FOR BINGAMAN AND HARKIN AMENDMENTS

Explanatory variable	Bingaman probit coefficient			Harkin probit coefficient
P Party[a]	-0.59 [-1.05][b]	-0.55 [-0.95]	-0.81 [-1.46]	-1.22 [-2.02]
C Tobacco production, 1987[c]	0.007 [0.88]	0.007 [0.86]	0.01 [1.32]	0.018 [1.34]
I ADA voting score, 1991[d]	-0.02 [-2.58]	-0.023 [-2.43]	-0.03 [-3.48]	-0.02 [-2.64]
T(3) Tobacco PAC contributions, 1987–92[e]	0.042 [1.92]	Not incl.[f]	Not incl.	0.016 [0.95]
T(2) Tobacco PAC contributions, 1987–1990[e]	Not incl.	Not incl.	0.014 [0.50]	Not incl.
T* Tobacco PAC contributions, 1987–92[e] (for 1991–92, *expected* contributions)	Not incl.	0.039 [1.69]	Not incl.	Not incl.
Constant	1.18 [1.48]	1.14 [1.33]	1.89 [2.55]	1.79 [2.17]
N	98	98	98	94
Pseudo R^2	.31	.30	.28	.20

NOTE: Dependent variable: 1 = vote to table the amendment;
0 = vote against tabling.
a. Party codes: 0 = Democrat; 1 = Republican.
b. Values in brackets are *t*-ratios.
c. In millions of pounds.
d. Ideology codes: 0 = most conservative; 1 = most liberal.
e. In thousands of dollars.
f. Not included.

I define compensated senators as those who received more tobacco contributions than expected; that is $T^* < T(3)$. I assume that senators behaving strategically in order to raise tobacco contributions for their election campaigns in 1992 should be more likely to oppose Bingaman than those senators not running. Among the thirty-nine senators who received larger than expected contributions, thirteen were facing reelection in 1992, and of these thirteen, ten voted to table Bingaman. Among the twenty-six remaining compensated senators not up for reelection, however, an identical proportion, twenty of twenty-six, voted to table Bingaman. Thus, not only were the rates of opposition to Bingaman the same regardless of whether senators were up for reelection, but the actual number of compensated senators with no strategic motivation who opposed Bingaman was exactly twice that of compensated senators with a strategic motivation who opposed Bingaman. This suggests that even though some senators were compensated for strategic votes, many more were compensated for apparently sincere votes.

Other potential biases threaten the credibility of even the coefficient for T^*. Most important among these is the likely influence of lobbying. Since contributions are often used to gain access for lobbying, lobbying and contributions should be positively correlated, and lobbying by itself should have an independent, marginal impact on voting. Lobbying by the tobacco industry, therefore, is a systematic factor relegated to the error term in the full model, which is likely to lead to an upward bias in the estimated coefficient for T^*.

One final question concerns the impact that tobacco contributions had on the actual share of yeas and nays. One way to address this question is to simulate the voting outcome under the assumption that the tobacco industry made zero campaign contributions. Procedurally, this involves multiplying the coefficients in table 11.4 with senators' actual values on each corresponding independent variable except campaign contributions, which is set to zero for each senator, and then summing these products. This value can then be transformed into a probability of voting yea. By comparing this predicted probability with the predicted probability of voting yea given *actual* campaign contributions, it is possible to estimate how many votes would have changed from yea to nay if the tobacco industry contributions decreased from the actual amounts given during the three election cycles to zero over the three cycles.

I have applied this procedure to voting on the Bingaman amendment using the money coefficient, T^*. The money coefficient for voting on the Harkin amendment is not statistically different enough from zero to make the procedure meaningful. For the Bingaman amendment, however, the simulation suggests that the outcome *assuming no campaign contributions from the tobacco industry whatsoever* would have been a 49–49 tie, instead of the 55–43 margin that actually prevailed.[4] The motion to table would have failed on a tie vote; however, Vice-President Quayle, then president of the Senate, would have had an opportunity to vote and break the tie. Given Quayle's general conservatism, it is likely that he would have voted to table. Thus, the campaign contributions from the tobacco industry may have made the margin a bit wider, but it is quite unlikely that money determined the policy outcome.

Conclusion

The possibility that special interests control public policies through campaign money poses a serious threat to the health and well-being of the political system. Since campaign money may have potentially debilitating effects on the democratic principles of accountability, representation, and political equality, the failure to diagnose and treat any maladies associated with campaign money can be damaging to the health of the political system. It can be equally damaging, however, to report maladies that do not exist.

In the case of tobacco contributions and tobacco policy, the diagnosis reported in the *JAMA* indicates that the public's health would improve substantially if only the campaign finance system were reformed or if members of Congress would voluntarily stop accepting campaign contributions from the tobacco industry. In contrast, the analysis reported in this essay indicates that even if campaign contributions were eliminated altogether, tobacco policies themselves would not change.

That tobacco money did not determine the Senate's policy on the Harkin and Bingaman amendments does not necessarily mean the tobacco lobby is ineffective, or that interest groups in general hold little sway over congressional policy decisions. The analysis presented here establishes only that on two roll-call votes in the U.S. Senate, campaign contributions from the tobacco industry were not instrumental in determining the outcomes. This is due primarily to the fact that larger ideological considerations came into play on these roll-call decisions. Thus a better prescription for changing tobacco policy than to eliminate or restrict campaign contributions is to advocate the election of liberal legislators and the defeat of conservative legislators. Unfortunately, the *JAMA* study's misdiagnosis of the problem in this case diverts attention away from efforts to find the true causal explanations for the nation's tobacco control policies, or to find other solutions to the nation's health problems.

Notes

1. Analyses of Senate roll calls have two additional advantages over analyses of House votes. First, much better measures of constituency factors are generally available at the statewide level than at the congressional district level. Second, given the Senate's six-year term, it is much easier to separate electoral considerations from legislative considerations.

2. The estimation technique for table 11.1 is probit. Each coefficient can be interpreted as the change in a standard normal variable, Z, given a unit change in the value of the independent variable.

3. This scenario leaves unanswered the question of why, after having already received money, the legislator feels any obligation to reciprocate by helping the group. In general, it is unclear what, if any, implicit contracts between legislators and groups would lead to quid pro quo behavior (McCarty and Rothenberg 1996).

4. To determine the change in votes, I compared the predicted votes given full contributions to predicted votes given zero contributions for senators whose votes were correctly predicted by the model.

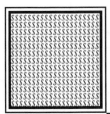

Jack Bonner
and
Howard Marlowe

Comments on the Congressional Connection

Jack Bonner, Bonner and Associates

We are putting Congress, interest groups, and lobbyists under a microscope at a very historic time. Today's Congress is doing things that have not been done before, and interest groups have had an important role in this development. We can gain insights into the roles of interest groups in contemporary congressional politics by drawing lessons from American political history. We can also deepen our understanding of how Congress and its members behave by trying to put ourselves into the mind-set of a typical member.

Health-care reform is the epitome of special interest politics. This issue has been on the political agenda for a long time and played up by every group in town. Some turn up the rhetoric to make it seem like a life-and-death matter. Once President Clinton took office, "inside the Beltway" special interest groups—the ones that most people in Washington pay so much attention to—were making the case for health-care reform, leading everyone to presume it was going to pass. Yet, what members of Congress began to hear from some interest groups and citizens back home, some of whom wrote in spontaneously, was distinctly out of step with what they were hearing from many high-powered Washington lobbyists. As members received more messages from constituents expressing their fear about what might happen to the nation's health-care system, they began to withdraw their support for the president's program. Consequently, this major policy proposal, which would have affected one-seventh of the nation's economy, was defeated. And, it was killed entirely. Other major issues, such as welfare reform and the budget, would be subject to compromise, but health-care reform was defeated entirely. Members have not forgotten this experience. It exemplifies an "explosion of democracy" that has taken place in American politics. This "explosion" affects how legislators do their jobs and how the modern Congress operates.

History is replete with other examples in which interest groups have mobilized at the local level. The Vietnam War protests and the civil rights movement were catalysts that caused sea changes in the way things happened in Washington. They were tied to some very emotional causes and some very emotional events. The nightly newscasts portrayed protests and the gruesome events that were occurring in the South in the case of civil rights, on the one hand, and body bags coming home from Vietnam on the other. These images were seared on the minds of Americans. That isn't happening now, but the role of special interests and the change in the direction of national policy is probably even more profound.

The reason for the magnification of the influence of interest groups is an explosion in participatory democracy that is now occurring. As a result of grassroots mobilization, members of Congress are paying more attention than ever to what interest groups back home think about the world. Members have found that if they are not attentive to their constituencies on important policy issues, such as health care, they will get burned. They witnessed the defeat of very important members, such as Speaker of the House Tom Foley (D-Wash.) and the long-time House Judiciary Committee Chairman Jack Brooks (D-Tex.). These and many others were not returned to Washington after the 1994 elections for one reason: they failed to pay attention to groups back home. Republicans and Democrats in Congress have learned from this lesson, reaching out to a wide variety of interest groups at the early stages of the 104th Congress and continuing to consult with them.

In particular, groups with the local chapters are sought out by the congressional leaders in Congress because they can deliver a local connection. These groups can deliver and receive opinions from back home, and this is what members remember. An anecdote from when I worked for the late Senator John Heinz (R-Pa.) illustrates this point. A lobbyist for the U.S. Chamber of Commerce was frequently coming to speak with the senator because Heinz sat on the Finance Committee. The lobbyist would say, senator, we would like you to vote this way or that way. When he would leave, Heinz would say, "Call up the Philadelphia Chamber and the Pittsburgh Chamber and see what the hell they think about it." Those were the Chamber leaders that the senator paid attention to. A smart legislator will look outside the Beltway—to the folks back home.

One of the keys to the interest group connection is a group's ability to produce examples of local policy impact. Members always want to know how policies influence folks back home. They want real examples told in real words by real people. A group that has only a small staff can have an immense impact if it can get an example of how an issue plays out on "Main Street," somewhere back in a member's district. If the example is credible, it will carry a great deal of weight with an individual member. If the group can forge a local connection with a large number of members, it will be able to influence the actions of the entire Congress.

Another important key to the interest group connection is credibility, which is often gauged by the sheer size of the group an organization represents. Groups with large numbers are important for two reasons. One is the political cover that they can provide for the member. Legislators who can say that they are taking a position that senior citizens and the AARP—a 33-million member organization—endorse have significant political cover. The other is that they can endorse the members' reelection. Groups that endorse candidates are very important, especially if their supporters listen to them. Groups that are both large and make endorsements are especially powerful; they get credibility both from their size and from the fact that their endorsement could have a huge impact on an election. For these reasons, it is important for inside the Beltway groups to involve their local members. Groups that have been successful at this, such as the insurance agents, will find Congress more responsive to their views than groups without grassroots support.

The budget process offers some lessons about how political leaders should deal with interest groups. Speaker of the House Newt Gingrich (R-Ga.) understood the advantage of organizing groups with strong "district power," bringing them into the legislative process early, responding to their views, and limiting the access and time that opposing groups had in the process. Gingrich did something that Clinton should have done better during the health-care debate. Ultimately, the president's program failed, and Gingrich got much of what he wanted.

Howard Marlowe, Marlowe and Company

Lobbyists tend to be caught up in the events of the moment. We do not often see clearly the changes that are taking place in Congress, nor do we have a sufficient appreciation of the lessons we can learn by examining historical trends in the legislative process. I welcome this opportunity to take the time to offer a perspective on our work. Over the past two or more decades that I have been involved with Congress, I have observed a marked increase in the number and sophistication of interest groups seeking to lobby Congress. The media and others dub these groups with the pejorative name "special interests." But we are a nation of special interests, and it is the job of members of Congress to mold the power jostling of these groups into what they determine to be the national interest.

During the past two decades, the role of political money in the legislative process has grown considerably. Members of Congress need outrageous sums of money to get reelected. Their easiest sources for these funds are interest groups and their lobbyists. But there has been a countervailing trend during this period—the growth of grassroots lobbying. Many interest groups that either do not have or choose not to use significant financial assets have relied on their ability to mobilize their membership to influence legislation. While I fear that this movement has not grown fast enough to offset the growing distrust of government as an institution, it clearly has had a powerful effect on lobbying techniques. I also regret that some interests possessing significant political assets have chosen to use their financial resources to manufacture grassroots support, or what then Senator Lloyd Bentsen (D-Tex.) labeled "astroturf lobbying" more than a decade ago. This type of ersatz, orchestrated mobilization does little to instill either the confidence of Congress in the lobbying profession or the public's trust of government. It is merely another example of the ability of money to buy influence.

Having made these observations, I believe that we must take the legislative process as we find it and try to understand what trends are developing. I am particularly pleased by the topics pursued in the chapters in this section of the volume, because they deal, in part, with two areas of concentration of my lobbying practice: the nonprofit sector and the appropriations process. Normally, the appropriations process would be completed by 1 October; from a lobbyist's perspective, the period between 1 June and 1 October is the season to be jolly. Thirteen appropriations bills make their way to the floor pulled by twenty-six of Santa's strongest helpers. These twenty-six "elves" are very special—so important, in fact, that they are reverently called "cardinals." The cardinals deliver presents that are also very special: thirteen appropriations bills that must pass, in one form or another, by 1 October. Lobbyists normally look at this period as the congressional Christmas season because appropriations bills offer opportunities for getting clients their slice of the federal money pie. They are also an opportunity for the naughty to get presents along with those who are nice (i.e., when privileged insiders manage to attach legislative riders to spending bills in violation of congressional rules).

Since the 1994 elections, much of the fun has been taken out of Christmas. It is too superficial to ascribe this lack of joy merely to the drive for a balanced budget and the scarcity of federal funds. The fight for dollars has historically favored existing programs and strong interests over new programs and weak interests. Since 1994, a relatively strong Republican congressional leadership has been in power whose priorities are in direct conflict with President Clinton and the desires of many special interests. Because of the GOP leadership's strong pull, Clinton and many liberal interest groups have been greatly restricted in their efforts to move their agendas. Put another way, those twenty-six cardinals have been effectively demoted. Centralized, top-down leadership has been trying to dictate spending priorities that leave the new Republican cardinals with little latitude to act with the independence to which their Democratic predecessors had become accustomed over the past forty years.

Today, Congress is demonstrating a large measure of discipline by setting budget-deficit targets based on fairly realistic economic forecasts. For lobbyists, the pay-as-you-go system, created in 1990, means that any interest group that wants to increase its share of the pie either has to come up with a matching tax increase (politically unthinkable) or take the funding from another interest group's project in the budget (politically difficult). Lobbying for new spending is usually a waste of a client's money. Most of us work simply to hold down the decrease in a favorite appropriation from last year's level. The same goes for authorizations. In fact, a good argument can be made that the authorizing committees have lost more clout than the Appropriations committees. Between having to make early budget estimates of the cost of programs within their jurisdiction and the centralized policy agenda set by the leadership (especially in the House), the days of powerful authorizing committee chairmen are rapidly fading.

Amid these changes, the Appropriations committees have managed to retain a relative measure of importance, but now the lobbying game has been reduced to one of defensive tactics. The climate of fiscal constraint, the complexity of the budget and appropriations processes, and the problems resulting from a stronger, centralized congressional leadership have themselves made lobbying a challenge. But lobbyists will soon have to contend with yet another level of misery—the presidential line-item veto. How this will work when it takes effect in 1997 remains to be seen, but it promises to lock the 105th Congress in fierce battles with the president.

Within Congress today, the degree to which interest groups are being manipulated by the Republican leadership is significant. While the leadership's ability to choreograph the support of interest groups appears to have declined sharply since the first months of the 104th Congress, it is clear that there is now a dual role for interest groups. Some use their power as "influencers," while others are called on to be "cheerleaders." I hope further research leads to a better understanding of the factors that cause some interest groups to perform one of these roles and not the other, and what factors cause some groups to shift from one role to the other.

A number of clients I represent are in the nonprofit sector. Many of these organizations tout the lobbying power of their membership and their own credibility as their primary political resources because they are not permitted by law to engage in political campaign activities. Some nonprofits have had notable successes, such as environmental groups. Nevertheless, it is fair to conclude that most have been rather ineffective in using their membership assets in an effective manner. Some years ago, I served as associate director of legislation for the AFL-CIO, which at the time had over 15 million members. That was also the period of the Reagan presidency, one in which a large chunk of that membership supported Mr. Reagan, despite his anti-union policies. I believe the AFL-CIO and the nonprofit sector share a common weakness: they believe they have a corner on the truth. When you know what the truth is, you do not have to work to convince others that you are right. You risk telling yourself that everyone should know what the truth is. If they don't, it is only a matter of time before they must see the light.

The labor movement has spent many years cursing the darkness. It was assumed that once a Democrat occupied the White House, truth would once again prevail. But while there was a marked improvement with the election of Bill Clinton, few in labor would say that their political fortunes have significantly improved. It has taken the lessons of repeated beatings from those who were thought to be friends to convince labor that new tactics are needed. Chief among those tactics has been the return to their grassroots and a realization that rank-and-file union members need to be educated about issues and motivated to act. While money is often referred to as "the mother's milk of politics," money is not the be-all and end-all for congressional lobbyists. From my point of view, money is neither the best nor the only means of obtaining access. Those groups who curse the access gained by interests with money too often fail to take advantage of their own nonfinancial assets. In failing to do so, they cede power and influence to their opponents.

While much of what takes place in Congress is a battle for political power among competing interests, we are in a period when the battle is motivated to a significant extent by forces seeking to redefine the role of government. Nonprofits usually favor a more activist government in which their role as a partner of government has importance. The business community usually favors a less activist role in which government regulates less. The outcome of this battle is decided on an issue-by-issue basis by various interest groups who use both Washington and grassroots lobbying to make their voices heard. Who these groups are and how they use their power deserves further study and analysis.

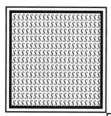

Part IV

The Executive Connection

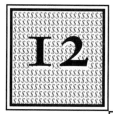

12   Eric M. Uslaner

Lobbying the President and the Bureaucracy

INTEREST groups and the executive don't go well together. We rarely hear much about how such groups influence the president and when we do, we wish we hadn't. The two presidents most closely connected to interest groups were Warren Harding and Richard M. Nixon. Harding's secretary of the interior signed over priceless oil reserves in Teapot Dome, Wyoming, and Elk Hills, California, to two oil company executives in 1921. In return the secretary received $125,000 in bribes. He was ultimately convicted of bribery in 1929. Harding died while in office in 1923, but people still remember how the interior secretary—and other administration officials —sold public policy for cash.

No one ever charged Nixon with either bribery or knowledge of it. But he was forced to resign—the only president ever to do so—because of his involvement in the Watergate scandal. The affair involved a 1972 burglary at the Democratic National Committee headquarters in Washington, D.C. The bungled break-in was financed at least in part by illegal cash contributions to the Nixon reelection effort. We never found out what, if anything, the donors wanted for their money, or if they ever approached Nixon directly. But the amounts were, by the standards of the time, very large, and some contributions were made by friends of the president.

Lobbyists rarely get direct access to the White House. Interest groups and chief executives have fundamentally different styles. Lobbyists build support for their programs through informal contacts and the provision of information (Milbrath 1963). Presidents have access to as much information as they need—often more than they can handle. They also have little free time to chat with representatives of all manner of interests. Moreover, interest groups and presidents have different agendas. Lobbyists usually press for special benefits for their groups. They have narrow agendas. Presidents often do not have either the time or the interest to get involved in the details that motivate lobbyists. They are more concerned with the big picture of policy.

Different agendas dictate different strategies. If you want something that will disproportionately benefit your own group, you don't want to shout about it. Many people will find it hard to understand how your special interest really benefits everyone (even if it does). So lobbyists pursue an "inside" strategy of talking to key decision makers and keeping the details out of the public eye. When presidents tackle broad issues, they want public support. And no other office gives them the immediate access to the public. The president is the only nationally elected official, so he has what Theodore Roosevelt called a "bully pulpit." In recent years, chief executives have increasingly relied on television addresses to the nation to build support for policies. They "go public" (Kernell 1986). How Ronald Reagan addressed the nation in 1981 to rally public support for his budget *over the heads of members of Congress* is a prime example of this "outside" strategy. Presidents thrive on publicity. Lobbyists generally shun it. Presidents go outside, interest groups inside.

The different worlds of lobbyists and presidents hardly means that interest groups play only a minor role in the executive branch. Instead, we must look elsewhere for group influence in the executive branch. One source of group pressure is to turn the lobbying process around. Sometimes the president can be a lobbyist himself, pressuring Congress to adopt his policies. And the chief executive is just one member of a huge executive establishment that includes cabinet departments and all manner of independent agencies. These agencies are gold mines for lobbyists. They are largely invisible to the public. The policies they produce are similarly hidden from public view. So an inside strategy works well. We almost never hear of bureaucracies such as the Small Business Administration. Even people who have heard of this agency cannot say much about what it does. So we do not know whether its policies benefit only client groups or make us all better off. This is the perfect scenario for groups to get their way.

Presidents as Lobbyists

The following chapters by Gary Andres and Ernest Wilson focus on presidents as lobbyists. The White House has an agenda that it seeks to get through Congress. There is a famous line that suggests executive dominance in American politics: "The president proposes, the Congress disposes." Yet presidents must pursue their agendas vigorously. Victory is hardly automatic. So they become chief lobbyists as well as chief executives.

How critical is the president? There is little consensus. Andres opts for a powerful chief executive: "More than anything or anyone else, the key determinant of success or failure of the legislative affairs office is the president himself." The president does not attend to details, but he selects the men and women who negotiate with Congress and sets the parameters for how much leeway they have. Presidents in trouble often replace their key staff members. Yet their staffs reflect each president's own style. Simply changing the lobbyists will lead to no more success than a baseball team owner's swapping managers without replacing the weak players.

Andres served as an insider in the Bush administration. He sees things close up. But some political scientists who stand back a bit are less convinced that insiders are so powerful. George Edwards III (1980, 1989), Jon R. Bond and Richard Fleisher (1990), and Mark A. Peterson (1990) doubt that presidential lobbying skills matter. Bond and Fleisher carefully consider alternative presidential styles. They argue that proposing—and the style of proposers—matter less than who does the disposing. The laws we get reflect the composition of Congress. Presidents win when they have a large number of devoted supporters on Capitol Hill. Presidents do not need to mobilize their core supporters. The loyal will stick with the White House through thick and thin. Andres recognizes this when he argues that "lawmakers of the President's party will normally support his position if doing so does not violate any long held philosophical view and is consistent with previous votes." But he adds: "Others, however, need cajoling and convincing. That's where the White House legislative affairs office spends most of its time and must get creative."

Until recently, most academic studies have not found much of an impact for executive lobbying. Peterson (1990, 276) argues that "the evidence of diminished Presidential influence in Congress has less to do with any plausible scenario of declining presidential talent than with extensive contemporary changes in the institutional, political, economic, and policy contexts of American politics." American politics is more fragmented and polarized. Presidents now find it difficult to get controversial agendas through Congress. And Congress is composed of independent entrepreneurs whose electoral success does not depend on the fate of the president.

Yet context isn't everything. Peterson argues that presidential style and skill have indirect effects on legislative success. Style and skill reveal themselves in a president's priorities. Presidents are more likely to prevail on issues that are central to their agendas. High-priority issues energize the White House staff and the Legislative Liaison Office. They also rouse up support among the core supporters in the president's ideological base (Peterson 1990, 160–71). Sullivan (1991) conducted a quantitative analysis of how well presidents are able to mobilize support for their proposals. He looks at White House "head counts"—expectations of who would support and who would oppose the president on upcoming roll calls—and compares them to the actual congressional votes. Presidents who concentrated on a relatively small agenda were more likely to swing votes in their favor from the Congress. Covington, Wrighton, and Kinney (1995) showed that presidents are most likely to win on items on their agenda. Covington (1987) found that members of the House were more likely to cast votes on issues that Presidents John F. Kennedy and Lyndon B. Johnson placed high on their agendas. The White House Office of Congressional Relations was able to mobilize its base. Palazollo and Swinford (1994) and Uslaner (1995) show that presidential lobbying on the North Atlantic Free Trade Agreement (NAFTA) in 1994 helped pass the accord in the House of Representatives.

The message is clear: keep yourself focused. Ernest Wilson's chapter shows that low-priority issues get weak lobbying efforts. He attributes many of the policy failures in Bill Clinton's White House to the low priority the administration gave to foreign policy. But the foreign policy and NAFTA cases also show the limits of White House strategic planning. Why did the Clinton administration give such a low priority to foreign policy? Mostly because the American public is not terribly interested in foreign policy these days (Spanier and Uslaner 1994, chap. 5). Why did presidential lobbying work on the North American Free Trade Agreement? Because President Clinton targeted those swing members who were *already most likely to back him* (Uslaner 1995). Presidents don't just set their agendas. They don't just decide to lobby. They are constrained by the larger political environment, including public opinion, their base in Congress, and the range of interested parties in the interest group universe.

Interest Groups and the Bureaucracy

Executives lobby. But they are also lobbied. Most interest groups do not have the high profiles that would give them access to the Oval Office. And they often find, especially on foreign policy, that the Executive Office of the President is not the most hospitable environment for their causes (Spiegel 1985). Presidents and their staffs look at the larger picture. They often have their own ideologies and interests and will not risk being seen as the tool of "special interests." Presidents want to be seen as representatives of the entire nation.

But that is hardly the case with the rest of the executive branch. The cabinet departments and independent agencies are designed to deal with narrower issues. The Department of Agriculture administers farm programs, not school construction. It would be surprising if narrow executive departments did not come to represent the interests that it regulates. And this is precisely what William Gormley finds in the next chapter. Our regulators often come from the very industries they are supposed to regulate. And regulators with ties to industry are not the independent watchdogs of business (or labor) that we expect them to be. Instead, it becomes difficult to tell the regulators from the regulated. This is the "capture theory" of regulation, where agencies become the tools of the industries they are supposed to regulate (Bernstein 1955). Writ large, American politics is one of "interest group liberalism" (Lowi 1979). Congress and the president delegate authority to lower-level administrators, who are captured by special interests. Government is not a neutral arbitrator among groups. Instead, both the legislative and executive branches are designed to represent the well-organized and the well-off at the expense of the more diffuse interests of the larger society. The Department of Agriculture represents farmers (Lowi calls it "Little Sir Echo"), not the interests of all Americans.

Why do we let this happen? Mostly, we have little choice. Many groups in American society—consumers, the poor, the less-educated—are poorly organized. They have neither the resources nor the skills to participate widely in politics (Verba, Schlozman, and Brady 1995). The more affluent often see a clearer stake in government policy. They are more easily mobilized. And they have the resources to influence both Congress and the bureaucracy. Bureaucrats, legislators, and interest groups form a community of interests. Groups lobby—and ultimately capture—the agencies that are supposed to regulate them. The groups provide key support for the agencies when bureaucrats seek higher funding levels from Congress. Congress gives interest groups the policies (such as agriculture price supports) they want, and bureaucrats work to ensure that the programs meet group demands. Groups then reward members of Congress with electoral support. So everyone gains something and nobody—except the disorganized mass of citizens—loses anything. This is the idea of an "iron triangle" involving the bureaucracy, congressional committees, and interest groups. The triangle also goes by other names: subsystem, policy whirlpool, and subgovernment (Freeman 1955, 6).

Whatever we call it, we should recognize that the iron triangle works only because it is out of the public eye. Few bureaucrats (or members of Congress) would wish to announce that they have been captured, or even that they were devoted adherents to the cause of any special interest. The iron triangle reflects policymaking on *distributive* policies, where government doles out goodies to interests. As long as everyone gets something, there is little debate over the merits of each program. Issues such as agriculture price supports, federal aid to the merchant marine, and defense contracting are rarely the subjects of strong ideological debates. These issues do not *appear to* transfer wealth from one group to another. Neither do they tell people (or groups) what they can or cannot do. Iron triangles simply dole out money in a quiet, bipartisan way.

The same players deal with each other year after year and make the same policy decisions year after year. Bureaucrats have life tenure, interest groups rarely go out of business, and members of Congress win reelection based on their ability to get bureaucrats to help their constituents and the support they receive from interest groups that benefit from federal largesse. This stability is bolstered by consensus: everyone makes a deal and no one makes a fuss. Each group "owns" its congressional committee or subcommittee, its little piece of turf in the federal bureaucracy, and its place in the group universe. Iron triangles are monopolies. Groups face no competition. Presidents are interlopers in this game. There is a new chief executive every eight years—and usually sooner. Presidents have little interest in constituency benefits—that is the realm of Congress and the bureaucracy. Walker (1991, 137) argues that iron triangles "protect the presidency from a potentially unmanageable flood of disputes." They give the president the cover to avoid taking controversial stands on popular programs such as public works or agriculture price supports. Congress makes the policy, claims the benefits, and removes these issues from the presidential agenda. And it's a good thing too. When presidents get involved—as Jimmy Carter and Ronald Reagan did—it is often to raid the purse of distributive benefits for other programs or tax reductions. And they rarely win in a direct confrontation with Congress on distributive issues. Groups recognize the president's dilemma and stay away from the White House. When interest group representatives need information or form coalitions, they go first to Congress. Presidents and cabinet officers rank near the bottom of both lists (Schlozman and Tierney 1986, 274–75).

Iron triangles were the dominant mode of policymaking from the 1940s to the 1970s. Then the political world changed. New issues arose and new interest groups came into being. Building a dam was no longer a simple deal among the Army Corps of Engineers, the House and Senate Interior committees, and the construction firms (Maass 1951). Now environmentalists got involved, and the stakes changed dramatically. Would the dam harm endangered species? What would it do to water quality? During the energy crises of the 1970s, scores of groups suddenly developed intense interest in where they were going to get their oil, gas, coal, electricity, and nuclear energy. As Jones (1979, 105) argued: "the *cozy little triangles* ... had become *sloppy large hexagons*" (emphasis in original).

The booming 1960s led to the rise of a new constellation of issues. A wealthy country could afford to pay more attention to the environment, civil rights, consumer protection, and all sorts of issues that involve either regulation or redistribution of resources. Walker (1991, 63–70) details the rise of interest groups in American politics in the 1960s and 1970s. The biggest growth spurt came from citizen groups—representing people who had previously had little voice in the policy process. All of a sudden groups that had previously had no opposition found themselves face to face with adversaries (Gais, Peterson, and Walker 1984). Iron triangles were replaced by "issue networks," bureaucrats, staffers, and group representatives linked by expertise in a policy area. In each policy domain, there might be many networks, not just one, and each would represent a different world-view. In this new world, consensus gives way to controversy. And long-standing alliances give way to shifting coalitions. By the 1980s, almost every interest group reported both allies and adversaries. A third of all group representatives said that their allies changed from one issue to another (Schlozman and Tierney 1986, 283). One classic iron triangle—agriculture—stumbled along with a modest degree of conflict. Another—energy—had become a very public whirlpool without lasting friends, but lots of lasting enmity (Salisbury, Heinz, Laumann, and Nelson 1987; Uslaner 1989). By the 1990s, even agriculture had become contentious as urban liberals, free-market conservatives, and environmentalists all ganged up on this formerly peaceable kingdom in a great raid on the sugar daddy of all subsidies. Many farm programs survived even the budget cuts of 1995–96, but not without bruising battles.

Interest Groups and the Executive: New Directions

From the 1940s through the 1960s, interest groups focused on the bureaucracy, not the White House. Lobbyists had supportive working agreements with bureaucrats. Often they even captured the regulators. The boom years led to greater conflict when the new kids on the block—citizen groups—pushed for government regulations. Consumer and environmental protection became increasingly prominent political issues and displaced the traditional distributive issues of the more consensual era. Then, as budgets tightened in the 1970s and thereafter, the remaining distributive issues became contentious. Special interests could get what they wanted as long as there was more than enough to go around. More stringent times meant greater controversy over who could raid the Treasury.

As more groups became active, their influence waned, as Gormley has noted in chapter 13. Tougher times have produced demands for budget cutting. Presidents now need to find funds for their pet projects wherever there is money. And this means that presidents are now becoming more involved in policy disputes over distributive issues. Demands for political reform have also pushed presidents into the group arena, as Gormley details. Jimmy Carter and Bill Clinton have been at the forefront of efforts to free government agencies from capture by restricting the jobs that former government officials can take in the private sector.

As the number of groups soars, the relative power of all groups de-clines. It is no longer easy to exercise influence within the bureaucracy, Gormley notes. So many groups are using different tactics. Both citizen and business lobbies are increasingly turning to litigation (Walker 1991). If you cannot win any more in Congress, transfer the conflict to the courts. Or, go directly to the White House. Under the old regime of iron triangles, the president was a peripheral player. Now he sets the agenda by dictating which groups get access to the executive branch.

Under the iron-triangle model, everyone got something. Liberals, con-servatives, Democrats, Republicans all shared in the booty. Now each pres-ident sets out an ideological agenda, providing access only to groups that are ideologically in sync with the administration's program. Carter started this politics of exclusion, but Ronald Reagan pushed this strategy to new heights. Groups that are shut out of the executive branch will go pleading to Congress when it is controlled by the opposition party—or to the courts when all seems stacked against them.

We now have a more contentious interest group environment. This makes it harder for groups to get their way and for presidents to lobby Congress. Groups are now more confrontational, and both the executive and legislative branches face more hostile environments. The public seems disgusted with all this backbiting, but it complicates the whole process by electing Congresses and presidents who seem destined to disagree with each other. Now groups are more closely identified with one party and one ideology than at any time in the recent past. This provides both opportuni-ties for the dominant coalition and severe problems for interests on the outside. As the in-groups and the out-groups exchange places frequently, the group universe looks more like a see-saw than a level playing field.

13 William T. Gormley Jr.

Interest Group Interventions in the Administrative Process: Conspirators and Co-Conspirators

THE IMPLEMENTATION of the Clean Air Act of 1990 troubled state governments and private corporations. Corporations objected to a car-pooling requirement that employers in nine smoggy cities take steps to encourage car pooling or the use of mass transit. State governments objected to an automobile emissions testing program in regions with exceptionally dirty air. Following tense conversations with governors and corporate officials, U.S. Environmental Protection Agency Administrator Carol Browner announced that participation in the car-pooling initiative would be voluntary and that smaller reductions in automobile emissions would be allowed (Lee 1996, 1). This episode illustrates how interest groups, including state governments, can influence the outcome of important decisions by federal agencies.

This chapter provides a broad overview of interest group involvement in decisions made by the federal bureaucracy. Students of bureaucratic politics and public administration differ in their assessment of the importance and the propriety of interest group interventions. According to some observers, interest groups are ubiquitous, importunate, and efficacious. According to others, interest groups are eclipsed by other important actors, such as legislators, political executives, and bureaucrats themselves. If interest groups do matter, a key normative concern is whether the constellation of interest groups active in particular proceedings or discussions is representative of the wider society. Another concern is whether interest groups support or undermine rational decision making.

Strategies and Tactics

Interest groups use a variety of techniques to influence decisions made by the federal bureaucracy. One of these is direct lobbying. Under the Administrative Procedure Act of 1946, federal administrative agencies must provide for a "comment" period as part of the rulemaking process. Although this does not necessarily imply an oral hearing, some statutes do require such a hearing. Regardless of statutory requirements, most federal administrative agencies have found it prudent to hold a hearing in which interest groups (and others) are free to participate. For their part, interest groups have often found these hearings to be excellent opportunities to state their views. According to Kerwin (1994, 203), they have found written comments to be even more efficacious.

A second technique is to influence the bureaucracy by influencing the Congress or particular members of Congress. For example, an interest group upset with a particular agency's policies or decisions can encourage a sympathetic member of Congress to hold an oversight hearing that puts the offending agency on the spot. Or an interest group can persuade a key member of Congress to threaten an appropriations reduction if the agency does not rethink its position. Or an interest group can convince a legislator to propose legislation that would clip the agency's wings, thus encouraging the agency to cry uncle. Studies show that legislative oversight of the bureaucracy can be effective (Aberbach 1990; Hedge and Scicchitano 1994). The connection between interest group activity and legislative oversight is less clear. What is clear is that interest groups work closely with congressional allies to reverse unfavorable decisions by administrative agencies. In 1995, for example, business groups helped convince Congress to cut the Environmental Protection Agency's enforcement budget and prohibit the Occupational Safety and Health Administration from issuing a workplace ergonomic rule, which would have set new standards to protect workers from repetitive strain injuries, such as carpal tunnel syndrome.

A third technique is to ensure that the top political executives who run the agency are supportive of the interest group's most cherished positions. In some instances, this may take the familiar form of the "revolving door," where someone who has worked for the interest group (or a related organization) is endorsed for a key political appointment. In other instances, the interest group may advise the agency or the White House personnel office that a particular nominee under consideration is unacceptable. Former broadcasting industry officials at the Federal Communications Commission are more sympathetic to the broadcasting industry and vote accordingly (Gormley 1979). Although the president's political party is a more powerful predictor of regulatory behavior than industry ties, regulatory commissioners who expect to accept a job with a regulated firm vote sympathetically during their final year in office (Cohen 1986). Thus the revolving door may matter more at the "exit" stage than at the "entry" stage.

A fourth technique is to mobilize a large constituency that initiates a letter-writing campaign or a series of personal visits to put pressure on the agency. That constituency may be geographic, occupational, or ideological in nature. The threat of electoral or budgetary reprisals may be sufficient to capture the agency's attention. According to Kerwin (1994, 203), the mobilization of grassroots support is one of several techniques that interest groups regard as effective.

These are not the only techniques that interest groups may employ to influence federal administrative agencies, but they illustrate an important point: interest groups can influence administrative agencies in a variety of ways, directly or indirectly, by shaping policies or personnel.

Alternative Perspectives

Scholars disagree on both the extent and the desirability of interest group influence in the administrative process. To some extent, these disagreements follow disciplinary fault lines. For example, economists have often stressed both the lopsided nature of interest representation and the pernicious consequences that flow from such representation. Olson (1971, 1982) has argued that narrow, special interests are far better represented than broader, more diffuse interests and that this asymmetric interest representation ultimately undermines economic growth. Stigler (1971) has argued that special interest groups, representing regulated firms or industries, tend to "capture" administrative agencies, especially regulatory agencies, and that this undermines economic efficiency. Niskanen (1971, 1990) has argued that federal administrative agencies, with strong support from loyal interest group constituencies, have sought larger budgetary appropriations than are warranted, to the detriment of taxpayers and the public good. If these critics are correct, then the relationship between interest groups and federal agencies, though symbiotic, does not serve the common good.

In contrast, legal scholars, such as administrative law experts, have often stressed both opportunities for interest groups to articulate diverse interests in society and the positive consequences of interest representation for public policy and for the legitimacy of our political system. Stewart (1975) has developed an interest representation model of administrative law that he regards as superior to models that stress legislative decision making or administrative expertise. Boyer (1981) has argued that efforts to enhance public participation in administrative decision making (e.g., through government funding of public interest groups) can result in a better balance of viewpoints and better agency decisions. And Rose-Ackerman (1995) has argued that the U.S. emphasis on robust interest representation in the administrative process ought to be emulated by other nations, even in policy domains where it is thought to promote conflict or delay, such as environmental policy. In general, administrative law scholars have viewed interest representation in positive terms. Although they have detected imperfections in our system, they have usually argued that some fine-tuning could resolve most remaining difficulties.

Political science perspectives on interest representation in the administrative process are more difficult to summarize, partly because the literature is richer and more nuanced. A number of political scientists have argued that special interest groups play a disturbingly prominent role in bureaucratic decision making (Schattschneider 1960; McConnell 1966; Lowi 1969). More subtly, Moe (1989) has argued that interest groups incorporate procedural constraints into statutes that ultimately make it difficult for administrative agencies to achieve their stated goals. Other political scientists, however, believe that the horrors of interest group politics have been greatly exaggerated (Aberbach and Rockman 1990).

Although schooled in the interest group tradition, a number of scholars have found it fruitful to abandon the concept of interest groups in favor of other broader categories. Heclo (1978) has argued that the policymaking process (including administrative decision making) can best be understood by thinking about "issue networks," which include interest groups but which include other actors as well. Similarly, Sabatier and Jenkins-Smith (1993) have utilized the construct of "advocacy coalitions" to advance a theory of the policymaking process. At the state level, I have sought to distinguish between conventional interest groups and proxy organizations, such as state attorneys general, that represent underrepresented interests in administrative proceedings (Gormley 1983). At the federal level, Salisbury (1984) has suggested that certain petitioners, such as state and local governments and corporations that intervene in the federal government's decision-making processes, should be thought of as "institutions" rather than interest groups, to distinguish them from membership-based organizations.

Trends

Over the past two to three decades, interest representation in the federal bureaucracy has changed significantly. The first, and most widely documented, change is that interest groups based in Washington, D.C., have become more numerous and more diverse. Private firms have established their own offices in the nation's capital (Schlozman 1984). Public interest groups, such as environmental groups, consumer groups, and women's groups, have proliferated (Walker 1983). State and local governments have beefed up existing organizations such as the National Governors Association and the U.S. Conference of Mayors (Camissa 1995) and, in many instances, have established their own outposts in our nation's capital as well. Numerous interests now possess the capacity to speak through an organization or a combination of organizations with headquarters in Washington, D.C. The potential for what Berry (1989) calls an "interest group society" is present.

A second important trend, however, has helped to undermine that potential. Beginning with the Nixon administration, presidents have undertaken significant initiatives to increase White House control over administrative rulemaking. Shortly after establishing the Office of Management and Budget (OMB), President Nixon issued an executive order institutionalizing "quality of life" reviews of proposed administrative regulations. Since that time, every president has established a procedure for OMB review of rules under consideration by the federal bureaucracy. President Reagan sharply accelerated this development by mandating that every major rule be accompanied by a cost-benefit analysis and by requiring that rulemakers take costs into account. OMB review has the potential to nullify or at least mitigate the effects of interest representation in administrative rulemaking. That is especially true of interests that call for stronger regulations whose benefits cannot be quantified or whose benefits do not exceed the corresponding costs.

A third trend has been to reduce opportunities for informal contacts between interest groups and the federal bureaucracy, including "ex parte contacts" while official proceedings are under way. A related development has been to discourage the "revolving door" between the private sector (broadly defined) and the executive branch. Jimmy Carter fired the opening salvo in the war against the revolving door by imposing restrictions on former government employees who wish to lobby the agency for which they used to work. Other presidents, including President Clinton, have supported and/or tightened such restrictions. In addition, President Clinton has issued an executive order prohibiting executive branch officials from meeting with lobbyists who do not meet strict registration requirements and has signed legislation requiring lobbyists to disclose their contacts with high-level executive branch officials. Changes in the tax code have also discouraged informal communication by increasing the costs of the legendary two-martini lunch.[1] All these reforms have worked to limit interest group interventions to on-the-record interventions in rulemaking proceedings and documented meetings between registered lobbyists and top agency officials.

A fourth trend, undoubtedly influenced by some of the above developments, has been for interest group influence in the federal bureaucracy to decline. Evidence from a longitudinal study of political appointees and senior civil servants within the federal bureaucracy supports the proposition that interest group influence has waned. In 1970, 33 percent of senior civil servants reported that interest groups wielded "a great deal of influence" over bureaucratic decision making; in 1986–87, only 14 percent of senior civil servants agreed with that proposition (Aberbach and Rockman 1990, 37). A key reason for the perceived reduction in influence is that contacts between interest group representatives and civil servants appear to have declined (Aberbach and Rockman 1990, 38). Of course, perceptions may be incorrect. Other social scientists, however, using different techniques and focusing more explicitly on policy outputs, have reached similar conclusions. For example, Heinz et al. (1993) believe that interest groups are participating more in the political process but enjoying it less. A key reason for this, they argue, is that interest groups are pitted against other interest groups, with somewhat unpredictable results.

Bureaucratic Differences

Though it is useful to consider overall trends, it is important to recognize their limitations. For example, executive orders empowering OMB to review rules and regulations, such as President Reagan's Executive Order 12291 and President Clinton's Executive Order 12866, have not applied to independent regulatory commissions such as the Federal Communications Commission and the Federal Trade Commission. Such agencies are therefore less subject to centralized oversight and presumably more vulnerable to interest group pressure. In contrast, administrative agencies that make foreign policy, such as the State Department, experience little sustained interest group pressure. Thus the sharp increase in interest group formation and representation that characterized the 1960s and 1970s may have bypassed agencies that deal with diplomacy, national security, and defense.

Several key differences in federal agencies affect the levels of interest group interactions found in the executive branch. First, administrative agencies deal with issues that differ in their salience; and salience affects the extent of interest representation. Administrative agencies that deal with issues of considerable interest to the general public can expect a variety of interest groups to come knocking on their door (Gormley 1986). This includes the Department of Health and Human Services (health and welfare issues), the Department of Education, and the Environmental Protection Agency. In contrast, agencies that confront issues with narrow appeal can anticipate relatively modest interest group participation. Such agencies include the Federal Deposit Insurance Corporation, the Securities and Exchange Commission, and the General Services Administration. Of course, salience varies somewhat over time. The savings and loan disaster, for example, temporarily increased the salience of financial regulation. Nevertheless, at any given point in time, agencies differ considerably in the degree to which they are exposed to interest group pressure.

Second, administrative agencies deal with issues that differ in their complexity; and complexity affects the effectiveness of interest representation (Gormley 1986). Special interest groups, with ample technical resources at their disposal, are well equipped to influence agencies that deal with arcane and esoteric issues. In contrast, public interest groups, with more meager resources, are often ill equipped to influence agencies that must weigh scientific evidence before making decisions. One exception to this general rule is environmental policy, where public interest groups have acquired sufficient technical expertise to challenge the factual foundations of business group arguments and the evidentiary basis for proposed administrative rules. Even in environmental policy, however, the clash of interests is often asymmetrical, to the detriment of public interest groups.

Third, administrative agencies differ in the extent to which their policy proposals benefit the few at the expense of the many. According to Wilson (1973), proposals with concentrated benefits and concentrated costs trigger interest group politics of the sort detected by Heinz et al. (1993), with one or more interest groups pitted against each other. But that is not the only possibility. In some instances, proposals benefit relatively narrow constituencies at the expense of taxpayers as a whole. In this familiar domain of "clientele politics," a single interest group or a cluster of like-minded interest groups has the potential to dominate the administrative policymaking process. Opportunities for clientele politics may well have diminished over time, as iron triangles have given way to issue networks. Nevertheless, there are examples of clientele politics even today, such as the USDA's agricultural marketing order program (Kerwin 1994, 207–8).

Fourth, administrative agencies differ in the extent to which their outputs can be monitored and their outcomes can be measured. Building on this insight, Wilson (1989) has developed a four-fold typology that yields four types of agencies: production agencies (observable outputs, measurable outcomes); procedural agencies (observable outputs, unmeasurable outcomes); craft agencies (unobservable outputs, measurable outcomes); and coping agencies (unobservable outputs, unmeasurable outcomes). Although Wilson does not link this typology to interest representation, one might argue that procedural agencies are most susceptible to interest group pressure. That is because interest groups can supply information to procedural agencies that looks highly relevant but that in fact is highly misleading (because it diverts attention from outcomes to outputs). Coping agencies may be the least manageable of all agencies, as Wilson contends, but that may insulate them from interest group pressure. Whatever entreaties interest groups submit to coping agencies, they cannot hope to constrain the behavior of street-level bureaucrats who enjoy enormous discretion (teachers, law enforcement officers, etc.).

Interest Group Effectiveness

Interest group interventions in administrative decision making range greatly in overall effectiveness. According to Aberbach and Rockman (1990), the effectiveness of such interventions has declined since 1970. Still, that does not tell us how effective such groups are, nor does it tell us which groups are more effective than others. It is useful to start with the presumption that well-funded business groups will be more effective than poorly funded public interest groups. That presumption seems reasonable enough. But not all business groups are well funded; nor is there enduring consensus among the many business groups that seek to affect the policymaking process. In addition, there are some extremely well-funded public interest groups, or these groups may have close ties to key agency officials, providing them with disproportionate access and influence.

Existing research suggests that both business groups and public interest groups have the capacity to influence federal administrative agencies. One survey of federal rulemakers found no difference in the perceived effectiveness of business groups and public interest groups (Furlong 1992). Perceptions may be mistaken. Another study, however, using behavioral methods, found that both business groups and public interest groups have influenced EPA decisions to continue or cancel the registrations of pesticides: when growers intervened, the EPA was more likely to continue registrations; when nonprofit organizations intervened, the EPA was more likely to cancel registrations (Cropper et al. 1990). Admittedly, this evidence comes from one set of issues addressed by one federal agency. Also, as noted earlier, environmental politics has for years been characterized by unusually feisty, resourceful, and efficacious public interest groups.

When I studied organizational effectiveness at the state level, I reached two interrelated conclusions: First, both business groups (public utilities) and citizens' groups (consumer groups, environmental groups) were effective participants in the administrative process (public utility commission decisions), but business groups were generally more effective. Second, citizens' groups' influence was largely confined to issues of relatively low complexity, such as redistributive issues that did not require reams of data on the cost of capital and rates of return on investment (Gormley 1983). If these findings are transferable to the federal level, they suggest that federal rulemakers, in the Furlong study, are perceiving greater balance in interest group representation than actually exists. They also suggest that environmental policymaking, in the Cropper et al. study, illustrates the upper bounds of effective citizen participation, rather than common patterns of participation.

Recent evidence supplied by Golden (1995) suggests an additional variable of considerable importance, specifically, whether the interest group supports or opposes the viewpoint of agency officials. When intervenors disagree, as they often do, agency officials respond to the viewpoint they find most congenial. This is true whether the disagreements involve business groups versus citizens' groups or business groups versus business groups. My own assessment of this phenomenon would be that interest group interventions in federal agency rulemaking proceedings constitute "catalytic controls" that do not pose a threat to agency autonomy or rational decision making (Gormley 1989). In contrast to coercive controls, catalytic controls require a bureaucratic response but do not require the bureaucracy to grant supplicants their precise request. That is, of course, especially the case when there are multiple supplicants with competing points of view. The upshot of this is that interest group interventions should have some impact—but not a dramatic impact—on rulemaking proceedings. And that is exactly what Golden finds: In seven of ten cases studied, there was some impact but not a great impact (Golden 1995, 56). In only two cases was there no impact at all.

Future Developments

Although the future of interest representation in federal administrative proceedings is difficult to predict, several developments are already apparent. The first is the effort by congressional Republicans to subject administrative rulemaking to greater congressional and judicial oversight. Under HR 9, which passed the House in March 1995, Congress would have a forty-five-day period in which to review administrative rules. Also, regulated firms would have additional opportunities to challenge rules in the federal courts: where a risk assessment and a cost-benefit analysis were prepared, firms could contest the technical quality of these findings; where such studies were not prepared, they could question whether the agency erred by not preparing them. Senate bill S 343, proposed by former Senators Robert Dole (R-Kans.) and Bennett Johnston (D-La.), included similar provisions. Although not brought to a vote, the bill might be revived in some form in the 105th Congress. At one level, these are efforts to encourage "forum-shifting" away from the federal executive bureaucracy and toward the legislative and judicial branches of government. At another level, they are attempts to augment the influence of regulated firms by multiplying opportunities to overturn a rule. In principle, public interest groups might also benefit from such opportunities, but regulated firms are more likely to be able to afford multiple interventions.

A second legislative proposal that has generated some interest on Capitol Hill would prohibit nonprofit organizations receiving federal funds from devoting more than 5 percent of their private resources to "political advocacy," including advocacy within the executive branch (Barr and Morgan 1995; Yang 1995). Championed by former Senator Alan Simpson (R-Wyo.) and Congressman David McIntosh (R-Ind.), among others, this proposal would almost certainly reduce the number and potency of interventions in administrative rulemaking proceedings by public interest groups. That would make interest representation in the administrative process even more asymmetric than it currently is. As Golden (1995) has noted, citizens' groups are far less likely to participate in administrative rulemaking proceedings than trade associations and private firms. If such legislation were to pass, public interest groups would be forced to cut back their lobbying activities, which would reduce their influence and, more important, deprive administrative agency officials of valuable information and advice.

A third and more benign development, already well under way, is to develop alternatives to administrative rulemaking. The most popular of these alternatives to date is "regulatory negotiation." Over the past decade and a half, a number of federal agencies have experimented with regulatory negotiation, in an effort to resolve policy differences among various interests in a less adversarial setting. The hope is that this will result in swifter, more amicable dispute resolution, with a lower likelihood of judicial review and judicial reversal. The Environmental Protection Agency, whose rules are almost always challenged in federal court, has been particularly enthusiastic about regulatory negotiation and has initiated a total of eighteen negotiated rulemakings, only two of which had to be aborted in midstream (Dalton 1993). It is difficult to know for sure whose interests are best furthered by regulatory negotiation. The philosophical premise, however, which many advocates accept, is that all parties ultimately benefit from a process that reduces posturing, encourages collective problem solving, and strives for win-win solutions. In a sense, the regulatory negotiation model embraces a more European-style approach to interest representation—the government invites relevant interests to participate in the administrative process not as petitioners or adversaries but as fellow problem solvers. Such a "corporatist" approach to interest representation presupposes that key interests can be readily identified, that all parties are capable of good faith, and that positive-sum game solutions can be found. If these conditions are present, regulatory negotiation holds considerable potential.

Negotiation does have its pitfalls, especially if multipolar conflicts are handled through bilateral bargaining between an administrative agency and a particular firm. For example, the Interior Department negotiated with the Murray Pacific Corporation, approving certain waivers from the Endangered Species Act; in return, the company agreed to cut no trees on 10 percent of its tree farm (Skrzycki 1996, 1). This may or may not be good public policy, but it effectively excludes other interested parties, such as environmental groups, from the administrative decision-making process.

Conclusion

It is natural for Americans to be apprehensive about interest groups. Certainly, our Founding Fathers were. They fretted about the mischiefs of faction and designed a political system that, they hoped, would make it difficult for factions to prevail. During the 1960s, there was some evidence to suggest that special interest groups dominated decision making within administrative agencies, especially regulatory agencies. During the 1970s, as public interest group participation mushroomed, it appeared that interest groups were busting out all over, resulting in more balanced interest representation but also in potential threats to reasoned decision making. During the 1980s, reasoned decision making became institutionalized, possibly at the expense of interest representation. Where does this leave us today? And where are we heading?

One possibility is that interest groups have declined in importance. That, at any rate, is the perception of federal civil servants, whose judgment deserves serious consideration. The root cause of that perception would seem to be that their contacts with interest groups are less extensive than they used to be. If legislation restricting lobbying by nonprofit organizations is passed, such contacts could diminish even further. There is, however, another possibility that needs to be further investigated, and that is that interest groups are as influential as ever but that they are increasingly acting through surrogates. When a congressional subcommittee chairperson extracts concessions from a federal agency, is he or she pursuing a personal agenda or an interest group agenda? When a federal court overturns an administrative agency decision, can that edict be traced to the ingenuity or perseverance of a particular interest group? When the Office of Management and Budget jawbones with an agency over a proposed rule, does that reflect technical objections to cost-benefit calculations or the reservations of an unnamed interest group? To understand interest groups better, we need to recognize that they often act in tandem with political institutions in an effort to influence other political institutions, such as the federal bureaucracy. If our research focus shifts in that direction, we may be better able to understand the complex relationship between administrative agencies and interest groups acting in concert with legislators, judges, and political executives.

Note

1. Tax-reform legislation enacted in 1986 reduced the deductibility of business lunches from 100 percent to 80 percent of expenses. Legislation enacted in 1993 further reduced that deductibility to 50 percent of expenses.

Gary J. Andres

Lobbying for the President: Influencing Congress from the White House

One of our darkest days as George Bush's Legislative Affairs team occurred in the fall of 1990 when we were informed during a GOP Leadership meeting on Capitol Hill that the President had just agreed to raise taxes. In addition to facing an angry mob of Republican Members, having to explain why we didn't know about the decision ahead of time only added insult to injury. For some reason, as I sat in that chaos filled room the late Bryce Harlow's (legislative affairs advisor to Presidents Eisenhower and Nixon) description of Congressional Affairs as an "ambulatory bridge across a constitutional divide" crossed my mind. In this case, however, the bridge had just blown up!

— Bush White House aide

MANAGING White House relations with Congress is a lot like landing a Boeing 747. Doing it right is routine, boring, and expected—not a feat that generates plaudits or praise. Yet doing it wrong can produce lots of sparks and heat, often leading to disastrous consequences for the president and his agenda. This chapter draws on my experience in the congressional relations operation of President George Bush, an operation that drew praise as well as criticism for the manner in which it worked with the Congress. It is my hope that at least two distinct audiences will learn from this chapter. First, I hope to add to the existing scholarly literature on how to structure, manage, and implement a White House lobbying program effectively. This research tends to fall into two broad categories.

Wayne (1978), Patterson (1988), and Gribbin (1989) provide detailed organizational analyses about the structure and operation of the White House Legislative Affairs Office. Conversely, much of the empirical literature (see, e.g., Covington 1987; Bond and Fleisher 1980) focuses less on the structure and operation of the Office of Legislative Affairs and more on other determinants of White House influence with Congress such as presidential popularity and party support in the House and Senate. This chapter falls into the first tradition, analyzing the structural determinants of a successful White House lobbying operation. It is also directed to current and future occupants of the White House Office of Legislative Affairs, and to those who organize it, with the hope that it will help those men and women replicate successes and avoid mistakes.

Structuring an Effective Office: Access to the President and Speaking for the President

The core of a successful White House lobbying operation is a structure that allows the principal Legislative Affairs staff direct, frequent, and meaningful access to the president. The structure must also provide a very clear picture to lawmakers that the Legislative Affairs office is the president's principal voice on Capitol Hill. The more layers of staff and bureaucracy separating the legislative operation from the president, or the larger the chorus of administration voices speaking for the president, the less successful the operation will be. A Legislative Affairs department isolated from direct contact with the Oval Office, or one that lacks the authority to speak for the White House, will lose credibility on Capitol Hill and serve the president poorly.

If the Legislative Affairs staff lacks direct access to the president, most legislators will interact with someone who does. Depending on the particular White House structure and the pattern of relationships within the building, it might be the chief of staff, the director of the Office of Management and Budget (OMB), or the National Security Adviser. Based on my discussions with current and former White House staff, circumvention of the Legislative Affairs office is one of the most common problems in managing congressional affairs since at least the Nixon administration. The president should take all steps necessary to ensure the problem is addressed swiftly, effectively, and regularly, if necessary.

Solving the problem is simple in principle, yet requires management, discipline, and direct support from the president. Ideally, all congressional calls or communications to any senior White House staff would be funneled through the Legislative Affairs office. In most cases, that is precisely how any congressional calls or communications to the president are handled by most recent White Houses. White House operators or other staff refer all calls from congressmen to the Legislative Affairs office and the legislative liaison staff perform an initial callback to determine if and when the president needs to get involved personally. A management directive from the president or chief of staff mandating that all congressional calls or correspondence to any White House staff get referred first to the Congressional Affairs office would go a long way toward ending uncoordinated and unauthorized interactions with legislators.

Controlling access in this way would raise the credibility of the Legislative Affairs office with lawmakers as well as help the office manage information flow between the White House and Capitol Hill. This structure would not eliminate contacts between Capitol Hill and non-Legislative Affairs White House staff, but it would manage them in such a way that the Congressional Affairs Department would know who is talking to the Hill, when, and on what legislative issues. Disasters in the legislative arena usually occur when the White House legislative team lacks information about agreements that other members of the administration reach with members of Congress. Sometimes the problems are small and manageable, but in other cases they can have long-term, devastating consequences.

The Bush administration's Environmental Protection Agency (EPA) created a small brush fire when it informed Congressman Henry Waxman (D-Calif.) that it supported one of his amendments during the markup of the Clean Air Act Amendments in 1989. The fragile coalition opposing the Waxman amendment included all of the Republicans and some of the most powerful Democrats on the House Energy and Commerce Committee, including then–House Energy and Commerce Chairman John Dingell (D-Mich.)—and presumably the White House. At least that is what the Legislative Affairs office was told.

Red-faced and angry, the White House Legislative Affairs office immediately tracked down the EPA officials responsible for communicating with Waxman and demanded that the agency correct the record. Fortunately, despite all the hullabaloo, the committee acted, and the White House position prevailed when the Energy and Commerce Committee defeated the Waxman amendment. This positive outcome occurred notwithstanding our inept communications display, but not before some embarrassing debate and angry back-room shouting matches between White House, EPA, and congressional staff. That was a minor blunder. At the other extreme, all four of George Bush's House lobbyists were blindsided in 1990 by a faxed press release from the White House while attending a meeting with members of the Republican leadership in the Capitol. An angry Republican law-maker read the fax aloud to the stunned audience of congressmen and White House lobbyists—the president had just agreed to raise taxes.

It is not rocket science, but executive branch decisions with congressional implications must be communicated to lawmakers in advance, through the Legislative Affairs office. Anything short of that is a disservice to the president and his allies on Capitol Hill. Frequent blunders, like the ones outlined here, will ultimately undermine the effectiveness of the president's lobbying operation and his stature with members of Congress.

William Bennett, President Reagan's secretary of education, implemented a congressional relations operation that instituted the two principles outlined earlier. First, his assistant secretary for legislative affairs had complete and unfettered access to the secretary. The assistant secretary had frequent, regular, and routine communication with the cabinet member to discuss congressional issues and problems. Second, Secretary Bennett laid down the law with the other senior staff—no communication, written or verbal, formal or informal, with members of Congress unless it was coordinated with the assistant secretary for legislative affairs.

This model went a long way toward creating a coordinated approach to Capitol Hill on behalf of the Department; it minimized blunders like those outlined earlier, and it raised the stature of the department's legislative arm because it was perceived to have access to the secretary and was a clear, consistent, identifiable voice on the Hill. According to one of Bennett's former assistant secretaries, this model was implemented because most of the senior staff at the department viewed themselves as "congressional affairs experts." "They were always anxious to work with Congress until something went wrong, then the Office of Legislative Affairs had to step in and pick up the pieces," said this former assistant secretary. "Coordinating all contact with the Hill through the Legislative Office helped alleviate many of these problems."

Harnessing Executive Branch, OMB Resources

With the proper level of organization and presidential support, the White House Office of Legislative Affairs has tremendous policy and political resources at its disposal throughout the executive branch of government. Cabinet members and the OMB director can help shape policies that benefit members of Congress; they can release information from the agencies that members can use for their political benefit, as well as engage in political activities such as traveling to a legislator's district and participating in a fund raiser.

Each department also employs an assistant secretary for legislative affairs, with an ample staff, that can join the White House legislative operation on lobbying key legislators prior to important votes. The departmental lobbyists follow issues as they meander through the committee process and often have unique insights into the political and substantive nuances included in legislation.

In conceptualizing the role of Legislative Affairs staff in managing executive branch lobbying, the word "harness" perhaps best captures the relationship, because if these executive branch resources are not organized and used appropriately, it can be counterproductive to the interests of the president. Failure to harness Congressional Affairs personnel in the other agencies not only squanders potential resources but can lead to the type of embarrassing coordination crises outlined in the previous section. As a further illustration, President Bush's OMB Director Richard Darman often dabbled in legislative affairs, creating a trail of problems for the White House Legislative Affairs office to clean up. Darman and most of his staff operated under the "one-way door principle." They sought information from the White House legislative staff to further their own objectives, but refused to parcel out any knowledge they had. Often, the White House liaison office had to step in and repair damage done by the OMB director and his staff to protect the interests of the president.

Direct intervention by the chief of staff or the president is the only way to remedy this problem. In the Bush White House, as is often the case, the Legislative Affairs office lacked the stature and clout internally to curtail the power of the OMB director's free-lancing on Capitol Hill. Failure to curb these abuses ultimately lessened the effectiveness of the Legislative Affairs office and harmed the president and his stature on the Hill. Raising the stature of the liaison office in the White House so that the assistant to the president for legislative affairs could prevent activities like those outlined above would go a long way toward remedying this problem.

Creating a Capitol Presence

A simple secret of success to any White House lobbying effort is visibility on Capitol Hill with members of Congress—legislators need to know when, where, and how to find Legislative Affairs personnel. A prominent cultural attribute of the Reagan and Bush Legislative Affairs operations was an active and visible presence in and around the Capitol whenever Congress was in session. "Working the steps or elevators," White House liaison personnel would literally stand on the Capitol steps where members would come in to vote or outside the elevators that led to the House and Senate chambers to discuss issues with legislators during and after roll-call votes in the House and Senate. This created an environment for the legislative liaison office to answer questions and communicate White House views to lawmakers directly and personally.

Many observers suggested Bill Clinton's first Legislative Affairs staff changed this practice, choosing to spend more time "downtown" at the White House compared to Capitol Hill. After several months of perceived invisibility, the Clinton crew began to hear criticism from Democratic congressmen suggesting they were treated better by the Reagan and Bush White Houses than their own party's president. In my opinion, one of the fundamental differences between the Republican White House staff from 1981 through 1992 and the Clinton Legislative Affairs office was the manner in which the individuals perceived the job. Reagan and Bush legislative liaison personnel viewed themselves as "lobbyists" for the president —choosing personnel to fill posts that, in many cases, previously held private-sector lobbying positions. I believe the Clinton White House perceived themselves differently. Most came directly from Capitol Hill or other political posts and maintained a staff mentality that almost disdained the word "lobbyist." Reagan and Bush Legislative Affairs offices wore the label of the president's "lobbyists" as a badge of honor, treating members and staff like peers while forcefully arguing the president's position on Capitol Hill and articulating legislators' views back to the White House.

This subtle, yet fundamental, difference in the way the Reagan and Bush teams versus the early Clinton team operated on Capitol Hill and the way each of them perceived their role was a major factor in the success of the respective operations. Successful future liaison operations should perceive themselves to be the president's lobbyists and interact with members and staff on a peer level. They should not avoid the rough-and-tumble of daily interactions with members of the House and Senate. Instead, they should establish a visible presence in the Capitol building.

Gaining Leadership Trust and Support

A key constituency, if not *the* key constituency, of any Legislative Affairs office is the congressional leadership of its own party. In the Bush White House, Legislative Affairs personnel worked daily, and usually hourly, with representatives of the Republican leadership in the House and Senate. Creating an environment of trust and reliance on the part of the president's party leadership is another key element of a successful White House legislative operation. Congressional leadership of the president's party should view the Legislative Affairs staff as its principal advocates in the White House. When the president is in the midst of personnel decisions, travel plans, or policy deliberations, the Legislative Affairs office should have a seat at the table, advocating the interests of the congressional leadership (which ideally represents the rank and file). Others in the White House can speak for the president's political friends, state party leaders, or the host of voices seeking the president's attention, but the Legislative Affairs office must speak effectively for the congressional leadership. Again, if members of Congress and specifically members in the leadership believe the legislative office is ineffective in representing congressional interests internally in the White House, lawmakers will turn elsewhere, ultimately undermining the effectiveness of the entire Legislative Affairs effort.

Conversely, once the president's party leadership in Congress trusts and relies on the Office of Legislative Affairs, the congressional leadership can help promote the president's agenda with the rank-and-file members of Congress. Garnering the absolute support of the congressional leadership is a key variable in successfully promoting the president's agenda with the remainder of the members. Any successful Legislative Affairs operation should work diligently toward earning the respect and trust of its party leadership in Congress. Such support will help ensure the rank and file consistently vote with the president as well.

Cultivating Relations with Members and Staff

One of the most difficult balancing acts for the White House lobbyist is how to advocate the president's position forcefully without crossing some line that turns a potential ally into an offended enemy. During the process of counting floor votes in the House and Senate, part of the White House cultural imperative was to "talk to the member." Too often industry lobbyists or others lose unexpectedly on key floor votes because of reliance on hearsay or guesses communicated by congressional staff concerning a member's position on a key vote. Any top-notch congressional relations operation encourages its personnel to deal directly and regularly with members of Congress in the process of gathering intelligence, communicating White House positions, and counting votes.

In some cases a member may leave his office on his way to vote, having told his staff he will follow the staff's recommendation to vote no. If the staffer passes on this information to lobbyists, he will be recorded that way on industry vote tallies. On his way to the floor, however, the White House staff may talk to the member and communicate the president's deep desire for the member to vote yes. Or the member might go to the floor and get buttonholed by his leadership, urging him to vote yes. Particularly in cases where the vote is not that salient to the member, direct personal communication with the congressman or senator is the only sure way to gauge his or her sentiment and potential vote.

Having said that, congressional staff are still an integral resource for the White House liaison office and play a critical role in the overall process. Ignoring their importance is a critical error. Cultivating good relations with key staff, taking their advice, and respecting their role is also critical in the development of an effective congressional relations strategy. Too often, however, lobbyists for government agencies or in the private sector rely too heavily or even exclusively on staff alone, often at their peril.

Successful congressional relations personnel will operate in both environments, with members and with staff. In doing so, the effective operation will deal appropriately with both groups, drawing on the resources and expertise of each. Judgment and common sense must guide activities in these areas. For example, talking about how a member will vote when staff indicates the boss is still undecided is a risk. If, however, the staffer tells you the office has just issued a press release indicating how the legislator intends to vote, there is usually no need to bother the member.

Frequent and regular White House Legislative Affairs office interactions with the member, to the exclusion of the staff, however, can also lead to negative results. In several cases White House personnel burned bridges with staff in a member's office by conveying the perception that they only "dealt with the member." This type of attitude and arrogance is counterproductive and should be avoided in any successful and effective liaison operation.

Several times during the Bush administration, White House Legislative Affairs personnel had to calm down angry congressional administrative assistants who had no knowledge the "boss" had just agreed to do a favor for the administration, like introduce a bill or cosponsor an amendment. Savvy and professional liaison personnel will always touch base with staff after making a request of the members directly so that everyone is in the communication loop.

Another attribute of a successful White House legislative office is "attention to the little things"—returning your phone calls every day before you go home, helping a junior congressional staffer by bringing his family into the White House for a tour of the Oval Office, faxing key staffers presidential position papers before they have to ask, or trying to find out why someone cannot get a satisfactory response to a constituent request to an agency. The list could go on and on. But the principle is the same. Pay attention to detail. Be courteous to people. And don't let even the smallest request go unattended. This philosophy and the implementation of it will cover a multitude of sins and help when you ultimately and inevitably engage in the bigger battles.

Shaping the Policy Agenda

White House liaison personnel are often criticized for lacking substance and sometimes relegated to the role of "messengers" in the vast array of policy issues of interest to the president and considered by the Congress. Liaison personnel often can only articulate the president's position on a bill and lack the substantive expertise to help shape compromises or debate the merits of an issue beyond a superficial level. This is a valid complaint and represents one of the greatest weaknesses liaison offices face in the legislative process. Yet in organizing a Legislative Affairs team of maximum effectiveness, it is a criticism that can and should be addressed.

Several factors contribute to this problem. The principal issue concerns the sheer number of floor votes in the House and Senate that occur daily on which the president or the administration stakes out a position. And if the primary task of the White House liaison office is to promote the president's position on floor votes and ensure this position prevails, it is difficult to find the time to invest in developing policy expertise in the midst of fighting one floor skirmish after another. White House legislative liaison staff routinely lobby members of the House and Senate on a wide array of issues on a daily basis. They may deal with a defense bill in the morning, transportation legislation on tap after lunch, and cap that off with an abortion vote at the end of the day. It is unrealistic to expect liaison staff to have much more than a passing knowledge of any of these issues, yet there are some steps the White House Legislative Affairs office could take to enhance its role in the policy process.

First, all liaison personnel should become experts in House and Senate floor procedure. Expertise in this realm cuts across all policy areas; it is a critical element in shaping ultimate policy outcomes and an essential part of the daily rhythm of Congress. It is often said that procedure shapes policy—nowhere is that more true than on the House and Senate floors. Second, the liaison office should divide up all major presidential initiatives and assign personnel in the office to become substantively competent in several policy areas. With the resources of the executive branch at their disposal, the White House could easily call on myriad experts to brief liaison personnel far in advance of potential floor votes. And if it is too busy during the week when Congress is in session, the White House should ask agencies to prepare detailed policy binders for the liaison staff to take home on the weekends as "homework." Ideally, someone in the office should be substantively competent on environmental legislation, banking policy, education, labor law, budget and appropriations issues, and so on. The effectiveness of the Legislative Affairs office will be enhanced considerably by raising the level of policy competence of the staff. Like the sure-fielding shortstop who enhances his slugging percentage, improved policy expertise enhances the individual lobbyist's performance as well as benefits the entire team.

Cajoling with Compassion

Effective legislative liaison personnel must constantly strive to find a balance in their lobbying activities. On one hand, if the lobbyist is too aggressive, members may feel threatened or turned off and vote against the president out of spite alone. On the other hand, those who simply "tally votes" without using all the legitimate tools of persuasion are equally ineffective. Using intimidation is rarely effective. One of the members of the Bush Legislative Affairs team was told by Chief of Staff John Sununu to take away tickets to a play in the president's box at the Kennedy Center from Congressman Ralph Regula (R-Ohio), who planned to vote against the president on a key piece of legislation. Regula said, "So what," went to Ticketron, ordered his own tickets, and voted against the president anyway. Not only that, but he continued to vote against the president on issues where he would have otherwise been supportive, just to spite us. It took a personal apology from the chief of staff to remedy the situation. That is an example of coercion gone awry!

Despite what some so-called interest groups or certain individuals in the media might suggest, most members of Congress determine their policy positions and cast votes based on a calculus that includes their own personal philosophy, the merits of the issue, the views of their constituents, and the position of their political party. That reality dictates the manner in which White House lobbyists approach members of Congress to solicit support. It also suggests the most appropriate and successful tactic in garnering support for the president's position—sound arguments consistent with a member's philosophical beliefs.

No matter how much we begged or the degree to which the president pleaded, about half the House Republicans rejected voting for a tax increase as part of the 1990 budget agreement. President Bush's budget deal struck with the Democrats at Andrews Air Force Base in the autumn of that year was, in the minds of many GOP lawmakers, the apotheosis of an administration gone amok, and there was nothing we could do about it. Congressman Bill Paxon (R-N.Y.) told me several days before the vote: "Don't talk to me; don't have a cabinet member talk to me; don't have the president talk to me. Since my days in the county legislature, I have never voted for a tax increase in my political career and I'm not going to start now." Many shared his sentiments.

Rallying the troops to join with conservative Democrats to defeat measures that, for example, spent too much money, were lax on crime, or overregulated the economy was much easier. These positions were consistent with members' history and philosophy, making the sales job for the Legislative Affairs office much easier and realistic. The reasons for presidential support or opposition by members of Congress are widely varied. There is an old Lyndon Johnson story that sheds some light on the ongoing relationships between presidents and members of Congress. When Johnson began pressing members for their support on a particularly contentious issue, he was told by a junior lawmaker, "Mr. President, I'll always support you when you're right on the issue." To which Johnson retorted: "I don't need you when I'm right on the issue, son. I need you now!" Lawmakers of the president's party will normally support his position if doing so does not violate any long-held philosophical view and is consistent with previous votes. Others, however, need a little cajoling and convincing. That's where the White House legislative affairs unit spends most of its time and must get creative.

Framing an issue in such a way that it becomes consistent with a member's philosophy or past history, answering questions where the substance might be murky to help alleviate particular concerns, augmenting the arguments with phone calls from the president or cabinet secretaries to express the gravity of the issue to the administration, coordinating with the party leadership in Congress, particularly the whip organization, urging other members to make the case to the wavering legislator. These represent the creative tactics employed by the liaison office to cajole members to support the president. Again, threats do not work. Sound arguments and creative tactics do.

One perennial problem faced by the White House Legislative Affairs office, as well as congressional party leaders, is the "squeaky wheel gets the grease" syndrome. This incentive to bargain, barter, and whine in exchange for every vote afflicts only a handful of members, but any successful congressional liaison operation must address it in order to survive. Like political campaigns, most floor votes in the House and Senate seem to stack up like this—40 percent support you no matter what; 40 percent oppose you no matter what; the battle revolves around the 20 percent undecided in the middle. Of the 20 percent, most genuinely grapple with the issue, trying to calculate what maximizes their political benefit, what is most consistent with past votes, and what is best for their district or state, among other considerations. Some members add a new dimension to the calculus—what additional promises, concessions, benefits can they get out of every vote. These "squeaky wheels" require an inordinate amount of time and energy on the part of the liaison staff and tend to be the same people on nearly every vote. Moreover, their leverage is directly proportional to the closeness of a given vote.

How to deal with this handful of members over the long term creates an interesting set of challenges for the White House. If you accede to their demands, they repeat the behavior because of your encouragement, emboldened to hold you hostage on other issues. If you do not, you risk losing. No formula or "one size fits all" cure can remedy this situation. Yet any successful White House, or even congressional whip operation, must acknowledge this problem and think creatively about how to address it in garnering long-term support.

The flip side of the squeaky wheel is the Jim Hansen syndrome. Congressman Jim Hansen (R-Utah), a quiet, hard-working conservative, never asked for anything; he only voted the right way from the standpoint of the Bush White House. He didn't play the squeaky wheel game and sometimes I felt that he should get a lot more credit than he did. The Jim Hansen syndrome underscores what's wrong with the system as it currently works. Congressmen and senators who simply "did the right thing" from the standpoint of the White House and never asked for anything in return are often neglected and ignored because the liaison office spends an inordinate amount of time fixing problems for the squeaky wheels.

Congressman Hansen was walking up the steps of the Capitol one day during a vote and because he was right in front of me I asked him if he planned to support the president's position on the next amendment. He looked at me, smiled, and said; "Of course I will. When don't I ever support the president? But you guys need to remember us loyalists out here from time to time. I sometimes feel like I should say I'm undecided just so people pay a little more attention to me."

An effective White House liaison office recognizes the perverse incentives that exist in the system. Sometimes members do have an incentive to play hard to get because they see the liaison office focusing so much attention on the squeaky wheels. The most loyal, helpful, and supportive members of Congress often receive the least amount of attention, and that is wrong. A successful White House staff anticipates the potential development of the Jim Hansen syndrome and takes steps to acknowledge, thank, and appreciate the loyal members of its party before they feel compelled to become squeaky wheels. Drafting a letter of thanks for the president's signature, recommending a thank-you call to the member from the president, inviting the lawmaker to the White House for lunch, or helping his or her constituents obtain a special White House tour are just a few small ways to say thanks to members who support the president's agenda.

Winning by Losing or Managing with the Majority

Whether or not the president's party controls the majority in Congress is another key variable in the operation of the Legislative Affairs office. Until the 1994 elections, all Democratic presidents since Kennedy have had the experience of same-party control of the House or Senate and usually both. By contrast, with the exception of Republican control of the Senate in the early 1980s, all Republican presidents since the 1960s lacked a majority in Congress.

Some of the Republican "wins" during the 1980s came about through constructing coalitions of Democrats and Republicans. Yet others came about through a phenomenon we called "winning by losing"—failing to achieve a majority, but winning by getting 146 votes in the House or 34 in the Senate to sustain a presidential veto. Managing congressional affairs under conditions where the president's party controls Congress versus those where it is in the minority does not influence many of the tactics suggested in this chapter for structuring an effective office. It is a difference, however, that warrants further review and study, particularly as it relates to strategic changes when the president's party controls one chamber, but not the other, or tactical changes when the president's party is almost completely overwhelmed from the standpoint of numbers, like President Ford in the House after the 1974 election versus Bill Clinton's situation following the 1994 elections, with nearly 200 Democrats in the House minority.

Certainly issues of coordination and scheduling of the party's agenda become much easier when the president's party controls Congress. With the majority, however, come new responsibilities and more members with which to deal. One of the problems inherent in addressing congressional-executive relations is that there are so few cases to study. One interesting avenue of inquiry would focus on the Clinton administration, which did have the experience of dealing with the Democrats in the majority and the minority between 1992 and 1996. Again, my suspicion is that few of the recommended tactics outlined in this chapter would change, yet the impact of the changes in party control on the Clinton administration's Office of Legislative Affairs would be a fruitful topic for further investigation.

Comparing the effectiveness of Legislative Affairs run out of "war room" operations versus the more traditional model using a general Legislative Affairs staff is another important area for further study. On issues such as the North American Free Trade Agreement, health-care reform, and the crime bill, the Clinton White House created operations separate from the traditional Legislative Affairs staff to promote the president's agenda in Congress. In each of these specific cases the White House created "war room" operations that included Legislative Affairs personnel, media, research, and political staff to garner votes, sometimes operating simultaneously in competition for media coverage and congressional attention. The effectiveness of these "war room" operations should be analyzed further by focusing on the specific conditions under which they operated and on the degree to which these operations enhanced the president's overall stature with Congress.

Conclusion

Weaving its way through all of my recommendations is a path leading directly to the Oval Office. More than anything or anyone else, the key determinant of success or failure of the Legislative Affairs office is the president himself. If the president chooses a skilled, respected, and competent lobbying team, and empowers these individuals to serve as the principal representatives of the White House on Capitol Hill and the primary links from lawmakers to the Oval Office, he will go a long way toward creating a successful Legislative Affairs operation. Allowing everyone and anyone to dabble in congressional affairs, without any consequences or internal discipline, is a recipe for ruin. The president, either personally or through his chief of staff, must enforce this principle or suffer the consequences. If the president, however, recognizes the significance of entrusting his lobbyists with the principal role of managing relations with the Congress, and implements sanctions when other White House staff violate that role, the Legislative Affairs staff will be well on its way to success.

Managing White House relations with Congress is a much more extensive and elaborate task than simply "lobbying" lawmakers. Successfully becoming the eyes, ears, and voice of the president on Capitol Hill and effectively communicating the preferences and interests of members of Congress internally at the White House is a complex journey, requiring a high degree of political acumen. More than one road leads to success. Yet effective construction of the "ambulatory bridge across a constitutional divide," as Bryce Harlow, chief of legislative affairs for Presidents Eisenhower and Nixon, aptly described the function of Legislative Affairs, should result in the president's answering yes to each of the following questions:

1. Has the Legislative Affairs team helped the president decipher and truly understand the nuances and politics of Congress better than he would without them?
2. Has the Legislative Affairs team effectively predicted and anticipated congressional attitudes and actions toward presidential initiatives for the White House?
3. Has the Office of Legislative Affairs built sufficient political capital with lawmakers so that members want to support the president?

Implementing the recommendations and observations presented in this chapter should significantly raise the probability of an enthusiastic yes to each of these questions.

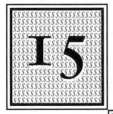

Ernest J. Wilson III

Interest Groups and Foreign Policymaking: A View from the White House

AT THE start of the Clinton administration the White House was buffeted by vast changes in the international system as well as substantial shifts in domestic politics.[1] Astute observers predicted that these broad shifts would provoke changes in key elements of U.S. foreign policymaking, especially where foreign and domestic issues converged. They anticipated the rise of new foreign policy issues (U.S. State Department 1992); the appearance of new foreign policy groups and voices (Clough 1994); and, implicitly at least, new political dynamics in the domestic politics of foreign affairs that would reshape access to the foreign policymaking agencies through lobbying and public engagement (Stanley Foundation 1996).

This chapter analyzes what actually happened in the domestic politics of foreign affairs during the first term of the Clinton administration. It discusses whether or not forecasts about new issues, new voices, and new politics came to pass. It describes some continuities and changes in the ways that external groups lobbied the White House on foreign affairs and the White House engaged and responded to interest groups on foreign policy. The chapter also presents a framework for understanding the role of interest groups in the White House foreign policy process.

Toward a Clinton Foreign Policy Doctrine?

There are certainly a priori political reasons to believe that this particular Democratic president and his administration would eagerly embrace these changes in order to advance their own domestic and international agendas.

During the presidential campaign, then-Governor Clinton attacked President Bush's policies as too captured by old Cold War ways of thinking. Clinton was comfortable, as was his vice-presidential candidate, Al Gore, with the newly prominent "global" issues such as the environment, population, and the information revolution. Many of the groups concerned with the global environment, sustainable development, and population planning that did not fare particularly well under the Republicans anxiously awaited Bill Clinton's administration, hoping it would turn the tide on budget cuts and inattention to the issues they judged important for U.S. foreign policy. Embracing change at home and abroad became the dominant theme in candidate Clinton's speeches.

Furthermore, Governor Clinton built his campaign for the White House partly on newly mobilized constituencies and nongovernmental organizations (NGOs) of women, minorities, and others whose international priorities differed in substance and style from more traditional foreign policy groups that had benefited from good White House access under Presidents Bush and Reagan. While many of the foreign policy advisers grouped around the candidate had deep roots in the foreign policy establishment (e.g., Council on Foreign Relations), there were enough exceptions to encourage nontraditional constituencies to believe that significant changes were afoot. One of the candidate's principal advisers, Anthony Lake, who went on to become assistant to the president for national security affairs, had been active in NGO foreign affairs organizations over the previous two decades.

Finally, the evolution of real-world events around the globe set the stage for informed observers to assume that substantial changes in the conduct of foreign policy were in the wings. This new context included the demise of the Soviet Union and the continued weakening of the military threat of Russia and China, the commercial assertiveness of rapidly developing economic markets around the world—the Asian "four tigers," for example—and the struggle for greater popular participation and government accountability around the globe, from South Africa to South Korea. Now that the constraints of the old conceptual framework of containment and anticommunism had crumbled, so the argument went, America was free to chart a new and more open and participatory foreign policy.

At home, the Clinton White House confronted tremendous demographic shifts along racial and ethnic lines; the greater involvement of women in the political economy; shifting voter allegiances across Democratic, Republican, and independent parties; and substantial changes in the structure and composition of the workforce. These shifts made conceivable the formation of new political alliances across policy issues, both domestic and foreign, creating new possibilities for the domestic politics of foreign policy. Thus the political orientations of the president and vice-president on new global issues such as international economics and the environment, and the appeal of these issues within their Democratic coalition, should have made the White House and the new administration more open to lobbying on newly important global issues and more amenable to forging new political ties through public engagement (Wilson 1994).

On the other hand, there were countervailing pressures on the president, especially given the 1992 electoral outcome, to stay away from major new foreign policy initiatives. Not the least of these was Governor Clinton's principal, and ultimately successful, line of attack on his opponent. He claimed that President Bush spent too much time on distant foreign affairs and not enough time on domestic bread-and-butter matters of immediate concern to the average citizen. With this successful appeal, Governor Clinton was elected president of the United States, but with only 43 percent of the popular vote, the fourth-lowest margin of victory in U.S. history. It was unclear at the outset how these contradictory imperatives would be resolved, and with what consequences. The White House could enthusiastically embrace new global issues or keep foreign policy at arm's length.

In brief, new global issues were brought to the high policy table as many predicted, including humanitarian intervention in Somalia, democracy protection in Haiti, and serious attention to environmental initiatives following the UN Conference on Environment and Development (UNCED), also known as the Earth Summit, in Rio de Janeiro in 1992. Second, nontraditional groups did gain greater access to policymakers in the White House and State Department. Nevertheless, no qualitatively new "politics of foreign policy" emerged on the national scene—the old elite did not wither away; new groups did not spring to ascendancy overnight; nor did the White House make a serious effort to engage politically in a sustained public campaign and debate over U.S. international commitments. Instead, there was a pattern of reluctant public engagement on foreign affairs. And since politics abhors a vacuum, into the political void stepped the new chairman of the Senate Foreign Relations Committee, Senator Jesse Helms (R-N.C.), and other harsh isolationist critics of U.S. engagement in global affairs. The newly elected Republican Congress then turned much of the post–Cold War foreign policy debate into haggling over budget cutting and closing government agencies (Sperry 1996). "Global" issues especially got short shrift from the presidential bully pulpit, although foreign commercial and trade policies were more successfully advanced.

Definitions and Research Strategy

I account for these outcomes in policy and politics by examining contextual, leadership, organizational, and constituency variables. By "contextual" variables I mean the structure of broad economic, political, and societal forces that frame and constrain political choices of governments and citizens. They include the distribution of power and authority in the global system and the beliefs and doctrines that grew from and supported it. This period saw a major shift in system power with the collapse of the Soviet Union and the weakening of the doctrine of "containment" that guided U.S. foreign affairs for five decades. Another contextual feature was the growth of world trade and the rise of new trading partners. Domestically, contextual factors included the radical shifts in membership and appeal between Republican and Democratic parties. And the most immediate contextual political factor was the thin, nonmajority win of President Clinton (DiClerico 1996, 19–23).

The "leadership" variable consists of actions taken by the president and his most senior foreign affairs advisers to establish policy priorities and allocate resources to achieve them. The uniqueness of the presidency is precisely its capacity to provide not only material resources but rhetorical resources to establish the national agenda. This is especially true in foreign affairs. In this field the president has great leeway. "Most Americans are content to let the president make foreign policy and they give him virtually unchallenged support ... as long as crises do not appear to get out of hand" (Uslaner 1991, 301).

"Organizational" factors refer to the ways in which these priorities are ordered and reflected in the allocation of staff time and responsibilities, and the effectiveness of the organization in setting priorities and achieving them—the degree to which the White House is organized to achieve the goals of the president and the extent to which the goals were achieved.

"Constituency" factors refer to the size and influence of domestic groups involved in foreign affairs. The literature on White House constituency relations in foreign affairs is modest. Bard concludes that "in the three most commonly used models of foreign policy making, the rational actor, organizational process and bureaucratic-politics models, there is little or no consideration given to the role played by interest groups in influencing policy outcomes" (Bard 1988, 5). There are at least two relevant comparative subliteratures available: those concerned with the politics of lobbying the White House, usually written to contrast with lobbying Congress; and those that contrast the politics of foreign policy with the politics of domestic policy (Uslaner 1991). It is worth briefly repeating the differences observed.

The White House Is Not Congress

As Peterson (1990) and others note, external interest group pressure on officials in the Executive Office of the President is perhaps less than half the story; the other half is the extensive public outreach in which the White House engages to pursue several different goals simultaneously: to keep itself informed, to legitimate the groups it engages, to demonstrate its commitments to its constituencies, to enhance its political standing, and to advance its own political agenda. Therefore, the term "public engagement" is as important as, if not more important than, "lobbying"—the latter term suggests groups outside the White House reaching in; the former, officials inside reaching out. This function, which has come to be named "public liaison," consists of identifying key groups and engaging them with the White House through correspondence, by sending White House officials to meet with them, and inviting them to White House briefings, meetings with senior administration officials, receptions, or other events.[2]

The differences between executive and legislative relations with society reflect the necessarily closed and restricted nature of White House operations, in contrast to congressional engagement and lobbying ties wherein interest group representatives can physically get into the lobbies and waiting rooms of the House and Senate. White House lobbying is almost a misnomer, since physical access to the building is extremely limited. It is a much more controlled environment. Also, Congress as a multimember, politically divided institution does less "public engagement" than the more focused White House.

Foreign Policy Is Not Domestic

This second truism recognizes the differences between the politics of foreign policy and of domestic policy. Uslaner and others have identified several key dimensions along which the two differ substantially. In foreign affairs, the stakes can be much higher (i.e., thermonuclear war); decisions are often irreversible; relationships are much less under control of American policymakers; decisions often need to be made very quickly; professional expertise is more centralized; and domestic interests and constituencies are less engaged (Uslaner 1991, 300).

The vast majority of what is done by the foreign policy staff at the White House (essentially, by the National Security Council or NSC staff) or at the State Department fits the Uslaner definition, especially in the new global areas of population, the environment, democracy, foreign aid, and U.S. humanitarian assistance. There are, however, some substantive issues where foreign and domestic politics are more similar, especially where interests and constituencies are more directly and deeply affected, as in trade and commerce (Destler 1992). The politics surrounding the North American Free Trade Agreement (NAFTA) and the Most Favored Nation (MFN) extension to China are examples.

Regrettably, it is difficult to establish a baseline for longitudinal analysis in these areas because there is very little empirical analysis available in the literature of White House lobbying on foreign affairs in previous administrations. Some descriptions are embedded within longer studies of particular foreign policy decisions and initiatives, but the documentation is thin.

Two Cases of the Politics of Global Affairs

We now examine lobbying and public engagement in several "global" policy issue areas. As president, Bill Clinton set three priorities as the foundations for his foreign policy. They were economics and creating jobs at home; restructuring U.S. strategic capacities; and promoting democracy, human rights, and global affairs. "Global affairs" included activities such as the environment, population, and foreign assistance. Clinton's foreign policy team made the argument that the new post–Cold War world required the United States to integrate these goals more effectively than in the past. Global, humanitarian, and economic conditions were imposing themselves more on American national interests, and global threats and opportunities needed to be addressed more seriously by the White House and State Department. A new undersecretary for global affairs was created at the State Department to take the lead on these issues and give them greater visibility. A former Democratic U.S. senator from Colorado, Tim Wirth, was the first incumbent of the new post. At the White House, the existing NSC Global Affairs directorate was beefed up with new staff positions and renamed Global Affairs and Multilateral Issues.

"Global Affairs" provides the analyst with a capacious window on the issues at hand. First, unlike traditional national security and defense areas, global policy issues are relatively new on the national agenda and hence should reveal more about the rise of new issues, voices, and "intermestic" politics—the merging of international and domestic political affairs. Second, concentrating on these areas will reveal one of the key differences between the presidency and the Congress, which is the power of the executive to set a new national agenda. Third, this is a foreign policy area where we would expect to find substantial differences between the administrations of Bill Clinton and George Bush. Finally, the relevant issues lack the same strong national constituencies as economic or security interests; therefore, the interaction between outside-in lobbying and inside-out public engagement should be especially close.

The cases we review share another important feature. Each was subject to an extensive presidentially mandated interagency review. When a new administration comes to office, the NSC invariably conducts extensive reviews of the state of the world, of current foreign policies in place, and whether or not the new administration should shift policy priorities, and if so, where and how. These reviews have been conducted as an affair of national security, closely guarded and closed to outsiders. The Clinton NSC opened up the interagency process (whose product is called a Presidential Review Document or PRD) seeking to make it more consultative and transparent. This newly opened window of opportunity allowed for greater NGO and other citizen involvement in global affairs.

A Structure for Public Engagement

At the start of the Clinton administration, the NSC staff was given some encouragement and latitude to conduct the national security reviews along two tracks, internal and external. The former consisted of a long series of interagency meetings among the relevant government agencies to catalogue and evaluate current U.S. government activities in the area and to arrive at a conclusion about new administration positions. It also served to push the bureaucracy more to consider the new administration's concerns in their programming. The second track involved public outreach and engagement, with the White House staff reaching out to leading groups active in the field under review and responding to lobbying efforts.

Some NSC directorates, like those responsible for Latin America, Middle East, and Global Affairs and Multilateral Issues, responded more positively than others to opportunities to engage in political outreach. These NSC offices regularly consulted various interests over the course of PRD assessments. From the Clinton White House's perspective, this approach improved the substantive content of possible policy recommendations; it permitted the White House to know the contradictory or complementary views of the community of interested groups and helped in persuading key constituencies of the administration's position.

The democracy and international programs review provided an ongoing political framework within which various constituencies, groups, and individuals could be brought into the White House to consult and interact with White House staff and representatives from the relevant government agencies. It is important to note that this process was initially handled entirely through the NSC and not through the Office of Public Liaison (although they would work together later). As word of the reviews circulated, outside organizations began their own lobbying efforts, sought one-on-one meetings at the White House, and invited NSC staff to meet with their members. To this extent the PRD process primed the pump for wider political engagement and direct lobbying.

Promoting Global Democracy

In his campaign for the presidency, Governor Clinton insisted that George Bush failed to pay adequate attention to human rights and democracy, and that if elected, he would give democracy the attention it properly deserved in the post–Cold War global environment. The Bush administration had rhetorically committed itself to democracy promotion and human rights protection and supported such organizations as the National Endowment for Democracy (NED). But Clinton seized on Bush's low-key human rights commitments in China and elsewhere to score political points in the election.

Once in office, President Clinton's NSC took a number of new steps, including appointing two directors in an expanded directorate for global affairs and multilateral issues, one for Human Rights, and one for Democracy. Among its policy reviews was one on democracy programs—PRD 26. New democracy and global affairs posts were also created at the State Department (a new undersecretary) and initially at Defense, at the assistant secretary level. Adding to the usual intergovernmental discussions among officials at the State Department, the U.S. Information Agency (USIA), and the U.S. Agency for International Development (USAID), the NSC staff began extensive external outreach activities of the type described above.[3]

Relevant Groups and Interests

Outside the White House, the promotion of democracy and human rights was at the top of the agenda of a small but committed group of very diverse organizations. Most were based in Washington or maintained offices there. They ran the gamut from organizations like Freedom House with roots in anticommunist causes and labor groups like the AFL-CIO under Lane Kirkland, to centrist think tanks like the Progressive Policy Institute, to liberal NGOs like Amnesty International. Also very active were quasi-nongovernmental organizations, such as the NED and its four affiliates—Center for International Private Enterprise (CIPE), National Democratic Institute (NDI), the International Republican Institute (IRI), and the Free Trade Union Institute (FTUI). They are independent of government but get almost all their funds from Congress. While sometimes criticized, their role in mobilizing democracy groups should not be underestimated. A senior official at state agreed that "we see a place for ... the expertise of private American institutions like the American Bar Association, the AFL-CIO, the U.S. Chamber of Commerce" (Goshko and Smith 1993).

Since there is a politically significant division of labor among groups, with some working mainly on human rights and others on democracy, the White House reviews included meetings with the full range of such organizations. These included leading regional organizations such as Africa Watch, Asia Watch (affiliated with Human Rights Watch), as well as missionary and church groups.

White House–Interest Group Relations

These groups also lobbied for general issues, such as the passage of treaties on the rights of the child and rights of women. They also pressed hard for U.S. sanctions against particular governments—Burma (Myanmar), Sri Lanka, Zaire, Nigeria, Romania, and others. The human rights groups tended to press hardest and most consistently on the administration to take concrete actions in particular countries, especially developing countries in Africa, Asia, and Latin America. The democracy groups, by contrast, tended to concentrate on actions with longer-term impacts, such as radio broadcasts to former Iron Curtain countries and China. While the democracy groups were neither large nor numerous, they did articulate positions appealing to the conservative elements of the Democratic Party that were important for Clinton's successful electoral coalition.

Administration Activities

The administration took a variety of actions in the area of human rights and democracy promotion, acting through interagency working groups on democracy, including the apex coordinating group, chaired by the assistant secretary for human rights, democracy, and labor. The actions in this area included the following:

1. Bilateral diplomatic pressure by the State Department. The administration was rewarded with good successes in Burma, Central America, and Mexico. It took firm stands in countries such as Nigeria, usually out ahead of European allies. In the Central African country of Cameroon, the U.S. government, for the first time, imposed sanctions in its Export-Import Bank (EXIM) financing because the final client was the local security forces, known for violating prisoners' rights. There were also efforts to wrestle with human rights and democracy in other more difficult cases, such as Chechnya and China. These tough cases were also driven largely by critics in Congress and NGOs who pressed for more muscular policies.
2. Pressures on multilateral organizations such as the World Bank and United Nations. At the UN Human Rights meetings in Vienna in 1993, the U.S. government was able to insert language into the final declaration expressing a strong human rights and democracy position. More so than in previous administrations, the U.S. executive directors to the World Bank and other regional development banks pressed to include democracy and human rights criteria for lending decisions in countries such as Nigeria where human rights practices appeared to violate international norms.
3. Pressures during trade and security missions. The late Commerce Secretary Ron Brown and other senior officials would raise human rights issues during trips abroad for other purposes of trade or national security.

4. Speeches by senior administration officials. On several occasions, such as the annual National Endowment for Democracy meetings, the president spoke directly on the role of democracy in his foreign policy.

5. Continuing to consolidate an interagency democracy and human rights bureaucracy within the White House, the State Department, USAID, USIA, the Department of Defense, and other agencies (Wilson 1994). Also by circulating information on "best practices" around the government, different agencies and bureaus could develop better programs in the field.

By 1994, the second year of the interagency review process, most interested groups had been consulted regularly, and there were fewer outreach efforts. Instead, more attention was given to seeking interagency agreement on a common democracy policy document. As the review dragged on through 1994, the external consultative meetings became less frequent as the relevant outside groups awaited some high-level and authoritative statement on democracy promotion, with growing skepticism. Still, the working group developed plans to publicize the administration's common position on democracy through a series of public events, speeches, and meetings. An accent on democracy, it was felt, would help demonstrate the moral compass of the administration, as it also pursued economic and commercial objectives.

The Turn Away from Public Engagement

In addition to lobbying the White House for substantive policy outcomes, and to promoting their legitimacy, constituency organizations were also lobbying the White House to help their own consolidation. To advance their lobbying efforts, disparate groups began to work together in new ways, not only to force the administration to adopt their policies but to press the White House to act politically to help create a more unified constituency. Some believed strongly that the constituency for global policies risked splintering under the centrifugal forces of a post–Cold War loss of clear strategic mission as well as from an increasingly tight federal budget that could pit groups against one another.

Therefore, in April 1993 the leadership of the NED and Freedom House sponsored a "Dialogue on Democracy" to encourage administration officials and representatives of human rights, democracy, and development groups to begin a process of bridge building to solidify support for a common policy agenda. Some of these groups had either opposed one another or proceeded on separate paths during the 1980s and early 1990s. The leadership of the groups argued that a joint effort should be welcomed by the administration because the resulting coalition could advance the president's own foreign policy goals. Some also feared that without clear administration leadership the groups would fall back on their warring ways.

The human rights, democracy, and development groups seized on these possibilities to press for more public engagement and White House leadership. The democracy bureaucracy generally supported this approach and tried to build internal support for a series of public events, speeches, and meetings on democracy. The initiative would indicate to allies and antagonists abroad that the administration took democracy seriously in its foreign policy. Despite this opportunity, however, the White House decided not to pursue this aspect of constituency building and public engagement. The document prepared by the interagency task force with outside consultation was shelved, and the public engagement components dropped.

Foreign Aid and Other International Resources

Lobbying and public engagement emerged as problematic in other global areas, such as humanitarian intervention and the reform of U.S. international assistance. In the administration's humanitarian intervention efforts, domestic politics was forced onto the White House by public and congressional reactions to the controversial, ambiguous, and highly visible events in Somalia, Haiti, and Bosnia. These events prompted some effort in the administration to convince the American public that the policies advanced America's interests. For foreign aid reform, by contrast, there was less immediate political imperative for public engagement.

As with democratization, the National Security Council–led review of all U.S. international programs, including foreign assistance, had internal and external components. As with democratization, there was wider consultation and involvement than in previous administrations; and as with democracy, there were some positive outcomes. But as with the democracy initiatives, the final product was ultimately stillborn when subsequent political commitments were not commensurate with the initial stated ambitions of the White House. This seems to confirm somewhat Larmon Wilson's close analysis of human rights initiatives under President Carter, where the early rhetoric was not matched by subsequent policy action (Wilson 1983).[4]

Administration Goals

The White House tasked all federal agencies to review international resource programs and their administrative, policy, and budgetary implications. The review sought information on more than 100 programs spread across two dozen departments, agencies, and banks, from the EXIM Bank and the Overseas Private Investment Corporation (OPIC) to USAID and USIA. While the core of this review—PRD 20—was to include a thorough top-to-bottom assessment of the mission of the USAID, it was felt that AID should not be reviewed in isolation from other organizations that transferred resources abroad.

Interest Groups

The groups interested in the delivery of resources abroad were more numerous than those concerned about democracy and human rights and spanned a wider range of interests and motives. General development organizations were especially active in this area. InterAction, an umbrella body of development-oriented groups, had more than 150 organizational members and a permanent staff in Washington and played a leading role in mobilizing ideas and interests on behalf of international programs. Their interests were material as well as intellectual, since many InterAction members received federal funding through USAID or USIA to undertake international work on behalf of the U.S. government. Think tanks and advocacy organizations such as the Overseas Development Council and Development Gap hosted seminars, lobbied the Hill and the White House, and pressed the State Department for a quick and expansive resolution of the proposed reforms. Regional organizations such as the Asia Foundation and the African American Institute relied heavily on federal funds and political backing for their programs and were active in Washington lobbying for more assistance for their respective regions. Professional groups such as the American Bar Association undertook their own reviews of U.S. foreign assistance and lobbied the White House to adopt their view. Business groups were relatively small players in the exercise, in part because they took positions different from the development groups on some key issues and decided that "foreign aid" was such a hopeless mess that they would concentrate on other targets.

With the exception of business, most groups that lobbied the White House shared a fear that foreign aid was losing its political viability and support, and they sought to convince lawmakers and administration officials to keep the programs on the policy agenda and funded at historical levels or higher. Most urged the administration to focus AID's energies on a few key themes such as sustainable development and to cut back the trade and security aspects of assistance. The U.S. Chamber of Commerce and other business groups disagreed strongly and argued to enhance AID's support for the American interests, but not in a sustained fashion.

From Launching to End Game

The two tracks—interagency and outreach—moved in tandem, but the opening months of the review were spent mainly with the White House instructing the international agencies to prepare substantive and budget reports on their activities. Within the White House, the review was co-directed by the National Security Council (NSC) and the National Economic Council (NEC), with support from the Office of Management and Budget (OMB). Soon thereafter, the White House reached out to the relevant interest groups and began the process of broad consultation. As with the democracy review, what began as more of a public engagement process expanded into a direct lobbying effort as more groups discovered the review and sought to protect their interests. "Outside-in" lobbying intensified as preliminary policy positions began to gore some oxen in Washington. For example, in the effort to create a new post–Cold War rationale for allocating resources, the White House decided to move away from a strictly country-by-country approach to use broad categories of policy goals to drive country priorities. Strong opposition came from regional organizations worried about losing earmarks for "their" region or country. Agents from aid-recipient countries also began to lobby the White House to oppose the shift.

One of the defining aspects of lobbying and public engagement in this global policy area was the White House decision to craft foreign assistance reforms through legislative as well as executive actions. The original law, the Foreign Assistance Act of 1961, had become an outmoded joke; most years, money for foreign aid was appropriated through continuing resolutions, not by passing a new bill. This time the administration, especially USAID, wanted to provide a new post–Cold War policy framework to guide future foreign assistance decisions.

By early 1994, the NSC had consulted enough NGOs and members of Congress and canvassed enough agencies to prepare a document for the president's review. This document—PRD 20—was discussed at a White House cabinet-level meeting with the heads of State, Commerce, NEC, NSC, USAID, EXIM, and senior officials from Defense. Among the organizational and substantive proposals was a recommendation to prepare a domestic political engagement campaign on international programs. This idea was accepted by the senior group and approved by the president. (Rejected was a more controversial proposal to create a new governmentwide coordinating body for international resource programs, based at the White House; rejecting it let State retain the lead in name, but not in fact, since other departments, such as Defense, did not consider State its leader.) Signed by the president, this agreement served as the basis for the subsequent legislative proposals that the administration submitted to Congress.

By choosing a legislative strategy, White House staff, along with officials at State and AID, spent much of their time briefing, negotiating with, and trying to avoid the many demands of members of Congress and their eager staffs. The tenor and intensity of the foreign assistance reform effort was greatly shaped by being a legislative proposal. There had to be hearings, rewrites, consultations with members, amendments, and alternative versions. Under these circumstances, the political dynamic that emerged was for coalitions to form around policy positions among likeminded NGOs, congressional offices, and the most relevant federal offices at State, AID, or Defense.

It is difficult analytically to ascertain the exact impact of White House lobbying or to distinguish between pressures from Capitol Hill and from the interest groups, since NGOs convince sympathetic members to query and pressure the White House by sending formal inquiries from Congress to the White House.

To be responsive to Congress, the White House did organize a number of Hill briefings for members and staff, including a senior meeting of the national security adviser, Anthony Lake, Secretary of State Warren Christopher, and AID Administrator Brian Atwood with congressional leaders and interested members. Also, Deputy Secretary of State Clifton Wharton put the reform process high on his personal agenda and chaired a key interagency group. Still, key senators were skeptical about the proposed reforms, especially with the 1994 elections on the horizon.

As it became apparent that international initiatives were in trouble on the Hill, and the budget picture became more dismal with every passing day, the White House and State Department tried to breathe a little life into administration engagement on foreign affairs. Compared to other departments, such as Housing and Urban Development or Defense, State's own public strategies were puny indeed. Even Treasury developed sophisticated public engagement campaigns to influence congressional votes on its funding for multilateral banks. Despite middle-level staff efforts, however, the State Department did not take seriously the threat to its own interests until well after the Republican landslide in the November midterm elections. Senior State Department officials sought to protect their nominal authority to coordinate all international programs, even though in effect other agencies rarely acceded to leadership by State. The result of its opposition to White House-led reforms to assume greater coordination and outreach responsibility (backed by Treasury, AID, OPIC, EXIM) was to thwart reforms for innovative interagency coordination, whether across economic, security, and human rights lines, or on more political issues such as public engagement. State's nominal authority remained intact, but foreign policy coordination and public engagement remained modest. Clarke (1988) ably describes some of the bureaucratic constraints on the Department of State's ability to lead bureaucratically or to overcome its culture and engage in political engagements.

To advance public engagement, the Overseas Development Council, perhaps the preeminent policy entrepreneur and think tank in Washington on these issues, launched a full-court-press to organize a major national conference on reforming U.S. international programs. They would offer the administration and others a highly visible national forum to set out their own proposals. But, as with public engagement on democracy, the conference and other outreach efforts were put on the back burner, waiting for clearance from various factions in the White House. In the end, the idea of a substantial outreach effort was quashed.

As the 1994 legislative agenda for the 104th Congress came to be increasingly crowded with impending health-care legislation and funding for the UN and humanitarian intervention, and as the State Department and the legislative affairs team at the White House backed further away from public engagement, the reform effort seemed more and more an orphan. Deputy Secretary Wharton's sudden departure from State deprived the reform initiative of a senior policymaker willing to seize the issue and push it forward. Without an overwhelmingly powerful constituency push, the inertia in the Senate would drag the bill, and the initiative, to an inconclusive end. The absence of a drop-dead action-forcing deadline also weakened the reform effort. Senate support for the reform wilted, and the bill died a natural death in the spring of 1994. USAID moved ahead with its more modest in-house reforms.

The nonengagement strategy of the White House on global issues such as democracy, foreign assistance, and humanitarian intervention contrasts sharply with the serious outreach and lobbying efforts surrounding trade and commerce issues. Regarding NAFTA, for example, the White House established a "war room" in the Old Executive Office Building (OEOB) to coordinate trade politics and trade policy. A sophisticated strategy of engagement was developed in the White House, led by the new NEC, with the backing of Commerce, the Office of the U.S. Trade Representative (OSTR), and other agencies. This included careful outreach to affected groups, including business, labor, affected minorities, and others.

The White House also proved responsive to lobbying from ethnic constituencies such as Jews and African Americans. The case of African Americans is especially striking since, unlike Jews, they were not taken seriously in previous administrations' foreign policy deliberations (Bard 1988, 57). Such groups as TransAfrica, the Congressional Black Caucus, and AfriCare, and individuals like Jesse Jackson and former Congressman William Gray, president of the United Negro College Fund, enjoyed unprecedented access to the National Security Council, to the Office of Public Liaison, and other units in the White House and were able to make their influence felt decisively on Haiti and South Africa policies. Also, in part because of the remarkable influence of Vice-President Gore, international environmental issues were given serious attention and a number of international environment initiatives were launched by the administration. Eventually, by the third year of the administration the ties between the Office of Public Liaison, the NSC, the Political Office, and Legislative Affairs improved, and domestic and international matters were better coordinated. A major foreign affairs initiative was, however, not on the table.

Conclusion

This chapter began with several assumptions drawn from the conventional wisdom about the domestic politics of foreign policy. The assumptions predicted higher prominence for new issues and new constituency groups, leading perhaps to a new kind of politics and political engagement. This chapter is not meant to be a detailed exploration of each assumption (or hypothesis) across all issue areas. Instead, it examined these three assumptions only in the context of several emerging substantive areas of global affairs. Still, some preliminary observations may be offered.

First, the White House did put global issues somewhat higher on the foreign policy agenda than in the past. Second, groups pressing global issues were granted greater lobbying access than in the past and were the target of more outreach by the White House. Third, there was not a substantial change in domestic political activity related to foreign affairs. A few new groups received more attention, but there was not a discontinuous break with previous White House interaction with policy interest groups.

Explaining Outcomes

The reasons for these outcomes were suggested at the start of this chapter. While this chapter has been mainly concerned with lobbying, lobbying alone cannot fully account for the political and policy outcomes we observed. A simplistic conclusion that the aid reform and prodemocracy constituencies were politically weak is certainly true, but it is also too thin. Outcomes were also shaped through the interaction of contextual factors, leadership, and organizational factors.

Despite the importance of international contextual factors that pushed toward a more vigorous foreign policy, such as the end of the Cold War and a yearning among many U.S. policy intellectuals for a new overarching framework to replace containment, other factors combined to block that outcome. By far the most important was the simple fact that Governor Clinton received only 43 percent of the popular vote in a three-way battle for the presidency that left him without a majority in most of the country's congressional districts. To win reelection he needed to move a significant bloc of voters to his camp, in a two-way race. And his foreign policy positions would not likely be the catalyst for such movement in the electorate. Even stronger constituency lobbying on global affairs probably would not change this basic fact.

Second, as governor of a small southern state, the new president had very little personal experience and appetite for foreign affairs. This decisively shaped the attention he personally gave to foreign policy issues, and it shaped his priorities.

Also, for the first two years of the Clinton administration the management of the White House was generally below par. The White House did not capture the synergies available between domestic and foreign affairs, reflected in the very autonomous status of each of the four major White House offices—NSC, Public Liaison, Legislative Affairs, and the Political Office. There was insufficient effort to leverage foreign affairs for domestic benefit, or domestic affairs to advance foreign interests. Nor was the secretary of state willing to go against the conservative and apolitical grain of the department's culture to press for wider and more sustained public engagement. This same elitist and apolitical perspective was brought into the NSC by officers seconded to the White House from the State Department and in fact is widely shared throughout the national security and foreign affairs community.

Finally, it is certainly the case that the constituencies interested in global affairs were much weaker than for many other issues, domestic or foreign. They lacked the membership size, financial resources, media visibility, and congressional clout of other interests. When the political heavies in the White House and departments refused to push global issues forward on the Hill, they invariably explained it by saying that the president had little to gain in policy or political terms from speaking out on global issues.

Findings

There were other nuanced and unanticipated findings that are worth noting:

1. Greater "access" to the White House does not automatically translate into greater influence over outcomes. Policy results desired by pressure groups may not occur, even with greater White House access. This is especially true when the goal is to influence the White House staff to alter the president's priorities and not just effect a particular policy outcome in a particular country or region.
2. The route to influence in the White House can start on Capitol Hill. Groups with marginal influence in the rough-and-tumble of Washington politics can amplify their influence by allying with sympathetic members of Congress, who in turn pressure the White House.
3. Marginal groups lobby the White House as much to legitimate an issue and get it on the policy agenda as to achieve a particular policy outcome. For many groups with global issues, the fact of meeting in the White House or OEOB is seen as desirable because it adds legitimacy to their claims of foreign policy importance.

4. There were substantial differences in the president's personal commitment to "new" foreign policy issues; he was much more involved in the politics of international economics than in global issues.

5. At the same time, policy issues without important constituencies are still important to U.S. foreign policy interests. Because a global issue lacks a large domestic constituency does not mean it is unimportant to the national security interests of the country and to the international and national standing of the president or to his capacity to conduct foreign policy effectively. "Orphan issues"—humanitarian relief, human rights, and pro-democracy engagements in Somalia, Haiti, and China—significantly affected the president's standing and his capacity to act in other more traditional foreign policy areas.

The challenge for presidential politics is twofold. Even "orphan issues" on occasion developed powerful guardians, as when the head of the African American lobby group TransAfrica went on a hunger strike, placed the president in a tough political box, and helped change U.S. foreign policy on Haiti. Second, international commitments with no deep domestic support can turn bad and tangle and sink administrations—as in Vietnam or Iran.

6. In policy terms, during periods of international transitions, the White House should commit itself to using the bully pulpit of the presidency to develop a national constituency for foreign policy. To do so requires marshalling organizational supports in the White House, changing the technocratic and antipublic engagement culture of the State Department, and linking with NGOs on a more consistent basis. In essence, the innovative public engagement strategy used with such success in support of the General Agreement on Tariffs and Trade (GATT), NAFTA, and the Summit of the Americas should be selectively applied to other areas as well, including global affairs and traditional security matters. As with all other issues involving the White House, however, these initiatives can be successful only if done at the behest of the president and subject to his own continuing involvement.

There is the serious risk that too much public engagement or excessive foreign policy lobbying will have negative effects on U.S. policy. Too much or inappropriate public engagement is just as bad or worse than too little, as we saw with the Iran-*Contra* scandal. As Anthony Lake and his coauthors wrote nine years before he became national security adviser, ". . . the making of American foreign policy has been growing far more political . . . as Americans—politicians and experts alike—have been spending more time, energy and passion in fighting ourselves than we have in trying as a nation, to understand and deal with a rapidly changing world" (Lake et al. 1995, 18).

Finally, these findings raise both methodological and conceptual questions about the domestic politics of foreign affairs for analysts who want to understand better lobbying the White House and other executive agencies. Questions of causality, for example, are difficult here as in any arena of political life. We cannot conclude with certainty which White House or State Department actions were prompted by lobbying or public engagement meetings with outside groups. One would need to develop more detailed case studies of possible influence and impact. For example the twists and turns on Haiti repatriation policy offer fruitful material to trace the impact of such groups as TransAfrica and the hunger strike of its leader, Randall Robinson, on policy outcomes.

There is also interesting work under way on the intersection between public attitudes toward foreign affairs, the behavior of politicians, and policy outcomes (Kull 1995; Rosner 1995). Beyond research strategies for case studies, questions of methods and models are also relevant here. Are our old pluralist, domestic-oriented models still sufficient in the light of the trends toward greater "intermestic" politics and lobbying? Are our current models sufficiently developed to analyze effectively the domestic politics of foreign policy, or will they need to be adjusted? What is the threshold between the old politics of foreign policy, and the new? What measurable indicators can be selected to show that we have reached a qualitatively different form or intensity of the domestic politics of foreign policy? These are issues that analysts of the domestic politics of foreign affairs should tackle seriously.

Notes

1. This chapter draws on the author's experience as a staff member on the National Security Council in the Clinton administration from 1993 through 1994 working on global and multilateral issues.

2. The origins of the Office of Public Liaison under Gerald Ford, and its subsequent growth, are described by Schlozman and Tierney (1986), Peterson (1990, 326–27), and Pika (1991).

3. Larmon Wilson points out the international and external approach of the Carter administration on human rights, the former involving "the bureaucratic struggle for influence among competing interests within the executive branch and between it and the legislative branch ... [and] the latter ... a human rights constituency outside the government that came to the fore in support of President Carter's commitment to human rights" (Wilson 1983, 191).

4. Larmon Wilson reports that as "the Carter White House worked to balance the commitment to human rights with other policy considerations, their

original rhetorical commitments to human rights had to be greatly modified and reduced in the crucible of foreign policy decision making. In fact, the commitment of every President to human rights appeared to assume a decreasing priority" (Wilson 1983, 179).

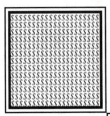

Michael J. McShane and Richard D. Otis Jr.

Comments on the Executive Connection

Michael J. McShane, TRW

LOBBYING in Washington in the late 1990s, and lobbying from an executive branch perspective in particular, has become an increasing complex job. Managing congressional affairs from an administration perspective is no easy task either. Nonetheless, some lessons may be equally shared with those who attempt to influence the policymaking process from the position of an organized interest and those who do so from within the White House. It is often the case that the problems encountered by the White House are exactly the problems we in corporate America face. I think the need for discipline is absolutely crucial. To have a totally successful government relations program you need to have the government relations program be part of the policy development process and contribute to developing a legislative agenda. This is absolutely true, but I am amazed how few companies and government agencies, including the White House, operate differently. It is crucial because if you do not have intelligence and guidance from government relations, how can you develop intelligent and thoughtful policy positions and the legislative and executive strategies to achieve them? Without insight and intelligence supplied by government relations, a really successful government relations program is difficult to create and maintain.

For example, Dr. Walker recounted the failure of the Carter energy package earlier in this volume. In the Carter administration, the Carter people (I was in the Carter White House and had worked on putting the Department of Energy together) went up to Capitol Hill to deliver to Congress this great plan to put together a national energy policy, a system designed like a Swiss watch. Many senators and congressmen from energy-producing states already had their own ideas about what they wanted for an energy policy. There were few, if any, significant conversations between the White House and Congress on the energy plan. In addition, there was precious little input into the Carter energy plan from the Congress through the White House congressional relations office. Needless to say, the plan just collapsed—dead on arrival—with no hope of resuscitation. A well-thought-out lobbying effort, launched well before the final plan was sent to the Hill, might have resulted in more acceptance of the plan and a greater chance of passing some form of energy policy. I think the same thing can be said about the Clinton health-care plan. There was very little input to the White House from the Hill and from the health-care industry and other organized interests around town. This led to the demise of that piece of legislation.

One final point on the importance of the Legislative Affairs apparatus in the White House: it is vital to make sure that everybody is on board for a policy and legislative strategy and that nobody is off freelancing. Control over agencies and the bureaucracies that run them is critical to having a successful administration. It is absolutely essential for an administration to grab hold of the bureaucracy and get their people in place as soon as possible after the elections. The Carter administration tried something called "cabinet government." They appointed the cabinet officers, then allowed the cabinet officers to appoint everyone down the line. What happened was people wound up being loyal to the cabinet officers, not necessarily the administration, and you had a lot of freelancing going on. A president needs his people in the political appointee positions, those Schedule C slots that are loyal to him personally as well as to his policies. There is a great story on LBJ that makes the point on how to handle this potential problem. Johnson had everybody joining his administration sign their letter of resignation before they were appointed. It was undated and remained in their personnel file. That was a wonderful way of maintaining discipline. LBJ said he wanted to do something; a cabinet officer came to him and said, "Mr. President, I really have some problems with this. I'm just not supportive of it." Johnson said, "Mr. Secretary, that's absolutely fine. You've got until noon to decide whether you're going to support me or not and if you don't, I'll accept your resignation." By quarter to twelve, the cabinet secretary had seen the error of his ways and was completely on board with the policy. What we had here was the discipline of the White House enforcing itself on the bureaucracy.

I will conclude with one final observation regarding the delineation between "special" interest groups and "public" interest groups. Special interest groups are generally characterized as big business, industry, and corporate America. Conversely, public interest groups are generally defined as those groups supporting a clean environment, consumer protection, and other social causes. The overarching premise is that special interest groups are not quite as good as public interest groups.

Much attention is paid to the power and the influence of big business and industry and the technical resources they possess, as if they are omniscient—a monolithic Goliath. Public interest groups, in contrast, are portrayed as the proverbial Davids—small, understaffed, and without the technical resources and the power to be heard, understood, or have any influence in the policymaking process. I challenge this perspective because I do not think that this is true at all. I think that public interest groups have extraordinary technical resources, significant political power, and the will to exercise that power. They also have powerful friends in Congress and in the administration.

One example of this is the now infamous snail-darter in Tennessee. Several large water projects on the Tennessee River were canceled because of the snail-darter. It was alleged that the snail-darter was an endangered species found only in a particular section of the Tennessee River where these water projects (e.g., dams, reservoirs) were to be built. It turns out that this little fish also lives in numerous places along the river and was safe and secure, even if the projects were built. The second example is the Alar scare involving apples. It was finally proved that the scare was the result of bad science put forward by public interest groups. Both decisions cost thousands of jobs and tens of millions of dollars. And both were initiated by public interest groups. This does not mean that public interest groups are always wrong. What it does mean is that public interest groups are not always right. Regarding whether special interest groups should have a role in the executive decision-making process, there is a bit of a constitutional problem with banning special interest groups from appearing before government regulators. The First Amendment to the Constitution does not reserve the right "to petition the Government for a redress of grievances" only to public interest groups. It gives that right to all citizens, including those who associate themselves with special interest groups.

Richard D. Otis Jr., American Plastics Council

If asked to think about decision making in Washington, D.C., most ordinary Americans would likely cringe and prefer to return to whatever they were doing. If they do think about it, they usually envision special interest groups and their lobbyists appealing to Congress for self-serving ends. It is an image of people and events the public has been given by both politicians and various interest groups who, in their own right, are part of the Washington game they often denigrate. Set aside for the moment whether the picture is accurate and notice that it does not include a significant but less known or understood range of activities undertaken by federal agencies.

Such executive branch activities may be grouped into two categories: (1) actions related to the relatively structured rulemaking process; and (2) a very broad range of far less structured decision-making activities including policy setting, developing agency research agendas, agency involvement in international negotiations, and the creation of "voluntary" federal programs. Under these two categories, agencies make decisions affecting every aspect of life in contemporary America, from individuals to businesses, small and large, nonprofit entities as diverse as universities and day-care centers and even government itself. Both can often be more complex, time-consuming, and difficult to affect or change—even by government officials—than the laws whose purpose they seek to implement.

From the First Amendment right to free speech to the election of citizen legislators, the right to petition our government, and the reservation of rights by states and the people, our system of government was founded on the active involvement of the people. There is little doubt that the public has a clear right to participate in governmental decision-making processes. Despite the negative picture many people have of lobbyists, a solid case can be made for their role in ensuring people's voices are heard and acknowledged. Often those who hold a negative view of lobbyists have a very different perspective when the issue at hand has direct personal relevance. They do not recognize the disconnection between an individual's acceptance of a broadly held societal myth and their own personal experience.

Public involvement in the rulemaking process has been clearly established under the Administrative Procedures Act (APA), first passed in 1946. While the details of its operation are the subject of a separate discussion, the reader should understand that the federal regulatory system was formulated to seek public comment and to provide an identifiable, clear mechanism for interested parties to affect the outcome. The existence of this process does not, however, mean that it was established or that it operates as a post-legislative, back-door mechanism for "special interests" to control or direct regulatory outcomes. Most of the time, the system operates quite to the contrary, as evidenced by the degree of litigation accompanying major regulations once they have been passed by Congress, implemented by the executive branch, and thrust on the public. How effective the APA is in truly ensuring that the public is involved in the rulemaking process and is able to affect agency decisions is an open question.

The second, broader category of agency activities is, by virtue of the range and variability from agency to agency, often harder to understand, more difficult to affect, and certainly less open to the public. Some structured opportunities for public involvement may occur under the Federal Advisory Committee Act (FACA), passed in 1972, and any number of "round tables," forums, or public meetings often held by agencies; however, these are voluntary actions on the part of federal agencies. The degree and nature of public involvement, if any, are at the sole discretion of the agency and, because the participants are chosen by the agency, are not necessarily truly representative of the public affected by the decision at hand.

The decision and rulemaking processes are generally not understood and often neglected by those seeking to affect government action. Lobbying Capitol Hill sounds more sexy than working with agency staff in a regional research laboratory. The mechanisms, tools, and ability to affect the outcome are probably even less well known and are employed effectively by a relatively limited but surprisingly diverse group of highly skilled artisans. They are often experienced insiders (including former career agency staff) with contacts, substantive knowledge of issues, patience, and resources. Although these systems are not intended to provide "special interest" with control over the regulatory outcome, those with the greatest understanding of the system and the ability to employ successfully the widest range of tools are clearly in a better position to have a greater effect.

Certain observers often try to place this diverse group of practitioners into simplistic categories. Inevitably they are characterized as groups at odds with each other—business versus public interest groups or powerless grassroots environmentalists versus big industry. There is always a certain presumption of good guy–bad guy or big guy–little guy relationships behind this thinking. The tale of David and Goliath negates one aspect of this fallacy. The repeated lack of common policy positions within the business community belies another. The notion that only self-proclaimed environmental groups care about the environment unmasks still another. Those involved in affecting agency decision making who fall prey to this model will underestimate the nature and capabilities of their opposition and fail to recognize potential allies. Skilled practitioners see beyond this simplistic categorization, but also recognize that characterization of one's opponents is a useful tool in its own right.

There are eight major capabilities that successful practitioners of executive branch lobbying should possess. They include a solid, detailed understanding of (1) how to set an agenda, construct the playing field, and determine the "rules" by which the game will be played (a well-planned, flexible strategy and properly executed tactical actions); (2) the formal and informal processes used by a specific agency; (3) when and at what step in the process to intervene; (4) the stakeholders involved in the issue (often, if an agency position has been written down, the game is lost—at best, it is an uphill battle); (5) the substance of the issue at hand; (6) various legal tools such as challenges as well as the applicable law underlying the planned agency action and the positions of other participants; (7) how to project and anticipate various players' likely actions (not only for opponents, but for different parts of an agency—if the policy staff disagree with you, the legal staff may not); and (8) the individual actors involved in the process (personalities matter in politics, even in executive agencies).

While less obvious, there are four additional characteristics of successful practitioners. These include (1) personal and professional integrity and credibility (including the ability to know when these are threatened); (2) personal relationships with the "opposition" (do not underestimate the role played by personal trust and a greater sensitivity toward motivation); (3) a recognition that people are people (faceless bureaucrats and heartless industry lobbyists have children and mortgages, too); and (4) a personal interest in the subject at hand (since many involved in the game are on a personal crusade, it helps to have a personal motivation as well). To the outsider, much of this sounds like a complex game and, indeed, it is. The stakes are often high and the complexity often difficult to manage. But, absent those who know how to play the game, we face a governmental decision-making system with few effective checks on its ability to constrain the public's right to be involved.

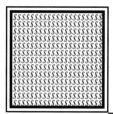

Part V

The Judicial Connection

16 Karen O'Connor

Lobbying the Justices or Lobbying for Justice?

"[JUSTICE] Black was huddled comfortably over his law books . . . when an old friend came through his doorway." "Tommy," Black called out in greeting Thomas G. Corcoran, a Roosevelt brain-truster from the old days. Corcoran was now a lawyer in private practice in Washington with a firm well known for its lobbying efforts on behalf of its corporate clients and "backstairs deals."[1] Black hadn't been in touch with Corcoran for several years. But Corcoran's daughter, Margaret, a former Black clerk, was experiencing a series of severe family and personal problems. Black assumed that was why his old friend had come to visit.

Black was thus shocked when Corcoran began to complain about a Court ruling the previous term. "No one came to the Supreme Court to lobby, even to 'put in a good word' for a petitioner," thought Black. "The mere mention of a pending case at a cocktail party was forbidden. Out-of-court contacts with Justices about cases were unethical." Now, here was Corcoran talking about a case that had a petition for rehearing pending. Aghast, Black got Corcoran out of his office as quickly as he could, cutting off his pleadings for his client.

A tenacious lobbyist, Corcoran didn't give up. He quickly made an appointment with Justice Brennan. Once in Brennan's office, he didn't waste time. "A grave injustice" had been done to his client by the Court, said Corcoran. Brennan, like Black, was astonished. What should he do? Remove himself from the case? After discussing the issue with his clerks and the rest of the justices, that's exactly what he did. Ironically, Brennan was originally inclined to accept the case for rehearing and the loss of his vote ultimately meant that the rehearing that Corcoran was so interested in failed by one vote and thus was never again heard.

Although incidents like this are everyday occurrences in the halls of Congress, the White House, and the executive branch of government, they are nearly unheard of in the halls of the Supreme Court. In the rarefied atmosphere of the Court, justices are considered to be immune from the mundane sorts of lobbying so common to the other branches of government. Overt lobbying of the Corcoran genre, for example, can actually be counterproductive. But that is not to say that the Court is immune from political pressures or the effects of organized pressure-group lobbying.

Noted interest group theorist Arthur A. Bentley (1908) was among the first to recognize that interest groups and organized interests viewed the judicial branch of government as a possible point of influence. According to Bentley, interest groups could exert their might in the nomination process as well as through actual participation in litigation. Yet few political scientists were quick to pick up on Bentley's recognition of the role of interest groups in the third branch of government. Conventional wisdom at the time, and indeed until the late 1960s and early 1970s, held that the courts were nonpolitical and above the fray of interest group politics—an idea that still informs many high school civics classes' treatment of the judiciary. As the works of Gregg Ivers and Wayne McIntosh and Cynthia Cates included in this section underscore, organized interests, be they corporations, interest groups, big business, or law firms, not only view access to the courts and litigation as important to the achievement of their goals or the goals of their clients, they also use a variety of forms of pressure, often not recognized as such in the interest group literature, to advance their goals.

In this chapter, the range of activities that organized interests engage in when they attempt to lobby the judiciary and the American legal system are explored (see table 16.1). When the Framers crafted Article III of the U.S. Constitution, creating the Supreme Court, they envisioned the Court as the "least dangerous branch" of government. To set it above the day-to-day machinations of politics, the Framers called for life appointment of all federal judges. True to separation-of-powers principles, however, the Framers left the selection of judges to an elected president and gave the U.S. Senate, whose members initially were chosen by state legislatures (prior to passage of the Seventeenth Amendment, which provided for the direct election of senators), the power to approve or disapprove the chief executive's recommendations. Thus, while the Court was to be somewhat removed from politics, its members often were those who survived a very political process. Presidents, elected officials themselves, often try to appoint jurists who share their political philosophy; and senators often have the wishes and desires of those they represent in mind when they cast their votes for

TABLE 16.1

TACTICS USED BY ORGANIZED INTERESTS
TO AFFECT THE JUDICIAL PROCESS

Internal group activities
  Nominations process
    Testifying before the Senate Judiciary Committee
    Submitting statements to the Senate Judiciary Committee
    Lobbying individual senators
    Conducting strategy sessions with members of Senate or their staff
    Preparing witnesses
    Alerting group members about nomination and issues involved
    Organizing letter-writing, phone, fax, or e-mail campaigns[a]
  Litigation process
    Sponsoring test-case litigation
    Filing amicus curiae briefs
    Writing op-ed pieces to drum up support

Coalitional, intergroup activities
  Nominations process
    Coordinating activities with other groups including lobbying, media, etc.
    Participating in joint group strategy sessions
    Supplying staff or financial support to other groups
  Litigation process
    Coordinating litigation campaigns
    Holding informational meetings about pending cases
    Sharing information on cases
    Providing research and other support services
    Filing amicus briefs jointly
    Coordinating amicus briefs
    Coordinating phone blitzes[b]

External group activities
  Nominations process
    Getting the word out through op-ed pieces, television and radio
      appearances, etc.
    Conducting polls or other research aimed to build public awareness of
      nominee
  Litigation process
    Holding Supreme Court briefings on upcoming cases
    Holding press conferences or issuing press releases after oral argument
    Holding press releases after decisions are handed down
    Holding marches to highlight cases

This framework draws from DeGregorio and Rossotti (1994).
a. This may also be an external activity.
b. This may also be an internal activity.

prospective Supreme Court justices (Segal, Cameron, and Cover 1992).

Not only are the nine members of the Supreme Court survivors of a political selection process, they are also the targets of varied forms of overt and not so overt political pressures once on the Court. Be it marches in Washington, D.C., test cases, or media blitzes, it is impossible for the justices to remain entirely above the fray of politics. Many of the major issues of the day, including affirmative action, abortion, gay rights, and Internet access, are hot-button issues that not only are the objects of interest group conflict but often find their ultimate resolution in the halls of the Marble Palace, as the Supreme Court is often called. The justices not only are aware of the way the political winds are blowing, interest groups and other organized interests often believe that it is their duty to get their side of the issue before the Court whether it be in the form of paid newspaper or television advertising, test cases, amicus curiae (friend of the court) briefs, demonstrations, or letter-writing campaigns.

This chapter explores the range of activities employed by interest groups in the judicial system and seeks to explain how the points of access for groups in the system—including the selection of federal court judges, the initiation of cases, judicial decision making, and even how cases are interpreted by the media and public—are often the results of, or the objects of, organized pressure-group activity. To that end, the role of interest groups in the judicial appointment process is first discussed. Second, the strategies and tactics used by many organized interests to lobby the court—direct sponsorship of cases and the filing of amicus curiae briefs—is detailed by examining the litigation strategies of several interest groups as well as by focusing in greater detail on the interest group activity that has surrounded the abortion issue and its treatment in the courts. Third, the use of what I term "spin doctoring" is examined as an underexplored and underrecognized tactic of organized pressure groups to affect policy as well as for the purpose of more traditional organizational maintenance. Spinning is used by a wide variety of organized interests including the corporations and conservative religious groups discussed by McIntosh and Cates and Ivers. This mobilization of the law for policy and maintenance purposes, moreover, has been used with particular success by organized interests on both sides of the abortion debate in an array of arenas from the nominations process to reaction to judicial opinions (Craig and O'Brien 1993; O'Connor 1996).

The Role of Interest Groups in the Judicial Appointment Process

The extraordinarily controversial Robert H. Bork (1987) and Clarence

Thomas (1991) nominations to the U.S. Supreme Court highlighted the role and potential impact of organized interests in the appointment process (Simon 1992). Both nominations triggered intense pressure-group interest. Several political scientists have analyzed those nominations in an effort to understand more about how and why interest groups participate in the judicial nominating process in an effort to allow us to understand more about interest groups in general.

The first systematic study of the Bork nomination process (DeGregorio and Rossotti 1994), for example, studied 147 groups that other studies found to be active participants in one or more phases of the process (Bronner 1989; Pertschuk and Schaetzel 1989; McGuigan and Weyrich 1990). DeGregorio and Rossotti found that some groups adopt an "inside the Beltway strategy," involving their own members in making direct appeals to their elected representatives. Others adopt an "outside the Beltway strategy," seeking the support of the public through targeted media campaigns; while other organized interests act in some combination of the two strategies (DeGregorio and Rossotti 1994). They and others (DeGregorio and Rossotti 1995; Caldeira, Hojnacki, and Wright 1996; Lichtman 1990) have found that interest groups are a valuable source of information about judicial nominees for both senators and the public. Commenting on the informational role of interest groups and group alliances in the nomination process, one study concluded: "senators on most nominations will have a full range of information from various quarters" (Caldeira, Hojnacki, and Wright 1996, 23). It is important to keep in mind that most groups involved in the process intend that like-minded men and women reach the Supreme Court. Once there, any one individual may play a key role in shaping the future of policies of key import to a group; thus, many groups are compelled to enter the judicial process at this early stage.

In addition to attempting to manipulate the press, media, and therefore public opinion in the judicial nominating process (Caldeira, Hojnacki, and Wright 1996; DeGregorio and Rossotti 1994, 1995), organized interests also participate extensively in the formal confirmation process. The Bork nomination, in particular, was taken as a call to arms for many liberal groups that believed that the Bork appointment would tip the Court in a conservative direction and bring with it a retreat from earlier liberal decisions on race, affirmative action, gender, and abortion. Bork, moreover, was an easy target for liberals. Not only had he played a pivotal role in the Watergate affair by firing the special prosecutor at Richard M. Nixon's request, he also served in that administration as U.S. solicitor general, where he defended or advocated many conservative positions before the U.S. Supreme Court. He also had a significant paper trail; as a law professor he had written extensively on controversial issues and had concluded that the right to privacy—the legal doctrine that the Court had used to justify its abortion rights decision in *Roe* v. *Wade* (1973)—could not be justified from his reading of the Constitution.

Similarly, the nomination of Clarence Thomas triggered severe consternation among liberal interest groups. Clarence Thomas, like Bork, had a long record of conservatism. But, during the Thomas hearings, the traditional coalition of liberal African American groups such as the National Association for the Advancement of Colored People (NAACP) parted ways with liberal groups it traditionally cooperated with to support the nomination of only the second African American to the Court. Women's rights groups, however, turned out in full force against the Thomas nomination, especially after Anita Hill's charges of sexual harassment against Thomas were made public. Their efforts along with those of other traditionally liberal groups, however, were not enough to derail the Thomas nomination.

Several studies of these two nominations have focused on the 147 groups that *claim* to have participated to one degree or another in the Bork and Thomas confirmation battles (Caldeira, Hojnacki, and Wright 1996; DeGregorio and Rossotti 1994, 1995).[2] Here, only *actual* formal participation in the Senate confirmation hearings of the nine sitting justices of the Supreme Court and the unsuccessful Bork nomination are considered as measures of interest group activity in the confirmation process.[3]

Over the years, a variety of liberal and conservative groups, as well as the American Bar Association, law professors, and attorneys from prestigious law firms, have testified for or against Supreme Court nominees. They know that the appointment of a single justice to the U.S. Supreme Court can, and often does, have major ramifications on their long-term interests and goals. Since Justice John Paul Stevens was appointed to the Court by Gerald R. Ford in 1975, 170 pressure groups have testified for, against, or about the ten nominations that have resulted in Senate confirmation hearings.[4] The Bork nomination attracted the most formal, public, interest group involvement with eighty-six groups testifying or submitting formal statements to the Committee (see table 16.2). The Thomas nomination was the next most controversial—at least in terms of the number of groups testifying for or against his nomination. Sixty-eight groups testified or filed written statements against Bork; forty-six did so against Thomas. Table 16.2, however, graphically reveals how idiosyncratic those two nominations were. Most nominations have generated far less pressure-group interest or public action.

Moreover, fifteen groups publicly participated in four or more hearings by testifying or filing a prepared statement with the committee.[5] Only one group, however, has appeared to give testimony in all ten hearings, the American Bar Association. It enjoys a unique role in the process as consideration of its recommendations are actually considered part of the formal confirmation process.

TABLE 16.2
INTEREST GROUPS AND LAW PROFESSORS APPEARING
IN SELECTED SENATE JUDICIARY COMMITTEE HEARINGS

Nominee	Year	Interest groups		Law professors		Law firms		ABA Rating	Senate Vote
		Lib.	Cons.	Pro	Con	Pro	Con		
Stevens	1976	2	3	—	—	0	0	Well-Q	98–0
O'Connor	1981	8	7	—	—	0	0	Well-Q	99–0
Scalia	1986	5	7	2	—	2	1	Well-Q	98–0
Rehnquist	1986	6	13	1	1	4	0	Well-Q	65–33
Bork	1987	18	68	20	26	15	8	Well-Q[a]	42–58
Kennedy	1987	12	14	4	—	4	0	Well-Q	97–0
Souter	1990	13	18	0	1	3	0	Well-Q	90–9
Thomas	1991	30	46	8	9	3	0	Q[b]	52–48
Ginsburg	1993	6	5	1	—	0	0	Well-Q	96–3
Breyer	1994	8	3	5	4	0	1	Well-Q	87–9

SOURCE: Data collected by author from Senate Judiciary Committee hearings reports.
a. 4 Not qualified.
b. 2 Not qualified.

The American Bar Association and
the Legal Profession

The American Bar Association was founded in 1878 but did not come to play a formal role in the selection of Supreme Court justices, as well as other judges for the federal bench, until the creation of its Committee on the Federal Judiciary in 1946 (Grossman 1965). The ABA's Standing Committee on Federal Judiciary evaluates candidates for the federal judiciary and then grades their qualifications for the bench. Ideally, the committee would like to screen candidates before they are formally nominated, but presidents have been loath to give up this near-veto power to a professional association. President Gerald R. Ford, however, forwarded fifteen names to the committee for its screening before he nominated John Paul Stevens.

The ABA rates potential Supreme Court justices as "Well Qualified," "Not Opposed (or Qualified)," or "Not Qualified." Votes of "Not Opposed" or "Not Qualified" are very rare, and generally are a harbinger of trouble in the U.S. Senate, as was the case with the Bork nomination. In 1982, when Ronald Reagan nominated Robert Bork to the U.S. Court of Appeals, Bork received the ABA committee's highest rating. In 1987, however, although ten members of the committee found him "Well Qualified," four members rated him "Not Qualified" based on their concerns about the conservative votes he might cast (Carter 1994, 163). Clarence Thomas was rated as "Qualified" for the Court of Appeals in 1989 and then "Qualified" for the Supreme Court, with two members rating him "Not Qualified," less than two years later.[6]

During the Reagan and Bush administrations the ABA committee almost lost its screening role. Republicans charged that ideological considerations were creeping into committee evaluations, "which raised the question of whether the committee deserved a special role, different from that of other interest groups" (Carter 1994, 163; Fein 1992).

Conservatives and Republicans were not alone in their criticism of the special role the ABA plays in the nomination/confirmation process. Several interest groups including the liberal Public Citizen and the conservative Washington Legal Foundation filed suit challenging the ABA committee's holding of closed meetings, arguing that under the Federal Advisory Committee Act, it was obligated to hold open meetings. Opposing this interpretation of the act was the U.S. Department of Justice, the ABA, and the liberal Alliance for Justice, a coalition of more than 100 liberal public interest groups. Ultimately, the Supreme Court ruled that the ABA was not covered by the act, thereby allowing the committee to continue its deliberations in private (*Public Citizen v. United States DOJ* 1989).

While having the most direct impact, the ABA is not the only represent-ative of the legal profession involved in the judicial nomination/confirma-tion process. Law professors and legal scholars, too, have tried to influence federal judicial appointments, although their participation is not institu-tionalized as is that of the ABA. In 1932, for example, President Herbert Hoover nominated the widely respected Benjamin Cardozo for the Su-preme Court at the urging of legal scholars. Conversely, legal scholar Louis Pollack apparently made some impact on the Senate Judiciary Committee considering G. Harrold Carswell's nomination to the Court by Richard M. Nixon when he commented that Carswell presented "more slender legal credentials than any nominee for the Supreme Court put forth in this cen-tury" (Baum 1981, 30).

Legal scholars are frequent witnesses in Senate Judiciary Committee hearings on prospective Supreme Court justices, although only one law professor, Gerard Casper of Stanford University, appeared before the Sen-ate Judiciary Committee more than twice in any of the ten nominations an-alyzed here. For example, in the Bork hearings, forty-six law professors testified—twenty in favor of the Bork nomination and twenty-six against the nominee (see table 16.2). Many of these liberal appearances against Bork were carefully orchestrated by the Leadership Conference on Civil Rights, an umbrella organization representing about 180 underprivileged interests ranging from racial minorities to the elderly to religious minorities (Phelps and Winternitz 1992, 73–74) and the liberal Alliance for Justice. Its Judicial Selection Project, in fact, was created to monitor the federal judi-cial selection and confirmation process, and it routinely shares its findings with the ABA. The White House ultimately did organize legal experts on behalf of Bork, although it did so only at the last minute, having been caught off guard by the intensely negative reaction to Bork's nomination.

Seventeen law professors spoke during the Clarence Thomas hear-ings—eight for and nine against. The Bork and Thomas hearings, however, were somewhat of an anomaly. Justice Ruth Bader Ginsburg, a former law professor herself, for example, had but one law professor testify on her be-half—Herma Hill Kay—who was one of her coauthors on her seminal women and the law textbook (Davidson, Ginsburg, and Kay 1974).[7] Thus, while in general law professors are not routine actors in Senate confir-mation hearings, their collective efforts, especially when coordinated by liberal or conservative interest groups, are noteworthy. In the Bork and Thomas hearings, the appearances and testimony of law professors—pro and con—were well orchestrated and clearly part of liberal or conservative organized pressure-group attempts to influence judicial doctrine by in-fluencing the outcome of the confirmation hearings.

Law firms, too, are often participants in the Senate confirmation pro-cess. While the role of Washington, D.C., based law firms as "insiders" who also act as lobbyists in Congress and the executive branch agencies for their clients is well known, many of those "Gucci Gulch" lobbyists are lawyers, and many of them are associated with some of the city's biggest and most prestigious law firms (Birnbaum and Murray 1987). Law firms are not especially active in the public side of the Supreme Court judicial confirmation process (see table 16.1). Seven of the last ten formal nominees had representatives of law firms testify for or against them; only three nominees—Scalia, Bork, and Breyer—had any opposition from law firms, and by any measure, that opposition was minimal (a total of ten firms). Far more law firms felt compelled to testify on behalf of a nominee. Indeed, it is perhaps surprising that more firms do not see the need to go on the public record in favor of a justice that their firm will in all likelihood be arguing before at some point in the near future.[8]

The Strategies and Tactics of Organized Interests in the Litigation Process

Many Americans presume the members of the federal bench—appointed by the president and confirmed by the U.S. Senate—to be above the fray of politics. This is simply not so. Those who select judges are political and often select judges for political reasons. Once Ronald Reagan's advisers, for example, recognized that he was having trouble with appealing to women voters in the 1980 presidential campaign, Reagan publicly pledged to appoint a woman to the first vacancy that occurred on the U.S. Supreme Court. Before him, Richard M. Nixon pledged to appoint "strict constructionist" judges to the federal courts in an effort to appeal to southern voters in his 1972 reelection bid.

Senators, too, may cast their votes for or against prospective nominees based on reelection considerations and pressure from organized pressure groups (Segal, Cameron, and Cover 1992). Thus it is not surprising that an overtly political process often results in the selection of political people to the federal courts. But the Framers clearly intended unelected judges appointed for life to be above the day-to-day rough-and-tumble of politics. And in many ways they are. Lobbyists (Mr. Corcoran being a notable exception) don't lurk around the Great Hall of the Supreme Court waiting to talk to justices. Neither do they shower justices with unsolicited gifts or golfing trips in an effort to sway votes or to increase access. But organized interests do try to affect the Court's pronouncements on major issues, as well as set the Court's agenda. One study of Washington, D.C., based interest groups, for example, found that 72 percent of the groups surveyed "fil(ed) suit or otherwise engaged in litigation" (Schlozman and Tierney 1988, 355).

The two most common forms of interest group lobbying of the Supreme Court, direct sponsorship and the filing of amicus curiae, or friend-of-the-court briefs, actually have many similarities to the other activities of organized interests discussed elsewhere in this volume. Moreover, the very nature of the rules of the Supreme Court encourage interest groups to participate in the litigation process. The Court, for example, selects and decides "only those cases which present questions whose resolution will have immediate importance far beyond the particular facts and parties involved." Said Chief Justice Vinson to lawyers of their role in the process: you "represent your clients, but [more crucially] tremendously important principles, upon which are based the plans, hopes and aspirations of a great many people throughout the country."

Test Cases and Direct Sponsorship

Richard C. Cortner once remarked that "cases do not arrive at the doorsteps of the Supreme Court like orphans in the night," and he was correct (1975, iv). In fact, the majority of important constitutional cases decided by the Supreme Court are brought by organized interests in the form of test cases (O'Connor and Epstein 1984, 72). One of the most common and most widely reported techniques used by interest groups to lobby the judiciary is the sponsorship of test cases. As early as the early 1900s, the National Consumers' League (NCL), a group of well-to-do women concerned about the long hours and low wages worked and earned by poor women, convinced Louis Brandeis, later to become the first Jewish justice on the U.S. Supreme Court, to take over the defense of Oregon's maximum-hour law for women.

At the urging of the Oregon Consumers' League, the Oregon state legislature had passed a law prohibiting women from working more than ten hours a day (Vose 1959; O'Connor 1980). The NCL's sponsorship of the litigation was limited to defense of the statute at the Supreme Court level. *Muller* v. *Oregon* (1908), however, was to become famous because its members collected all sorts of sociological and medical evidence to include in its brief to bolster the NCL's claims before the Court that long hours of work were deleterious to women's health. This "Brandeis brief"—a brief hallmarked by submission on nonlegal data to convince the Court to find for a particular party—is now commonly used by all sorts of interest groups who attempt to convince the Court of the negative (or positive) implications of the case at hand.

More common is the kind of sponsorship of the genre engaged in by the National Association for the Advancement of Colored People (NAACP). As early as 1939, the NAACP created a separate, tax-exempt litigating arm (Kluger 1976; Wasby 1995) and decided to launch a full-blown attack on racial discrimination in housing and public schools from the trial court level. First, it began litigation that culminated in *Shelley* v. *Kraemer* (1948). In *Shelley,* the NAACP successfully convinced the Supreme Court that state enforcement of racial restrictive covenants was unconstitutional state action violative of the Fourteenth Amendment (Vose 1959). Later, a series of test cases designed to whittle away at the separate but equal doctrine that had been enunciated by the Supreme Court in *Plessy* v. *Ferguson* (1896) (which had been used as the legal basis to allow the maintenance of state-sanctioned segregation in education and public accommodations), culminated in *Brown* v. *Board of Education of Topeka, Kansas* (1954). In *Brown,* where Thurgood Marshall convinced the Court that race-based classifications should be suspect, the NAACP's Legal Defense and Educational Fund showed how important the bringing of carefully orchestrated cases could be in a group's ability to bring about desired national policy change. For politically disadvantaged groups such as the NAACP, litigation was certainly a more feasible and realistic way of obtaining its goals than resorting to more traditional forms of lobbying.[9]

Since that time, the role of interest groups in sponsoring litigation has often been studied (Epstein and Kobylka 1992; Greenberg 1974; Ivers 1995; McIntosh 1985; Olson 1984; Wasby 1995). This tradition is continued in the chapters that follow. The McIntosh and Cates chapter is unusual in that it treats large corporations as organized interests but properly points out the potential for increased interest group and corporate involvement in free speech cases as the forms of communication available to all expand exponentially on a monthly basis. The recent passage by Congress of the sweeping Telecommunications Act, for example, caused a strange array of interest group bedfellows to seek an immediate order from the federal courts to enjoin its enforcement. Similarly, the Ivers chapter highlights how the conservative American Center for Law and Justice has affected not only the organizational environment of church-state law and litigation but also the legal strategies and tactics of other groups.

Sponsorship of cases, while costly, is the preferred tactic of many interest groups—if they have the financial resources and personnel to effectuate such a strategy. When funds are scarce, or when cases come to the Court that may affect a group's overall litigation strategy or involve an issue with which it is interested, organized pressure groups often file amicus curiae briefs.

Friends of the Court

It is not only by sponsoring cases that interest groups lobby the Court for policy change. They also file amicus curiae briefs in an effort to inform the Court of their views on the possible implications of the decision, as well as to urge adoption of their favored resolution of legal disputes. While originally envisioned to be a friend of the court and neutral regarding the parties, amici are now more appropriately viewed as friends of one of the participants to the litigation. Says political scientist Samuel Krislov, the amicus is no longer "a neutral amorphous embodiment of justice, but is an important participant in the interest group struggle" (Krislov 1963, 703), as they afford a way for groups, like lobbyists on the Hill, to provide information to decision makers.

Today, amicus briefs may be filed by interest groups and other interested parties for a variety of reasons including that they are unhappy with the type or quality of argument being made by the parties or they are requested to do so by one of the parties. Often, like-minded groups use amicus filings as a way of presenting arguments that cannot be made by the party to the lawsuit. Others believe it is imperative to show the Court, the public, and their members that they are strongly committed to certain positions (O'Connor 1980).

Nowhere can the range of interest groups and organized interests that participate in litigation as amici be seen more clearly than in abortion cases (Behuniak-Long 1991). In 1989, for example, a new record was set for the number of amici filed in a single case in *Webster* v. *Reproductive Health Services,* a challenge to a series of restrictions passed by the Missouri state legislature severely limiting and/or regulating abortion rights as enunciated earlier by the Court in *Roe* v. *Wade* (1973). Thirty-three groups, including the U.S. government, filed amicus curiae briefs for themselves or on behalf of some other group or groups in support of the restrictive legislation (see table 16.3). In contrast, twenty-six groups filed amicus briefs, actually representing several hundred groups,[10] urging the Court to find the abortion restrictions unconstitutional. In addition, briefs in support of the Reproductive Health Center's challenge to the law were also supported by amicus briefs from several members of Congress and ten states.

Although political scientists have found that the number of amicus curiae briefs filed in support of certiorari positively affects the Court's decision to accept a case for full review and oral argument (Caldeira and Wright 1987, 1990), it does not appear that the number of groups filing amicus briefs necessarily indicates that the side with the most briefs, or those from the most influential interest groups, will win. In *Webster,* for example, where more briefs (as well as more groups in absolute numbers given the coalitional activity present) were filed on the side of the health center challenging the state statute, the Court ruled that all but one of the state's abortion restrictions were unconstitutional.

Interestingly, many of the interest groups that testified against Robert Bork or Anthony Kennedy had done so because they feared that the appointment of a conservative, pro-life justice could alter the delicate balance that existed on the Court and trigger a reversal or severe limitation of the Court's expansive abortion rights ruling in *Roe.* Judge Bork, in particular,

TABLE 16.3
INTEREST GROUP PARTICIPATION IN *WEBSTER*

For Missouri —
Counsel: William L. Webster, attorney general of Missouri

Supported by amicus curiae from
The U.S. Government
Alabama Lawyers for Unborn Children, Inc.
American Association of Prolife Obstetricians and
  Gynecologists
American Family Association, Inc.
American Life League, Inc.
Catholic Health Association of the United States
Catholic Lawyers Guild of the Archdiocese of Boston, Inc.
Center for Judicial Studies et al.
Covenant House et al.
Focus on the Family et al.
Holy Orthodox Church
Knights of Columbus
Lutheran Church–Missouri Synod et al.
Missouri Catholic Conference

For Reproductive Health Services —
Counsel: Frank Susman

Supported by amicus curiae from
American Civil Liberties Union et al.
American Jewish Congress et al.
American Medical Association et al.
American Psychological Association
American Public Health Association et al.
Americans for Democratic Action et al.
Americans United for Separation of Church and State
Association of Reproductive Health Professionals et al.
Bioethicists for Privacy
Catholics for a Free Choice et al.
Center for Population Options et al.
Committee on Civil Rights of the Bar of the City of New
  York et al.
22 international women's health organizations
American Nurses' Association et al.

National Legal Foundation
Right to Life Advocates, Inc.
Rutherford Institute et al.
Southern Center for Law and Ethics
Southwest Life and Law Center, Inc.
U.S. Catholic Conference
127 members of the Missouri General Assembly
American Academy of Medical Ethics
American Collegians for Life
Association for Public Justice
Catholics United for Life et al.
Christian Advocates Serving Evangelism
Doctors for Life et al.
Feminists for Life et al.
Free Speech Advocates
Human Life International
International Right to Life Federation
National Right to Life Committee, Inc.
New England Christian Action Council, Inc.
Right to Life League of Southern California, Inc.
Birthright, Inc.

National Coalition Against Domestic Violence
National Family Planning and Reproductive Health Association
National Association of Public Hospitals
Population–Environment Balance et al.
281 American historians
2,887 women who have had abortions
California National Organization for Women et al.
Canadian Abortion Rights Action League
National Association of Women Lawyers et al.
National Council of Negro Women, Inc. et al.
National Organization for Women
77 organizations committed to women's equality
Certain members of Congress
Congressman Christopher H. Smith et. al.
608 state legislators
Certain members of the Commonwealth of Pennsylvania
Briefs of amici curiae were filed for the states of California New York, Massachusetts, Colorado, Texas, Vermont, Louisiana, Arizona, Idaho, Pennsylvania

drew vociferous opposition because of his beliefs, articulated earlier, that the privacy doctrine, upon which the Court had based its decision in *Roe,* was seriously flawed. Most major pro-choice national organizations including the National Abortion Rights Action League (NARAL), Planned Parenthood, and the National Organization for Women (NOW) testified against Bork and/or Kennedy. Because Justice Kennedy voted with the majority in support of *Webster,* their fears were apparently well founded.

To illustrate further the role that interest groups play in the litigation process, and to underscore the connection between the appointment and decision-making stages of the judicial process, the litigation activities of the fifteen groups that testified in four or more Supreme Court confirmation hearings were examined in greater detail.[11] All fifteen interest groups participated in litigation either as a sponsor or amici from 1979 to 1996. Only one group, the United States Justice Foundation, participated in only one case (table 16.4). Of the fourteen other groups that participated in litigation, all but the Leadership Conference on Civil Rights participated in more than twenty-five cases. Four groups sponsored cases as well as participated as amici. Eleven of the fifteen groups filed amicus briefs in one or more cases involving abortion rights;[12] of those eleven, only the conservative Concerned Women for America submitted an amicus brief urging the Court to uphold abortion restrictions. Thus it appears that organized groups that could be termed "repeat players" in the Senate confirmation process were groups that were also "repeat players" before the Supreme Court, especially when abortion rights were at stake (Galanter 1975).

The Role of Interest Groups in Setting the Judicial Agenda

Organized pressure groups do not generally leave their interest in judicial lobbying at the courthouse door. Instead, many of them engage in a variety of other tactics (see table 16.1) designed to bring about favorable judicial results. Nevertheless, few studies of interest groups and the courts have considered the role of organized interests in setting the legal agenda outside the formal litigation process. This agenda setting may come in largely two forms: (1) attempts to manipulate the media and therefore public opinion in the judicial nominating process beyond the formal hearings, and (2) planned efforts to cultivate the media in an effort to sway the way legal issues are framed, discussed, and reported both before and after opinions are rendered.[13]

The Nominations Process
Liberal groups, for example, carefully orchestrated media campaigns

against both Robert Bork and Clarence Thomas (Garment 1988; Simon 1992). In the Bork case, many national groups including NARAL, NAACP, and the AFL-CIO urged their members to write to their senators to urge them to vote against the nomination. NARAL members, sporting "Borkbuster" buttons, planned "a series of demonstrations and letter-writing and telephone campaigns during the August congressional recess in the home states of senators seen as important to the effort" (Bork 1990, 285). The range of activities open to interest groups in the judicial nominating process is vast, and different groups often utilize one or more strategies based on a variety of internal and external factors (see table 16.1; Caldeira, Hojnacki, and Wright 1996).

People for the American Way, for example, a group that has played an important role in the Court's treatment of First Amendment cases (Ivers 1995), mailed memoranda to editorial writers at nearly 1,700 newspapers across the nation in an effort to drum up grassroots opposition to Bork. Throughout the summer of 1989, moreover, "the hot, steamy days of July and August were filled with frantic activity—but only on the part of Bork's opponents" in the form of radio ads, print ads, and letter-writing campaigns carefully orchestrated to block his elevation to the Supreme Court (Bork 1990, 285).

Liberal groups admit to spending about $2 million on paid advertising to defeat Bork; pro-Bork forces estimate that their opponents spent closer to $10 to 15 million to defeat his nomination (Garment 1988). Nearly as much was spent in the Thomas proceedings. Interest groups clearly view the Court as a high stakes game.

Spinning the Issues and More

Organized pressure groups also are involved in what can be called "spin control." Spin control generally takes one of two forms: (1) interest groups either try to affect media reporting of legal issues or pending cases, or (2) they attempt to put a positive or negative spin on a judicial decision immediately after it is handed down much in the way campaign aides try to spin reporters after major presidential debates (Hagstrom 1993; Omicinski 1992). Of the fifteen groups that participated in more than four Senate confirmation hearings, five conducted press briefings on upcoming cases (see table 16.4). The ABA publishes what it terms a neutral *Supreme Court Preview*, a scholarly analysis of pending cases, so that is not considered spin here. The NOW Legal Defense Fund, in contrast, holds an annual press briefing in August for the press where it goes over the Supreme Court's upcoming agenda.

Ten of the fifteen groups either held press conferences or issued statements immediately after oral arguments were completed before the Court. Often, their lawyers emerge from the courthouse and go immediately

TABLE 16.4

LITIGATION AND MEDIA ACTIVITIES OF SELECTED ORGANIZED INTERESTS

| | Litigation activities | | Spin control activities | Press conferences / releases | |
	Sponsor	Amicus	Briefings on upcoming cases	After oral argument	After decisions
ABA		•	•		•
ADA		•	•		•
AFJ		•			
AFL-CIO	•	•		•	•
CCR	•	•		•	•
CWA		•	•	•	•
LCCR		•		•	•
IIPC		•		•	•
MALDEF	•	•		•	•
NARAL		•		•	•
NCDL		•		•	•
NOW/LDF	•	•	• [a]	•	•
NWPC		•	•	•	• [b]
WLDF		•	•	•	•
USJF		•		•	•

SOURCE: Data collected by calls to all groups during April 1996.

a. But not lately.

b. In conjunction with other organizations.

284

to hordes of media waiting for comment on how the oral argument went. This kind of activity allows an organization to put its own spin on how the justices appeared to react to their arguments and to grab the headlines or sound bites on that day's news. And even more dramatically, only one organization, the Alliance for Justice, which has most recently turned its attentions to the judicial selection, *did not* hold press conferences or issue press releases after major decisions of interest to the group were released.

NARAL has been one of the most prominent users of these kinds of tactics. In addition to calling press conferences and issuing statements, it went much further than most groups to put its spin on how the abortion issue was being played around America. In 1989, for example, after *Webster v. Reproductive Health Services* was docketed for Supreme Court review, it launched a major national campaign to let women know that *Roe* was in jeopardy and that access to safe, legal abortions was in peril. Working closely with other groups, including Planned Parenthood and NOW, NARAL designed a two-part strategy. The first was to let women know about *Webster*. The second part of the strategy was to educate the public to understand that even if *Roe* was not overturned, *Webster* could be a major setback, depending on the kinds of state restrictions the Court was willing to allow. NARAL's scheme was to get Americans to ask, "Who decides?" in an effort to alter how the debate was being framed by changing how abortion was dealt with on the public agenda (O'Connor 1996).

To that end, NARAL launched a massive print and television advertising campaign using a series of well-crafted advertisements aimed at the general populace as well as decision makers. One included photos of a young girl growing up. As the photos stop abruptly in the girl's late teen years, an announcer intoned, "She grew up in the '50s and died in the '60s, a victim of illegal abortion" (Tribe 1992, 174). By trying to stress the possibility that abortion could soon revert to being illegal, NARAL and pro-choice forces tried to shape the way abortion was being debated.

Although the justices of the Supreme Court cannot be the object of conventional lobbying techniques, pro-choice groups also brought their "Who Decides" campaign to the Court by launching an unconventional letter-writing campaign. The justices' chambers were inundated with mail from irate women. Although the Court normally receives about 1,000 pieces of mail a day, the volume soon reached 40,000 pieces of mail a day, effectively stalling the Court's communications systems. Said Toni House, the Court's Public Information Officer, "I hope they [the letter writers] understand this is not a popularity contest. We are not keeping score of who favors abortion and who does not. While people have a right to write the court I hope that they do not expect that the enunciation of their opinion will have any effect on the justices" (quoted in Craig and O'Brien 1993, 65).

At the same time, pro-choice groups also sponsored a march on Washington, D.C., drawing over 300,000 participants to convince the Court and the nation that women did not want to see abortion rights put in jeopardy by the Supreme Court. And on 26 April 1989, the day *Webster* was argued before the Court, both pro-choice and pro-life demonstrators (who also had filed amicus briefs) were out in full force in front of the Court where "passions ran high as competing protestors squared off at the courthouse steps, chanting, singing and screaming at each other" (Simon 1992, 128). Thus the range of activities that groups engage in to lobby the Court are clearly not limited to the ones most frequently studied by scholars. And many of these activities have yet another purpose: marches and the like help build group solidarity and organization maintenance.

Organization Maintenance

While influencing the course of public opinion and judicial decision making, the participation of most groups involved in the process often has another, more immediately selfish goal. Interest groups, in fact, often use the courts, be it involvement in the nominations process, decisions, or spin on those decisions, for institutional maintenance purposes. Liberals and conservatives alike send mass mailings to their members or potentially interested individuals asking for funds to "fight a nomination" or "wage a judicial war or litigation battle." People for the American Way, for example, sent out over 4 million letters soliciting funds to help it stop the Bork nomination and it reportedly raised nearly $2 million. Similarly, NARAL raised millions in its campaign against Bork's confirmation, as well as with its "Who Decides?" campaign, ostensibly launched to help it litigate in *Webster*. In addition to its direct-mailing effort, it ran full-page advertisements in local newspapers headlined "What women have to fear from Robert Bork." The advertisement also included a form to be cut out and mailed in with a contribution to help NARAL's lobbying activities (O'Connor 1996). Thus the kinds of activities that surround court-focused pressure-group activity often have a positive by-product for groups as they help them raise revenues and build member solidarity and support.

Conclusion

As this chapter and the two that follow it underscore, interest group involvement in the activities of the third branch of government are extensive and in many ways similar to those used to lobby the other branches of government. Interest groups try to get "their" supporters—or at minimum their sympathizers—on the federal bench and often spend just as much money, if not more, than special interests do to get friendly legislators elected to Congress or the presidency.

Interest group involvement in the judicial process does not stop there.

Organized pressure groups, either individually or in coalitions, bring issues to the Court for its resolution in ways not all that different from how special interests get sympathetic lawmakers to propose legislation. Groups often seek out plaintiffs to bring test cases and then ask similarly minded groups for their support, be it financial, technical, or in the form of individual or coordinated amicus curiae briefs. Thus, at the litigation stage, parallels can be drawn to the activities of groups who seek out lawmakers to sponsor legislation. Groups often seek out an issue and then find plaintiffs to allow them to make their case as it wends its way through a judicial system that contains just as many potential roadblocks as the lawmaking process does to potential legislation.

Groups involved in litigation as a mechanism to achieve their policy goals are perhaps most like other groups in their external activities. They often go beyond the courts to reach out to their members and the mass public through mailings, as well as television and print advertisements. Thus it is time to reintegrate the study of interest groups that participate in the judicial process into the broader study of interest group politics.

Acknowledgments

The author would like to thank Ron Shaiko and Gregg Ivers for their helpful comments and suggestions on this paper. I would also like to thank Elliott Slotnick for first raising the idea of spin control in the context of Court reporting. A special note of thanks goes to Jess Waters at American University for her outstanding research assistance, especially plowing through thousands of pages of Senate Judiciary Committee testimony.

Notes

1. All quotes here and the entire vignette are drawn from Bob Woodward and Scott Armstrong (1979, 88–96).

2. This information was culled from several sources and surveys conducted with group officials. See Caldeira, Hojnacki, and Wright (1996); DeGregorio and Rossotti (1994, 1995).

3. This measure is used because it is one that forces groups to go on the public record where potential justices can easily see which groups, law firms, or individuals are for or against them by reading or seeing the public record of their confirmation proceedings.

4. A list of these groups is available from the author. Some groups testified or filed statements about candidates without taking sides. These appearances are not included in this analysis.

5. Those fifteen groups are Alliance for Justice, American Bar Association, Americans for Democratic Action, the AFL-CIO, Center for Constitutional

Rights, Concerned Women for America (a conservative group), International Association of Police Chiefs (generally a conservative group), NARAL, National Association of Criminal Defense Lawyers, Leadership Conference on Civil Rights, Mexican American Legal Defense Fund, NOW and NOW LDF, National Women's Political Caucus, United States Justice Foundation, and the Women's Legal Defense Fund.

6. The number voting "Qualified" was not released. It is known that at least one member did not vote.

7. Ginsburg did have the help of her friends, many of them law professors, before her nomination. In fact, her husband orchestrated a concerted letter-writing campaign to the president on her behalf (Randolph 1993).

8. What is not revealed in table 16.1 is the somewhat surprising fact that of the twenty-five total firms that publicly became involved in the confirmation process, only ten were D.C. firms; the remaining fifteen were outside the Beltway firms. Thus at least in this stage of the legal process few law firms attempted to intervene publicly in the process. This, of course, is not to say that they did not participate in the process in other ways, including preparing prospective nominees for their confirmation hearings, helping other testifiers produce their statements, or prepping them for their testimony on behalf of or against a nominee.

9. This is not to imply that only disadvantaged groups resort to litigation to obtain their goals. As McIntosh (chap. 18) and others (Epstein 1985) point out, all sorts of organized interests may see litigation as conducive to attainment of their objectives.

10. The "et al." in table 16.3 can often indicate numerous other groups signing on to the brief to indicate their support.

11. The name of each group was run in the briefs file of LEXIS.

12. Only the ABA, International Association of Chiefs of Police, National Association of Criminal Defense Lawyers, and the U.S. Justice Foundation did not become involved in the abortion issue, at least in terms of participating in litigation before the Supreme Court.

13. Vose (1959) and others, however, have noted the tendency of some groups to flood the law reviews with articles urging particular judicial interpretation of the Constitution or statutes as a form of pressure-group activity.

Gregg Ivers

Please God, Save This Honorable Court: The Emergence of the Conservative Religious Bar

SHORTLY before he was to begin his historic confrontation in a Dayton, Tennessee, courtroom with Clarence Darrow over the meaning of the Bible and its place in American public education, William Jennings Bryan told a throng of assembled supporters that the *Scopes* trial was more than just his personal effort to save "the Christian Church from those who are trying to destroy her faith." With charm and charisma pouring from the shadow where he stood, Bryan announced that his case posed an equally disturbing question: Can a minority use the courts to force its ideas upon the schools and the larger society? Majorities acted with the natural self-restraint that the Constitution required. If the Godless were indeed a majority, then by all means elect them. And if they were not, then was it fair to have the courts impose their will on an unwelcoming citizenry through constitutional edict (Ginger 1958, 90)?

To Bryan, of course, the answer was no. Today a movement of Christian evangelicals and fundamentalists three generations removed from the *Scopes* trial of the 1920s seeks to frame a legal debate on issues of church and state in the same manner. Through skill and determination, today's conservative Christians have the potential to leave their mark on the constitutional relationship between church and state with far greater success than any of their predecessors.

This chapter addresses three major questions in an effort to place the rise of the conservative religious legal movement in the broader context of how organized interests use the litigation process and what they hope to gain from it. How has the environment of organized interests in Supreme Court church-state litigation changed since the tumultuous era associated with Chief Justice Earl Warren? Second, who are the leaders and organizations that constitute this law-based movement of Christian conservatives, and how do they use the litigation process to advance their interests? This question is directly linked to the third: How has the entrance of Pat Robertson's litigation arm, the American Center for Law and Justice (ACLJ), affected not only the organizational environment of church-state law and litigation but the legal strategies and tactics of other conservative religious organizations as well?

The Rise of Religious Conservatives in the Litigation Process

Political scientists, legal scholars, and students of social movements have created a substantial body of scholarship that attests to the influence of organized interests in the litigation process. For some time, the theoretical and empirical approach that scholars emphasized in their research on the role of organized interests in the courts was on the decidedly minoritarian nature of this litigation. From the early work of Arthur Bentley (1908) through the later work of Clement Vose (1958, 1959), whose pioneering and still-classic book, *Caucasians Only,* provided the first extended treatment of how constitutional litigation could serve as far more than a mechanism for conflict resolution, one theme remained consistent: organized interests who represented constituencies disadvantaged in the political branches of government could bypass those majoritarian channels and demand their constitutional rights through litigation. And, consistent with the pattern of "forum shopping" common in litigation work, how organized interests chose to assert their presence in the courts varied based on their resources and how much they were willing or able to spend. The choices available ranged from direct sponsorship, the most expensive and arguably most potent option, to the submission of *amicus curiae,* or friend of the court, briefs, a much less expensive choice but one not without its advantages, to providing research and other support services to other actors. Whatever the choice, organized interests could be successful in forcing recalcitrant political bodies unresponsive to the needs of political minorities to engage in fundamental change (e.g., Ivers 1995, 1992; Epstein and Kobylka 1992; Epstein 1985; O'Connor and Epstein 1983; O'Connor 1980; Cortner 1968; Barker 1967; Harper and Etherington 1953; Yale Comment 1949).

Much of this research has centered on the work of the NAACP Legal

Defense Fund's litigation campaign from the late 1930s through *Brown* v. *Board of Education* to end state-enforced racial segregation and the difficulties associated with the judicial implementation of that landmark decision (Wasby 1995; Tushnet 1987; Vose 1959, 1958, 1955). Other important contributions to the literature on interest group-sponsored litigation featured analysis on legal efforts to revolutionize the law include sex-based equality (O'Connor and Epstein 1983; O'Connor 1980), criminal procedure (Medalie 1968), First Amendment freedoms (Ivers 1995; Swanson 1990; Sorauf 1976), and environmental regulation (Hassler and O'Connor 1986). In each case, liberal groups used the courts to advance policies that would not win approval by the majoritarian branches of government. Even conservatives who opposed the policy objectives of these groups admitted that they had been effective in using the courts to advance their organizational interests. Eventually these conservative interests also entered the litigation arena, a development that has received comprehensive attention (Epstein 1985). I attempt to describe below how these broad changes in the litigation environment have affected church-state law and politics.

If there is one feature that illustrates just how much the interest group environment has changed in church-state litigation over the past twenty-five years, it is the now ideologically plural, confrontational nature that characterizes the process. During the first major period of constitutional change in the law of church and state, litigation was dominated by three major national organizations, each of which took a strong "separationist" interpretation of the Establishment Clause of the First Amendment, which has been interpreted by the Supreme Court to forbid direct financial assistance to religion and formal sponsorship of religious activities in public settings.[1]

From the late 1940s, when the Court decided *Everson* v. *Board of Education* (1947), through the late 1960s, when the Court decided *Flast* v. *Cohen* (1968), three groups were the driving forces behind every landmark lawsuit: the American Jewish Congress, the American Civil Liberties Union (ACLU), and Americans United for Separation of Church and State (AU). These groups fought state-sponsored prayer in public schools, tax-supported assistance to parochial schools, and other government programs that appeared to advance the interests of religion.

The conceptual and intellectual framework and legal strategies to execute it in this line of cases rested with one man, Leo Pfeffer, and the organizational structure that sustained him during this period, the American Jewish Congress (Sorauf 1976). To understand just how thoroughly Pfeffer dominated the development of church-state law and litigation during a career that spanned four decades (1945–85) as both a scholar and litigator, consider that he either represented the plaintiffs or appeared as the counsel of record for organizations appearing as amici curiae in over half of the Establishment Clause cases decided by the Supreme Court during this period. This is a record of law building unsurpassed by any other public interest lawyer in the twentieth century, including that of Thurgood Marshall during his tenure with the NAACP (Ivers 1995; Krislov 1985). As Samuel Krislov (1985, 421) has commented, "No one comes to mind, to rival Pfeffer's intellectual dominance over so vital an area of constitutional law for so extensive a period in this combination of pleading and intellectualizing. His corpus of work comes close to meeting the components ... for a successful constitutional reform movement—articulated theory, extensive litigation over time, pragmatic flexibility, and patient and persistent step-by-step strategy." Over time, Pfeffer's presence extended beyond the institutional confines of the American Jewish Congress to the entire network of organizations that advocated strict separation between church and state, including the ACLU, AU and, to a lesser extent, such major Jewish organizations as the American Jewish Committee and the Anti-Defamation League of B'nai B'rith (Ivers 1995).

Conservative organizations that went to court to oppose the American Jewish Congress, the ACLU, AU, or other organizations within the liberal, separationist orbit during this critical period in constitutional development were a scarce presence, and few even filed amicus curiae briefs. In fact, not even *Engel* v. *Vitale* (1962) and *Abington* v. *Schempp* (1963), the landmark cases decided in 1962 and 1963 outlawing, respectively, the recitation of state-composed prayers, whether mandated or voluntary, and state-sponsored Bible reading in the public schools, attracted conservative amici to support the schoolboards' arguments that such activities were constitutional. Instead, the litigation environment was dominated by the American Jewish Congress, the ACLU, and the AU, with crucial and regular support from other liberal Jewish and Protestant organizations. Other than an occasional amicus curiae brief from the United States Catholic Conference (USCC), which participated in parochial school aid and released-time for religious instruction cases, and occasional ad hoc coalitions of parents' groups, conservative opposition was virtually nonexistent (Ivers 1995, 66–188).

From 1969 to 1980, the litigation environment became somewhat more diverse, but for the most part it remained dominated by liberal, separationist groups. What little opposition did exist came from the USCC and other lay Catholic organizations. They were joined on occasion by an Orthodox Jewish group, the National Commission for Law and Public Affairs (COLPA), which supported state subsidies for religious education.

Although some Protestant organizations were active in the litigation process during this period, these organizations had a decidedly separationist bent. The Baptist Joint Committee on Public Affairs (BJC), for example, has represented the interests of numerous Baptist churches and conventions nationwide exclusively on religious liberty issues since 1962 and the National Council of Churches (NCC) has represented the voices of more than thirty religious denominations on a diverse palette of social and public affairs issues since the end of World War II. Supported by other mainline Protestant agencies representing Presbyterians, Methodists, Congregationalists, and Unitarians, the participation of American Protestantism in matters of church-state law and litigation came in support of the separationist position before the Supreme Court. In contrast, conservative Protestant organizations remained silent during this period (Ivers 1992). That would soon change.

Since 1980, conservative religious organizations have become regular participants in Supreme Court church-state litigation. Like their liberal counterparts, religious conservatives have relied chiefly on participation as amici curiae to represent their interests in litigation, but have not flinched from sponsorship if the cause merited such involvement. The organizational environment of church-state litigation has undergone a transformation from one that was dominated by civil liberties and Jewish organizations, which often worked together, to one characterized by a much greater degree of religious and ideological pluralism. Christian evangelical and fundamentalist organizations with histories as far back as their liberal counterparts, such as the Christian Legal Society (CLS) and the National Association of Evangelicals (NAE) founded in 1943, entered into the thick of litigation politics as never before. Also present were newer conservative groups, such as the Rutherford Institute, founded in 1982, with sophisticated legal programs of their own.

Evangelicals and fundamentalists had been involved in church-state issues before, primarily in aggressive editorial attacks in the mass and specialized media, the manipulation of public opinion, or pressuring Congress to rescind the Court's decisions through legislation or constitutional amendment (Keynes and Miller 1989). During this latter period, however, evangelicals and fundamentalists became involved in litigation at an exponential rate. Through the Court's 1990 term, for example, 55.1 percent of its Establishment Clause cases drew amicus briefs from interest groups on both sides, a figure nearly double the rate in cases decided from 1969 through 1979 terms (Ivers 1992).

Prior to 1980, the only one of these self-identified Christian evangelical or fundamentalist groups to submit an amicus brief was the CLS, and that came in an eminently forgettable case, *Jones* v. *Wolf* (1979), concerning the regulation of labor disputes between unions and churches (Ivers 1990). More recently, between the 1990 through the 1997 Supreme Court terms, religious conservatives have appeared regularly as amici in church-state litigation, participating at rates equal to and in some cases more than liberal interests. In an even more dramatic departure from the past, religious conservatives have sponsored several crucial cases that the Court has decided in their favor. As Karen O'Connor notes in chapter 16, the ability of groups to sponsor cases allows them to direct and control litigation strategy in a fashion impossible through participation as amicus curiae. The latter, while useful and sometimes influential in shaping how the Court might view the legal issues in a case, does not allow an organization to engage in the most fundamental strategic concerns involved in the litigation process, including the selection of clients, the development of a factual record, and the management of the appeals process. Case sponsorship permits much great control over the dynamics involved in complex constitutional litigation. The increased presence of conservative religious groups in church-state litigation has proven no exception to this rule.

The rise of religious conservatives in the litigation process is a consequence of the mobilization of evangelical Christians in the late 1970s and early 1980s, one that extended far beyond previous activities of such public figures as the Reverend Jerry Falwell and his now-defunct Moral Majority (Wilcox 1992; Moen 1989; Hertzke 1985; Reichley 1985). Religious conservatives, encouraged by the election of Ronald Reagan, awoke from a long period of political slumber fully prepared to enter high-powered Washington politics, including an arena once the almost exclusive domain of liberal and moderate religious denominations—the courts. This development startled the network of mainline religious lobbies that for so long had represented ecumenical dialogue in public affairs. Moreover, the Christian conservatives who came to Washington in the late 1980s were better organized, more sophisticated in their political and legal capabilities, and better financed than ever before.

Who, or What, Is the Religious Right?

The Religious Right is a term often used by reporters, direct-mail fund raisers, academics, and organized interests to describe religious conservatives who are open about the role that their Christian faith plays in their lives and their willingness to engage the political process based on that faith, and who seek very conservative public policies. In reality, the Religious Right is no more of a monolith than the "secular left" Christian conservatives have pledged to undo as a force in American society. Conservative religious organizations do share a common view about the role of religious values in education or the need to protect the religious rights of Christians who feel oppressed by the workings of the administrative state and what they perceive to be the often thoughtless regulations secular society places on their "God-given" rights. This leaves religious conservatives in a position no different from their older and more well-established liberal opponents. Previous research on the differences between like-minded organizations on the appropriate strategies, tactics, and policy outcomes to pursue through litigation concludes that the idea of a monolithic movement of religious conservatives or liberal secularists is largely myth (Ivers 1995, 1992; Sorauf 1976).

Diversity exists within the conservative Christian legal community. Just as some liberal, separationist organizations would rather negotiate with a school administrator than threaten a lawsuit, there are conservative lawyers who prefer the same. And just as many ACLU affiliates are ready to go to court at the drop of a hat, while other liberal groups, such as the Anti-Defamation League of B'nai B'rith, prefer to resolve a dispute through community relations professionals, so too do conservative groups differ in their eagerness to litigate.

The most visible conservative Christian legal organization is the American Center for Law and Justice (ACLJ), formed by the Reverend Pat Robertson as a counterpart to the ACLU. The ACLJ is directed by Jay Sekulow, who seeks a more public profile through the sponsorship of high-profile lawsuits, frequently holding press conferences and being available to the print and television media for interviews and commentary. Yet there are also volunteer attorneys working with the CLS who seek to resolve problems quietly, such as misunderstandings between students and their school principals. For every case that the ACLJ envisions as ripe for Supreme Court review, literally hundreds of cases are resolved with a letter or phone call by other organizations. These strategic differences within the conservative legal community sometimes result in acrimony and off-the-record but rarely unprintable remarks, yet this is no different from strategic differences among liberal civil liberties and religious organizations.

The formation of the ACLJ has led to increased media attention to the rise of conservative public interest law firms that specialize in religious liberty cases. In July 1995, the *New York Times* published an article on the emergence of conservative religious organizations as increasingly prominent players in church-state law and litigation (Niebuhr 1995, 1). The formation of the ACLJ, the Liberty Counsel, and the Becket Fund for Religious Liberty has expanded the number of groups active in conservative Christian legal activity and has increased the number of groups that are willing to litigate on church-state issues.

Older organizations such as the CLS, the NAE, and the Rutherford Institute are now more active than in the past in Supreme Court church-state litigation, but historically their preference has been to participate as amici curiae, a far less effective method of influencing the dynamics of law and precedent. The decision to pursue an amicus strategy is a combination of cost-consciousness and membership expectations. With limited financial resources and staff available to devote to long-term litigation projects, conservative religious organizations are often compelled, like their liberal opponents, to resort to the more cost-effective alternative of participation as amicus curiae. Equally important are the wants and expectations of organizational membership. Legal and professional staff that work for organizations dependent on membership for the brunt of their funding are not always able to act independently of their donors' interests (Ivers 1995, 1992).

Another aspect in which these older organizations differ from the newer ones is in their desire for publicity. Several interviews with members of the conservative religious bar conducted for this chapter pointed to a preference for what one CLS attorney called "informal" settlements—letters and phone calls to the offending parties, legal summaries designed to inform schools officials of students' rights, and assistance to paralegals and lawyers from private firms working on a case who do not possess church-state expertise. Such a view stands in contrast with another that emerged during an interview with an attorney from the Becket Fund. When asked if the fund preferred initiating lawsuits or pursuing informal settlements, the response of this attorney was that "we do not take cases that we intend to settle at the local level. If you start doing that, you find your organization becoming nothing more than a free legal clinic."[2] Thus the strategic choices that conservative religious organizations find themselves utilizing in the litigation process, choices between sponsorship, participation as amicus curiae, or working less visibly to settle conflicts through negotiation, are consistent with the legal approaches discussed earlier in this chapter that were traditionally the province of liberal groups.

To summarize, the full-blown entrance of religious conservatives into the legal arena has convulsed the dynamic that once drove church-state law and litigation, a development that is consistent with the more general rise of the conservative public interest bar over the past two decades. It is fair to state that if you were a high school principal twenty-five years ago and a church-state lawyer came knocking on your door, he or she was likely to have handed you an ACLU or American Jewish Congress business card on the way out. Today, the odds are even or better that the attorney might be someone who works for the CLS or the Rutherford Institute or the ACLJ, and a few principals may find themselves caught between the demands of both sets of attorneys. As populated and diverse as the conservative religious bar has become, the ACLJ has emerged as the most public of these organizations active in church-state law and politics.

The American Center for Law and Justice

One of the reasons for the controversy surrounding the ACLJ is its founder, Pat Robertson. Robertson is perhaps best known for his televangelism ministry, the 700 Club, and for his failed presidential bid in 1988, but he has also built a conglomerate of business, religious, and political enterprises that is simply staggering in scope and wealth. Although Robertson failed to win the White House in 1988, he raised more money than any previous candidate for a presidential nomination and finished second in the Iowa caucuses. While Robertson quickly faded as a factor in the Republican nominating primaries after Iowa, the voter base he organized and tapped into for his support in 1988—Christian conservatives—has since become a powerful nominating constituency in Republican politics and the membership base of the Christian Coalition. Headed until 1997 by Ralph Reed, who decided to forgo an academic career as a college professor and historian for the chance to launch a political movement of Christian conservatives, the Christian Coalition has been extremely successful in flexing its muscle in the electoral and legislative processes.

Like many Christian conservative activists, Robertson has long believed that a large reservoir of registered voters exists who feel that something has gone terribly wrong in American public life: liberal abortion policies, the absence of religious values and expression in public life, cultural permissiveness, and the rotting of public education. Robertson believes that a majority of Americans share his views, and has asked himself and his millions of supporters the same question that William Jennings Bryan asked during the *Scopes* trial: Can a minority use the courts to force its ideas upon the schools and the larger society? His answer came in the formation of the ACLJ, which he created in 1991.

The ultimate objective of the ACLJ, as described in one its first newsletters, is to "tear down" the "fictitious wall" of separation created by the "ACLU and its left-wing allies." When he first proposed the idea, Robertson foresaw the ACLJ as a civil liberties organization for evangelical Christians, one that would "set the agenda for religious freedom in America during this decade" (Fournier 1992). Robertson, moreover, had no interest in following the model for religious conservatives created by the CLS, but instead that of his archrival and mortal enemy, the ACLU. Robertson chose the controversial but successful Jay Sekulow to serve as the ACLJ's general counsel. Just as Ralph Reed was able to communicate the religious fervor that animates much of the Christian Coalition's public policy work in secular terms, Sekulow, who, in *Board of Westside Schools* v. *Mergens* (1990), had just won a unanimous decision in the Supreme Court on behalf of the right of student religious clubs to meet in public schools, would soon do the same in courtrooms across the land.[3]

Interviews conducted for this chapter, as well as information culled from secondary sources, confirm Sekulow's claim that he heads the most aggressive and confrontational of the Christian law firms. With a yearly budget of $8 million, a staff of 13 attorneys and over 500 lawyers around the country who are ready to act as the equivalent of Paul Revere's Minutemen when religious liberty cases are referred to them through informal channels, the ACLJ is already larger and wealthier than its older and more established allies in the cause. One of Sekulow's first public actions after taking the ACLJ helm was to publish an op-ed piece in the *Wall Street Journal* the day after the Court's 1992 decision in *Lee v. Weisman* (1992), which upheld a thirty-year line of decisions prohibiting state-sponsored religious devotionals in public schools. Sekulow insisted what the Court had really said was that schools were prohibited from inviting clergy to direct prayer, but students were free to organize devotionals during school events as long as participation was voluntary. While Sekulow's arguments that students have free speech rights to organize religious services in public schools have not yet found their way back to the Supreme Court, several states have enacted statutes authorizing some form of student-initiated prayer in public schools. Two lower federal courts have issued conflicting rulings on the constitutionality of these laws, increasing the probability that the Court will eventually hear arguments on the issue.

In truth, there was absolutely nothing in the Court's opinion to indicate that Sekulow's article captured its true intent. But the article, along with the 10,000 faxes the ACLJ sent to school districts around the nation arguing precisely that point, provided the impetus for the subsequent drive to introduce, with reasonable success, state laws allowing "student initiated" prayers during public school events. That schools must take some role in assisting students and providing guidelines for such religious activities raises a more difficult constitutional question than perhaps Sekulow and the ACLJ wish to acknowledge. Like almost all other recent Establishment Clause cases that have involved some question whether religious activities are permissible in public buildings or other public spaces, religious conservatives have framed the debate as a free speech issue and not about governmental preference for or establishment of religion. There is a considerable disagreement on this point among constitutional scholars and church-state activists. Nonetheless, it is difficult to deny that such groups as the ACLJ, the CLS, and others in the conservative religious bar have been influential in shaping the constitutional terms of debate.

While the ACLJ's approach to litigation has thus far proven quite successful, there is reason to believe that perhaps its penchant for credit claiming, a desire to pursue lawsuits when perhaps alternative forms of dispute resolution are more appropriate, and its reputation as the most politically driven of the major conservative Christian law firms may pose a problem in the future. The internal cohesiveness of a social movement, as well as the success of that movement to organize around external goals, depends in large part on the power of a single group or individual to represent the various needs of the organizations that comprise it. When a single organization or a single individual can dominate an area of law and litigation, such as Thurgood Marshall and the NAACP and Leo Pfeffer and the

American Jewish Congress once did, it makes it much easier to determine the course of action and control organizational rivalries. There were plenty of occasions when the organizational allies, as well as their own constituencies, of the NAACP and American Jewish Congress disagreed with their decision making. But because of the public reputations of Marshall and Pfeffer, and the need to present their opponents with the illusion of unanimity, such disagreements were usually squelched in public (Wasby 1996; Ivers 1995; Tushnet 1987). Neither Sekulow nor anyone else in the conservative religious legal movement has yet to earn such credentials.

Organizational rivalries have not yet pushed religious conservatives into confrontation with one another. The enemy is still out there. But as these organizations continue to proliferate, the chances will increase that, despite agreement on the need to reintroduce state assistance into the religious choices that individuals make about their education and how to conduct their politics, the appearance of unity may well disintegrate into a dispute over just who is the most qualified to carry out God's work on earth—or at least in the courts.

There is also something else different about the new wave of conservative litigation. Racial equality and the elimination of organized prayer in school were distinctly minoritarian positions. The landmark racial discrimination and religion cases were, of course, about individual rights, but they were about minority rights as well. Prohibiting state-imposed segregation protected individuals at the expense of majority rule, but it also protected African Americans as a group from the white majority. Religious conservatives today see their cause as being about individual rights, as when a schoolchild is erroneously told that he or she cannot read the Bible during study hall or lunch. But deep down, all of it—the legislative work, the lawsuits, and the electioneering—is also about restoring, in their eyes, what they view as the rightful place of Christian—and hence majoritarian —values in American public life, values usurped by an unfeeling, arrogant minority of secular humanists and civil libertarians out-of-touch with mainstream values. Many of the policies promoted by the Christian conservative legal organizations command the support of a majority of Americans, but some groups advocate positions that few Americans find palatable (Jelen and Wilcox 1995; Wilcox 1996).

Conclusion

For some time, the public interest and religious organizations that dominated the arena of church-state law and litigation viewed religious conservatives and the smattering of organizations that represented them in such conflicts. Religious conservatives were portrayed as politically naive and unschooled in the complex constitutional requirements of the Establish-

ment Clause. Rather than address what religious conservatives believed
were legitimate issues of discrimination and disrespect for their First
Amendment rights, liberal separationists sought to paint them as theocrats
bent on replacing our secular constitutional principles with canon law di-
rectives. As a powerful fusion of religious and secular conservative interests began to merge in the late 1970s into a powerful public interest law
movement in its own right, bringing with them a constitutional vision that
has been accepted in considerable part by the Supreme Court, the powerful
nucleus of liberal, separationist civil liberties and religious organizations
that had once dominated the church-state arena began to recognize and
contend with their legal and political sophistication.

The rise of conservative religious law firms and public interest organizations over the past two decades has had a transformative effect on how
church-state litigation is conducted. Once the domain of liberal, separationist organizations, the courts are now more plural and confrontational
than ever before. For religious conservatives as well, participation as amicus curiae is no longer the sole means of representation in the litigation
process. Well-financed, publicity-conscious, sophisticated, and ever more
aggressive, the conservative religious bar has become more willing to identify and sponsor plaintiffs whose complaints have the potential to reshape
constitutional law. Just how far-reaching the impact of the conservative religious bar will be on the dynamics of the litigation process and, by extension, church-state relations, is certain to attract the interest of students of
religion, politics, and the courts.

Acknowledgment

The author would like to thank Daniel J. Weiss, a 1995 graduate of
American University and currently a student at the University of Chicago
Law School, for his research assistance. He also conducted personal interviews with several representatives of the organizations discussed in this
chapter.

Notes

1. In general, a "separationist" or "absolutist" position on the Establishment Clause is associated with the belief that government should provide no
financial aid or support to religious institutions and religious practices in public
settings. For example, an absolutist would oppose all forms of religious worship
in public schools, laws that authorized moments-of-silence for student prayer or
provided public funds to religious schools for remedial education programs
geared to economically disadvantaged students. The reader is cautioned to remember, however, of the risk associated with using adjectives such as these, as

well as others (conservative, liberal) to describe a complex set of political and/or constitutional viewpoints. Considerable differences exist among like-minded individuals and organizations that consider themselves absolutist on the Establishment Clause.

2. Personal interviews conducted by Daniel J. Weiss with Nathan Forrestor, Becket Fund, 25 April 1995; and Frederick Claybrook, Christian Legal Society, 17 March 1995. Quote is taken from the Forrestor interview.

3. Sekulow has argued and won two major cases in the Supreme Court that have substantially broadened the rights of religious clubs and organizations to meet in the public schools. *Lamb's Chapel* v. *Center Moriches School District,* 113 S.Ct. 2141 (1993) and *Board of Education of Westside Schools* v. *Mergens,* 496 U.S. 226 (1990).

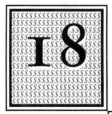

Wayne V. McIntosh and Cynthia L. Cates

Interest Groups and the Courts: Free Speech for Corporations

" '60 Minutes' Kills Piece on Tobacco Industry: CBS Fears Lawsuit, Cites ABC Settlement." This was the headline for a story appearing in the 10 November 1995 edition of the *Washington Post*. The CBS newsmagazine had been instructed not to air an interview already taped and scheduled to run on the next Sunday's (12 November) show. "We were told [by CBS lawyers] that we couldn't put the piece on," Mike Wallace, the veteran *60 Minutes* correspondent who conducted the interview, said. "In the final analysis, they are the publishers.... We argued with the attorneys and we lost."

The interview was with a former tobacco company research scientist and vice-president, Jeffrey Wigand, who had worked for Brown & Williamson, one of the nation's largest cigarette manufacturers. Wigand possessed detailed inside information and was set to dispute the public position of industry executives by revealing that the addictive qualities of nicotine had been known for decades.

Earlier in the year ABC News had run a story, based on an inside source dubbed "Deep Cough," suggesting that the tobacco companies "spiked" cigarettes with nicotine in order to guarantee their consumer market and had done so for a long time. In response, Philip Morris and R.J. Reynolds filed a $10 billion libel suit. Within months, ABC settled, agreeing to pay the cigarette manufacturers' legal costs for their trouble and instructing its news division to issue a public apology for the story. CBS killed its piece, even though Brown & Williamson had not even threatened litigation. Moreover, on the same morning that the *60 Minutes* story hit the newswires, KCBS, one of the network's largest affiliates in California, yanked from the airwaves an antismoking advertisement it had been running for weeks.

Where is the First Amendment in all of this? The fact of the matter is that it is largely irrelevant. What about freedom of the press? Even if they were willing to defend themselves, and even if they were ultimately successful, ABC and CBS would face years of litigation and spend millions of dollars in legal fees and court costs. The media would be defending a constitutional principle and the tobacco industry, its market. No contest; the First Amendment loses. As for the public's right to know and to receive information, the public has a right to receive only that information that media sources are willing to provide. Media owners can claim their own First Amendment right to publish or not publish whatever they please because they retain editorial control over their publications.

ABC made the mistake of running its story and immediately faced a withering onslaught from tobacco lawyers. The example was not lost on CBS, which, merely anticipating similar treatment, exercised self-censorship and did not allow its story to be broadcast. This scenario is repeated across the country by owners of newspapers, newsletters, magazines, radio and television stations, and cable outlets, not nearly as deep-pocketed as parent companies of ABC and CBS, who engage in self-censorship for fear of being sued. Similarly, small group representatives and ordinary citizens are cowed from giving public testimony regarding unscrupulous practices by merchants, landlords, and companies for the same reasons. They simply cannot afford to defend against what has come to be known as Strategic Litigation Against Public Participation (SLAPP) suits.

The point of all this is that most of the parties discussed above are corporations, rather than individuals. And the censors of speech are corporations, rather than governments.

This chapter assesses the influence of corporations and their umbrella trade associations in constitutional development, with a focus on the speech clause of the First Amendment. Communication technology has exploded to encompass a wider range of activities, as confirmed by the provisions of the Telecommunications Act of 1996, and the First Amendment has been carried with it. Emord (1991, xiii) argues that only a "self-governing media marketplace" can guarantee that "our freedom of speech and press [will] retain its meaning and protected status in the new media age." But the historical trend of all markets is to consolidate, merge toward oligopolistic control, with fierce measures instituted to ward off competition, and we see the same trend occurring in the information marketplace. Instead of moving toward a free-form environment, we are likely headed toward one of tighter restrictions on discourse within corporate-controlled environments. Like the Internet, the First Amendment has been hailed as a great source of freedom for individuals, but corporations have worked hard to convert it to their own use and to secure it among their constellation of resources. And thus we must take heed of veteran journalist Bill Moyers's qualified assertion that "the computer will democratize communications if we make sure that there is public access to it and it's not controlled just by a handful of powerful corporations" (Moyers 1995).

In this chapter we consider a constitutional issue, which is prime real estate for judicial action. A wide array of social science investigations have clearly established that interest groups make extensive use of the courts to achieve their policy goals. In this regard, the First Amendment has attracted more than its share of group-sponsored litigation. The conflict is over what kinds of speech the First Amendment guarantees. What is at stake will become more clear as you read through the chapter.

The next section makes the case for examining corporations as interest groups in the judicial process and assesses their strategic position. It is followed by a brief discussion of competing First Amendment visions. Finally, the last section assesses recent corporate-sponsored activities before the U.S. Supreme Court.

Interest Groups, Corporations, and Courts

Having established long ago (in *Santa Clara County*, 1886) that a corporation is a person for constitutional purposes under the Fourteenth Amendment, business-sector lawyers set immediately to work developing an extensive portfolio of individual constitutional rights for their corporate-person clients (e.g., Rivard 1992). Formation of a constellation of rights and liberties for people lagged far behind, but by the 1930s a number of advocacy organizations had entered the fray. The legendary work and strategy of Thurgood Marshall, when he represented the NAACP Legal Defense Fund (e.g., Kluger 1976), and the American Civil Liberties Union (ACLU), incessant champion of First Amendment rights of unpopular minorities, is at least vaguely familiar to most students of politics and law. Epstein (1985) argues that the litigation successes of 1950s and 1960s "public interest" organizations, expanding rights of minorities, women, workers, criminal defendants, and the like, eventually produced a mirror-image effort from the ideological right, and the 1970s and 1980s found new entities deploying their own court-centered strategy as a judicial counterweight.

This is an interesting phenomenon where the courts have played host to clear, sometimes dramatic, political jousting and tit-for-tat. It is also not surprising that it has received the lion's share of scholarly attention. Setting up shop under the influence of seminal works by the likes of Bentley (1908) and Truman (1951), students of the process generally begin with the presumption that interest groups represent a popular constituency (see, e.g., Vose 1955, 1957, 1958, 1959, 1966; Manwaring 1962; Barker 1967). Large or small, an interest group is a collection of similarly minded individual members. As a consequence, the interest group-like effort of corporations and their trade associations in the judicial arena has been largely overshadowed by the more spectacular and theatrical clashes between right- and left-leaning population-based organizations, whose differences in philosophy are both stark and familiar.

Most assessments of interest groups in litigation focus on the institutional role of the Supreme Court of the United States in the broad scheme of government (Vose 1981). Research below the High Court level is primarily devoted either to the strategies employed by some especially visible group, such as the ACLU, NAACP, and NOW (e.g., Halpern 1976; O'Connor 1980; Wasby 1983), or to the influence of organizations in developing a specific constitutional issue, such as civil rights, the death penalty, or the rights of the disabled (e.g., Olson 1981, 1984; Sorauf 1976; O'Connor 1980; Epstein 1985; Vose 1959; Way and Burt 1983). Most interest group research focuses exclusively on advocacy organizations, while corporations receive only cursory attention.

We know that individual large corporations and industry umbrella organizations influence public policy as a matter of routine (Coleman 1982). To say that they effectively lobby legislatures and executive agencies at all levels of government is to state an accepted political truism. We take for granted that they are fierce players in the legislative and rule making processes and that they play hard ball. What we do not take for granted is their policy effort and influence in the judicial process.

Corporations are creatures of law. Legal defense is a major part of doing business, and it is built into their design. Major businesses and the industry associations that represent them have deep pockets, which means that they have the necessary resources to devote to sustained effort wherever it is required. And, most important, under U.S. and state tax codes a corporate player can write off its litigation expenses as a legitimate cost of doing business, an advantage decidedly not accorded to individuals.[1] Moreover, corporations are not burdened with public interest baggage. Ideology is an inefficient distraction, witnessed by the fact that in politics business groups support "winners" regardless of ideological tilt. They enter politics to win, not to make noise. Similarly, they sell services and products to all. We are all consumers, no matter what our politics. The corporate eyes are fixed on one prize—profits. And courts and the process of litigation have always been a central part of the overall corporate political strategy. It should not be surprising, then, that corporations have inevitably plundered the jewels of successful constitutional development crafted by organizations claiming to represent the interests of individual constituencies and litigating under a public interest banner. Let us not forget, the First Amendment places restrictions on government, so both real-person and corporate-person Davids face the same Goliath.

The corporate First Amendment strategy has been facilitated by several beneficial factors. First, unlike the realities faced by Marshall and his colleagues in other population-based organizations, corporations are not trying to affect a reversal of policy in the face of hostile majorities, or even significant and powerful minorities. Their tack has been to extend legal principles already established or to pursue modifications (rather than wholesale reversal) in existing principles.[2] And the respectability and social power of corporations tends to make any free speech claims they present seem more legitimate and less radical than those of the individuals who typically seek protection under the First Amendment.

Second, corporations are created for the express purpose of accumulating resources. Among major market actors, at least, the resource problem has been solved, a fact that situates them in stark contrast to even the most successful population-based advocacy organizations. Such groups are perpetually strapped for cash, which is a ceaseless distraction away from a unified policy vision. Some of their effort must go to maintenance of the membership.[3] Indeed, if successful, the corporate litigant can serve two purposes at once—influencing legal principle in advantageous ways also enhances their business pursuits. And they enter the legal arena with history on their side. As Galanter (1975) points out, and many others demonstrate with specific research (e.g., Scheingold 1974; Rosenberg 1991; Halpern 1995), the "haves" do eventually "come out ahead."

Reporting on the 1987 term of the Court, for example, Epstein (1991, 355) notes that "conventional wisdom certainly holds that public interest groups and civil rights/liberties groups dominate litigation. Although they are supporting players, ... they are far from the leading participants. That distinction belongs to commercial groups and governmental interests." In fact, among all cases decided by the Court in 1987, it was not even close. Commercial and business entities topped the list of both litigation sponsors and amicus curiae participants. And while she does not report a breakdown of the type of participants involved, Epstein finds that all the Court's "freedom of expression" cases drew amicus curiae attention, and better than three-quarters of them were directly sponsored by interest groups (at 357–59). Similarly, Caldeira and Wright (1988, 1990), having assessed amicus curiae interjections over a series of terms, place corporations and business, trade, and professional associations among the most active participants at both the certiorari and plenary stages. In fact, scattered evidence indicates that corporations have a long history of intense involvement in the judicial policy process (see, e.g., Wolfskill 1962; Vose 1959, 1972).

It is easy to understand the litigation efforts of groups like the ACLU in promoting the notion of free speech. Indeed, the ACLU was founded expressly for that purpose. But it is much less clear what role corporations have in the judicial debate over free speech.

Free Speech: A Variety of Resources

Free speech may be a basic human need. Call it fundamental to "the . . . spirit,"[4] to "individual self-realization" (Redish 1982, 514), to private "autonomy" (Fried 1992, 233), to personal "fulfillment" (Emerson 1970, 6), to "human dignity" (Smolla 1992, 9); the ability to speak one's piece is transcendent among those elements that make a person a person.[5]

No matter what track one chooses—individual autonomy, marketplace of ideas, democratic self-governance, or some combination of the three (see e.g., Tribe 1988, 785ff), the individual is the key. Indeed, the individual is a central component of liberal theory foremost in the calculus of the Founders, Federalists and Anti-Federalists alike, and in the rationalizations of theorists who have pondered the core purpose of the First Amendment.

Certainly, individuals have not always prevailed when seeking protection of their expression in the courts. Nonetheless, the clear thrust of First Amendment doctrine over the past fifty years has been to expand individual liberty of expression, despite overwhelming community sentiment to the contrary. Hence, Gregory Johnson can publicly burn the American flag because "the government may not prohibit the expression of an idea simply because society finds the idea itself offensive or disagreeable" (*Texas* v. *Johnson* 1989, 414). Similarly, Clarence Brandenburg can express his racial bigotry, even advocate violence, in terms that would offend the conscience of all but his own small band of colleagues (*Brandenburg* 1969), and Robert Stanley has the right to possess unambiguously obscene materials that even the most libertarian among us would find repugnant (*Stanley* 1969).

Most, if not all, of this expansion of First Amendment coverage can be attributed to the litigation efforts of interest groups, especially the ACLU, which has been heavily criticized even by its supporters for defending the rights of individuals of the Johnson-Brandenburg-Stanley ilk. Supreme Court justices, while being pressed to extend their own logic and thereby expand the realm of protected expression, have proceeded with something far less than a unified theme. Indeed, the *New York Times* publication of the Pentagon Papers is protected on the basis of the theory of democratic self-government (*New York Times Co.* v. *U.S.* 1971), Brandenburg and Johnson are refuged by the marketplace theory, and Stanley is upheld on the notion of individual autonomy.

One can criticize the Court for lack of theoretical clarity and for tendering opinions whose logic, when placed side by side, are difficult to reconcile. But trying to articulate the various tenets of liberalism often leads in conflicting directions. The general thrust of the First Amendment, though, has it that people, as individuals, are the driving force in society. Viewpoints, beliefs, philosophies, and the like should be freely expressed. Government, instead of being in the business of suppression, should be open. The collective will of individuals is to be reflected in government business and policy. In this scheme of things, institutions (e.g., families, neighborhoods, churches, corporations, universities) play a mediating role, take an intermediary position, between individuals and their government. Institutions and corporations exist for human purposes, to promote the goals and ends of the people who create them. People create organizations to act more effectively in the political policy process. People create corporations to act more efficiently and effectively in the economic marketplace. Indeed, the corporate body is but an extension and expression of its human entrepreneurs. While this is the case across the range of rights issues, it is particularly true with regard to free speech under the First Amendment. Free speech is personal, delegated directly and solely to individuals under the wording of the Constitution. The focal point, however, is undergoing significant change, as corporations are horning in on the free speech universe.

In their approach to the law, philosophers and law professors generally derive a principle, which then leads them to a conclusion or outcome. Interest groups, in contrast, begin with an outcome and use a principle to support it. Corporate litigants have proven to be quite adept at incorporating all three visions of the First Amendment to promote their cause.

Free Speech and the Information Marketplace

First Amendment jurisprudence has experienced several periods of development during the course of the twentieth century. Interestingly, the notion of free speech lay constitutionally dormant for nearly one and one-half centuries. "From the adoption of the First Amendment (1791) to the beginning of the basic legal transformation (1919), a variety of social and religious activists demanded recognition of freedom of speech," notes David Kairys (1990, 237). Indeed, Kairys continues, prior to the Great Depression era, "one spoke publicly only at the discretion of local, and sometimes federal, authorities, who often prohibited what they, the local business establishment, or other powerful segments of the community did not want to hear.... The primary periods of stringent enforcement and enlargement of speech rights by the courts, the 1930s and the 1960s, correspond to the periods in which popular movements demanded such rights" (237–38).

Abrams (1919) represents the opening point, where two justices broke from the pack to give judicial voice to the notion that individuals should be protected from government actions restricting their speech. From that point the notion gradually picked up adherents, ultimately claiming a full complement of justices, and probably reaching a climax around 1969 in *Brandenburg*.[6] The Court, obviously, has not stopped taking on individual speech cases, but since *Brandenburg*, it has primarily been broadening the landscape with such issues as the public-private forum distinction (c.f. *City of Ladue* v. *Gilleo*, 1994; *Forsyth County* v. *Nationalist Movement*, 1992), symbolic speech (c.f. *Tinker* v. *Des Moines School District*, 1969; *Texas* v. *Johnson* 1989), the right not to speak, and the right to receive information.

The last two—the rights not to speak and to receive information—initially were found to be important liberty offshoots of the general speech guarantee accorded to individuals; the first to protect them from forced allegiance to an orthodox point of view, and the second to enhance their access to a full menu of information choices. (Each involves individual privacy interests as well.) Once conceived, however, these First Amendment seeds have led to multiple-right births. The press is clearly implicated in the second, since it is in the information distribution business. Indeed, it has become quite difficult to distinguish between the First Amendment's "press" and "speech" clauses. As Chief Justice Burger noted in 1978, "The speech clause standing alone may be viewed as a protection of the liberty to express ideas and beliefs, while the press clause focuses specifically on the liberty to disseminate expression broadly. . . . Yet there is no fundamental distinction between expression and dissemination" (*First National Bank of Boston* v. *Bellotti* 1978, Burger, C.J., concurring). Press owners, for their part, also possess speech rights, which means that they will naturally desire to exercise editorial control over content and will balk at dissemination of views with which they do not wish to be associated (i.e., the right not to speak). Finally, corporations may have views to express as well, and we should expect them to seek the same protections as those granted their individual and press constitutional siblings.

Indeed, since the introduction of the radio early in this century, followed more recently by broadcast television, cable television, computer networks, and multimedia communications mergers (combining newspapers, motion picture studios, book and magazine publishers, television and radio, telephone and computer networks under one roof), communication and information have been transformed into market commodities, owned and distributed by corporations. Quite naturally, the First Amendment is of primary importance.

The right of editorial control over content of information disseminated over the mass media has been a matter of legal contention that media corporations have, in the long run, won. In response to the introduction of radio as a mass communications medium, the Federal Communications Commission (FCC) was created by the federal government to regulate the industry on the theory that because the broadcast spectrum was finite, broadcasters were utilizing a public resource and thus had an affirmative obligation to serve the public interest. This public interest theory was extended to cover the television broadcast industry, and as the number of stations proliferated and the promise to put a television in every home seemed a virtual reality, it eventually led to the promulgation of the Fairness Doctrine in 1959 (Section 315(a), 47 U.S.C., 1959). In essence, the Fairness Doctrine required broadcasters to seek out issues of local importance for reporting to the public and to air differing views on those controversies. In 1968 the FCC amended the regulations further to require broadcasters to provide free air time to individuals whose personal integrity or honesty had been called into question by earlier coverage, to issue a public response (Section 73.1930, 47 C.F.R., 1968).

These regulations were obviously considered by broadcast owners to be an affront to their own First Amendment rights (not to mention their Fifth Amendment property rights). In 1969 a Pennsylvania radio station challenged the doctrine before the Supreme Court, arguing that "the First Amendment protects any broadcaster's desire ... to broadcast whatever they choose, to exclude whomever they choose ... and to refuse to give equal weight to the views of opponents" (*Red Lion* 1969, plaintiff's brief). Nonetheless, the Court unanimously upheld the constitutionality of the Fairness Doctrine's personal attack right of reply component.[7] Having lost in the courts, media corporations focused on the direct alternative, appealing to the FCC itself to repeal the regulation. In 1987 a commission dominated by Reagan appointees, who were in the midst of a deregulation spree, unanimously did precisely that (*Syracuse Peace Council*, 2 FCC Rcd. 5043, 1987). Thus, broadcasters acquired editorial control over the content of their broadcasts, a right that was unsuccessfully argued before the Supreme Court in 1969.[8] This means that, like individuals and the print media, broadcast corporations possess a right not to speak.

A major part of the impetus behind the creation of the FCC and the commission's system of regulations discussed above was the notion that the public has a right to receive information. Indeed, the *Red Lion* Court noted that "it is the right of viewers and listeners, not the right of the broadcasters, which is paramount" (390). Moreover, the print media have successfully utilized this line of argument to assert their right to publish. For example, Justice Black wrote separately in *New York Times Co. v. U.S.* to emphasize the point: "In the First Amendment the Founding Fathers gave the free press the protection it must have to fulfill its essential role in our democracy. The press was to serve the governed, not the governors. . . . The press was protected so that it could bare the secrets of government and inform the people" (717, Black, J., concurring).

The information age has seen the conversion of expression into a commodity, which is packaged and traded in a marketplace similar to the marketing of other goods and services (e.g., Collins and Skover 1993). And this requires a large-scale medium of conveyance if the expression is to reach an audience of consumers. Commodification of expression also has another important side. Media corporations are not merely in the expression business for the sake of expression dissemination. They are in the business of delivering audiences to their sponsors and advertisers. Hence, in practical economic terms it is difficult to distinguish a media corporation from any other.

Corporations have a long history of exerting influence in state, local, and national political arenas. Moreover, once radio and television provided access to mass audiences, corporations were quick to make use of the media to persuade consumers to buy their products. The same techniques are available for the purpose of political persuasion. In 1976 the Court struck down limitations on expenditures on behalf of a presidential candidate, made independently by individuals and organizations alike, as an unconstitutional restriction on political speech (*Buckley* 1976; and see *FEC* v. *NCPAC* 1985). Hence, in the *Buckley* Court's view, independent cash expenditures to promote a political candidate is the constitutional equivalent of speech.

It does not require a great stretch to see that corporations might use the mass media to attempt to influence outcomes of state and local ballot initiatives and referenda. Two years later the Court entertained that very issue in a case originating in Massachusetts. For a number of years the state legislature had seen its attempts to win voter approval of tax referendums thwarted, with large corporations waging massive advertising campaigns to defeat the measures. Finally, the lawmakers legislated a ban on such expenditures, so long as a referendum did not directly affect corporate assets. The corporations sued, and the Court, in *First National Bank of Boston* v. *Bellotti* (1978), struck down the legislation. Justice Powell, speaking for the Court, reasoned in part,

> If the speakers here were not corporations, no one would suggest that the state could validate silence of their proposed speech. It is the type of speech indispensable to decision-making in a democracy, and this is no less true because the speech comes from a corporation rather than an individual. The inherent worth of the speech in terms of its capacity for informing the public does not depend upon the identity of its source, whether corporation, association, or individual.

The corporate litigants in this case argued that their speech rights actually promoted all three primary purposes of the First Amendment. Corporate-sponsored advertising campaigns enhance the autonomy and dignity of individual citizens by protecting them from a paternalistic government that insults their intelligence by attempting to restrict their information choices, provides a greater array of alternative viewpoints in the idea marketplace where individuals are free to choose for themselves, and the political speech uttered over the mass media by the business community is "indispensable to decision-making in a democracy."

The final frontier for corporate lawyers is to secure all speech for their clients with the same degree of protection granted to individuals. To the corporation, this means full inclusion of commercial speech under the First Amendment umbrella. Traditionally, product advertising did not cross the First Amendment threshold. In 1942, for example, the Supreme Court unanimously found that commercial speech was not worthy of First Amendment protection (*Valentine* 1942). And thirty years later, in 1974, the FCC explicitly excluded commercial speech from the Fairness Doctrine because it does not "inform the public on any side of a controversial issue [nor does it offer] a meaningful contribution to public debate" (*Fairness Report*, 48 FCC 2d1).

History notwithstanding, a wedge for commercial speech was put into place the following year by the Supreme Court. In *Bigelow* (1975) the Court upheld the right of a Virginia newspaper to publish an advertisement for a New York abortion clinic, finding that "the advertisement ... did more than simply propose a commercial transaction. It contained factual material of clear 'public interest.'" Hence, a state legislature cannot "bar a citizen of another State from disseminating information about an activity that is legal in that State." During the very next term, the Court went a major step further, explicitly welcoming commercial speech into the First Amendment domain. In response to a consumer advocacy group's claim that citizens have a right to receive pricing information on prescription drugs, the Court struck down a ban against advertising by pharmacists, finding that "free flow of commercial information" is "indispensable" to individual recipients' ability to make rational economic decisions (*Virginia State Bd. of Pharmacy* 1976, 765).

Note that the successful blows on behalf of commercial speech were landed by a small newspaper and a traditional interest group. But note also that the Court's reasoning created a perfect opening for corporations to locate product and service advertising squarely within the First Amendment zone of protection by advocating that only the "free flow of commercial information" will serve the public interest. After all, individual citizens not only have a right to receive information, but access to commercial information is "indispensable" in much the same way that access to political information is "indispensable" (*First National Bank of Boston* v. *Bellotti*). Since 1976 this is precisely what has occurred, and although commercial speech has yet to be fully embraced as deserving highest-tier status under the First

Amendment,[9] the corporate community has made significant inroads in that direction.[10]

A significant indicator of the corporate strategy to appropriate the First Amendment free speech clause is the fact that the major advertising and manufacturing trade associations have recruited one of the most prominent speech attorney advocates, Burt Neuborne.[11] Professor Neuborne has a long history of arguing cases before the U.S. Supreme Court, primarily as a representative of the American Civil Liberties Union. His line of attack as a civil liberties advocate has been a consistent one, in which he has often argued, in the face of government restriction, for further development of the citizen's right to receive information. Since at least 1990, however, Neuborne has also filed amicus briefs on behalf of advertisers and major manufacturers. That he can represent both with essentially the same set of arguments is quite revealing.

For example, in 1983 Neuborne argued that a congressional ban on editorializing by broadcasters receiving public money violated viewers' First Amendment "rights to express and to receive the views of noncommercial broadcasters on issues of public interest and importance" in an amicus brief prepared on behalf of the ACLU (*FCC v. League of Women Voters of California* 1984; Brief on Behalf of the American Civil Liberties Union, as Amicus Curiae, filed 13 September 1983). Six years later, in *Webster* (1989), Neuborne, again representing the views of the ACLU and several other organizations (Brief Amici Curiae of the American Civil Liberties Union, the National Education Association, People for the American Way, the Newspaper Guild, the National Writers Union, and the Fresno Free College Foundation, filed 30 March 1989), argued against a state restriction on abortion counseling, reasoning that a state cannot accomplish a policy goal by silencing speech and thereby restricting the flow of information to potential hearers. "In effect, Missouri attempts to use medical censorship as a device to manipulate the behavior of poor women," despite the fact that "the Supreme Court has repeatedly recognized that the right to speak includes the right to receive information" (at note 17 and accompanying text). Neuborne then submits that the government policy in question not only threatens the autonomy rights of individuals but also the integrity of the democratic process:

> In a world where literally millions of Americans depend upon government-funded programs to provide them with critical guidance in areas as diverse as medical care, law, and higher education, the prospect of state manipulation of the free flow of information and advice from government-funded professionals to individual hearers in the name of advancing "state policy" poses an intolerable threat to First Amendment values. One of the ultimate purposes of the First Amendment is the protection of the individual's capacity for in-

formed and autonomous choice. That capacity is seriously undermined when the state is permitted to censor the flow of publicly funded professional information and advice. Under such a regime, hearers are given the illusion of autonomous choice; but the reality of control rests with the state.... Under our Constitution the state lacks the power to turn its workforce into a propaganda machine that parrots the party line.[12]

By 1992 Neuborne was representing a very different set of parties, although the thrust of his legal position had not changed, even if his clientele base had broadened.[13] In *City of Cincinnati v. Discovery Network, Inc.* (1993), the brief amici filed on behalf of the Association of National Advertisers (and several other trade associations) assails a local ordinance against free-standing newsracks, located on public property and holding commercial advertisements, as an affront to democratic process, the autonomy rights of individual citizens, and a subversion of the marketplace of ideas.[14]

The assertion by Cincinnati that commercial speech is less important than noncommercial speech is wrong, both at the level of society and the individual. The First Amendment protects political democracy and free markets by assuring the uncensored flow of information on which each depends. Political democracy requires robust free speech protection in order to assure that voters receive information needed to make an informed choice. Free markets also depend upon informed choice.... Consumers vote with their dollars, just as citizens vote with their ballots. If government can casually control the flow of information to voters, the free political choice at the core of a functioning democracy is imperilled. Similarly, if government can casually control the flow of commercial information to consumers, the free market choice at the core of our economic system is imperilled. Moreover, from the standpoint of an individual hearer, it is often demonstrably more important to receive information about a product critical to health or happiness than to receive noncommercial information.[15]

Finally, to demonstrate the compatibility between the First Amendment free speech rights of individuals and corporations, the Association of National Advertisers filed an amicus brief with the Supreme Court in late 1993 to support Margaret Gilleo's litigation against the City of Ladue (*City of Ladue v. Gilleo* 1994). She was seeking the right to place a sign displaying a political message on the front lawn of her home in the face of a local ordinance prohibiting such displays (although certain types of signs were permissible). The brief, again presented by Professor Neuborne, begins with the following statement:

Ordinarily, ... A.N.A. has appeared as amicus curiae to urge that commercial speech be accorded an appropriate level of free speech protection. In this case, the City of Ladue has reversed the usual order of speech regulation by treating commercial speech more favorably than noncommercial communication. While A.N.A. applauds Ladue's recognition of the importance of commercial speech, A.N.A. continues to believe that it is constitutionally impermissible for government to differentiate among categories of speech on the basis of content in the absence of an overwhelming social need. Moreover, where, as here, a municipality seeks to eliminate a long-established and pervasive means of communication—the display of signs and symbols on private property—in the name of aesthetics, the municipality threatens both commercial and noncommercial speech.[16]

Ms. Gilleo did ultimately win her case, and while one cannot say with certainty that support from the commercial sector tipped the scales of justice in her favor, it surely did not hurt. More important, the position taking in this litigation strengthens the case being made by corporation lawyers as they argue that protection of speech rights in the corporate community enhances speech rights afforded to all.

Conclusion

It is clear that corporations have utilized the process of litigation in much the same way as other interest groups in order to influence the shape of First Amendment free speech doctrine. The fact that they have done so without facing hostile majorities has simplified the problem. Indeed, the strategy has been to incorporate all three basic visions of the First Amendment to extend the logic of precedents established in individual rights cases. Moreover, recruitment of one of the long-time champions of individual civil liberties to argue their case only adds to the high credibility they already enjoy. The corporate strategy is not one of the "stalking horse" looking to make a hostile takeover bid, but one of a "white knight" proposing a friendly merger. Their approach has been successful more often than not and has won the full allegiance of at least one current member of the Supreme Court who generally takes a consistent pro–civil liberties position in First Amendment cases. Indeed, Justice John Paul Stevens wrote a separate concurrence in a 1995 commercial speech case involving government restrictions on beer labeling that finds him in substantial agreement with the corporate position (*Rubin* v. *Coors* 1995, Stevens, J., concurring).

Clearly, corporations and the umbrella trade and business associations that represent them are significant judicial players, even in the constitutional civil liberties domain. Centralization of the information industries has occurred coterminously with changes in doctrine recognizing more corporate speech rights. Is this mere coincidence, or is there a cause-effect relationship?

As we move into an era where speech takes place primarily under corporate auspices, will the true relevance of the First Amendment decline? After all, the Constitution applies to government censorship and/or restriction, not to similar controls imposed by private concerns. The right not to speak has been invoked as critical to media corporations, which naturally want to exercise editorial control over information disseminated under their banner, and to their corporate sponsors who do not wish to be associated with particular viewpoints or modes of expression. One can easily see how this might conflict with the public's right to receive information. The November 1995 editorial decision by CBS to nix a *60 Minutes* interview with former tobacco company executive Jeffrey Wigand and local affiliates' election to ax antismoking ads provide an important case in point. The interview finally did air on *60 Minutes* on Sunday, 4 February 1996—but only after the *Wall Street Journal* had provided CBS with legal cover by publishing transcripts of Wigand's trial testimony in their newspaper.

Notes

1. For example, Houck (1984, 1448) reports that, as of 1982, "American corporations write off an estimated $3.7 billion annually in this fashion."

2. The elevation of commercial speech did require reversal of existing doctrine. However, it was a consumer advocacy group, not a corporation or trade association, that won the reversal (*Virginia State Bd. of Pharmacy* 1976).

3. Organizational incentives, such as promoting a positive public image and self-perpetuation, loom large for such groups. Epstein's (1985) discussion of the actions by the conservative public interest law organizations, like the National Legal Foundation and its seven regional affiliates, illustrates this phenomenon. Mass-membership groups, which are becoming increasingly dependent on external sources of funding, must also be attentive to the wishes of significant patrons when designing their political strategies. Gelb and Palley (1982, 48–50), for example, found that women's groups undertook projects and activities in order to maintain or acquire foundation support. Also see O'Connor (1980, 118–19).

4. Justice Thurgood Marshall, writing for the Court in *Procunier* (1974, 497).

5. While the varying use of terms such as dignity, self-realization, and autonomy apparently makes more than semantical difference to some authors (see especially Redish 1982), for the purposes of this brief exposition we treat them as synonymous.

6. That *Brandenburg* represents the ultimate in individual protection against government encroachment is, of course, arguable.

7. But see *CBS v. Democratic National Committee* (1973), where the Court upheld a broadcaster's right to refuse access to an advertiser.

8. This was a right that had already been clearly established for the print media in *Miami Herald Publishing Co. v. Tornillo* (1974).

9. Commercial speech is still subject to regulation, but regulations must be "limited to measures designed to protect consumers from fraudulent, misleading, or coercive sales techniques" (*Central Hudson Gas and Electric Corp.* v. *Public Service Commission*, 1980, 574, Blackmun, J., concurring).

10. In the nineteen years since the Court explicitly recognized in *Virginia Pharmacy* that commercial speech is entitled to First Amendment protection, it has repeatedly struck down restrictions on dissemination of commercial speech, while referring to the consumer's right to receive information relevant to making economic choices in a range of contexts.

11. Compare this cooptation strategy with Twiss's (1942) discussion of the mobilization of legal talent by the corporate community during the New Deal era.

12. Burt Neuborne, Brief Amici Curiae of the American Civil Liberties Union, the National Education Association, People for the American Way, the Newspaper Guild, the National Writers Union, and the Fresno Free College Foundation (filed 30 March 1989). Citations included in the original brief have been omitted here.

13. Neuborne has not abandoned the ACLU. Quite the contrary, he now represents both his old constituency and his new one. Compare, e.g., his briefs filed for the ACLU in *Hurley* (1995) and *Turner Broadcasting System* (1994), with those filed on behalf of advertisers and manufacturers in *Rubin* v. *Coors* (1995) and others discussed in the text.

14. Brief Amici Curiae of Association of National Advertisers, Inc.; American Association of Advertising Agencies; National Association of Manufacturers; Grocery Manufacturers of America, Inc.; and National Food Processors Association in support of respondents (filed 1 June 1992).

15. Citations included in the original brief have been omitted here.

16. Brief Amicus Curiae of the Association of National Advertisers, Inc., in support of respondent (filed 13 December 1993).

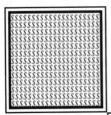

Alan Morrison
and
Robert A. Katzmann

Comments on the Judicial Connection

Alan Morrison, Public Citizen Litigation Group

ALEXIS de Tocqueville said 150 years ago, "nearly any policy issue of any importance at all ends up in the courts." Tocqueville's statement is probably truer today than it was then. Thirty years ago American corporations did not sue each other, and they sued the government only once in a while, and only as a last resort. Litigation was simply not considered a course of action for nice people. Things have changed drastically over the past few decades.

The second point that I want to make is that the corporations and the religious right groups involved in recent litigations are different from the NAACP, the ACLU, and Public Citizen. In many of these earlier cases, interest groups were representing a minority interest against a majoritarian principle. That is, they were trying to defeat in the courts that which the legislature has provided.

The opposite has occurred in recent years because there is more majoritarian influence in the political system. The interesting thing about the religious right is that none of their cases would have been necessary but for the fact that Leo Pfeffer and his colleagues at the American Jewish Congress were successful thirty and forty years ago, making local boards of education feel compelled to act. Currently, the issues that school boards face are the opposite of the issues decided under the Warren court.

It is inconceivable, for example, that fifty years ago anyone at the University of Virginia would have tried to stop Ron Rosenberger from publishing *Wide Awake: A Christian Perspective at the University of Virginia,* a magazine financed with university funds. Yet during the 1990s some law-yer at the university who was well versed in First Amendment law said that the Establishment Clause prevents the university from allowing *Wide Awake* to be published. Then Mr. Rosenberger brought his challenge, rely-ing on the precedents set in free speech cases—many won by the ACLU —to defeat the University of Virginia.

The question in *Rosenberger v. University of Virginia* (1995) should not have hinged on whether this was an Establishment Clause case or a free speech case. The question should have hinged on how relevant Court deci-sions hinged on the facts of the case, which hardly makes it into a great con-stitutional confrontation between these two First Amendment clauses. That is, the appropriate question should have been, "Is this a magazine that a reli-gious group is using to actively proselytize for members, or is this a philo-sophical magazine that has chosen to focus on religious topics?" This is largely a factual question that should properly have been sent back to the dis-trict court, just like the creche case out in Ohio should have been sent back there for trial. The *Rosenberger* opinion is quite remarkable because its outcome did not turn on whether the university could give money to an or-ganization that was actually proselytizing individuals to join a religious group. Nobody on the Supreme Court said that Virginia could do that.

Third, it is absolutely true that many more corporations, trade associa-tions, and other business entities were filing amicus briefs in the Supreme Court during the 1990s than the 1960s. But filing briefs is not the equiva-lent of increasing influence, and on that there is no way that we can meas-ure it for certain. Nonetheless, it seems pretty clear from the justices' state-ments, public and private, that having a large number of amicus briefs on one side or the other does not make any difference at all. The question is, What do they add? Have they got something different to say? Most of the time the answer is no. Most of the individuals who file amicus briefs do so because they want to use them in fund-raising appeals to show that their group is "fighting evil incarnate." The briefs are merely written to demon-strate that the group is in some way involved in the battle. As a result, most of them are "me too" briefs that say little that is important or original.

These briefs do not add much to the judicial decision making because they are filed by amateurs and Supreme Court litigation is confined to ex-perts. In fact, one of the problems with Supreme Court litigation is that many of the lawyers involved are not experts, and this encourages some in-dividuals to file amicus briefs. Some individuals, for example, file briefs be-cause they believe that a school board is doing the right thing, but its attor-ney does not fully understand the issues involved in a relevant religious controversy. In a few cases, the filers have made a correct assessment, but most of the time the briefs are filed for publicity and fund-raising reasons. As a result, most of briefs rarely impress the justices.

Lest we start to worry that the costs of litigation have enabled corporations to run over the Supreme Court as Hitler marched through the plains of France with tanks ablaze, it is important to recognize that there are two notable areas where the corporate front has been strongly united and has produced virtually no results. The first one is in the area of punitive damages. For a number of years corporations have been trying to knock away at punitive damages, and they have been almost universally unsuccessful. There was a little chink a couple years ago in *Honda* v. *Oberg* (1996), but it was the most minor chink. It applied to one state. It set aside a rule of the Supreme Court of Oregon under which it would not review punitive damage awards and the Supreme Court of the United States said, "No. Due process requires that you at least look at them. We have no idea what you are going to say after you look at them, but you have to at least agree to look at them." So they are going to go back and look at them. With that exception, corporations have been terribly unsuccessful on that issue.

They have been unsuccessful in part because there are two problems for business in these cases. First, they can be accused of trying to "make a federal case out of every single punitive damages award," which is something that the Supreme Court will go a long way to prevent. Second, the Court understands defendants do not like the magnitude of some settlements because they have too many zeroes, but it wants to know what the standard should be deciding an appropriate award, and on what theory that standard is based. The problem for corporations is that no one has provided either an appropriate standard or a theory for one. In fact, the business community has been seriously divided on which formulas to ask the Court to apply. The Court has decided not to venture into this swamp, leaving it to the states to make these decisions. The second area where corporations have been notably unsuccessful under the First Amendment is in the area of corporate contributions to election campaigns and independent expenditures in support of candidates for elected office. In *First National Bank of Boston* v. *Bellotti* (1978), the Supreme Court said that it was unconstitutional for a state to forbid a corporation from making independent expenditures on a substantive ballot initiative. The Court had said other seemingly encouraging things in other contexts, and so efforts were made to try to knock out the federal statute that prohibits corporations from making contributions directly to candidates. The lower courts still said no, and the Supreme Court never took that issue. The Court did, however, rule in *Austin* v. *Michigan Chamber of Commerce* (1990) that corporations could not even make independent expenditures if the legislature prohibited it because that might be a means of avoiding the contribution limitation.

It is also appropriate to focus on commercial speech cases. The Public Citizen Litigation Group has been very active in this area. I argued the *Virginia State Bd. of Pharmacy* v. *Virginia Citizens Consumer Council* (1976) case; my firm wrote the amicus brief in *Bigelow* v. *Virginia* (1975). We succeeded in these two cases to move the discussion away from a pure First Amendment editorial issue to a listener right to receive issue. The term "right to receive" does not mean a right to receive in the sense that you have information and I have the right to get it from you, or that I have a right to make you say what I want to hear. It means only that the state cannot stand in the way if you freely want to express certain ideas to me.

That is exactly what happened in the *Virginia Pharmacy* case. The state of Virginia said, largely at the behest of the pharmacists of Virginia who did not want competition, that advertising—truthful advertising—of prescription drug prices was unlawful. When we filed that case, we knew two things. One is that the First Amendment argument would be much better received by the Court from the listening/receiving side, rather than from the speaker. (Of course, we also knew that you cannot have people listening unless you have people speaking.) Second, we knew that our victories would apply not just to pharmacists but to doctors and lawyers—which included legal advertising and therefore also extended to commercial speech with all of its ramifications.

It is not surprising that the ACLU was supportive in those efforts or that the ACLU and Burt Neuborne are coming in on that side and using those cases. I guess the only thing that is disappointing to me on the ACLU's performance is on the issue of tobacco where they have refused to accept that tobacco inflicts harm on people that makes it different in kind from any of the harms in any of the other cases. In my view the Supreme Court will never accept the proposition that the government must ban a product—tobacco—before it can discourage it through limiting the amount, type, nature, or location of advertising. Hopefully, Congress will pass a law limiting tobacco advertising, or the FDA's proposal to limit cigarette advertising directed to children will become law, and then there will be a constitutional test of this proposition.

The one great thing about pontificating about Supreme Court litigation is that you know that no one can ever refute you when you say that your work had a particular effect because there are no double-blind experiments. We do not write a brief one way and have a case argued this way and then write a brief another way and have the case argued the other way and see which result is better. It just does not, fortunately, happen that way.

Robert A. Katzmann, Governance Institute*

As interest groups turn increasingly to the courts to further their policy objectives, their attention as to who sits on the bench has become more in-

---

* Robert A. Katzmann is also a professor at Georgetown University.

tense (Katzmann 1997). Given the role of the Supreme Court in a wide range of high-profile areas—such as race, abortion, gender, property rights, and criminal justice—it is not surprising that groups organized around such subjects would seek to influence judicial appointments.

An oft-stated pronouncement is that the Bork nomination injected a new element in the confirmation process: organized interests mobilized in opposition. In fact, the tradition of interest group involvement is a long one; for example, the NAACP and AFL-CIO actively sought in 1930 to defeat John J. Parker because of his callousness, allegedly in matters of race and labor (Goings 1990). What is new in the past twenty-five years is the increasing number of groups that, believing they have a stake in the complexion of the federal judiciary, have created mechanisms to monitor judicial appointments closely. And even more recently, interest groups have changed the nature of lobbying techniques (Silverstein 1995; Caldeira 1988–89).

In the past generation, groups, at first mostly liberal, were created to advance particular causes—for instance, environmentalism, civil rights, women's rights, disability rights. These organizations used litigation as one prong in a political strategy to achieve their ends (O'Connor 1980; Epstein 1993). In the 1980s, conservative groups arose as well, and turned to what they perceived to be an increasingly sympathetic judiciary to secure their purposes. Many of these various groups, recognizing the importance of the courts, began to monitor judicial appointments, supporting and opposing particular candidates. Indeed, Linda Greenhouse, the Supreme Court reporter of the *New York Times,* observes that following major decisions, she is sometimes inundated by "huge stacks of faxes" from all sides, seeking to offer their "spin" on the case (Greenhouse 1996). At times, groups point to their lobbying activities with regard to nominees as part of their fund-raising campaigns.

The intensity of interest group attention to the judiciary is symbolized by the changing character of the confirmation hearing itself—from a time forty years ago when interest group testimony was sometimes nonexistent to more recent times when hearings dates are specifically set aside to take testimony from scores of organizations. In 1956, for example, William J. Brennan Jr. was questioned for a total of three hours, over two days of hearings (with *no* interest group testimony before the full committee). Eleven years later, the Senate Judiciary Committee quizzed Thurgood Marshall, a politically controversial nominee, for about seven hours—with only *one* interest group representative testifying (*Thurgood Marshall Hearings* 1967). In 1987 Robert Bork answered questions for thirty hours over four and a half days; the hearings themselves lasted for twelve days, including eighty-seven hours of testimony taken from 112 witnesses, 86 of whom represented interest groups (*Robert H. Bork Hearings* 1987).

Interest group activity takes a variety of forms: carefully scrutinizing the records of nominees and potential nominees; disseminating packets of information to the media in praise of, or in opposition to, particular candidates; lobbying senators; preparing suggested questions for senators to pose to the nominees; and media advertising. An example of group impact occurred during consideration of G. Harrold Carswell's nomination when the Washington Research Project brought to Senate attention information that the nominee had helped establish a private corporation to take over an all-white public country club to evade desegregation (Totenberg 1988).

With the confirmation proceedings of Robert Bork came a new dimension to interest group activity. In addition to trying to influence senators directly, several groups sought to reach public opinion directly (DeGregorio and Rossotti 1994). Bork's opponents—such as People for the American Way, the Leadership Conference on Civil Rights, the Alliance for Justice, and the National Abortion Rights Action League—undertook an extensive media campaign that included advertisements on television and radio and in the newspapers. These tactics, which liberals used in an effort to defeat Bork, were borrowed from campaigns of the right to defeat state judges subject to election or retention votes. And, in fact, conservative groups sought to respond to the offensive against Bork. When Clarence Thomas was nominated, the Conservative Victory Committee and Citizens United mounted television spots to neutralize possible opponents of the nominee—Senators Edward Kennedy, Joseph Biden, and Alan Cranston (Shaiko 1994, 185).

Those who undertake such media efforts obviously hope that it stimulates grassroots reaction that will affect senators. The extent to which such efforts influence the Senate is not easily discernible. But these activities add a new dimension to the confirmation process, one that deserves further reflection.

Media advertising seeks to advance causes and is not designed to be a factually accurate, objective presentation. Commentators across the spectrum have noted, as Ruth Bader Ginsburg reported, "egregious example[s] of the misinformation" such campaigns can breed (Ginsburg 1988). The most extreme form of such political campaigns is manifested by television and radio advertisements, offering sound-bite attacks of a nominee's purported views. In such circumstances, the potential for distortion of a nominee's view is great. Indeed, a sitting judge who is nominated to fill a higher court vacancy is not in a position to defend himself or herself; such activity would run counter to traditional and necessary norms that constrain judges from joining the political fray.

In a society in which interest groups play an important and highly beneficial role, and in which First Amendment protections properly adhere, curbing lobbying activity is not (as some have suggested it is) the remedy for curtailing the excesses of a few organizations. Perhaps it would be useful if a consensus could be fashioned, perhaps under the aegis of a neutral forum, in which the principal groups across the political spectrum agreed to a set of voluntary norms as to the nature of media advertising in the confirmation process. For their part, political and interest group leaders should forcefully condemn any excesses as injurious to both the political and judicial processes. Lapses in fairness are symptomatic of a larger problem deserving attention—the sometimes absence of civility in public life.

In the era of the "permanent campaign" in which groups and interests are engaged in ongoing media-oriented attempts to influence policy across the branches and levels of government, we would be Polyannas if we did not recognize that the intensity of such efforts will produce occasional excesses. But recognition and discussion of such practices can perhaps reduce their occurrence. After all, those who have among the strongest interest in maintaining a vital independent judiciary are the very groups that turn to it for the resolution of disputes.

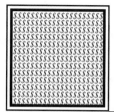

Part VI

Conclusion

Paul S. Herrnson, Clyde Wilcox, and Ronald G. Shaiko

Interest Groups at the Dawn of a New Millennium

THE CHAPTERS in this volume have demonstrated many of the connections between interest groups and government, between interest groups and political parties, and among interest groups. These connections are myriad and complex. They reflect the interplay of group goals, resources, and structures, as well as the institutional structures of government, the decentralized nature of the parties, and the rules regulating interest group activity. The complexity of interest group arrangements give insights into the sophistication of many interest group organizations; they change their strategies and tactics in response to changing institutional arrangements and political realities.

Interest Group Connections

The research presented here demonstrate a number of lessons about interest group politics. First, interests participate in virtually every arena of American politics. Groups are active in many aspects of the electoral process and seek to influence the executive, legislative, and judicial branches of government. Second, the institutional and political environments in which interests operate influence how they organize and the activities they carry out. When groups move from the legislative arena to try to influence the bureaucracy, for example, they must rely on different resources and use different tactics. Groups that specialize in judicial politics are organized in ways that are quite different from those that specialize in legislative politics.

Third, most groups, whether they are organized as PACs, lobbies, grassroots groups, or in other forms, are pragmatic. They use multifaceted strategies, adapting their tactics to suit new objectives and political circumstances. Groups forge, strengthen, and dissolve connections with various public officials, political institutions, and constituencies in order to pursue their goals better.

Combined, these conclusions suggest considerable fluidity in the interest group universe. Groups reorganize their priorities and make adjustments to their strategies and tactics when there are changes in institutional arrangements, group resources, or the regulatory regime.

In the electoral arena, groups forge connections with policymakers by helping with their electoral campaigns. The U.S. system of candidate-centered elections creates considerable uncertainty for candidates, who must assemble their own coalitions, raise their own money, and reach out to diverse groups of voters. The chapters in the first section show that groups play an important role in elections, providing money, volunteers, voters, and the infrastructure to reach those voters. By helping candidates, these groups gain access to key members of Congress, including party leaders, committee chairs and ranking members, and influential policy entrepreneurs. They gain more limited access to presidents and presidential candidates, but have ready access to party officials out of government who tend to be grateful for the support they provide to party committees and candidates.

Corporations, trade associations, and labor unions are highly skilled at adapting their strategies to suit the changing political conditions they encounter. During the 1980s, many business groups decided that the Republicans, with whom they agreed on most taxation and regulatory issues, would probably remain the minority party in the House for the foreseeable future. As a result, most corporate and trade association PACs switched from a pro-Republican pattern of contributions designed to elect a free market-oriented Congress to an incumbent-oriented pattern intended to give them access to powerful House Democrats.

The lobbyists associated with these PACs also learned that they could accomplish some of their goals by working with House Democratic leaders and officials in a GOP-led executive branch. Once the 1992 election led to the installation of a Democratic president, some business leaders found themselves shut out of the White House, and more than a few doubled their congressional lobbying efforts. The 1994 GOP takeover of Congress created new incentives for business-oriented PACs to switch their contributions to favor leaders of the newly installed Republican-led Congress. Even some labor groups, which have traditionally given the vast majority of their contributions to Democratic candidates, redirected some of their PAC money toward Republicans. Nevertheless, PACs did not completely abandon House Democrats because they recognized the possibility that Democratic leadership could return to Congress and wanted to continue to curry favor with the Democratic-led administration.

Of course, money is not the only resource that enables groups to form connections on the Hill. The relationship between members of Congress and lobbyists can be thought of as an exchange of needed resources. Members value the technical and political information that lobbyists provide, while interest groups need Congress to enact their preferred policies.

From the 1980s through the early 1990s, most liberal organizations enjoyed easy access to powerful congressional leaders but were shut out of the decision making that took place in the higher echelons of the Republican-dominated executive branch. Most conservative groups had to contend with the opposite situation: they were warmly received by the Reagan and Bush White Houses but had only limited sway with congressional Democrats. Following the 1994 elections, the situation was reversed. Conservative groups became the new congressional insiders, and liberal groups found that they were more likely to get a warm reception from the chief executive, members of the cabinet, and other executive branch officials.

In the Congress, groups form connections with other groups in order to approach the legislature more effectively. These coalitions were even more important in the new Republican Congress because at least initially the GOP centralized power, limited the access of interest groups, and even sought to limit the resources and actions of lobbyists for certain groups. Coalitions are more important and more difficult to assemble because of the constraints of policymaking in a zero-sum budgetary politics. Where once groups could logroll to win support for additional spending, they now must work with allies to protect sectors of the budget while competing with these same allies for their slice of the budgetary pie.

The strategies and tactics employed by organized interests to form connections in the executive branch are different from those used in Congress. The constituency connection that links members of Congress with interest groups simply does not exist in executive agencies. The policy preferences of the president motivate political appointees in the executive branch. Policies and institutional norms that may or may not coincide with the current administration drive the efforts of career bureaucrats. Lobbyists must understand the policy dynamic that exists between the White House, the executive agencies and departments, the relevant political appointees, and the career bureaucrats who actually implement public policy.

The information that interest groups provide through sanctioned executive agency channels (such as public comments in the rulemaking process) or through informal communications with agency officials is often more technical or scientific, reflecting the substantive complexity of the issue rather than its political complexity. Interest group access to the president and the White House staff has been facilitated in recent years by the proliferation of task forces, advisory offices, and commissions created within the Executive Office of the President. The Office of Science and Technology Policy, the Advisory Committee for Trade Policy and Negotiation, and other offices have served to link private-sector interests with policymaking entities within the White House organization.

Presidents are less often subjected to the narrow, particularistic lobbying that occurs in Congress, but they do need interest group support to get reelected and to enact their policies. Presidents seeking reelection need groups to mobilize voters on their behalf and to provide soft money to help fund their campaigns. Presidents seeking to pass key legislation need groups to mobilize their members and lobbyists behind their proposals and to help win the support of key legislators. Beyond the access points mentioned above, the Office of Public Liaison also provides an important nexus for the presidents and the interest group community (Seligman and Covington 1996).

Interest group connections with the judiciary are very different from those with the legislative and executive branches. Lobbyists do not speak with justices on the Supreme Court. They must instead use test cases and file amicus briefs in an attempt to influence judicial opinions. As such, many of the key resources of groups—especially membership and lobbying skill—are useless when approaching the courts. But money is still useful, for judicial politics are quite expensive. Repeat players such as corporations and groups that specialize in legal action are advantaged, for they are able to litigate to affect the rules in areas such as standing.

Interest Groups and Political Reform

Political reform has had a major impact on interest group politics. Long gone are the days when industrialists and other interest group leaders handed members of Congress bags full of cash in return for casting congressional votes to turn over mining rights on huge tracts of mineral-rich land, grant corporate tax breaks and subsidies, or support some other form of legislation from which business, labor, or some other group would gain significant benefit. Even legendary icons such as Daniel Webster wrote on Senate stationery to the president of the Second Bank of the United States, asking for his "usual retainers" to ensure his support (Sachs 1996). Mark Twain, in his fictional account of members of Congress, typified the conventional wisdom when he wrote "A Congressional appropriation costs money.... A majority of the House committee, say $10,000 apiece —$40,000. A majority of the Senate committee, the same each, say

$40,000; a little extra to one or two chairmen of one or two such commit-
tees, say $10,000 each ... there's $100,000 gone to begin with" (Twain
1899, 192).

In contrast, the scandals of the 1990s involve smaller sums and in many
cases do not even involve violations of law. The "book deal" that led to the
demise of House Speaker Jim Wright (D-Tex.) in 1989 and the check-
bouncing scandal at the House bank that resulted in the early retirements
and defeats of numerous congressmen in 1992 are cases in point. The Webster example contrasts even more sharply with allegations that PAC contributions of $5,000 or less are used to "buy" members' votes. Political re-
forms have reduced the level of corruption in American politics, including
the level of bribery, quid pro quos, and payoffs that involve special interests.

Political reforms have not, probably cannot, and should not eliminate
the influence of organized interests. Nevertheless, reform must be an ongoing process if it is to keep corruption at a minimum and limit the avenues
that organized interests can use to influence the political process. Individuals, politicians, and organized interests have time and time again proven
themselves capable of adapting to institutional reform and structural
changes in government. Problems arise when a small number of groups are
able to dominate the political system.

Interest group responses to the Federal Election Campaign Act of 1974,
the gift ban, lobby reform, and the movement toward centralization of
power in Congress have all demonstrated that groups are adept at altering
the methods they use to participate in the political process. The FECA, for
example, prohibited corporations, trade associations, unions, and other
groups from contributing treasury monies to federal candidates, but it laid
the groundwork for the skyrocketing number of PACs formed in the late
1970s and 1980s. Moreover, the law was eviscerated in 1996 by court rulings that now allow groups to use their treasury funds to carry out issue
advocacy campaigns. This has resulted in a small sector of society that represents a limited number of viewpoints providing a disproportionate
amount of the money that is spent in election campaigns.

Similarly, the Lobbying Disclosure Act of 1995 introduced major improvements in the disclosure and reporting of interest group lobbying activities, and the gift ban, also passed in 1995, curbed the practice of using
expensive meals, vacations, and gifts to gain access to federal lawmakers.
Yet, less than two years after their passage, these reforms are being tested
by some lobbyists and lawmakers. Interest group representatives have
learned to work around the gift ban's prohibitions against lobbyists "win-
ing and dining" members by reporting their epicurean encounters as campaign contributions. Portions of the Lobbying Disclosure Act have come
under challenge in the Senate, where members have proposed some "tech-

nical" amendments that would relax reporting requirements (Bradley 1996). Some reformers advocate full disclosure of expenditures on grass-roots lobbying and issue advocacy campaigns, neither of which is covered by current campaign finance and lobbying laws.

The creativity and pragmatism of politicians and lobbyists limit the possibilities for major political reform. When old routes of political influence are shut down, these individuals have often blazed new ones. Sometimes they have benefited from assistance provided by the courts. The connections between government officials and group representatives seem impossible to sever. As the FECA, the gift ban, and lobby reform demonstrate, interest groups and politicians eventually find ways to challenge and maneuver around political reforms without directly breaking the law. Political reforms typically reroute streams of influence rather than dry them up. Journalists, scholars, reformers, and ordinary citizens must be continually vigilant to prevent a small portion of society from amassing too much political clout.

Future reforms are bound to influence how interest groups operate, but the politics of reform dictate that it will be difficult to enact a major restructuring of the environment in which PACs and lobbies function. Virtually every Congress since the 1970s has debated changes in the campaign finance system, for example. During the 104th Congress, members of the House and Senate introduced over sixty campaign finance reform proposals including some that would have banned PAC contributions and provided candidates with free television broadcast time, and others that would have done away with all contribution and spending limits (Cantor 1996). All these bills fell far short of enactment, as did their forerunners in previous congresses. With the exception of the enactment of the 1976 and 1979 amendments to the FECA, no major change in the campaign finance system has been enacted into law. Most of the major changes that have taken place in the legal environment of campaign finance have come from the courts, rather than Congress.

A number of dynamics make it difficult for Congress to reform the laws that govern campaign finance and lobbying. Philosophical disagreements over the role of money in politics, the right to petition the government, and freedom of speech that reflect broad tensions over the roles that money, lobbying, and the government should play in politics and society are a major stumbling block. Partisan concerns, some of which reflect disagreements in philosophy and some based on considerations of political expedience, make it difficult for Democrats and Republicans to agree on the kinds of reforms that should be enacted. Differences in the financing of House and Senate campaigns and the operations of the two chambers typically lead to interchamber disagreements (Magleby and Nelson 1990). These are frequently exacerbated by the threat of a presidential veto or more subtle forms of White House involvement. The efforts of Common Cause, Public Campaign, and other so-called public interest groups that whip up popular opposition to incremental change in favor of "all or nothing" reforms make it difficult for members of Congress to back modest improvements and give them excuses for opposing most campaign finance legislation.

Perhaps the biggest obstacle to campaign finance reform is that those who enact the reforms know that they will have to live under them. With the exception of the few legislators who are appointed to fill out a predecessor's term, every member of Congress has some claim of expertise on campaign finance. Members arrive in the House or Senate by way of elections, and fund raising was a major component of virtually all their campaigns. Their expertise, varied experiences, and obvious self-interest make it extremely difficult for legislators to agree on a reform program. While many are concerned with improving the campaign finance system, their notions of what constitutes improvement reflect both their political experiences and their calculations about how change will affect their future campaigns.

Similar calculations influence lawmakers' thinking about other areas of political reform, including lobbying reform. Proposals to change the way interest groups and politicians approach one another, exchange information, mobilize legislative and public support for their preferred projects and career aspirations have the potential to advantage some to the detriment of others. They almost always result in at least some unanticipated outcomes that influence relationships of power and ways of doing things. Successful politicians—that is, those who are in power—have strong motivations to resist the efforts of reformers. Legislators believe that they are capable of using their own judgment to weigh the evidence and arguments presented by lobbyists.

As a result, political reforms are enacted infrequently and usually in response to widespread public outrage. Early twentieth-century campaign finance reforms prohibiting banks and corporations from making contributions to federal candidates and imposing ceilings and disclosure requirements on other contributions were passed in response to Progressive era protests against the power of big business (e.g., see Alexander 1992, chap. 3). The FECA was passed after Watergate investigations revealed many improprieties in the financing of President Richard Nixon's 1972 reelection campaign. The Lobbying Disclosure Act of 1995 and the gift ban were passed in the wake of the "Keating Five" scandal in the Senate, the post office and banking scandals in the House, and record levels of public hostility and anger at Congress (e.g., see Bowman and Ladd 1994). It is unlikely that a legislative coalition in favor of reform can be built in the absence of a major showing of public displeasure. Without public sentiment threatening the electoral security of those who fail to support reform, politicians are unlikely to change the campaign finance system fundamentally. The gulf that separates legislators on reform issues is too wide and their sense of self-interest too strong.

Moreover, should Congress and the president succeed in enacting further political reform, interest groups seeking to influence the elections and the policymaking process and politicians in need of campaign contributions and technical or political information will undoubtedly find ways to work around the reform's intent without violating the law. As long as interest group representatives wish to influence the regulations, budgetary, appropriations, courtroom decisions, public decrees, and other outputs of members of Congress, the president, executive branch officials, and the courts, they will search for ways to present their cases to the government. As long as politicians rely on interest groups for technical expertise and assistance with building legislative coalitions and developing electoral support, they will find more or less convenient ways for lobbyists to state their views. As regulatory regimes mature, those who operate under them test them, overturning some statutes in the courts and unearthing loopholes that enable them to work around the intent of others. What at first appear as small leaks in a regulatory structure can turn into a flood of activity that may eventually call into question the legitimacy of the framework itself.

Interest Groups, Reform, and American Democracy

The general unwillingness and practical inability of reformers to construct regulatory regimes that shut out organized interests from the political process was anticipated by the Framers of the Constitution. When they created a decentralized government that featured many points of access and embraced the property values associated with capitalism, they laid the foundation for a political system that rewards individuals and groups that are able to mobilize people and money. The Framers recognized that groups would have unequal numbers and financial resources and that this would lead to inequalities in the representation of their views. They speculated that the only way to prevent this outcome completely would be to deprive individuals of the freedom to use their talents to advance their interests and express their views—an approach that was repugnant to their notions of liberty.

Rather than attempt to constrain individual liberty, the Framers constructed a political system that utilized a series of checks and balances to prevent any one group from tyrannizing others. The chartering of a national bank, the Louisiana Purchase, and other early decisions that put the nation on the road toward a large commercial republic also encouraged the development of a diverse population made up of individuals who had overlapping interests. The Framers believed that overlapping interests and group memberships would force individuals and organized groups to cooperate with each other in pursuit of their common goals, to respect each others' rights and liberties, and to understand that mutual cooperation and respect were needed to maintain the political system that defended those rights and liberties. The current interest group system is far from perfect, but by connecting individuals to government and allowing a diversity of views to be expressed in the public arena, it helps protect some of Americans' most fundamental values—the rights of individuals to liberty, equality, and the pursuit of happiness. Interest group connections to the federal government fall short of the high standards set by reformers, but by facilitating political representation and participation, the interest group connection makes important contributions to American democracy.

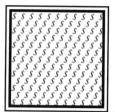

References

Aberbach, Joel. 1990. *Keeping a Watchful Eye*. Washington, D.C.: Brookings Institution.

Aberbach, Joel, and Bert Rockman. 1990. "What Has Happened to the U.S. Senior Civil Service?" *Brookings Review* 8:35–41.

Adams, Gordon. 1981. *The Politics of Defense Contracting: The Iron Triangle*. New York: Council on Economic Priorities.

Alexander, Herbert E. 1992. *Financing Politics: Money, Elections, Political Reform*. Washington, D.C.: CQ Press.

Alexander, Herbert E., and Monica Bauer. 1991. *Financing the 1988 Election*. Boulder, Colo.: Westview Press.

Alexander, Herbert E., and Anthony Corrado. 1995. *Financing the 1992 Election*. Armonk, N.Y.: M.E. Sharpe.

Almond, Gabriel, and Sidney Verba. 1963. *The Civic Culture*. Princeton: Princeton University Press.

American Society of Association Executives (ASAE). 1996. *Associations in a Nutshell*. Washington, D.C.: American Society of Association Executives.

Anderson, David. 1993. "Religious Groups Favor Health Reform." *Washington Post*, 2 October.

Anderson, Jack. 1996. *Inside the NRA: Armed and Dangerous*. New York: Dove Books.

Arnold, Mia. 1995. Personal interview. National Organization for Women. 24 August.

Arnold, R. Douglas. 1990. *The Logic of Congressional Action*. New Haven: Yale University Press.

Arterton, F. Christopher. 1993. "Campaign '92: Strategies and Tactics of the Candidates." In *The Election of 1992*, ed. Gerald M. Pomper. Chatham, N.J.: Chatham House.

Bach, Stanley, and Steven S. Smith. 1988. *Managing Uncertainty in the House of Representatives*. Washington, D.C.: Brookings Institution.

Bard, Mitchell. 1988. "The Influence of Ethnic Interest Groups on American Middle East Policy." In *The Domestic Sources of American Foreign Policy: Insights and Evidence*, ed. Charles W. Kegley Jr. and Eugene R. Wittkopf. New York: St. Martin's Press.

Barker, Lucius. 1967. "Third Parties in Litigation: A Systematic View of the Judicial Function." *Journal of Politics* 29:41–69.

Barnes, Fred. 1995. "Revenge of the Squares: Newt Gingrich and Pals Rewrite the '60s." *New Republic*, 13 March, 23–29.

Barr, Stephen. 1995a. "Nonprofits Fight Limits on Lobbying: GOP Bill Would Restrict Nonprofit Groups, Expand Definition of Lobbying." *Washington Post*, 19 September, A1, A7.

———. 1995b. "Negotiations Fail on Curbing Nonprofit Groups' Lobbying." *Washington Post*, 26 October, A14.

———. 1996. "GOP's Star Witness, 'Mr. X,' Details Lobbying by Agency." *Washington Post*, 16 May, A27.

Barr, Stephen, and Dan Morgan. 1995. "Spending Bill Deadlocks Over GOP Proposal to Restrict Nonprofits." *Washington Post*, 15 September, A4.

Baum, Lawrence. 1981. *The Supreme Court*. Washington, D.C.: CQ Press.

———. 1990. *American Courts: Process and Policy*. 2d ed. Boston: Houghton Mifflin.

Baumeister, E.J. 1992. "Regional Views of Foreign Policy." *Foreign Policy* 88:38–56.

Behuniak-Long, Susan. 1991. "Friendly Fire: Amici and *Webster* v. *Reproductive Health Services*." *Judicature* 74:261–70.

Bentley, Arthur F. 1908. *The Process of Government*. Chicago: University of Chicago Press.

Berke, Richard. 1995. "Republicans Spurning the Big-Business Label." *New York Times*, 11 May, B11.

Bernstein, Marver. 1955. *Regulating Business by Independent Commission*. Princeton: Princeton University Press.

Berry, Jeffrey M. 1977. *Lobbying for the People*. Princeton: Princeton University Press.

———. 1984. *The Interest Group Society*. Boston: Little, Brown.

———. 1989. *The Interest Group Society*. 2d ed. Glenview, Ill.: Scott, Foresman/Little, Brown.

Biersack, Robert. 1994. "Hard Facts and Soft Money: State Party Finance in the 1992 Federal Elections." In *The State of the Parties: The Changing Role of Contemporary Politics*, ed. Daniel M. Shea and John C. Green. Lanham, Md.: Rowman and Littlefield.

Birkby, Robert H., and Walter Murphy. 1964. "Interest Group Conflict in the Judicial Arena." *Texas Law Review* 42:1018–48.

Birnbaum, Jeffrey H. 1992. *The Lobbyists: How Influence Peddlers Get Their Way in Washington*. New York: Times Books.

Birnbaum, Jeffrey H., and Alan S. Murray. 1987. *Showdown at Gucci Gulch: Lawmakers, Lobbyists, and the Unlikely Triumph of Tax Reform*. New York: Random House.

Black, Duncan. 1958. *The Theory of Committees and Elections.* Cambridge: Cambridge University Press.

Blomquist, Brian. 1996. "Hill GOP to Take New Swing at Campaign-Finance Reform." *Washington Times,* 24 June, A3.

Blum, Joan. 1995. Personal interview. National Abortion Rights Action League. 17 August.

Bond, Jon R., and Richard Fleisher. 1980. "The Limits of Presidential Popularity as a Source of Influence in the U.S. House." *Legislative Studies Quarterly* 5:69–78.

———. 1990. *The President in the Legislative Arena.* Chicago: University of Chicago Press.

Bork, Robert H. 1990. *The Tempting of America.* New York: Free Press.

Bornemeier, James. 1995. "Bipartisan Bid to Revamp Endangered Species Act Introduced in House." *Los Angeles Times,* 8 September, A3.

Bowman, Karlyn, and Everett Carll Ladd. 1994. "Public Opinion toward Congress: A Historical Look." In *Congress, the Press, and the Public,.* ed. Thomas E. Mann and Norman J. Ornstein. Washington, D.C.: Brookings Institution.

Boyer, Barry. 1981. "Funding Public Participation in Agency Proceedings: The Federal Trade Commission Experience." *Georgetown Law Journal* 70:51–172.

Bradley, Jennifer. 1996. "Feingold Blocks Revision of Lobby Disclosure Law." *Roll Call,* 23 September.

Brant, Martha. 1995. "The Alaskan Assault: Congress Clear-Cutting Regulation with the GOP." *Newsweek,* 2 October, 44.

Bronner, Ethan. 1989. *Battle for Justice: How the Bork Nomination Shook America.* New York: Norton.

Brown, Clifford W. Jr., Lynda W. Powell, and Clyde Wilcox. 1995. *Serious Money: Fundraising and Contributing in Presidential Nomination Campaigns.* New York: Cambridge University Press.

Browning, Graeme. 1996. *Electronic Democracy: Using the Internet in American Politics.* Wilton, Conn.: Online, Inc., Pemberton Press.

Bruck, Connie. 1995. "The Politics of Perception." *New Yorker,* 9 October, 50–76.

Burkett, Elinor. 1996. "Politics: In the Land of Conservative Women." *Atlantic Monthly,* September, 19–24.

Burrell, Barbara C. 1994. *A Woman's Place Is in the House: Campaigning for Congress in the Feminist Era.* Ann Arbor: University of Michigan Press.

Caldeira, Gregory A. 1988–89. "Commentary on Senate Confirmation of Supreme Court Justices: The Role of Organized and Unorganized Interests." *Kentucky Law Journal* 77:538.

Caldeira, Gregory A., Marie Hojnacki, and John R. Wright. 1996. "The Informational Roles of Organized Interests in the Politics of Federal Judicial Nominations." Paper prepared for delivery at the 1996 annual meeting of the Midwest Political Science Association.

Caldeira, Gregory A., and John R. Wright. 1987. "Organized Interests and Agenda Setting in the U.S. Supreme Court." *American Political Science Review* 82:1109–26.

———. 1990a. "Amici Curiae Before the Supreme Court: Who Participates, When, and How Much?" *Journal of Politics* 52:782–806.

————. 1990b. "The Discuss List: Agenda Building in the Supreme Court." *Law and Society Review* 24:807–35.

Camissa, Anne. 1995. *Governments as Interest Groups: Intergovernmental Lobbying and the Federal System.* Westport, Conn.: Praeger.

Cantor, Joseph E. 1996. "Campaign Finance Legislation in the 104th Congress." *CRS Report to Congress,* updated 5 April.

Carothers, Thomas. 1994. "The NED at 10." *Foreign Policy* 95:123–38.

Carter, Stephen L. 1994. *The Confirmation Mess: Cleaning Up the Federal Appointments Process.* New York: Basic Books.

Center for Responsive Politics. 1988. *PACs on PACs: The View from the Inside.* Washington, D.C.: Center for Responsive Politics.

Chaplain, Sheila. 1993. "Special Interests, Firms Offer Up Loans, Gifts, In-Kind Help." *Legal Times,* 11 January, 1.

Chappell, Henry. 1981. "Campaign Contributions and Voting on the Cargo Preferences Bill: A Comparison of Simultaneous Equation Models." *Public Choice* 36:301–12.

————. 1982. "Campaign Contributions and Congressional Voting: A Simultaneous Probit-Tobit Model." *Review of Economics and Statistics* 62: 77–83.

Chinoy, Ira. 1997. "In Presidential Race, TV Ads Were Biggest '96 Cost By Far." *Washington Post,* 31 March, A19.

Clarke, Duncan H. 1988. "Why States Can't Lead." In *Domestic Sources of American Foreign Policy,* ed. Charles W. Kegley and Eugene W. Wittkopf. New York: St. Martin's Press, 142–48.

Clausen, Aage R. 1972. *How Congressmen Decide: A Policy Focus.* New York: St. Martin's Press.

Claybrook, Frederick. 1995. Personal interview. Christian Legal Society. 17 March.

Clough, Michael. 1994. "Grass-Roots Policy Making, Say Good-Bye to the Wise-Men." *Foreign Affairs,* January/February, 2–7.

Cohen, Jeffrey. 1986. "The Dynamics of the 'Revolving Door' on the FCC." *American Journal of Political Science* 30:689–708.

Cohen, Richard E. 1992. *Washington at Work: Back Rooms and Clean Air.* New York: Macmillan.

Coleman, James. 1982. *The Asymmetric Society.* Syracuse: Syracuse University Press.

Collins, Ronald K.L., and David M. Skover. 1993. "Commerce & Communication." *Texas Law Review* 71:697.

Common Cause. 1992. "Clinton and Democrats Raise Nearly $20 Million in Soft Money during the Presidential General Election Period; Bush and Republicans Raise $12.4 Million, According to Reports Filed with FEC." Press release, 17 December.

————. 1993. "Soft Money for President Clinton & Democratic National Committee Tops $29 Million during 1991–1992 Election Cycle." Press release, 3 March.

Congressional Budget Office. 1990a. *Pay-As-You-Go Budgeting.* U.S. Congress. Staff memorandum, March.

————. 1990b. *The 1990 Budget Agreement: An Interim Assessment.* U.S. Congress, December.

Congressional Record, 8 February 1995, E303–4.

———, 24 February 1995, H2182.

———, 7 April 1995, H4419.

———, 10 May 1995, H4675.

———, 30 June 1995, H1388.

———, 17 July 1995, H7016.

———, 18 July 1995, E1455–56.

———, 1 August 1995, H8135.

———, 2 August 1995, H1688.

———, 3 August 1995, H8388–97.

———, 7 August 1995, H1695.

———, 12 September 1995, H8789–90.

———, 13 September 1995, H1773.

———, 21 September 1995, H9406.

———, 27 September 1995, H9566.

———, 29 September 1995, H9716.

———, 10 October 1995, H9766.

———, 8 November 1995, H11910–11.

———, 5 December 1995, H13942.

———, 6 December 1995, H14141–42.

———, 13 December 1995, H14373.

Conway, Margaret M. 1991. "PACS in the Political Process." In *Interest Group Politics,* 3d ed., ed. Allan J. Cigler and Burdett A. Loomis. Washington D.C.: CQ Press.

Corrado, Anthony. 1992. *Creative Campaigning: PACs and the Presidential Selection Process.* Boulder, Colo.: Westview Press.

———. 1996. "The Changing Environment of Presidential Campaign Finance." In *In Pursuit of the White House,* ed. William G. Mayer. Chatham, N.J.: Chatham House.

Cortner, Richard C. 1968. "Strategy and Tactics of Litigants in Constitutional Cases." *Journal of Public Law* 17:287–307.

———. 1975. *The Supreme Court and Civil Liberties Policy.* Palo Alto, Calif: Mayfield.

Covington, Cary R. 1987. "Mobilizing Congressional Support for the President." *Legislative Studies Quarterly* 12:77–95.

Covington, Cary R., J. Mark Wrighton, and Rhonda Kinney. 1995. "A 'Presidency-Augmented' Model of Presidential Success on House Roll Call Votes." *American Journal of Political Science* 39:1010–24.

Craig, Barbara Hinkson, and David M. O'Brien. 1993. *Abortion and American Politics.* Chatham, N.J.: Chatham House.

Cropper, Maureen, Bill Evans, Steve Berardi, Maria Soares, and Paul Portney. 1990. *An Analysis of EPA Regulation of Food-Use Pesticides.* Washington, D.C.: Resources for the Future.

Cushman, John H. Jr. 1996. "G.O.P. Backing Off from Tough Stand over Environment." *New York Times,* 26 January, A1, A8.

Dahl, Robert A. 1956. *A Preface to Democratic Theory.* Chicago: University of Chicago Press.

Dalton, Deborah. 1993. "The Negotiated Rulemaking Process: Creating a New Legitimacy in Regulation." *Review of European Community and International Environmental Law* 2.

Danner, Dan. 1995. Personal interview. National Federation of Independent Business. 7 September.

Davidson, Kenneth, Ruth Bader Ginsburg, and Herma Hill Kay. 1974. *Sex Based Discrimination.* St. Paul, Minn.: West.

Davidson, Roger H. 1981. "Subcommittee Government: New Channels for Policy Making." In *The New Congress,* ed. Thomas Mann and Norman Ornstein. Washington, D.C.: American Enterprise Institute.

———. 1995. "Congressional Committees in the New Reform Era: From Combat to Contract." In *Remaking Congress: Change and Stability in the 1990s,* ed. James A. Thurber and Roger H. Davidson. Washington, D.C.: CQ Press.

DeGregorio, Christine. 1997. *Networks of Champions: Leadership, Access and Advocacy in the U.S. House of Representatives.* Ann Arbor: University of Michigan Press.

DeGregorio, Christine, and Jack E. Rossotti. 1994. "Resources, Attitudes and Strategies: Interest Group Participation in the Bork Confirmation Process." *American Review of Politics* 15:1–19.

———. 1995. "Campaigning for the Court: Interest Group Participation in the Bork and Thomas Nomination Processes." In *Interest Group Politics,* 4th ed., ed. Allan J. Cigler and Burdett A. Loomis. Washington, D.C.: CQ Press, 215–38.

DeGregorio, Christine, and Kevin Snider. 1995. "Leadership Appeal in the U.S. House of Representatives: Comparing Officeholders and Aides." *Legislative Studies Quarterly.*

DeParle, Jason. 1995. "The First Primary." *New York Times Magazine,* 16 April, 33.

Destler, I.M. 1992. *American Trade Politics.* 2d ed. New York: Twentieth Century Fund.

DiClerico, Robert. 1996. "Assessing the Clinton Presidency: The Risks of Context and Character." *Extensions* (Journal of the Carl Albert Congressional Research and Studies Center), Spring, 19–23.

Doyle, Richard, and Jerry McCaffrey. 1991. "The Budget Enforcement Act of 1990: The Path to No Fault Budgeting." *Public Budgeting and Finance* 10 (Spring).

Drew, Elizabeth. 1983. *Politics and Money: The New Road to Corruption.* New York: Macmillan.

Drinkard, Jim. 1996. "Millions Spent to Lobby the U.S.," *Philadelphia Enquirer,* 23 September 1996, A1.

Dunn, Charles W. 1989. *Religion in American Politics.* Washington, D.C.: CQ Press.

Ebersole, Luke Eugene. 1951. *Church Lobbying in the Nation's Capitol.* New York: Macmillan.

Edsall, Thomas B. 1996. "GOP Plans Counteroffensive on Labor." *Washington Post,* 22 March.

Edwards, George C. III. 1980. *Presidential Influence in Congress.* San Francisco: W.E. Freeman.

————. 1989. *At the Margins: Presidential Leadership of Congress.* New Haven: Yale University Press.

Egan, Timothy. 1995a. "Industries Affected by Endangered Species Act Help a Senator Rewrite Its Provisions." *New York Times,* 13 April, A20.

————. 1995b. "In the Northernmost State, Politics Takes a Pugilistic Turn." *New York Times,* 31 August, A18.

Ehrenhalt, Alan, Renee Amrine, and Philip D. Duncan. 1987. *Politics in America: The 100th Congress.* Washington, D.C.: CQ Press.

Emerson, Thomas I. 1970. *The System of Freedom of Expression.* New York: Vintage Books.

Emord, Jonathan W. 1991. *Freedom, Technology, and the First Amendment.* San Francisco: Pacific Research Institute for Public Policy.

Engelberg, Stephen. 1995. "100 Days of Dreams Come True for Lobbyists in Congress." *New York Times,* 14 April, A12.

Epstein, Edwin M. 1969. *The Corporation in American Politics.* Englewood Cliffs, N.J.: Prentice Hall.

Epstein, Lee. 1985. *Conservatives in Court.* Knoxville: University of Tennessee Press.

————. 1991. "Courts and Interest Groups." In *The American Courts: A Critical Assessment,* ed. John B. Gates and Charles A. Johnson. Washington, D.C.: CQ Press.

————. 1993. "Interest Group Litigation during the Rehnquist Court Era." *Journal of Law and Politics* 9:639–717.

Epstein, Lee, and Joseph F. Kobylka. 1992. *The Supreme Court and Legal Change: Abortion and the Death Penalty.* Chapel Hill: University of North Carolina Press.

Fallows, James M. 1989. *More Like Us: Putting America's Native Strengths and Values to Work to Overcome the Asian Challenge.* Boston: Houghton Mifflin.

Faucheux, Ron. 1995. "The Grassroots Explosion." *Campaigns and Elections,* December/January, 21–25, 53.

Federal Election Commission. 1993. "Democrats Narrow Financial Gap in 1991–92." Press release, 11 March.

————. 1995. "PAC Activity in 1994 Elections Remains at 1992 Levels." Press release, 31 March.

————. 1996a. "Record." April, 8.

————. 1996b. "PAC Activity Increases in 1995." Press release, 4 April.

————. 1997. "FEL Reports Major Increases in Party Authority for 1995–96." Press release, 19 March.

————. 1997. "PAC Activity Increases in 1995–96 Election Cycles." Press release, 22 April.

Fein, Bruce. 1992. "The ABA: Just Another Interest Group." *Texas Lawyer,* 21 October.

Fiorina, Morris P., and Kenneth A. Shepsle. 1989a. "Formal Theories of Leadership: Agents, Agenda Setters, and Entrepreneurs." In *Leadership and Politics,* ed. Bryan D. Jones. Lawrence: University Press of Kansas.

————. 1989b. "Is Negative Voting an Artifact?" *American Journal of Political Sci-*

ence 33:423–39.

———. 1990. "A Positive Theory of Negative Voting." In *Information and Democratic Processes,* ed. John Ferejohn and James Kuklinski. Urbana: University of Illinois Press.

Fisher, Louis. 1985. "Ten Years of the Budget Act: Still Searching for Controls." *Public Budgeting and Finance,* Autumn.

Foreman, Christopher H. Jr. "Grassroots Victim Organizations: Mobilizing for Personal and Public Health." In *Interest Group Politics,* ed. Allan J. Cigler and Burdett A. Loomis. Washington, D.C.: CQ Press.

Forrester, Nathan. 1995. Personal interview. Becket Fund. 25 April.

Fournier, Kevin A. 1992. "Statement for the Defense: Tear Down This Wall!" *Law & Justice* 1, no. 3.

Fowler, Linda L., and Robert D. McClure. 1989. *Political Ambition.* New Haven: Yale University Press.

Fowler, Linda L., and Ronald G. Shaiko. 1987. "The Grassroots Connection: Environmental Activists and Senate Roll Calls." *American Journal of Political Science* 31:484–510.

Frankel, Glenn. 1996. "Tobacco Industry Switches Brands." *Washington Post,* 15 March, A1.

Freeman, J. Lieper. 1955. *The Political Process.* New York: Random House.

Frendreis, John P., and Richard A. Waterman. 1985. "PAC Contributions and Legislative Behavior: Senate Voting on Trucking Deregulation." *Social Science Quarterly* 66:401–12.

Fried, Charles. 1992. "Exchange: Speech in the Welfare State: The New First Amendment Jurisprudence: A Threat to Liberty." *University of Chicago Law Review* 59:225.

Fritsch, Jane. 1995. "Decisions on Gifts Defended by Dole." *New York Times,* 2 September, 1, 30.

Furlong, Scott. 1992. "Interest Group Influence on Regulatory Policy." Ph.D. dissertation. Washington, D.C.: American University.

Gais, Thomas. 1996. *Improper Influence: Campaign Finance Laws, Political Interest Groups, and the Problem of Equality.* Ann Arbor: University of Michigan Press.

Gais, Thomas L., Mark A. Peterson, and Jack L. Walker. 1983. "Interest Groups, Iron Triangles, and Representative Institutions in American National Government." *British Journal of Political Science* 14:161–85.

Galanter, Marc. 1975. "Why the 'Haves' Come Out Ahead: Speculations on the Limits of Legal Change." *Law & Society Review* 9:95–160.

Garment, Suzanne. 1988. "The War against Robert H. Bork." *Commentary,* January.

Gelb, Joyce, and Marian Lief Palley. 1982. *Women and Public Policies.* Princeton: Princeton University Press.

George, Alexander H. 1980. *Presidential Decision Making in Foreign Policy: The Effective Use of Information and Advice.* Boulder, Colo.: Westview Press.

———. 1995. "The President and the Management of Foreign Policy: Styles and Models." In *The Global Agenda: Issues and Perspectives,* 4th ed., ed. Charles W. Kegley and Eugene W. Wittkopf. New York: McGraw-Hill,

107–26.

Gimpel, James G. 1996. *Legislating the Revolution: The Contract with America in its First 100 Days.* Needham Heights, Mass.: Allyn and Bacon.

Ginger, Ray. 1958. *Six Days or Forever? Tennessee v. John Thomas Scopes.* New York: Oxford University Press.

Ginsberg, Benjamin, Walter R. Mebane, and Martin Shefter. 1995. "The Presidency and Interest Groups: Why Presidents Cannot Govern." In *The Presidency and the Political System,* 4th ed., ed. Michael Nelson. Washington, D.C.: CQ Press.

Ginsberg, Benjamin, and Martin Shefter. 1995. "The Presidency, Interest Groups, and Social Forces: Creating a Republican Coalition." In *The Presidency and the Political System,* 3d ed., ed. Michael Nelson. Washington, D.C.: CQ Press.

Ginsburg, Ruth Bader. 1988. "Confirming Supreme Court Justices: Thoughts on the Second Opinion Rendered by the Senate." *University of Illinois Law Review* 101:115–17.

Goings, Kenneth W. 1990. *The NAACP Comes of Age: The Defeat of Judge John H. Parker.* Bloomington: Indiana University Press.

Golden, Marissa. 1995. "Interest Groups in the Rulemaking Process: Who Participates? Whose Voices Get Heard?" Paper presented at the Third National Public Management Conference, Lawrence, Kansas.

Goldstein, Joshua. 1995. *PACS in Profile.* Washington, D.C.: Center for Responsive Politics.

Goldstein, Kenneth M. 1995. "Tremors before the Earthquake: Grassroots Communications to Congress before the 1994 Election." Paper presented at the annual meeting of the American Political Science Association, Chicago.

Gormley, William Jr. 1979. "A Test of the Revolving Door Hypothesis at the FCC." *American Journal of Political Science* 23:665–83.

———. 1983. *The Politics of Public Utility Regulation.* Pittsburgh: University of Pittsburgh Press.

———. 1986. "Regulatory Issue Networks in a Federal System." *Polity,* Summer, 595–620.

———. 1989. *Taming the Bureaucracy: Muscles, Prayers, and Other Strategies.* Princeton: Princeton University Press.

Goshko, John, and R. Jeffrey Smith. 1993. "Details of Clinton's 'Democracy' Programs Slowly Begin to Emerge." *Washington Post,* 5 May, A28.

Graber, Mark A. 1996. *Rethinking Abortion: Equal Choice, the Constitution, and Reproductive Rights.* Princeton: Princeton University Press.

Greenberg, Jack. 1974. "Litigation for Social Change: Methods, Limits, and Role in Democracy." *Records of the New York City Bar Association* 29:9–63.

Greenhouse, Linda. 1996. "Essay: Telling the Court's Story: Justice and Journalism at the Supreme Court." *Yale Law Journal* 105:1537–53.

Greenhouse, Steven. 1994. "Clinton Is Faulted on Political Choices for Envoy Posts." *New York Times,* 13 April, A15.

Greider, William. 1992. *Who Will Tell the People: The Betrayal of American Democracy.* New York: Touchstone Books.

Grenzke, Janet M. 1989. "PACs and the Congressional Supermarket: The Currency

Is Complex." *American Journal of Political Science* 33:2–24.

———. 1990. "Money and Congressional Behavior." In *Money, Elections, and Democracy*, ed. Margaret Latus Nugent and John R. Johannes. Boulder, Colo.: Westview Press.

Gribbin, William J. 1989. "The President and the Congress: The Office of Legislative Affairs." In *Mandate for Leadership III*. Washington, D.C.: Heritage Foundation, 39–50.

Grier, Kevin B., and Michael C. Munger. 1986. "The Impact of Legislator Attributes on Interest Group Campaign Contributions." *Journal of Labor Research* 7:349–61.

———. 1991. "Committee Assignments, Constituent Preferences, and Campaign Contributions." *Economic Inquiry* 29:24–43.

Grossman, Joel B. 1965. *Lawyers and Judges: The ABA and the Politics of Judicial Selection*. New York: Wiley.

Guth, James L., John C. Green, Lyman A. Kellstedt, and Corwin E. Smidt. 1995. "Onward Christian Soldiers: Religious Activist Groups in American Politics." In *Interest Group Politics*, ed. Allan J. Cigler and Burdett A. Loomis. Washington, D.C.: CQ Press.

Hagstrom, Jerry. 1993. "So Now It Can Be Told." *National Journal*, 20 March, 703.

Hall, Richard L. 1993. "Participation, Abdication, and Representation in Congress." In *Congress Reconsidered*, 5th ed., ed. Lawrence Dodd and Bruce Oppenheimer. Washington, D.C.: CQ Press.

Halpern, Stephen C. 1976. "Assessing the Litigative Role of ACLU Chapters." In *Civil Liberties: Policy and Policymaking*, ed. Stephen L. Wasby. Lexington, Mass.: Lexington Books.

———. 1995. *On the Limits of Law: The Ironic Legacy of Title VI of the 1964 Civil Rights Act*. Baltimore: Johns Hopkins University Press.

Hansen, John Mark. 1985. "The Political Economy of Group Membership." *American Political Science Review* 79:79–96.

Hardesty, Rex. 1976. "The Computer's Role in Getting Out the Vote." In *Labor in American Politics*, ed. C. Rehmus, D. McLaughlin, and F. Nesbitt. Ann Arbor: University of Michigan Press.

Harper, Fowler V., and Edwin Etherington. 1953. "Lobbyists before the Court." *University of Pennsylvania Law Review* 101:1172–77.

Hassler, Gregory L., and Karen O'Connor. 1986. "Woodsy Witchdoctors vs. Judicial Guerillas: The Role and Impact of Competing Interest Groups in Environmental Litigation." *Boston College Environmental Law Review* 13:487–525.

Havens, Harry. 1986. "Gramm-Rudman-Hollings: Origins and Implementation." *Public Budgeting and Finance* 6:4–24.

Heclo, Hugh. 1978. "Issue Networks and the Executive Establishment." In *The New American Political System*, ed. Anthony King. Washington, D.C.: American Enterprise Institute.

Hedge, David, and Michael Scicchitano. 1994. "Regulating in Space and Time: The Case of Regulatory Federalism." *Journal of Politics* 56:134–53.

Heinz, John, Edward Laumann, Robert Nelson, and Robert Salisbury. 1993. *The*

Hollow Core: Private Interests in National Policy Making. Cambridge: Harvard University Press.

Herrnson, Paul S. 1988. *Party Campaigning in the 1980s.* Cambridge: Harvard University Press.

———. 1994. "The National Committee for an Effective Congress: Liberalism, Partisanship, and Electoral Innovation." In *Risky Business? PAC Decision-making in Congressional Elections,* ed. Robert Biersack, Paul S. Herrnson, and Clyde Wilcox. Armonk, N.Y.: M.E. Sharpe.

———. 1997. "Money and Motives: Party, PAC, and Individual Spending in House Elections." In *Congress Reconsidered,* ed. Lawrence C. Dodd and Bruce I. Oppenheimer. Washington, D.C.: CQ Press.

———. 1998. *Congressional Elections: Campaigning at Home and in Washington.* 2d ed. Washington, D.C.: CQ Press.

Hertzke, Allen D. 1988. *Representing God in Washington: Religious Interest Groups in the American Polity.* Knoxville: University of Tennessee Press.

Hicks, Robyn. 1994. "Grassroots Organizations in Defense of Mother Nature: The Clean Water Action Vote Environment PAC." In *Risky Business? PAC Decisionmaking in Congressional Elections,* ed. Robert Biersack, Paul Herrnson, and Clyde Wilcox. Armonk, N.Y.: M.E. Sharpe.

Hojnacki, Marie. 1995. "Organized Interests as Coalition Members." Paper prepared for presentation at the annual meeting of the American Political Science Association, Chicago.

Houck, Oliver A. 1984. "With Charity for All." *Yale Law Journal* 93:1415.

Hula, Kevin. 1995. "Rounding Up the Suspects: Forging Interest Group Coalitions in Washington." In *Interest Group Politics,* 5th ed., ed. Allan J. Cigler and Burdett A. Loomis. Washington, D.C.: CQ Press.

Ivers, Gregg. 1990. "Organized Religion and the Supreme Court." *Journal of Church and State* 32:775–93.

———. 1992. "Religious Organizations as Constitutional Litigants." *Polity* 25:243–66.

———. 1995. *To Build a Wall: American Jews and Separation of Church and State.* Charlottesville: University of Virginia Press.

Jackson, Brooks. 1988. *Honest Graft: Money and the American Political Process.* New York: Knopf.

Jackson, John E., and John W. Kingdon. 1992. "Ideology, Interest Group Scores, and Legislative Votes." *American Journal of Political Science* 36:805–23.

Jacob, Herbert. 1995. *Law and Politics in the United States.* 2d ed. New York: HarperCollins.

Jacob, Paul. 1995. Personal interview. U.S. Term Limits. 16 August.

Jacobson, Gary C. 1987. *The Politics of Congressional Elections.* 2d ed. Boston: Little, Brown.

Jacoby, Mary. 1996. "House, Senate GOP Join Forces to Push Bill Banning Lobbying by the Executive Branch." *Roll Call,* 14 March, 10.

Jelen, Ted G., and Clyde Wilcox. 1995. *Public Attitudes on Church and State.* Armonk, N.Y.: M.E. Sharpe.

Jones, Charles O. 1979. "American Politics and the Organization of Energy Decision Making." *Annual Review of Energy* 4:99–121.

————. 1994. *The Presidency in a Separated System*. Washington, D.C.: Brookings Institution.

Joyce, Phil. 1993–94. Memos on budget process legislation (to Robert Reischauer and others), 22 January 1993–1 September 1994.

Judis, John. 1995. "The Contract with K Street." *New Republic* 4:18–25.

Kairys, David. 1990. "Freedom of Speech." In *The Politics of Law: A Progressive Critique*, ed. David Kairys. New York: Pantheon.

Katzmann, Robert A. 1997. *Courts and Congress*. Washington, D.C.: Brookings Institution/Governance Institute.

Kau, James B., and Paul H. Rubin. 1982. *Congressmen, Constituents, and Contributors: Determinants of Roll Call Voting in the House of Representatives*. Boston: Martinus Nijhoff.

Keating, David. 1995. Personal interview. National Taxpayers Union. 24 August.

Kee, James Edwin, and Scott V. Nystrom. 1991. "The 1990 Budget Package: Redefining the Debate." *Public Budgeting and Finance* 10:4.

Kegley, Charles W., and Eugene W. Wittkopf, eds. 1995. *The Global Agenda: Issues and Perspectives*. 4th ed. New York: McGraw-Hill.

Kellman, Laurie. 1995. "GOP Renews Effort to Hamper Lobbying: Planned Parenthood, YMCA Targeted." *Washington Times*, 29 September, A8.

Kernell, Samuel C. 1977. "Presidential Popularity and Negative Voting." *American Political Science Review* 71:44–66.

————. 1986. *Going Public*. Washington, D.C.: CQ Press.

Kerwin, Cornelius. 1994. *Rulemaking: How Government Agencies Write Law and Make Policy*. Washington, D.C.: CQ Press.

Kessler, Daniel, and Keith Krehbiel. 1995. "Dynamics of Cosponsorship." Manuscript. Graduate School of Business, Stanford University.

Key, V.O. Jr. 1964. *Politics, Parties and Pressure Groups*. 5th ed. New York: Crowell.

Keynes, Edward, and Randall K. Miller. 1989. *Prayer, Bussing, and Abortion*. Durham, N.C.: Duke University Press.

Kingdon, John W. 1989. *Congressmen's Voting Decisions*. 3d ed. Ann Arbor: University of Michigan Press.

Klinkner, Philip A. 1994. *The Losing Parties: Out-Party National Committees, 1956–1993*. New Haven: Yale University Press.

Kluger, Richard. 1976. *Simple Justice: The History of Brown v. Board of Education and Black Americans' Struggle for Equality*. New York: Knopf.

Knickerbocker, Brad. 1995. "GOP Budget Hawks Peck at Endangered Species Regulations." *Christian Science Monitor*, 20 July, 3.

Koford, Kenneth. 1989. "Dimensions in Congressional Voting." *American Political Science Review* 83:949–62.

————. 1990. "Spatial Models of Legislative Choice." *Legislative Studies Quarterly* 84:259–319.

Krehbiel, Keith. 1995. "Cosponsors and Wafflers From A to Z." *American Journal of Political Science* 39:906–23.

Krislov, Samuel. 1963. "The Amicus Curiae Brief: From Friendship to Advocacy." *Yale Law Journal* 72.

Kuklinski, James H. 1978. "Representative-Constituency Linkages: A Review Article." *Legislative Studies Quarterly* 4:121–40.

Kull, Steven. 1995–96. "What the Public Knows that Washington Doesn't." *Foreign Policy* 101:102–15.

Kuntz, Phil, and Glenn Burkins. 1996. "Worried by AFL-CIO's Election Funds, Business Groups Ready Their Own War Chest." *Wall Street Journal,* 10 May, A12.

Lacayou, Richard. 1995. "This Land Is Whose Land?" *Time,* 23 October, 68–72.

LaHaye, Beverly. 1995. Personal interview. Concerned Women for America. 17 August.

Langbein, Laura I. 1986. "Money and Access: Some Empirical Evidence." *Journal of Politics* 48:1052–62.

———. 1993. "PACs, Lobbies, and Political Conflict: The Case of Gun Control." *Public Choice* 77:551–72.

Langbein, Laura I., and Mark A. Lotwis. 1990. "The Political Efficacy of Lobbying and Money: Gun Control in the U.S. House, 1986." *Legislative Studies Quarterly* 15:413–40.

Lau, Richard R. 1982. "Negativity in Political Perception." *Political Behavior* 4:353–75.

———. 1985. "Two Explanations for Negativity Effects in Voting Behavior." *American Journal of Political Science* 29:119–38.

Lee, Gary. 1995a. "Environmentalists Try to Regroup." *Washington Post,* 22 April, A3.

———. 1995b. "Environmental Groups Launch Counterattack after Losses on Hill." *Washington Post,* 19 August, A6.

———. 1995c. "GOP Pushes Superfund Rewrite: Democrats Say Plan Would Free Industry from Cleanup Responsibility." *Washington Post,* 27 October, A9.

———. 1996. "Compromising on Clean Air." *Washington Post,* 24 February, A1.

LeLoup, Lance T., Barbara Luck Graham, and Stacy Barwick. 1987. "Deficit Politics and Constitutional Government: The Impact of Gramm-Rudman-Hollings." *Public Budgeting and Finance* 7:83–103.

Lewis, Charles. 1996. *The Buying of the President.* New York: Avon Books.

Lichtman, Judith. 1990. "Public Interest Groups and the Bork Nomination." *Northwestern University Law Review* 84:978.

Little, Thomas H., and Samuel C. Patterson. 1993. "The Organizational Life of the Congressional Parties." *American Review of Politics* 14:39–70.

Loomis, Burdett A., and Allan J. Cigler. 1991. "Introduction: The Changing Nature of Interest Group Politics." In *Interest Group Politics,* 3d ed., ed. Allan J. Cigler and Burdett A. Loomis. Washington, D.C.: CQ Press.

Love, Alice A. 1995a. "Lobbyist-Written Bills Not Unique to GOP Congress." *Roll Call,* 17 April, 1, 42.

———. 1995b. "A Lobby War on 'Ending Welfare for Lobbyists.'" *Roll Call,* 18 September, 10, 18.

Lowi, Theodore J. 1964. "American Business, Public Policy, Case Studies, and Political Theory." *World Politics* 16:677–715.

———. 1969. *The End of Liberalism.* New York: Norton.

———. 1979. *The End of Liberalism.* 2d ed. New York: Norton.

Maass, Arthur. 1951. *Muddy Waters: The Army Corps of Engineers and the Na-*

tion's Rivers. Cambridge: Harvard University Press.

McCarty, Nolan, and Lawrence S. Rothenberg. 1996. "Commitment and the Campaign Contribution Contract." *American Journal of Political Science* 40:872–904.

McConnell, Grant. 1966. *Private Power and American Democracy.* New York: Knopf.

McCool, Daniel. 1989. "Subgovernments and the Impact of Policy Fragmentation and Accommodation." *Policy Studies Review* 8:264–87.

McGuigan, Patrick, and Dawn H. Weyrich. 1990. *Ninth Justice: The Fight for Bork.* Lanham, Md.: University Press of America.

McIntosh, Wayne V. 1985. "Litigating Scientific Creationism, or Scopes I, II, III. . ." *Law and Policy* 7:375–85.

Madison, James, Alexander Hamilton, and John Jay. 1988. *Federalist Papers,* ed. Garry Wills. New York: Bantam Books.

Magleby, David B., and Candice J. Nelson. 1990. *The Money Chase: Congressional Campaign Finance Reform.* Washington, D.C.: Brookings Institution.

Makinson, Larry. 1995. *The Price of Admission: Campaign Spending in the 1994 Elections.* Washington, D.C.: Center for Responsive Politics.

Malbin, Michael. 1981. "Delegation, Deliberation, and the New Role of Congressional Staff." In *The New Congress,* ed. Thomas E. Mann and Norman J. Ornstein. Washington, D.C.: American Enterprise Institute.

Mann, James. 1993. "America and China's MFN Benefits: 1989–1994." In *Public Engagement in U.S. Foreign Policy after the Cold War: Final report of the eighty-third American Assembly held at Arden House, Harriman, New York, 3–6 June,* 23–25. New York: The Assembly.

Manwaring, David. 1962. *Render unto Caesar: The Flag Salute Controversy.* Chicago: University of Chicago Press.

Marcus, Ruth. 1992. "Bush Camp Files Complaint against Horton Ad Maker." *Washington Post,* 15 July, A9.

———. 1996a. "Political Ads Test the Limits." *Washington Post,* 8 April.

———. 1996b. "Party Spending Unleashed: Justices Say Independence from Candidate Is Key." *Washington Post,* 27 June, A1, A6.

Marcus, Ruth, and Guy Gugliotta. 1996. "Number of Lobbyists Who Register Doubles." *Washington Post,* 16 March, A4.

Marsden, George M. 1980. *Fundamentalism and American Culture.* New York: Oxford University Press.

Maskell, Jack. 1995. "Restrictions on Lobbying Congress with Federal Funds." *CRS Report* 95-382 A, 3 March.

Mathews, Jessica. 1995. "Battle for the Environment." *Washington Post,* 27 November, A21.

Mayhew, David. 1974. *Congress: The Electoral Connection.* New Haven: Yale University Press.

Medalie, Richard C. 1968. *From Escobedo to Miranda: The Anatomy of a Supreme Court Decision.* Washington, D.C.: Lerner Book Co.

Milbrath, Lester W. 1963. *The Washington Lobbyists.* Chicago: Rand McNally.

Miller, George. 1995a. "Authors of the Law." *New York Times,* 24 May, A21.

———. 1995b. "Purse Put to the Test: Special Interests Find Cover in Budget Reconciliation." *Washington Post,* 26 September, A1, A4.

Moe, Terry. 1989. "The Politics of Bureaucratic Structure." In *Can the Government Govern?* ed. John Chubb and Paul Peterson. Washington, D.C.: Brookings Institution.

Moen, Matthew C. 1989. *The Christian Right and Congress.* Tuscaloosa, Ala.: University of Alabama Press.

Mollison, Andrew. 1994. "Health Care Reform: Religion Mixes with Politics in Debate over New System." *Atlanta Journal and Constitution,* 16 February.

Moore, Stephen, Sidney M. Wolfe, Deborah Lindes, and Clifford E. Douglas. 1994. "Epidemiology of Failed Tobacco Control Legislation." *Journal of the American Medical Association* 272:1171–75.

Morgan, Dan. 1995. "Shifting Stance on Environment Puts GOP's Lewis on the Spot." *Washington Post,* 7 December, A19.

Morrison, Bob. 1995. Personal interview. Family Research Council. 14 August.

Moyers, Bill. 1995. *Larry King Live (CNN).* Interview transcript, 29 June.

Mueller, John. 1992. "Democracy and Ralph's Pretty Good Grocery: Elections, Equality, and the Minimal Human Being." *American Journal of Political Science* 36:983–1003.

Nelson, Candice J. 1994a. "The Business-Industry PAC: Trying to Lead in an Uncertain Electoral Climate." In *Risky Business? PAC Decisionmaking in Congressional Elections,* ed. Robert Biersack, Paul S. Herrnson, and Clyde Wilcox. Armonk, N.Y.: M.E. Sharpe.

———. 1994b. "Women's PACs in the Year of the Woman." In *The Year of the Woman: Myths and Realities,* ed. Elizabeth Adell Cook, Sue Thomas, and Clyde Wilcox. Boulder, Colo.: Westview Press.

Niebuhr, Gustav. 1995. "Conservatives' New Frontier: Religious Liberty Law Firms." *New York Times,* 8 July, 1.

Niskanen, William. 1971. *Bureaucracy and Representative Government.* Chicago: Aldine/Atherton.

———. 1990. "Bureaucracy and Representative Government." In *The Budget-Maximizing Bureaucrat,* ed. Andre Blais and Stephane Dion. Pittsburgh: University of Pittsburgh Press.

Norquist, Grover. 1995. Personal interview. Americans for Tax Reform. 7 August.

O'Connor, Karen. 1980. *Women's Organizations' Use of the Courts.* Lexington, Mass.: Lexington Books.

———. 1996. *No Neutral Ground: Abortion Politics in an Age of Absolutes.* Boulder, Colo.: Westview Press.

O'Connor, Karen, and Lee Epstein. 1983. "The Rise of Conservative Interest Group Litigation." *Journal of Politics* 45:479–89.

———. 1984. "The Role of Interest Groups in Supreme Court Policymaking." In *Public Policy Formation,* ed. Robert Eyestone. Greenwich, Conn.: JAI Press, 63–81.

Olson, Mancur. 1971. *The Logic of Collective Action.* Cambridge: Harvard University Press.

———. 1981. "The Political Evolution of Interest Group Litigation." Paper presented at the annual meeting of the American Political Science Association.

———. 1982. *The Rise and Decline of Nations.* New Haven: Yale University Press.

———. 1984. *Clients and Lawyers: Securing the Rights of Disabled Persons.* Westport, Conn.: Greenwood Press.

Omicinski, John. 1992. "De Tocqueville Would Be Shocked by 'Spin Doctors.'" *Gannett News Service,* 22 October.

Palazollo, Daniel J., and Bill Swinford. 1994. " 'Remember in November?' Ross Perot, Presidential Power, and the NAFTA." Paper presented at the annual meeting of the American Political Science Association, New York.

Patterson, Bradley H. Jr. 1988. *The Ring of Power.* New York: Basic Books.

Penner, Rudolph G., and Alan J. Abramson. 1988. *Broken Purse Strings: Congressional Budgeting 1974–1988.* Washington, D.C.: Urban Institute Press.

Pertschuk, Michael, and Wendy Schaetzel. 1989. *The People Rising: The Campaign against the Bork Nomination.* New York: Thunder's Mouth Press.

Peterson, Mark A. 1990. *Legislating Together.* Cambridge: Harvard University Press.

Petracca, Mark P., ed. 1992. *The Politics of Interests: Interest Groups Transformed.* Boulder, Colo.: Westview Press.

Pfeffer, Leo. 1981. "Amici in Church-State Litigation." *Law and Contemporary Problems* 44:83–110.

Phelps, Timothy M., and Helen Winternitz. 1992. *Capitol Games.* New York: Hyperion.

Pianin, Eric. 1995. "Hill Leaders Agree on 7-Year Budget." *Washington Post,* 23 June, A1.

Pika, Joseph A. 1991. "Opening Doors for Kindred Souls: The White House Office of Liaison." In *Interest Group Politics,* 3d ed., ed. Allan J. Cigler and Burdett A. Loomis. Washington, D.C.: CQ Press.

Pons, Michael. 1995. Personal interview. National Education Association. 29 August.

Poole, Keith T. 1981. "Dimensions of Interest Group Evaluations of the U.S. Senate, 1969–1978." *American Journal of Political Science* 25:49–67.

Poole, Keith T., and Steven Daniels. 1985. "Ideology, Party, and Voting in the U.S. Congress, 1959–1980." *American Political Science Review* 79: 373–99.

Poole, Keith T., Thomas Romer, and Howard Rosenthal. 1987. "The Revealed Preferences of Political Action Committees." *American Economic Review* 77:298–302.

Posner, Michael. 1994–95. "Rally Round Human Rights." *Foreign Policy* 97:133–39.

Randolph, Eleanor. 1993. "Ginsburg's Spouse Says He Arranged Letter Campaign." *Washington Post,* 17 June, A17.

Rauber, Paul. 1996a. "An End to Evolution: The Extinction Lobby in Congress Is Now Deciding Which Species Will Live and Which Will Die." *Sierra,* January/February, 28–32, 123.

———. 1996b. "Eco-Thug: Richard Pombo." *Sierra,* January/February, 16.

Rauch, Jonathan. 1994. *Demosclerosis: The Silent Killer of American Government.* New York: Times Books.

Redish, Martin H. 1982. "The Value of Free Speech." *University of Pennsylvania Law Review* 130:591.

Reed, Ralph. 1995. Personal interview. Christian Coalition. 14 September.

Regens, James L. "Congressional Cosponsorship of Acid Rain Controls." *Social Science Quarterly* 70:505–12.

Reichley, A. James. 1985. *Religion in American Public Life.* Washington, D.C.: Brookings Institution.

Reischauer, Robert D. 1991. Speech given at the National Tax Association's 84th Annual Conference on Taxation. Williamsburg, Va., 11 November.

Rich, Spenser. 1987. "Welfare-Overhaul Bill Passes Big Test." *Washington Post,* 16 December, A10.

———. 1988. "Realities May Bar Boost in Social Spending, Deficits Eating Up Next President's Leeway." *Washington Post,* 20 July.

Rieselbach, Leroy. 1995. "Congressional Change: Historical Perspectives." In *Remaking Congress: Change and Stability in the 1990s,* ed. James A. Thurber and Roger H. Davidson. Washington, D.C.: CQ Press.

Rimmerman, Craig A. 1994. "New Kids on the Block: The WISH List and the Gay and Lesbian Victory Fund." In *Risky Business? PAC Decisionmaking in Congressional Elections,* ed. Robert Biersack, Paul S. Herrnson, and Clyde Wilcox. Armonk, N.Y.: M.E. Sharpe.

Rivard, Michael D. 1992. "Symposium: Contemporary Issues in Administrative Adjudication: Comment: Toward a General Theory of Constitutional Personhood: A Theory of Constitutional Personhood for Transgenic Humanoid Species." *UCLA Law Review* 39:1425.

Roberts, Susan. 1993. "Further Feminism and Female Representation? The Role of Women's PACs in Recruitment." Paper presented at the annual meeting of the Midwest Political Science Association.

Robert H. Bork Hearings, U.S. Senate Committee on the Judiciary. 1987. Washington, D.C.: Government Printing Office.

Rohde, David W. 1991. *Parties and Leaders in the Post-Reform House.* Chicago: University of Chicago Press.

Romer, Thomas, and James M. Snyder Jr. 1994. "An Empirical Investigation of the Dynamics of PAC Contributions." *American Journal of Political Science* 38:745–69.

Rose-Ackerman, Susan. 1995. *Controlling Environmental Policy: The Limits of Public Law in Germany and the U.S.* New Haven: Yale University Press.

Rosenberg, Gerald N. 1991. *The Hollow Hope: Can Courts Bring about Social Change?* Chicago: University of Chicago Press.

Rosin, Hanna. 1995. "Fern Trampling." *New Republic,* 3 July, 12–14.

Rosner, Jeremy. 1995–96. "The Know Nothings Know Something." *Foreign Policy* 101:116–29.

Rubin, Irene S. 1993. *The Politics of Public Budgeting: Getting and Spending, Borrowing and Balancing.* 2d ed. Chatham, N.J.: Chatham House.

Ruffner, Frederick G., ed. 1988. *Encyclopedia of Associations.* Detroit: Gale Research Co.

Sabatier, Paul, and Hank Jenkins-Smith, eds. 1993. *Policy Change and Learning: An Advocacy Coalition Approach.* Boulder, Colo.: Westview Press.

Sabato, Larry J. 1984. *PAC Power: Inside the World of Political Action Committees.* New York: Norton.

Sachs, Richard C. 1996. "The Lobby Disclosure Act of 1995: A Brief Description."

CRS Report for Congress 96-29, 4 January.

Salant, Jonathan D. 1996. "Conventions Pay Off for Corporations." *Congressional Quarterly Weekly Report,* 17 August, 28–30.

Salant, Jonathan D., and Richard Scammon. 1995. "Senate Bans Lavish Gifts from Interest Groups." *Congressional Quarterly Weekly Report,* 29 July, 2237–38.

Salisbury, Robert. 1969. "An Exchange Theory of Interest Groups." *Midwest Journal of Political Science* 13:1–32.

———. 1984. "Interest Representation: The Dominance of Institutions." *American Political Science Review* 78:64–76.

———. 1990. "The Paradox of Interest Groups in Washington—More Groups, Less Clout." In *The New Political System,* 2d ed., ed. Anthony King. Washington, D.C.: American Enterprise Institute.

Salisbury, Robert H., John P. Heinz, Edward O. Laumann, and Robert L. Nelson. 1987. "Who Works with Whom? Interest Group Alliances and Opposition." *American Political Science Review* 81:1217–34.

Salwen, Kerin. 1994. "Labor Unions Consider How to Spend Funds in Drive for Health-Care Reform." *Wall Street Journal,* 2 February.

Schattschneider, E.E. 1960. *The Semi-Sovereign People: A Realist's View of Democracy in America.* New York: Holt, Rinehart, and Winston.

Scheingold, Stuart A. 1974. *The Politics of Rights: Lawyers, Public Policy, and Political Change.* New Haven: Yale University Press.

Schick, Allen. 1981. *Reconciliation and the Congressional Budget Process.* Washington, D.C.: American Enterprise Institute.

———. 1988. "Proposed Budget Reform: A Critical Analysis." In *Proposed Budget Reform: A Critical Analysis,* U.S. Senate Committee on Government Affairs, 100th Cong., 2d sess. Washington, D.C.: Congressional Research Service and Library of Congress, April.

Schiller, Wendy J. 1995. "Senators as Political Entrepreneurs: Using Bill Sponsorship to Shape Legislative Agendas." *American Journal of Political Science* 39:186–203.

Schlozman, Kay. 1984. "What Accent the Heavenly Chorus? Political Quality and the American Pressure System." *Journal of Politics* 46:1006–32.

Schlozman, Kay Lehman, and John T. Tierney. 1986. *Organized Interests and American Democracy.* New York: Harper & Row.

———. 1988. "More of the Same: Washington Pressure Group Activity in a Decade of Change." *Journal of Politics* 45: 351–75.

Schroedel, Jean Reith. 1986. "Campaign Contributions and Legislative Outcomes." *Western Political Quarterly* 40:371–89.

Segal, Jeffrey A., Charles M. Cameron, and Albert D. Cover. 1992. "A Spatial Model of Roll Call Voting: Senators, Constituents, Presidents, and Interest Groups in Supreme Court Confirmations." *American Journal of Political Science* 36:96–121.

Seligman, Lester G., and Cary R. Covington. 1996. "Presidential Leadership with Congress: Change, Coalitions, and Crisis." In *Rivals for Power: Presidential-Congressional Relations,* ed. James A. Thurber. Washington, D.C: CQ Press.

Sellers, Charles G. 1965. "The Equilibrium Cycle in American Two-Party Politics." *Public Opinion Quarterly* 29:16–37.

Shaiko, Ronald G. 1994. "Le PAC, C'est Moi: Brent Bozell and the Conservative Victory Committee." In *Risky Business? PAC Decisionmaking in Congressional Elections,* ed. Robert Biersack, Paul S. Herrnson, and Clyde Wilcox. Armonk, N.Y.: M.E. Sharpe, 181–95.

————. 1995. "Lobby Reform: Curing the Mischiefs of Faction?" In *Remaking Congress: Stability and Change in the 1990s,* ed. James A. Thurber and Roger H. Davidson. Washington, D.C.: CQ Press.

————. 1996. "Changing the Washington Culture: Lobby Disclosure and the Gift Ban." *Extension of Remarks: APSA Legislative Studies Section Newsletter* 19:1–2, 11.

Shair, Yossi. 1995. "Multicultural Foreign Policy." *Foreign Policy* 103:69–91.

Shear, Jeff. 1995. "The Ax Files." *National Journal,* 15 April, 924–27.

Sheffner, Benjamin. 1996. "GOP Shatters Money Record for 1996 Races." *Roll Call,* 14 March, 22.

Silberman, Jonathan, and Garey Durden. 1976. "Determining Legislative Preferences on the Minimum Wage: An Economic Approach." *Journal of Political Economy* 84:317–29.

Silverstein, Mark. 1995. *Judicious Choices: The New Politics of Supreme Court Confirmations.* New York: Norton.

Simon, Paul. 1992. *Advice & Consent: Clarence Thomas, Robert Bork, and the Intriguing History of the Supreme Court's Nomination Battles.* Washington, D.C.: National Press Books.

Sinclair, Barbara. 1983. *Majority Leadership in the U.S. House.* Baltimore: Johns Hopkins University Press.

————. 1995. *Legislators, Leaders, and Lawmaking: The U.S. House of Representatives in the Postreform Era.* Baltimore: Johns Hopkins University Press.

————. 1997. *Unorthodox Lawmaking: New Legislative Processes in the U.S. Congress.* Washington, D.C.: CQ Press.

Skrzycki, Cindy. 1996. "Slowing the Flow of Federal Rules." *Washington Post,* 18 February, A1.

Smith, Richard. 1995. "Interest Group Influence in the U.S. Congress." *Legislative Studies Quarterly* 20:89–139.

Smolla, Rodney A. 1992. *Free Speech in an Open Society.* New York: Knopf.

Sorauf, Frank J. 1976. *The Wall of Separation.* Princeton: Princeton University Press.

————. 1988. *Money in American Elections.* Glenview, Ill.: Scott, Foresman.

————. 1992. *Inside Campaign Finance: Myths and Realities.* New Haven: Yale University Press.

Spanier, John, and Eric M. Uslaner. 1994. *American Foreign Policy Making and the Democratic Dilemmas.* 6th ed. Needham Heights, Mass.: Addison Wesley.

Sperry, Roger L. 1996. "Diplomatic Disorder." *Foreign Affairs,* July, 16–22.

Spiegel, Steven L. 1985. *The Other Arab-Israeli Conflict.* Chicago: University of Chicago Press.

Staggenborg, Suzanne. 1991. *The Pro-Choice Movement: Organization and Activism in the Abortion Conflict.* New York: Oxford University Press.

Stanley Foundation. 1996. "Assessing the Clinton Presidency: The Risks of Context and Character." *Extensions* (Journal of the Carl Albert Congressional Research and Studies Center), Spring, 19–23.

Stewart, Richard. 1975. "The Reformation of American Administrative Law." *Harvard Law Review* 88:1667–1811.

Stigler, George. 1971. "The Theory of Economic Regulation." *Bell Journal of Economics and Management Science* 2:3–21.

Stokes, Donald E., and Gudmund R. Iverson. 1962. "On the Existence of Forces Restoring Two-Party Competition." *Public Opinion Quarterly* 26:159– 71.

Stone, Peter H. 1995. "Follow the Leaders." *National Journal,* 24 June, 1640–44.

Sullivan, John L., Earl Shaw, Gregory E. McAvoy, and David G. Barnum. 1993. "The Dimensions of Cue-Taking in the House of Representatives: Variation by Issue Area." *Journal of Politics* 55:975–97.

Sullivan, Terry. 1991. "The Bank Account Presidency: A New Measure and Evidence on the Temporal Path of Presidential Influence." *American Journal of Political Science* 35:686–723.

Swanson, Wayne R. 1990. *The Christ Child Goes to Court.* Philadelphia: Temple University Press.

Tate, David. 1981. "Reconciliation Breeds Tumult as Committees Tackle Cuts: Revolutionary Budget Tool." *Congressional Quarterly Weekly Report,* 23 May, 887–91.

Teasley, Mary Elizabeth. 1995. Personal interview. National Education Association. 29 August.

Thelwell, Raphael. 1990. "Gramm-Rudman-Hollings Four Years Later: A Dangerous Illusion." *Public Administration Review* 50:190–97.

Thurber, James A. 1987. "Budget Continuity and Change: An Assessment of the Congressional Budget Process." In *Studies of Modern American Politics,* ed. D.K. Adams. Manchester, England: Manchester University Press, 80.

———. 1989. "Budget Continuity and Change: An Assessment of the Congressional Budget Process." In *Studies in U.S. Politics,* ed. D.K. Adams. Manchester England: Manchester University Press, 78–118.

———. 1991a. "Delay, Deadlock, and Deficits: Evaluating Congressional Budget Reform." In *Federal Budget and Financial Management Reform,* ed. Thomas D. Lynch. Westport, Conn.: Greenwood Press.

———. 1991b. "Dynamics of Policy Subsystems in American Politics." In *Interest Group Politics,* 3d ed., ed. Allan J. Cigler and Burdett A. Loomis. Washington, D.C.: CQ Press.

———. 1991c. "The Impact of Budget Reform on Presidential and Congressional Governance." In *Divided Democracy: Cooperation and Conflict between the President and Congress,* ed. James A. Thurber. Washington, D.C.: CQ Press, 145–70.

———. 1995a. "If the Game Is Too Hard, Change the Rules: Congressional Budget Reform in the 1990s." In *Remaking Congress: Change and Stability in the 1990s,* ed. James A. Thurber and Roger H. Davidson. Washington, D.C.: CQ Press, 130–44.

———. 1995b. "Remaking Congress after the Electoral Earthquake of 1994." In *Remaking Congress: Change and Stability in the 1990s,* ed. James A. Thurber and Roger H. Davidson. Washington, D.C.: CQ Press.

———. 1995c. "Republican Centralization of the Congressional Budget Process."

Extension of Remarks: APSA Legislative Studies Section Newsletter, December.

———. 1996. "Political Power and Policy Subsystems in American Politics." In *Agenda for Excellence: Administering the State,* ed. B. Guy Peters and Bert A. Rockman. Chatham, N.J.: Chatham House, 38–75.

Thurgood Marshall Hearings, U.S. Senate Committee on the Judiciary. 1967. Washington, D.C.: Government Printing Office.

Tocqueville, Alexis de. 1835. *Democracy in America.* New York: Harper & Row (1966).

Tonelson, Alan. 1994–95. "Jettison the Policy." *Foreign Policy* 97:121–32.

Totenberg, Nina. 1988. "The Confirmation Process and the Public: To Know or Not to Know." *Harvard Law Review* 101:1213–17.

Tribe, Laurence. 1988. *American Constitutional Law.* 2d ed. Mineola, N.Y.: Foundation Press.

———. 1992. *Abortion: The Clash of Absolutes.* New York: Norton.

Truman, David B. 1951. *The Governmental Process.* New York: Knopf.

Tushnet, Mark V. 1987. *The NAACP's Legal Strategy against Segregated Education, 1925–1950.* Chapel Hill: University of North Carolina Press.

Twain, Mark. 1899. *The Gilded Age: A Tale of To-Day.* Hartford, Conn.: American Publishing Company.

Twiss, Benjamin. 1942. *Lawyers and the Constitution: How Laissez Faire Came to the Supreme Court.* Princeton: Princeton University Press.

U.S. Department of State. 1992. *State 2000: A New Model for Managing Foreign Affairs.* Washington, D.C.: Government Printing Office.

Uslaner, Eric M. 1989. *Shale Barrel Politics.* Stanford, Calif.: Stanford University Press.

———. 1991. "A Tower of Babel on Foreign Policy." In *Interest Group Politics,* 3d ed., ed. Allan J. Cigler and Burdett A. Loomis. Washington, D.C.: CQ Press, 299–318.

———. 1995. "Trade Winds: NAFTA, the Rational Public, and the Responsive Congress." University of Maryland: Mimeo.

Verba, Sidney, Kay Lehman Schlozman, and Henry E. Brady. 1995. *Voice and Equality: Civic Voluntarism in American Politics.* Cambridge: Harvard University Press.

Vose, Clement. 1955. "NAACP Strategy in Restrictive Covenant Cases." *Case Western Reserve Law Review* 6:101.

———. 1957. "National Consumers' League and the Brandeis Brief." *Midwest Journal of Political Science* 1:178–90.

———. 1958. "Litigation as a Form of Pressure Group Activity." *Annals of the American Academy of Political and Social Science* 319:20–31.

———. 1959. *Caucasions Only: The NAACP and the Restrictive Covenant Cases.* Berkeley: University of California Press.

———. 1966. "Interest Groups, Judicial Review, and Local Government." *Western Political Quarterly* 19:85.

———. 1972. *Constitutional Change.* Lexington, Mass.: Lexington Books.

———. 1981. "Interest Groups and Litigation." Paper presented at the annual meeting of the American Political Science Association.

Walker, Jack. 1983. "The Origins and Maintenance of Interest Groups in America." *American Political Science Review* 77:390–406.

———. 1991. *Mobilizing Interest Groups in America: Patrons, Professionals, and Social Movements.* Ann Arbor: University of Michigan Press.

Wasby, Stephen L. 1983. "Interest Group Litigation in an Age of Complexity." In *Interest Group Politics,* ed. Allan Cigler and Burdett Loomis. Washington, D.C.: CQ Press.

———. 1984. "How Planned Is 'Planned Litigation'? " *American Bar Association Research Journal* 1:83–118.

———. 1995. *Race Relations Litigation in an Age of Complexity.* Charlottesville: University Presses of Virginia.

Watzman, Nancy, and James Youngclaus. 1996. *Capital Lobbying: Money Played Its Part in 1995.* Washington, D.C.: Center for Responsive Politics.

Way, Frank, and Barbara J. Burt. 1983. "Religious Marginality and the Free Exercise Clause." *American Political Science Review* 77:652.

Wayne, Leslie. 1996. "Loopholes Allow Presidential Race to Set a Record." *New York Times,* 8 September, A1, A2.

Wayne, Stephen J. 1978. *The Legislative Presidency.* New York: Harper & Row.

Weiss, Dan. 1995. Personal interview. Sierra Club. 17 August.

Weisskopf, Michael. 1993. "Energized by Pulpit or Passion, the Public Is Calling; 'Gospel Grapevine' Displays Strength Over Military Ban." *Washington Post,* 1 February, A1.

Welch, William P. 1982. "Campaign Contributions and Legislative Voting: Milk Money and Dairy Price Supports." *Western Political Quarterly* 35: 478–95.

West, Darrell M. 1996. "Harry and Louise Go to Washington." *Journal of Health Politics* 21:35.

West, Darrell M., and Richard Francis. 1995. "Selling the Contract with America: Interest Groups and Public Policymaking." Paper presented at the annual meeting of the American Political Science Association, Chicago.

Wilcox, Clyde. 1992. *God's Warriors: The Christian Right in Twentieth-Century America.* Baltimore: Johns Hopkins University Press.

———. 1994. "Coping with Increasing Business Influence: The AFL-CIO's Committee on Political Education." In *Risky Business? PAC Decisionmaking in Congressional Elections,* ed. Robert Biersack, Paul S. Herrnson, and Clyde Wilcox. Armonk, N.Y.: M.E. Sharpe.

———. 1996. *Onward Christian Soldiers: The Christian Right in Politics.* Boulder, Colo.: Westview Press.

Wilson, Ernest J. III. 1994. "Double Diversity: The Intersection of Big Changes at Home and Abroad." In *Beyond the Beltway,* ed. Daniel Yankelovich and I.M. Destler. New York: Norton, 155–74.

Wilson, James Q. 1973. *Political Organizations.* New York: Basic Books.

———. 1989. *Bureaucracy: What Government Agencies Do and Why They Do It.* New York: Basic Books.

Wilson, Larmon. 1983. "Human Rights in United States Foreign Policy: The Rhetoric and the Practice." In *Interaction: Foreign Policy and Public Policy,* ed. Don C. Piper and Ronald J. Terchek. Washington, D.C.: American Enterprise Institute, 178–208.

Wittman, Marshall. 1995. Personal interview. Christian Coalition. 17 August.

Wolfskill, George. 1962. *The Revolt of the Conservatives: A History of the American Liberty League, 1934–1940*. Boston: Houghton Mifflin.

Woliver, Laura R. 1993. *From Outrage to Action: The Politics of Grassroots Dissent*. Urbana: University of Illinois Press.

———. 1995. "Mobilizing and Sustaining Grassroots Dissent." Paper presented at the annual meeting of the American Political Science Association, Chicago.

Woodward, Bob, and Scott Armstrong. 1979. *The Brethren: Inside the Supreme Court*. New York: Avon Books.

Wright, John R. 1985. "PACs, Contributions, and Roll Calls: An Organizational Perspective." *American Political Science Review* 79:400–414.

———. 1990. "Contributions, Lobbying, and Committee Voting in the U.S. House of Representatives." *American Political Science Review* 84:417–38.

———. 1996. *Interest Groups and Congress: Lobbying, Contributions and Influence*. New York: Allyn and Bacon.

Yale Comment. 1949. "Private Attorneys-General: Action in the Fight for Civil Liberties." *Yale Law Journal* 58:574–98.

Yang, John E. 1991. "Budget Battle Set to Begin on New Terrain." *Washington Post,* 3 February, A12.

———. 1995. "Plan Limiting Nonprofits is Labeled 'Extreme.' " *Washington Post,* 29 November, A4.

Yang, John E., and Steven Mufson. 1991. "Package Termed Best Circumstances Permit." *Washington Post,* 29 October, A4.

Court Cases Cited in Text

Abington v. Schempp, 374 U.S. 203 (1963).

Abrams v. U.S., 250 U.S. 616 (1919).

Austin v. Michigan Chamber of Commerce, 494 U.S. 652 (1990).

Bigelow v. Virginia, 421 U.S. 809 (1975).

Board of Education of Kiryas Joel School District v. Grumet, 114 S. Ct. 2481 (1994).

Board of Education of Westside Schools v. Mergens, 496 U.S. 226 (1990).

Bowsher v. Sinar, 106 S.Ct. 3181 (1986).

Brandenburg v. Ohio, 395 U.S. 444 (1969).

Brown v. Board of Education of Topeka, Kansas, 347 U.S. 483 (1954).

Buckley v. Valeo, 424 U.S. 1 (1976).

Capitol Square Review Board v. Pinette, 115 S. Ct. 2440 (1993).

CBS v. Democratic National Committee, 412 U.S. 94 (1973).

Central Hudson Gas and Electric Corp. v. Public Service Commission, 447 U.S. 557 (1980).

Church of Lukumi Babalu Aye v. City of Hialeah, 113 S. Ct. 2217 (1993).

City of Cincinnati v. Discovery Network, Inc., 113 S. Ct. 1505 (1993).

City of Ladue v. Gilleo, 114 S. Ct. 2038 (1994).

Colorado Republican Federal Campaign Committee v. Federal Election Commission, U.S. 64 U.S.L. 4663 (1996).

Engel v. Vitale, 370 U.S. 421 (1962).

Everson v. *Board of Education,* 330 U.S. 1 (1947).
FCC v. *League of Women Voters of California,* 468 U.S. 364 (1984).
FEC v. *NCPAC,* 470 U.S. 480 (1985).
First National Bank of Boston v. *Bellotti,* 435 U.S. 765 (1978).
Flast v. *Cohen,* 392 U.S. 83 (1968).
Forsyth County v. *Nationalist Movement,* 505 U.S. 123 (1992).
Honda Motor Co. v. *Oberg,* 116 S. Ct. 1847 (1996).
John Hurley and South Boston Allied War Veterans Council v. *Irish American Gay, Lesbian, and Bisexual Group of Boston,* 115 S. Ct. 2338 (1995).
Jones v. *Wolf,* 443 U.S. 595 (1979).
Lamb's Chapel v. *Center Moriches School District,* 113 S. Ct. 2141 (1993).
Lee v. *Weisman,* 112 U.S. 2649 (1992).
Mergens v. *Board of Westside Schools,* 496 U.S. 226 (1990).
Miami Herald Publishing Co. v. *Tornillo,* 418 U.S. 241 (1974).
Muller v. *Oregon,* 208 U.S. 412 (1908).
New York Times Co. v. *U.S.,* 403 U.S. 713 (1971).
Plessy v. *Ferguson,* 163 U.S. 537 (1896).
Procunier v. *Martinez,* 416 U.S. 396 (1974).
Public Citizen v. *United States Department of Justice,* 491 U.S. 440 (1989).
Red Lion Broadcasting v. *FCC,* 395 U.S. 367 (1969).
Roe v. *Wade,* 410 U.S. 113 (1973).
Rosenberger v. *University of Virginia,* 115 S. Ct. 2510 (1995).
Rubin v. *Coors Brewing Company,* 115 S. Ct. 1585 (1995).
Santa Clara County v. *Southern Pacific Railroad,* 118 U.S. 394 (1886).
Shelley v. *Kraemer,* 334 U.S. 1 (1948).
Stanley v. *Georgia,* 394 U.S. 557 (1969).
Texas v. *Johnson,* 491 U.S. 397 (1989).
Tinker v. *Des Moines School District,* 393 U.S. 503 (1969).
Turner Broadcasting System v. *FCC,* 114 S. Ct. 2445 (1994).
Valentine v. *Christensen,* 316 U.S. 52 (1942).
Virginia State Bd. of Pharmacy v. *Virginia Citizens Consumer Council,* 425 U.S. 748 (1976).
Webster v. *Reproductive Health Services,* 492 U.S. 490 (1989).
Zobrest v. *Catalina Foothills School District,* 113 S. Ct. 2462 (1993).

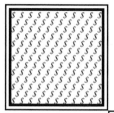

Index

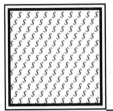

About the Contributors

Gary J. Andres is partner and vice-president of The Dutko Group, Inc., a multiple-client, public affairs consulting firm. He served as deputy assistant to the president for legislative affairs in the Bush White House from 1989 to 1992.

Jack Bonner is founder and president of Bonner & Associates, a firm specializing in organizing and conducting grassroots campaigns at the federal, state, and local levels on legislative and regulatory issues. He is also an adjunct professor at American University. He has been referred to as the "King of Grassroots" by National Public Radio and as the "guru" of grassroots by *Fortune* magazine.

Colton C. Campbell is adjunct assistant professor of political science at the George Washington University. He specializes in Congress's utilization and development of temporary commissions and the growing use of alternative mechanisms in formulating policy outside the traditional legislative process.

Cynthia L. Cates is assistant professor of political science at Towson State University, where she teaches judicial process and court policymaking. Formerly, she was a senior analyst with the U.S. Advisory Commission on Intergovernmental Relations, specializing in the impact of federal court decisions on state and local governments.

Christine DeGregorio is associate professor of government at American University. She is the author of *Networks of Champions: Leadership, Access, and Advocacy in the U.S. House of Representatives.*

Roger H. Davidson is professor of government and politics at the University of Maryland, College Park. His books on Congress and national policymaking include *Congress and Its Members.* He is co-editor of the *Encyclopedia of the U.S. Congress* and a fellow of the National Academy of Public Administration.

James G. Gimpel is associate professor of government and politics at the University of Maryland, College Park. He is the author of *Legislating the Revo-*

374

lution and *National Elections and the Autonomy of American State Party Systems.*

Donald L. Goff is president of Conventional Wisdom, a public affairs consulting firm. He previously served as director of federal government affairs and PAC director for AT&T. He is also an adjunct professor at American University.

William T. Gormley Jr. is professor of government and public policy at Georgetown University. He is author of several books, including *Taming the Bureaucracy,* which won the Louis Brownlow Book Award from the National Academy of Public Administration.

Paul S. Herrnson is professor of government and politics at the University of Maryland, College Park. He is the author of *Congressional Elections: Campaigning at Home and in Washington* and *Party Campaigning in the 1980s.* He is also co-editor of *Risky Business? PAC Decisionmaking in Congressional Elections.*

Gregg Ivers is associate professor of government at American University. He is the author of *To Build a Wall: American Jews and the Separation of Church and State* and *Redefining the First Freedom: The Supreme Court and the Consolidation of State Power.*

Robert A. Katzmann is Walsh Professor of American Government, professor of law, and professor of public policy at Georgetown University; he also heads the Governance Institute and is a visiting fellow at the Brookings Institution. He is author of several books, including *Courts and Congress, Regulatory Bureaucracy: The Federal Trade Commission and Anti-Trust Policy,* and *Institutional Disability: The Saga of Transportation Policy for the Disabled.*

Wayne V. McIntosh is associate professor of government and politics at the University of Maryland, College Park, specializing in law and politics. He is author of *The Appeal of Civil Law.*

Michael J. McShane is director of government relations at TRW, Inc. He is an active member of the Democratic Leadership Council (DLC) and served as an adviser to the Clinton-Gore reelection campaign in 1996.

Howard Marlowe is president of Marlowe and Company, a multiple-client lobbying firm representing a variety of private and governmental entities. He is a past president of the American League of Lobbyists. He is also an adjunct professor at American University.

Ellen S. Miller is the executive director of Public Campaign, a nonprofit, nonpartisan advocacy organization that works with citizen groups in state-based efforts to take special interest money out of U.S. elections. She served as executive director of the Center for Responsive Politics from 1984 to 1996.

Alan Morrison is founder and director of Public Citizen Litigation Group. He has appeared before the U.S. Supreme Court on numerous occasions, litigating a variety of public interest issues.

Candice J. Nelson is associate professor of government at American University and academic director of the Campaign Management Institute. She is the co-author of *The Money Chase: Congressional Campaign Finance Reform* and

The Myth of the Independent Voter, and co-editor of *Campaigns and Elections, American Style.*

Karen O'Connor is professor of government and department chair at American University. From 1977 to 1995, she taught at Emory University, where she won the university's Distinguished Teacher award. Her most recent publications are *American Government: Roots and Reform, No Neutral Ground: Abortion Politics in an Age of Absolutes,* and *Women, Politics and American Society.*

Richard D. Otis Jr. is director of federal government relations at the American Plastics Council. Prior to joining the Council, he worked at the Environmental Protection Agency.

Ronald G. Shaiko is associate professor of government at American University and academic director of the Lobbying Institute. He is the author of *Voices and Echoes for the Environment: Public Interest Representation in the 1990s and Beyond* and *The Art and Craft of Lobbying.*

James A. Thurber is professor of government at American University and director of the Center for Congressional and Presidential Studies. He is editor or co-editor of a number of publications, including *Rivals for Power: Presidential-Congressional Relations, Remaking Congress: The Politics of Congressional Stability and Change,* and *Campaigns and Elections, American Style.*

Eric M. Uslaner is professor of government and politics at the University of Maryland, College Park. His books include *The Decline of Comity in Congress* and *American Foreign Policy-Making and the Democratic Dilemmas.*

Charls E. Walker is one of the deans of the Washington lobbying profession. He came to Washington almost forty years ago as an assistant to the secretary of the treasury in the Eisenhower administration. After serving as executive director of the American Bankers Association for six years, he opened his own lobbying firm in 1973. Almost a quarter-century later, he remains involved in a wide range of policy issues, particularly tax policy and energy issues.

Stephen J. Wayne is professor of government at Georgetown University. He is author of numerous books including *The Road to the White House, The Legislative Presidency, Presidential Leadership,* and *The Politics of American Government.*

Clyde Wilcox is professor of government at Georgetown University. His recent books include *Serious Money: Fundraising and Contributing in Presidential Nomination Campaigns* and *Second Coming: The Christian Right in Virginia Politics.*

Ernest J. Wilson III is director of the Center for International Development and Conflict Management at the Univerity of Maryland, College Park, where he is also associate professor of government and politics. In 1993–94 he worked in the White House as director of international programs and resources in the National Security Council.

John R. Wright is professor of political science at George Washington University. He is author of *Interest Groups and Congress: Lobbying, Contributions, and Influence,* as well as numerous articles on interest groups and lobbying.